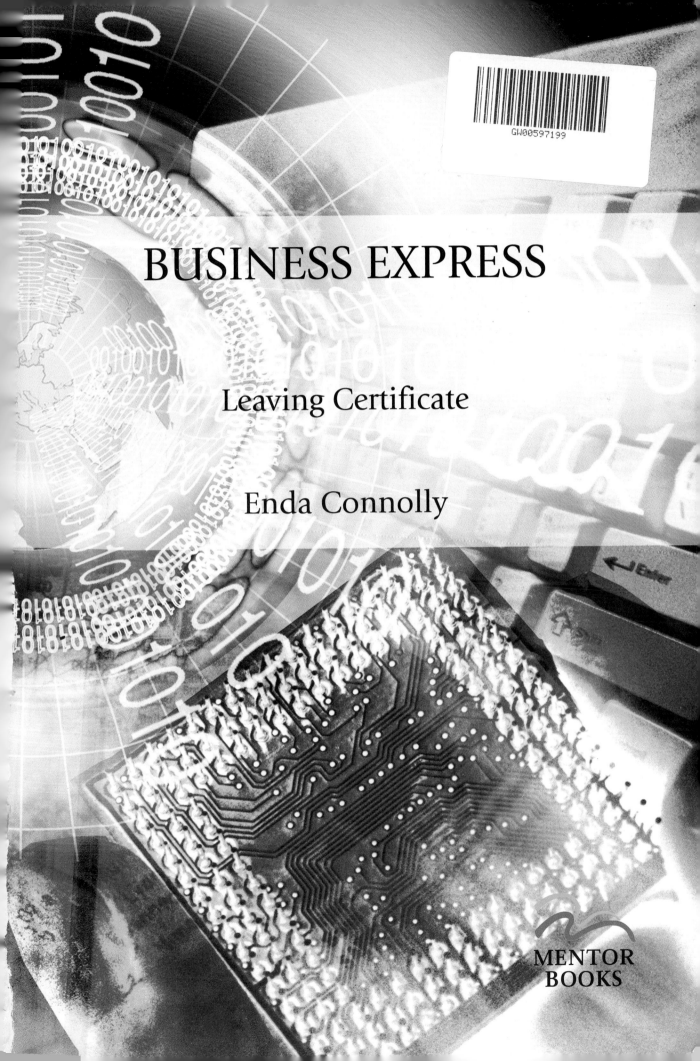

BUSINESS EXPRESS

Leaving Certificate

Enda Connolly

MENTOR BOOKS

Mentor Books
43 Furze Road,
Sandyford Industrial Estate,
Dublin 18.
Tel. (01) 295 2112/3
Fax. (01) 295 2114
e-mail: admin@mentorbooks.ie
www.mentorbooks.ie

The paper used in this book is made from the wood pulp of managed forests. For every tree felled, at least one tree is planted, thereby renewing natural resources.

ISBN: 978-1-906623-66-1
Copyright © Enda Connolly 2011

Edited by: Una Whelan
Design and Layout: Kathryn O'Sullivan
Cover design: Kathryn O'Sullivan

5 7 9 10 8 6

Printed in the EU

Acknowledgements

Thinkstock, Vitz Drinks, Bóthar, Trócaire, Greenpeace, IBEC, ISME, Ben & Jerry's, National Consumer Agency, Dunnes Stores, Riverdance, Ford, ESB, Virgin Group, Irish Defence Forces, Aer Lingus, Getty Images, NASA, Sony, Mercedes–Benz, AIB Bank, Bus Éireann, Intel, Microsoft, Nutzwerk, Toyota, the Equality Authority, Viking Splash Tours, Sugru, Amazon, PlayStation, AIB, Lucozade, Tesco, Lidl, Aldi, Intel, Toyota, Aviva, VHI, Cuisine de France, Mr Crumb, Coca-Cola, Pepsi Co, Ballygowan, Irish Breeze, Pizza Hut, Bord Bia, Cully & Sully, the Gleeson Group, Volkswagen, SEAT, Audi, Skoda, Sadolin, Cadbury's, Goodfella's, Super Valu, Centra, SPAR, Domino's Pizza, Jacob Fruitfield, Ribena, The Body Shop, BMW, Ryanair, Unilever, Glanbia, Kellogg's, Enterprise Ireland, Aer Arann, Supermac's, Erin, Birds Eye Foods, Pfizer, Companies Registration Office, Volvo, Virgin Group, Sunway Holidays, daft.ie, Baldwin's Farmhouse Ice Cream, Donegal County Enterprise Board, Shell Oil, Airtricity, Seahorse Aquariums, Eircom, Largo Foods, Airbus, Kingspan, Harley-Davidson, RTÉ, IDA Ireland, the Kerry Group, Fairtrade.

Contents

To Anne, Nia and Siún –
for your love and patience.
I owe you big time!

Chapter 1
Introduction to People in Business

Key Study Questions

Case Study

Organic Fanatic

Gary Lavin was in a shop buying a sandwich and looking for a healthy alternative to the rows of sugary drinks on offer. Other than mineral water, he could not find anything he liked. This gave him the idea for starting his own soft drinks **business**.

Using his own savings as **finance**, Gary spent the following 18 months researching his idea and developing a business plan for his enterprise. When everything was ready, he launched his company, Vitz Drinks, and started selling his own range of low-calorie, vitamin soft drinks sold under the Vit Hit **brand name**. The drinks were a success and Gary became a successful **entrepreneur.**

He then saw an opportunity for another range of soft drinks using organic fruit juice. To develop and successfully launch this new product, he realised that he needed more money. He did not want to use any more of his savings and did not want to take out a large **loan.** Instead, he decided to sell a 17% share of the business to an **investor** in return for €250,000 in cash. This extra **equity finance** allowed Gary to launch the Organic Fanatic range of soft drinks. This new range of products also proved very successful and his drinks are now distributed in thousands of retail outlets throughout Ireland as well as being **exported** throughout Europe.

1. What is business?

Business is about producing goods and services and supplying them to customers. The food you eat, music you listen to, books you read, and clothes you wear, are all designed, produced, distributed and sold by businesses.

A business *is any organisation set up to provide goods and services. A business can be commercial or non-commercial.*

Commercial businesses *provide goods and services to make a profit for the owners.* Profits are made when a business takes in more money from sales than it has to pay out in costs.

> Examples: Vitz Drinks, Sony, Dunnes Stores and Volkswagen.

Non-commercial businesses *(also known as social enterprises or not-for-profit businesses) exist to meet some needs other than making a profit.* Many not-for-profit businesses do not charge for the services they provide. Instead, they generate revenue from other sources such as fundraising, donations or government grants.

Working for a Just World

> Examples: Charities such as Bóthar, Trócaire, campaigning organisations such as Greenpeace and sporting organisations such as the GAA.

OL Short Q1

2. Who are the stakeholders involved in business?

Business stakeholders include:
- **Entrepreneurs**
- **Investors**
- **Employees**
- **Managers**
- **Producers**
- **Customers**
- **Suppliers**
- **Government**

Stakeholders *are the different groups of people who are directly affected by how a business is run.* The stakeholders in Vitz Drinks business are Gary Lavin (the entrepreneur), his investors, employees, consumers, banks, suppliers, government and wider society.

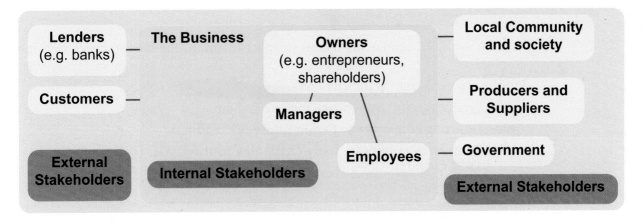

Fig. 1 Different types of business stakeholders.

Entrepreneurs

Entrepreneurs *are people who take the initiative to turn an idea into a business.* Commercial entrepreneurs like Gary Lavin see an opportunity to make a profit but also take the risk that the business might fail. They could be wasting their time and lose the money they put in. Social entrepreneurs, like the founders of Bóthar and Greenpeace, want to provide some service or achieve some goal that they believe is important to society.

> Entrepreneurs and investors need each other. The entrepreneur needs the investor to provide the finance to start and grow a business. The investor needs the entrepreneur to establish a successful business that will generate a reasonable financial return for the investor's money.

Bóthar
HELPING PEOPLE TO
HELP THEMSELVES

Investors

Often entrepreneurs will not have enough money to start a business. **Investors** *are the people who provide a business with the finance it needs.* This finance can come from owners' capital, loan capital from banks or grants from State agencies.

★ **Owners' capital** *is money invested by people or companies. In return they become part owners of the business and are entitled to a share in future profits.* Owners' capital is *also known as* **equity capital**.

> **Example:** Gary Lavin invested his own savings into his soft drinks business and also secured finance from investors in exchange for a share of the business.

★ **Loan capital** finance is provided by banks or other lenders and has to be repaid, with interest, within a certain period of time.

★ **Grants** are usually provided by State agencies such as Enterprise Ireland or County Enterprise Boards. **A grant** *is a gift of money that does not have to be repaid as long as certain conditions are met, such as creating a certain number of new jobs.*

7

Employers and employees

As soon as the entrepreneurs recruit people to work in the business they become employers.

Employers *recruit staff to work for them.* **Employers' rights** include:

* ✱ Recruiting employees when they need them
* ✱ Directing employees to perform the work required
* ✱ Dismissing employees fairly (according to the Unfair Dismissals Acts 1977 to 2007)

Employers' responsibilities include:

* ✣ Providing a written contract of employment
* ✣ Paying wages as agreed in the contract of employment
* ✣ Providing safe working conditions
* ✣ Complying with all employment laws

> **Example:** Gary employs staff to produce and sell his soft drinks. He wants hard-working and enthusiastic staff who will contribute their skills to the long-term success of the business. Gary can reward his staff financially with wages and bonuses, and non-financially with extra holidays and flexible working hours.

Employees *are recruited by businesses to assist in the business in return for a wage.* **Employees' rights** include:

* ★ Receiving a written contract of employment
* ★ Being paid the agreed wage
* ★ Working in a safe and healthy workplace
* ★ Freedom to join a trade union

Employees' responsibilities include:

* ❖ Following instructions (as long as they are reasonable and legal)
* ❖ Doing a fair day's work for a fair day's pay
* ❖ Being honest and loyal in their work

Managers

Managers *are the people responsible for running the business and achieving its goals.* They must:

* ◆ **Plan, organise** and **control** all aspects of the business including people, finance and equipment
* ◆ Have the **leadership, motivation** and **communication skills** needed to manage staff and to communicate effectively with stakeholders.

> **Example:** As the business grows, Gary will have to take on managers to help him cope with producing and selling his expanding range of drinks in Ireland and abroad.

Producers and suppliers

Producers *are the businesses that make products to sell to customers.* They transform raw or recycled materials, machinery, finance and human effort (labour) into finished products for sale.

> Example: Vitz Drinks produce soft drinks.

Suppliers *are the businesses that supply the raw materials needed by the producer.*

> Example: Suppliers provide the organic fruit, water, bottles and labels needed to make Vitz Drinks range of products.

Service providers *are businesses that supply the services needed by a business.* These services include insurance, banking, telecommunications and transport.

Consumers

Customers *are people who purchase goods from a business for their own use **or for resale** to others.*

> Example: Someone buying a bottle of Vitz Drinks' Organic Fanatic is a customer. Centra and SuperValu are also customers when they buy Vitz Drinks products for resale in their stores.

Consumers *are a type of customer who buy goods and services **purely for their own use**, not for resale.*

> Example: A person buying a bottle of Organic Fanatic from a shop for their lunch is a consumer.

Customers and consumers are the most important people in business because they provide the entrepreneur with a market and possible profits.

Society

Society *refers both to the local community where the business is located and to wider society, both nationally and globally.* Society wants businesses to behave in a socially responsible manner and not to damage the environment or the welfare of others. This means not infringing on other people's rights or welfare, such as by selling dangerous products or generating pollution.

Government

Government *refers to local and national authorities that set the rules and regulations by which businesses must operate.* Changes in government laws or taxes can affect how a business is run and what profits are earned. The government wants businesses to:

* Provide **jobs**
* Pay their fair share of **taxes**
* Obey the **law**

In return, the government provides services such as schools, hospitals, roads and policing needed by business and society.

OL Short Q2, 3, 4, 5

OL Long Q1, 2, 3

HL Short Q1, 2, 4

3. What are interest groups?

Stakeholders in business may be represented by interest groups. **Interest groups** *are organisations representing people (or stakeholders) who share a common interest or goal.* Also known as **pressure groups,** they try to influence the behaviour and decisions of others by engaging in lobbying, negotiation, boycotts or legal actions.

Lobbying *refers to a deliberate effort by interest groups to influence decision-makers by promoting a particular point of view.* It is often done through requesting meetings and generating favourable media coverage for the interest group on radio, television, print media and the Internet.

Business interest groups and trade associations

Business interest groups *represent the interests of businesses.*

> Examples:
> ★ **IBEC** *(Irish Business and Employers Confederation) is the main organisation representing large- and medium-sized businesses in Ireland.* It attempts to influence trade unions, the Irish government, the European Union and wider society on issues relevant to its members such as legislation, taxation and employee pay and conditions. It also provides advice to its members on economic and business matters. **The Small Firms Association** *speaks for and advises small businesses.* It is part of IBEC.
> ★ **Irish Small & Medium Enterprises (ISME)** *speaks for and advises small- and medium-sized enterprises.* It is independent of IBEC.
> ★ **Chambers of commerce** *aim to protect and promote businesses located in their area.* **Example:** Killarney Chamber of Commerce.

Trade Associations *are business interest groups that represent businesses involved in similar types of activities.*

> Examples:
> ✳ The **Society of the Irish Motor Industry (SIMI)** represents garages and car dealers.
> ✳ The **Food and Drink Industry Ireland (FDII)** is the main trade association for food and drink manufacturers in Ireland. It can represent Vitz Drinks.
> ✳ **RGDATA** represents the interests of independent grocery retailers.
> ✳ **Irish Association of Health Stores (IAHS)** represents the interests of health food shops.

IBEC

IRISH SMALL AND MEDIUM
ENTERPRISES ASSOCIATION LTD

CHAMBERS
IRELAND
IN BUSINESS FOR BUSINESS

Other stakeholder interest groups

There are also many other interest groups representing stakeholders such as employees, consumers, environmental and other specialist interests in the local community and wider society.

* **Trade unions** *are organisations that represent the interests of employees in a business on issues concerning pay or conditions of employment.*

> Examples: SIPTU, ASTI, TUI. **The Irish Congress of Trade Unions (ICTU)** *represents the interests of all trade unions and their members nationally.* It is a very important interest group as it is in regular discussions with IBEC, the government and the EU on issues affecting employees. Most trade unions in the country are members of the ICTU.

* **The National Consumer Agency** *is a State agency set up to ensure consumers are aware of their rights and that legislation protecting consumers is obeyed.*

* **The Consumers Association of Ireland** *represents and lobbies on behalf of consumer interests.* It is independent of the government. Members of the public can support this organisation by becoming members.

* **Environmental and specialist interest groups** are also important in business. They represent the interests of members of society who want to prevent undesirable activities or to promote some cause they believe is important.

> Examples: Greenpeace, the GAA.

| OL Short Q6, 7, 8 |
| OL Long Q6, 7 |

| HL Short Q5, 6, 7 |
| HL Long Q4, 5 |

GREENPEACE

Case Study

BEN & JERRY'S
Big Adventure

After leaving school, best friends Ben Coen and Jerry Greenfield did not exactly become roaring successes. Ben dropped out of five different colleges before trying his hand at a variety of jobs including pottery teacher, cleaner, security guard and taxi-driver. Jerry wanted to be a doctor but twice failed to get into college and ended up with a job he disliked.

Ben and Jerry eventually decided to become **entrepreneurs** and go into business together making ice cream. They completed a simple course in ice cream making and passed with flying colours. With investment from €6,500 in savings and a €3,000 bank loan they bought an ice-cream machine and rented an old petrol station that they converted into an ice cream 'scoop-shop'.

During the summer their shop filled with customers. Ben & Jerry's quirky flavours, rich ingredients and chunky fillings were an instant hit with **consumers** and sold out nearly every day. In winter they would go around selling the ice cream to restaurants. Within three years, they had moved to new and larger premises and were selling the ice cream in pint tubs to shops and restaurants for miles around.

In the competitive ice-cream market, the larger and well-established Haagen Dazs company took exception to Ben & Jerry's growth in the luxury end of the market and started competing aggressively against them. However, Ben & Jerry's adopted a **competitive approach** to dealing with their larger rival by retaliating with their own, more effective advertising and publicity campaign. Haagen Dazs backed down and Ben & Jerry's Ice Cream was now well established in consumers' minds.

Since starting up, Ben & Jerry's has grown into a business with thousands of employees and global sales of over hundreds of millions of euro. They have developed their own style of business management that involves having a **co-operative approach to stakeholder relationships**. For instance, the business has a staff committee, known as the 'Joy Gang', responsible for making the business as happy a place to work as possible. Dairy farmers are paid well for supplying high-quality milk. The company strives to be environmentally friendly and nearly everything in the factory is recycled. Furthermore, every year employees are encouraged to do some voluntary community work during work hours and 8% of profits are given to charities in the local community.

Some cynics say it all seems too good to be true. They claim that this 'right-on' attitude and hippie packaging is just a marketing ploy to win customers from rivals. Ben and Jerry respond that caring is central to business success. 'It helps profitability,' says Jerry, insisting that the two can go together.

Recall and Review

1. Identify the stakeholders in Ben and Jerry's business.

4. What relationships exist between the different stakeholders in business?

In business, the relationships between stakeholders have the following characteristics:

* Stakeholder relationships are based on having **different needs**
* Stakeholder relationships **can be competitive**
* Stakeholder relationships **can be co-operative**
* Stakeholder roles and relationships **can be dynamic/change over time**

● Stakeholder relationships are based on having different needs

Each stakeholder in business has different needs and depends on other stakeholders to satisfy those needs.

Stakeholder	Needs	Offers in return
Entrepreneurs / Owners	• Profit • Finance and support • Skilled workers • Minimal risk	• Goods and services • Employment and wages • Taxes • Share of profits • Interest on loans
Investors	• Profit on investment • Possible share in the ownership	• Finance
Employers	• Honesty • Reliability • Motivation and hard work	• Pay and conditions • Training • Promotional opportunities
Employees	• Good pay and conditions • Secure employment • Opportunities to develop	• Skills and qualifications • Hard work and motivation • Honesty and reliability
Producers	• Reliable suppliers • Loyal customers • Profitable business	• Right quality • Right prices
Suppliers	• Reliable customers who pay on time • Profitable business	• Products and services
Customers	• Quality goods and services • Fair and affordable prices	• Payment for goods/services • Loyalty and repeat business
Society	• Local jobs • No damage to local community, wider society or the environment • Support and sponsorship	• Favourable public opinion • Socially responsible brand image
Government	• Tax revenue for government • Goods and services for society	• Tax incentives • Grants, business advice and support • Infrastructure and services

5. What is the difference between co-operative and competitive relationships?

Consumers will benefit. From improved quality. improved customer service. Better choice. Better value for money, Once business in the same line are competing

• Stakeholder relationships can be competitive

The relationship of a business with its different stakeholder groups can be either competitive or co-operative.

The **competitive approach** *views the relationships between different stakeholders as being a win/lose one. It assumes that only one party can win and therefore stakeholders must compete to gain a commercial advantage over the other.*

eg employers compete for promotion.

> A **competitive** approach is **suitable** for dealing with **rival firms** in the marketplace.

> **Competitive approaches see business as a win/lose relationship. This approach is best suited to dealing with rivals in the marketplace.**

Example: Ben & Jerry's adopt a competitive relationship with rival ice cream producers. This involves monitoring the prices and products offered by rivals to ensure that their business remains competitive and attractive to consumers.

> The **competitive approach can be unsuitable** for dealing with **business stakeholders** as it can damage the reputation of the business.

Producers in the same line of business sometimes get together and co-operate with each other to protect their specific industry against outside threats to encourage economic development and to create jobs for the benefit of the community

Example: If Ben & Jerry's decided to lower its quality standards to save money it could damage the reputation of the business among customers and cause a drop in sales and profits. This could result in some employees being made redundant, reduced orders for suppliers and service providers, and a drop in tax revenue for the government.

• Stakeholder relationships can be co-operative

> **A co-operative approach sees business as a win/win relationship. This approach is best suited to managing relationships between stakeholders.**

A **co-operative (or partnership) approach** *views the relationships between different stakeholder groups as potential win/win situations for all sides.* A business with a co-operative attitude will seek opportunities to work in partnership with **stakeholders** and not against them.

eg employees working together to get the job done.

Example: During a recession, a partnership approach between employers and employees in a business may result in them working closely together to save the business, such as employees agreeing to take a pay cut to reduce costs and employers agreeing not to make any staff redundant.

• Stakeholder roles and relationships can be dynamic / change over time

Changing roles: As a business grows, the roles of different stakeholders can change over time.

Example: Ben and Jerry started off simply as consumers of ice cream, then became entrepreneurs and managers of their own ice cream business. As the business grew and new products were developed, they had to become employers of staff. To reward and motivate these staff, shares could be sold to their employees. This would make the employees also investors in the business.

Changing relationships: Sometimes rival firms may switch from a competitive approach to a co-operative approach with each other.

> **Example:** Normally Gary Lavin's Vitz Drinks would have a competitive relationship with rivals. However, it could also adopt a co-operative relationship with rivals to encourage more people to choose Irish soft drinks brands instead of imported brands. This would benefit all the firms producing soft drinks in Ireland.

OL Short Q9, 10

OL Long Q4, 5, 8, 9, 10

HL Short Q3, 9

HL Long Q1, 6, 7

Describe one example of a Co-operative relationship and source of conflict. For (1) Investor and Entrepreneur
- *entrepreneur gives open transparent and honest information to the investor e.g accurate business plans / cash flow forecasts, and in return provides a reasonable rate. Conflict: If entrepreneur gives false information to the investor defaults on loan repayments, reinvests profits rather than give a return on Investor may want greater return out of profits. Investment*

Examples of Competitive and Co-operative Approaches to Business Relationships

Competitive Approach	Co-operative (Partnership) Approach
Where a business seeks to exploit other stakeholders	Where a business seeks to work with stakeholders so that both sides gain
Employees: Treated by the business as an expense that must be tolerated rather than as partners in success. Wages are kept as low as possible and employee input into decision-making is minimal.	**Employees:** Seen as partners in building a successful business and receive fair wages, good working conditions and possibly a share in the profits or ownership.
Investors: May be provided with exaggerated or misleading financial information to persuade them to invest.	**Investors:** Provided with honest and complete financial information that will help to build trust.
Customers: Viewed as wallets to be emptied rather than clients with genuine needs. Low-quality goods may be sold while advertising may be misleading or deceptive.	**Customers:** Relationship is based on reliability, quality and value. Close attention is paid to market research and maintaining high standards. This helps to build long-term customer loyalty, sales and profits.
Suppliers: Viewed as adversaries from whom the toughest possible terms should be squeezed.	**Suppliers:** Receive fair prices and conditions in order to build a reliable long-term business relationship.
Government: Taxes may be evaded or laws not fully complied with.	**Government:** Complying with all laws and ensuring that taxes are paid as required.
Society: Needs or demands of local community or wider society may be ignored to cut costs, e.g. not installing adequate pollution controls or ignoring the concerns of local residents.	**Society:** The support and goodwill of the local community and wider society are regarded as crucial to the long-term success of the business.

Supplier and purchasing manager - Co-operative situation Supplier provides good quality raw materials, Components and finished goods to the purchasing manager who pays on time and offers a fair price. Conflict - if poor quality materials are provided / poor after sale services offered by Supplier. The purchasing manager fails to pay for goods

6. How can conflict in business be resolved?

Conflict *occurs when the interests of different people in business are in disagreement. This results in one party wanting to achieve something (e.g. increase in wages) which is in conflict with what another party wants (e.g. reduce costs).*

If conflict does arise, those involved may attempt to ignore it in the hope that it will go away. Alternatively, they may try to 'bully a solution' by using their power and influence to force their own way. However such responses are unsuitable as the disagreements that gave rise to the conflict will remain and resentment and conflict are likely to surface again in the future. Ongoing conflict can damage the reputation of a business.

Resolving conflict

A business can best avoid conflict by respecting stakeholders and adopting a co-operative approach to business. However, when conflict does occur between people in business, two basic strategies can be followed – non-legislative and legislative.

Non-legislative ways to resolve conflict

❖ **Talk** and see if a solution can be reached. If not, then some negotiations may be required. **Negotiating** *means getting all sides in a dispute or conflict to explain their position, understand their differences and then bargain to arrive at a resolution that is acceptable to both sides.* If negotiations are not working, it may be necessary to involve a **third party**.

❖ **Seek help** from a third party. Third parties are outside bodies that can help to resolve conflict, such as industry trade associations. Third parties may also be willing to provide arbitration. **Arbitration** *means getting a third party to listen to all sides and then to recommend a solution.*

e.g travel agents with Customers for holidays

Legislative ways to resolve conflict

❖ **Use a State conflict resolution agency.** The government has set up different State agencies to enforce the law and to help resolve conflicts that can arise between stakeholders.

For conflicts between **consumers and businesses**:
- National Consumer Agency
- Small Claims Court

For conflicts between **employers and employees**
- Labour Relations Commission
- Labour Court
- Equality Authority
- Employment Appeals Tribunal

❖ **Use the law.** There are laws to assist in resolving conflict between different stakeholders in business.

For conflicts between **consumers and businesses**:

- Consumer Protection Act 2007 (See Chapter 2)
- Sales of Goods and Supply of Services Act 1980 (See Chapter 2)

For conflicts between **employers and employees**,

- Industrial Relations Act 1990 (See Chapter 3)
- Employment Equality Act 1998 (See Chapter 3)
- Unfair Dismissals Acts 1977 to 2007 (See Chapter 3)

HL Short Q8
HL ABQ
HL Long Q1, 2, 3

Key Concepts & Business Terms

After studying this chapter the student should be able to explain the following key concepts and business terms:

1. Business
2. Commercial business
3. Profits
4. Non-commercial businesses/ social enterprises / not-for profit businesses
5. Stakeholders
6. Entrepreneurs
7. Investors
8. Employers
9. Employees
10. Managers
11. Suppliers
12. Producers
13. Customers
14. Consumers
15. Society
16. Interest groups / pressure groups
17. Business interest groups
18. Lobbying
19. IBEC
20. Small Firms Association (SFA)
21. ISME
22. Chambers of commerce
23. Trade associations
24. Trade unions
25. ICTU
26. Competitive business relationships
27. Co-operative business relationships
28. Changing stakeholder roles over time
29. Changing stakeholder relationships over time
30. Conflict
31. Non-legislative ways to resolve conflict
32. Negotiation
33. Legislative ways to resolve conflict

useful websites

www.vitzdrinks.com
www.ibec.ie
www.isme.ie
www.sfa.ie

www.chambers.ie
www.benjerry.com
www.simi.ie

Leaving Certificate Practice Questions

Ordinary Level

Ordinary Level – Section 1 – Short Questions (10 marks each)

1. Distinguish between a commercial and a non-commercial business.
2. Explain the term 'business stakeholder'.
3. List **five** main parties involved in business.
4. Describe the role of the entrepreneur in business.
5. Explain the term 'investor' and give **two** examples of different types of investors.
6. Explain what is meant by the term 'interest group'.
   Give **two** examples of interest groups.
7. What do the following letters stand for: (a) IBEC, (b) ICTU, (c) ISME.
8. Distinguish between a trade association and a trade union.
9. Identify **two** possible causes of conflict in business.
10. Give **two** examples of a co-operative approach to business relations.

Ordinary Level – Section 2 – Long Questions

1. Describe the role played by **four** of the main parties in business. (20 marks)
2. Distinguish between a producer and a supplier and give **one** example of each. (20 marks)
3. Describe the relationship that exists between an employer and an employee. (20 marks) [LCQ]
4. Give **two** examples of possible sources of conflict that can arise between an employer and an employee. (20 marks)
5. Describe the relationship between a producer and a consumer and give **two** examples of possible sources of conflict that can arise between a producer and a consumer. (20 marks)
6. Explain the role of interest groups in business. (25 marks)
7. Outline **two** examples of interest groups in business. (15 marks)
8. Explain the reasons why it is important for entrepreneurs to listen to consumers. (15 marks)
9. Explain the benefits to consumers of competition between rival businesses. (15 marks)
10. Outline **two** examples of where a business may have a co-operative relationship. (20 marks)

Higher Level

Higher Level – Section 1 – Short Questions (10 marks each)

1. Distinguish between a consumer and a customer.
2. Explain the meaning of the term 'business stakeholders'.
3. Identify **two** parties in business and describe a competitive relationship between them. [LCQ]
4. Explain the role played by investors in business.
5. Illustrate the role of interest groups in business. [LCQ]
6. Identify **three** examples of special interest groups.
7. Distinguish between an interest group and a supplier.
8. Describe the difference between non-legislative and legislative conflict resolution.
9. Explain what is meant by a partnership approach to business.

Higher Level – Section 2 – Applied Business Question

GOLD MEDAL SPORTS

From a young age, Danielle Burke was always keen on tennis, basketball and other sports. After studying business at university, she decided to set up her own business manufacturing sports equipment. She financed the start-up using savings, a grant from her local County Enterprise Board and money from a group of shareholders who agreed to invest in the business in return for a 40% share of the ownership.

Over the years, the business has grown and become a very profitable producer of a wide range of sports goods and equipment. It employs dozens of staff in the local community and pays tax on its profits to the government. However, for her staff, Danielle is a tough manager to work for. Pay at Gold Medal Sports is poor and working hours are long. The business regularly has to recruit new staff to replace staff who leave for better work elsewhere.

Danielle is a tough negotiator and always looks for the best bargains from her suppliers. However, she has had problems with the quality of the raw materials coming from some of her suppliers. The equipment in her factory is also now out of date and prone to breaking down. This is affecting the quality standards of the goods produced and customers are not happy. Gold Medal Sports is now under increasing pressure from rival sports goods manufacturers in China and the Far East who can supply better quality goods at very competitive prices.

To respond to this threat, Gold Medal Sports needs modern, state-of-the-art production machinery. This will require a major investment of finance. Danielle has decided that for the next few years, all profits will be retained in the business to pay for modernisation of the factory. This means that there will be no dividends paid to the shareholders who invested in the business until the profitability of the business improves.

1. Describe how the different stakeholders can affect the future survival and success of Gold Medal Sports. Refer to the text in your answer. (20 marks)
2. Illustrate **one** co-operative relationship and **one** competitive relationship that exist between Gold Medal Sports and its stakeholders. Refer to the text in your answer. (30 marks)
3. Evaluate the possible benefits to Danielle of adopting a more co-operative relationship with the business stakeholders. (30 marks)

Higher Level – Section 2 – Long Questions

1. 'Business today is made up of relationships between different people.' Discuss the different relationships that occur in business. (25 marks)
2. Contrast the relationship that exists between entrepreneurs and investors in a business enterprise. (15 marks) [LCQ]
3. Analyse the relationship between:
   (a) entrepreneurs and investors.
   (b) entrepreneurs and society.
   (c) a producer and its suppliers.
   (d) a producer and its rival producers.
   (e) a producer and its consumers.
   (f) a producer and interest groups. (30 marks)
4. Discuss the role that interest groups can play in business. (15 marks)
5. Describe the benefits of membership of the following to a business:
   (a) IBEC,
   (b) chambers of commerce,
   (c) a trade association. (15 marks)
6. 'All relationships in business are competitive.' Evaluate this statement. Support your answer with **two** examples. (20 marks)
7. Describe a co-operative and a competitive relationship that would typically exist between a business and other business organisations. (20 marks) [LCQ]

Chapter 2
Resolving Conflict in the Marketplace

Key Study Questions

Case Study *Eimear goes car shopping*

Eimear is in the market for a new car. She says that she is happy to settle for 'something that is reliable, cheap to insure, good to drive and still looks well'. She is planning to visit a number of local car dealers to see what's available within her budget. Top of her list of car dealers that she wants to visit are Classy Cars and Delux Motors.

When Eimear sees a car that she likes, purchasing it will involve entering into a **legal contract** with the car dealer. To ensure that she gets a fair deal, Eimear will need to be aware of her **legal rights** as a **consumer** and the **legal responsibilities** of the car retailers.

1. What are the elements of a legally binding contract?

Most of the deals and agreements between the different stakeholders in business are contracts. **A contract** *is a legally binding agreement that can be enforced in a court of law.* This means that if a person breaks the agreement, the judge can order him/her to complete the contract or else pay compensation.

The law of contract *sets out the rules for proving when a contract exists and when it is finished (terminated).* The law of contract is important because it governs most of the relationships between stakeholders in business.

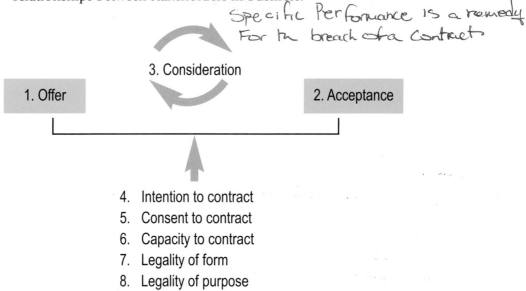

Specific Performance is a remedy for the breach of a contract

```
                    3. Consideration
   1. Offer                              2. Acceptance
```

4. Intention to contract
5. Consent to contract
6. Capacity to contract
7. Legality of form
8. Legality of purpose

Fig. 1 The elements of a legally valid contract.

Agreement: There must be a clear complete and unconditional offer and acceptance of that offer. E.g.

> A legal offer can be made verbally, in writing or by conduct.

1. Offer

Every contract must contain an **offer** to make a contract. This can be done in one of three ways:

1. **Verbally**, for example, 'I'll give you €10,000 for that car.'

2. **In writing** or by post.

3. **By conduct**, such as a customer handing over a magazine and money to a shop assistant at a checkout.

An offer is terminated if it is:

1. **Revoked**, that is, withdrawn **before** the other party has accepted it.

2. **Not accepted in time** where there is a time limit set by the offeror. For instance, CAO offers of college places only apply for a limited period of time and are terminated if not accepted when that time expires.

3. **Rejected** by the other party.

Example: Eimear visited the Classy Cars showrooms and saw a number of cars that she liked. After taking three of them for test drives, she decided that she wanted to buy the white Toyota and made an offer. The car is for sale for €25,000 and Eimear verbally tells the dealer that she is willing to pay €25,000.

Example: Suppose a car in a garage is mistakenly priced at €199 instead of the correct price of €19,999. If Eimear sees the car and insists on buying it at the display price then, legally, she is wasting her time. The garage is within its legal rights to refuse to accept an offer from a customer to buy goods displayed at the wrong price.

> **Important Note**
>
> An offer must not be confused with an invitation to treat. **An invitation to treat** *refers to an invitation to a customer to make an offer which can then be accepted or rejected.* Goods on display in a shop are regarded as an invitation to treat.

2. Acceptance

Acceptance means that the other person agrees to all the terms of the original offer without any conditions. **Acceptance** of an offer can be communicated in three ways:

HL Short Q1
HL Long Q1

1. Verbally
2. In writing
3. By conduct (e.g. a shop assistant taking the customer's money in exchange for a magazine).

> All offers to enter a contract which have been accepted must be honoured.

Example: Eimear has made an offer of €25,000 for the car that she liked. It is on special offer as it is the last one left in stock. The salesman at Classy Cars says that he will get back to Eimear with an answer because, he says, another customer is also interested in buying that particular car.

The next day the salesman from the garage phones to say that Eimear can have the car for €30,000. Eimear says no, the maximum she is willing to pay for the car is €25,000. She is annoyed at how she is being treated and tells the garage that she is no longer interested and is withdrawing her offer. The garage then say that they will accept her original offer of €25,000 and demand payment. Does Eimear have to pay?

The answer is no. Eimear did make an offer but it was not accepted. The garage then made a counter offer of €30,000 which she rejected so there was no longer any offer for the garage to accept.

3. Consideration

Consideration provides evidence of a contract.

Each party to a contract must give something of value to the other party. **Consideration** *is what each party offers the other as evidence of their agreement.* So long as Consideration exists, a Court of law will not question it's adequacy

Provided it is of some value

Example: Unhappy with her treatment by Classy Cars, Eimear went to Delux Motors instead. There she saw a silver Volkswagen that she liked. After a test drive, she made an offer to buy if the garage could supply the car in red. The garage verbally accepted Eimear's offer and asked for a deposit of €1000, as they would have to order the car from Germany. Eimear paid the deposit and in return Delux Motors provided a receipt and order confirmation. This exchange by each party provides the consideration for this contract.

4. Intention to contract

For a contract to be legally enforceable, there must be an intention to contract.

Intention to contract *means that the parties to the contract must have intended to create a legally binding contract that could end up in court if not fulfilled.* Contract law makes two important assumptions:

1. All **business agreements**, whether written or verbal, **are intended to be legally binding**.

2. All **social and private agreements are not intended to be legally binding**. This means, for instance, that you cannot sue a friend because they did not keep their promise to lend you their car for a holiday trip.

Example: The agreement between Delux Motors and Eimear is a business agreement and therefore assumed to be legally binding.

5. Consent to contract

Consent to enter a contract must be genuinely and freely given.

Consent to contract *means that each party must give genuine agreement of their own free will to the making of the contract.* Consent to enter a legally binding contract may not exist:

1. If a person is **pressurised against their will** into entering a contract. This can occur if physical or mental pressure **or intimidation** was used to force an agreement without genuine free choice or consent.

2. If a person enters a contract as a result of deliberate **misrepresentation** or dishonesty by others.

Example: If, after purchasing a car, Eimear discovers that the car was not new and that the mileometer has been illegally changed, then this would be a deliberate misrepresentation. According to the law, Eimear would be entitled to cancel the contract and get her money back.

3. If a **genuine mistake** can be shown to have happened.

6. Capacity to contract

Capacity *means that the people agreeing to the contract must have the legal right to do so.* People who do not have the legal right to enter into a contract are:

1. Anyone under 18, except for items considered normal purchases for such a person, such as clothes, music or food.

2. People who are intoxicated, insane or 'of unsound mind' at the time.

3. A company cannot enter into contracts which are outside its legally stated purpose as set out in its Memorandum of Association. For example, a company set up to sell cars cannot open a hotel as it would not have the legal authority to do so. If it did, it would be acting **ultra vires**.

> **Parties must have the legal capacity to enter into a contract.**

Company operating outside their powers.

> **Example:** Eimear is over 18 and is not insane so she has the legal capacity to enter into a contract. If she was 16 when she bought the car then the contract would be invalid.

7. Legality of form

Legality of form *means that certain contracts* **must** *be drawn up in writing before they can become legally binding.* These include hire purchase agreements, property sales and insurance policies. Other than these, most other contracts can be verbal or implied by conduct (e.g. handing over money).

> **Example:** If Eimear were buying the car on hire purchase, she would have to get a written contract. If she was paying cash, no written contract would be necessary to prove that a contract exists.

8. Legality of purpose

Legality of purpose *means that for a contract to be legally binding, it must be for a* **legal purpose** *and not involve committing any crime or breaking any law.*

> - **Contracts must be in a legally valid form.**
> - **Contracts must be for a legal purpose.**

OL Short Q1, 2, 3
OL Long Q1
HL Short Q2
HL Long Q2

2. How can a contract be terminated?

Termination of a contract *means it can no longer be legally enforced.* Contracts can be legally terminated by:

Specific.

Contracts can be terminated by
1. **Performance**
2. **Agreement**
3. **Frustration**
4. **Breach of contract**

1. **Performance** – where the parties involved fulfil all their obligations as agreed.

   Example: Once the car is delivered and the guarantee period expires, the contract between Eimear and Delux Motors is over.

2. **Agreement** – all the parties to a contract can agree to terminate a contract, whether or not the purpose of the contract has been achieved.

   Example: If Delux Motors had difficulty getting delivery of the car from the manufacturers in Germany, then both Eimear and the garage could agree to cancel the contract.

3. **Frustration** – where some unforeseen event(s) prevents the contract being completed. This could be due to a fire, an extreme weather event or the death or bankruptcy of any of the parties to the contract.

   Example: If a major fire in the Volkswagen factory means that production of cars is suspended indefinitely.

E.g 4. **Breach of contract** – where one of the parties breaks a condition of the contract. **A condition** *is an* **essential element** *of a contract.*

   Example: A condition of the contract between Eimear and Classy Cars is that the car to be delivered is in red. If the car that is delivered turns out to be pink or orange, then this would break an essential condition of the contract and Eimear could cancel the contract.

- A condition is an essential element.
- A warranty is non-essential.

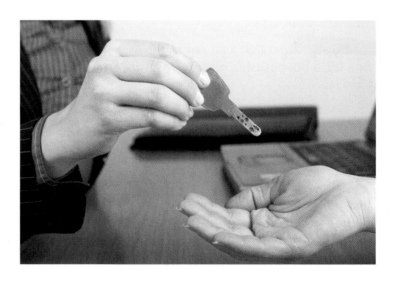

*A **warranty** is a **non-essential element** of a contract.* If a warranty is broken you are entitled to compensation, although the contract is still valid.

> **Example:** Suppose the car delivered to Eimear has a different brand of tyre to what is described in the sales brochure. This would only be a breach of warranty, as it does not interfere with the ownership or proper use of the car. The contract to purchase still stands but the garage should correct the breach of warranty before Eimear takes legal possession.

OL Short Q4, 12

HL Short Q3
HL Long Q3

3. What are the remedies for breach of contract?

When a condition of a contract is broken, you can:

1. **Rescind (cancel) the contract.** If a condition of a contract is broken, the injured party can refuse to honour it.

> **Remedies for breach of contract are:**
> 1. **Cancellation**
> 2. **Compensation**
> 3. **Specific performance**

> **Example:** A pink saloon car is delivered instead of a red coupé.

2. **Sue for financial compensation** for the losses incurred. This can be done by hiring a solicitor and taking the other party to court. If a warranty is broken, the contract can still be fulfilled but often at greater expense and inconvenience. Compensation can be sought for breaches of warranty but the contract cannot be cancelled.

3. **Seek 'specific performance'**, which means getting the court to order the other party to keep their side of the agreement.

OL Long Q2

HL Long Q4

Case Study

PIXAR
cancels contract with Disney

Pixar, the animation business responsible for producing Hollywood blockbusters such as *Toy Story*, *Wall-E* and *Up*, signed a **contract** with Disney Corporation. According to the contract, Pixar would make the movies while Disney would provide all the **advertising**, spin-off product merchandising and marketing promotions in exchange for a percentage share of the profits.

However, after a few years, Pixar became unhappy with the high **profits** that they had agreed in the contract to share with Disney. Pixar decided that it wanted to change this condition of the contract so that Disney would get a smaller percentage of the profits.

Not surprisingly, Disney was unwilling to change the contract, as it would mean giving up hundreds of millions of dollars in lost profits. Despite repeated efforts, Pixar could not persuade Disney to agree to a change in the contract.

Pixar decided that it had had enough. Under a legally binding **condition** of the contract, Pixar was obliged to make only a certain number of movies with Disney. Once the final movie was completed, the existing contract was fully **performed** and was **legally terminated**. After that, Pixar was free to undertake its own marketing and distribution and retain 100% right to all profits from its own movies.

Recall and Review

1. What are the elements of a legally binding business contract?
2. How can a company like Pixar terminate a contract?

4. What legislation protects consumer rights?

Caveat emptor *is a legal term meaning 'Let the buyer beware'.* Whenever a consumer buys a good or service they are expected to use a reasonable degree of common sense. If you subsequently have a complaint and want to take legal action, your case will fail if you have not followed this basic principle of consumer law.

Even if consumers have obeyed the 'caveat emptor' rule, there are many causes of conflict that can arise between a business and its consumers. These include the use of misleading advertising and selling poor quality goods and services.

Consumers' legal rights and sellers' responsibilities are set out in two important pieces of legislation:

1. The Sale of Goods and Supply of Services Act 1980.
2. The Consumer Protection Act 2007.

5. What is the Sale of Goods and Supply of Services Act 1980?

The Sale of Goods and Supply of Services Act 1980 sets out the law concerning the sale of goods and services.

The **Sale of Goods and Supply of Services Act 1980** *sets out:*

* *The* **legal rights of consumers** *when they purchase goods*
* *The* **legal responsibilities of retailers** *to consumers*
* *The* **legal remedies** *available*

This law applies to every consumer purchase of new goods from a legally registered business. It also applies to goods bought on hire purchase. The law does not apply to second-hand goods (except cars) or if you buy something from a friend or a private individual.

Evaluation:

The legal rights of consumers

1. **Goods sold must be of merchantable quality. Merchantable quality** *means that goods sold to consumers must be reasonably durable, even if they are sale items.*

   Example: A new car must not break down after travelling just five kilometres, cornflakes should be fresh and edible, or buttons must not fall off a shirt within days of purchasing it.

2. **Goods sold must be fit for the purpose intended.**

   Example: If a customer asks for a car with heated seats, then the seats must be heated. Similarly, if a consumer wants a waterproof jacket, then the jacket sold must be waterproof.

3. **Goods sold must be as described** by the salesperson/brochure/sample.

   Example: A car described as red in a brochure or sales agreement must not turn out to be pink when delivered to the customer.

4. **The buyer is entitled to legal ownership and quiet possession.** This means that the seller of the goods has the sole legal right to sell the goods. As a result, the buyer should enjoy quiet possession by being able to use the goods as they wish.

5. **Services** must be provided by a **competent person** with **skill** and using **due care and diligence.** Any **materials used** must be sound and fit for the purpose and be of merchantable quality.

   Example: A mechanic servicing a car should be properly trained and use proper tools and the correct spare parts.

6. **Consumers renting or buying on hire purchase** have the same rights as someone buying goods paying upfront with cash.

The legal responsibilities of retailers

1. **Retailers are legally responsible** for any defects in any product they sell, even if it is the manufacturer's fault.

2. **Retailers must respect all the legal rights of customers** (listed above).

3. **Complaints** must be dealt with by the seller even if they relate to a fault caused by the manufacturer.

4. **Signs pretending to limit the retailer's liability are illegal.** These include 'The shop does not accept responsibility for any faulty goods sold'; 'No money refunds'; 'Credit Notes Only'; 'Goods not Exchanged'. However, the consumer has no right to redress if:

   - The consumer is responsible for any fault.

- The consumer has simply changed their mind and wants to return the goods.
- The consumer failed to act reasonably promptly after buying the goods.

5. **Any product guarantees offered** are an additional benefit. They cannot restrict consumer rights as set out in law. Written guarantees must be clear and specific regarding:

- the goods covered
- who is offering the guarantee
- the duration of the guarantee
- the procedure for making a claim
- what remedy is offered.

6. It is illegal for retailers to demand payment for **unsolicited goods sent** to consumers. *These are goods that are sent to someone without having received an order.*
S/he has the right to keep the goods after 6 months if the sender has not collected them.

redress • **The remedies available** *if the sender has not collected them.*

when there is a delay between the purchase date and the actual complaint, or when the fault is of a minor nature then the consumer may only be entitled to partial refund or repair.

If the consumer has proof of purchase (such as a receipt) the remedies available depend on how serious the fault is.

1. **Repair** of the good if the fault is very minor (e.g. a small scratch on car paintwork). If the retailer offers a repair, the consumer can agree to the repair and still retain the right to a full refund if the repair is not satisfactory.

OL Short Q8, 9, 10

OL Long Q3

HL Short Q5

HL Long Q6

2. **Replacement** of the good if the fault is more serious

3. **Refund** of money. If the goods are not as described, not fit for the purpose intended or not of merchantable quality, then the consumer is entitled to a full refund from the seller, not just a replacement or a repair.

The consumer's rights lessen the longer s/he puts off making the complaint.

6. What is the Consumer Protection Act 2007?

The Consumer Protection Act 2007 sets out the law concerning the false or misleading promotion of goods for sale.	The **Consumer Protection Act 2007** *is the law that protects consumers from unfair business-to-consumer commercial practices. The Act bans practices that are unfair, misleading or aggressive towards consumers and are likely to impair a consumer's choice.* The Act does not apply to dealings between businesses. Specifically the Act:

★ **Prohibits false product descriptions.** Goods must not be sold with a false trade description. This applies to advertisements, shop notices or any claims made by a sales person, either written or verbal.

> **Examples:** (a) Second-hand cars being sold as new. (b) Cornflakes advertised as being the cheapest in town, when they are not. (c) A coat labelled 'waterproof' but which lets in the rain. (d) A dry-cleaning business that offers 'same day service' but in reality regularly takes three days. (e) Making false claims that a product can cure an illness.

★ **Prohibits false prices:** It is illegal to give false or misleading information regarding the past, present or future price of a product. Goods marked as being reduced in price in a sale must have been on sale at the original higher price for at least 28 consecutive days before the sale.

★ **Prohibits false or misleading advertising**.

> **Examples:** (a) Advertising a jumper as being 100% wool when it is really made of acrylic. (b) Offering 'free prizes' when it costs money to claim the prizes. (c) Running competitions when the top prize is not available.

★ **Prohibits businesses from engaging in aggressive practices** such as harassing, coercing, taking advantage of, or putting unfair pressure on a consumer.

> **Examples:** (a) Demanding payment for unsolicited goods. (b) Running 'pyramid schemes' where a person pays money but, instead of a product or service, their only benefit arises from persuading other people to join the scheme after them.

★ **Established the National Consumer Agency.**

National Consumer Agency

national **consumer** agency
gníomhaireacht náisiúnta **tomhaltóirí**

putting **consumers** first

The National Consumer Agency (NCA) *is the State agency that promotes consumers' awareness of their legal rights and ensures that consumer legislation is obeyed by businesses.* Specifically, the National Consumer Agency is responsible for:

- **Enforcing consumer laws.** The NCA does this by investigating suspected breaches of consumer law. It can issue on-the-spot fines to businesses for some breaches of consumer law. It can also bring repeat offenders to court. The agency has the power to enter business premises, accompanied by gardaí if necessary, to gather evidence.

- **Providing information and advice to the public** on their rights as consumers. The NCA does this mainly through its website (www.consumerconnect.ie), publications and telephone helplines.

- **Providing information and advice to businesses** on their legal responsibilities to consumers.

- **Advising the government** on how best to ensure that the welfare of consumers is protected.

- **Publishing a Consumer Protection List** of businesses found breaching consumer law.

OL Short Q5, 6, 7
OL Long Q5
HL Short Q6, 7
HL Long Q5, 7, 12

Evaluation: is very effective because it is a statutory body, is an advocate for the consumer and has enforced powers for example.

- The NCA can serve a compliance notice on a trader when it considers to have engaged in a prohibited activity.

- NCA may also apply to the court for an order that requires a business to pay compensation for any loss or damage to the consumer resulting from a offence.

Case Study

ElectroWorld's
Faulty Refrigerator

Eimear's boyfriend, Alan, recently bought his own house and has purchased a new fridge for his kitchen from ElectroWorld. The fridge was delivered but after a few days he noticed that the temperature control was not working correctly. Food was beginning to smell, go mouldy and had to be thrown out. Naturally, he was annoyed, but wondered what he should do, and whether he had any legal rights to back him up.

Alan contacted ElectroWorld and explained his complaint about his fridge to the manager. She apologised but said that unfortunately it was nothing to do with the shop. The manager claimed it was the manufacturer's fault and that Alan should contact them. She kindly gave him the manufacturer's telephone number and address in South Korea so that he could contact them.

While in ElectroWorld, Alan saw that they advertised their products as being the 'cheapest in town or your money back'. However, he now knew that the fridge that he bought could be purchased for €100 less in a shop across the street. When he pointed this out to the manager, she just laughed and said: 'It's just a bit of harmless advertising hype – people are not expected to take our ads seriously!'

Alan was really annoyed about this and wondered whether the store was breaking the law by making such misleading claims.

Recall and Review

1. Identify the elements of the Sale of Goods and Supply of Services Act 1980 that apply to Alan's situation.
2. Explain the legal responsibilities of ElectroWorld under the Consumer Protection Act 2007.
3. Outline the advice you would give Alan in dealing with this issue.

7. How can consumer complaints be resolved in a non-legislative manner?

> It is better to try to settle a business conflict without having to use the law. This can be done by talking to the other party or by seeking help.

Consumers who find themselves in conflict with a business over the way they have been treated have two **non-legislative** ways of resolving the issue:

1. Talk to the retailer
2. Seek help from a third party

● Talk to the retailer

Talk to the retailer as soon as possible when the difficulty arises. The best way of doing this is to:

* Know your legal rights as set out in law.
* Bring along a receipt as proof of purchase.
* Ask to speak to the manager and complain in a friendly but firm manner, insisting that your legal rights as a consumer be respected. (It is important to remember that an aggressive negotiation style can make matters worse.)
* If talking to the retailer does not work, write a formal letter of complaint to the retailer.

● Seek help from a third party

If discussing the situation with the retailer does not work, then consumers can ask a third party to assist. Organisations that can assist in resolving a consumer conflict are:

* National Consumer Agency (set up by the Consumer Protection Act 2007).
* Industry trade associations (e.g. Society for the Irish Motor Industry).
* Consumers' Association of Ireland.
* Financial Services Ombudsman for complaints concerning financial institutions.
* Office of the Ombudsman for the Public Service.

Biúró an Ombudsman um
Sheirbhísí Airgeadais

Financial Services
Ombudsman

Consumers' Association of Ireland

The Consumers' Association of Ireland *is a non-commercial organisation set up to protect and promote the interests of consumers.* Members of the public must pay an annual membership fee to join and in return they receive a consumer magazine, *Consumer Choice*, and advice on consumer rights. The association's main activities are:

✪ Publishing reports and surveys into consumer products and services.

✪ Highlighting problem areas where the interests of consumers are being neglected and seeking improved product quality standards.

✪ Running a consumer advice service to help members with consumer problems and complaints. For a small fee the association's solicitor will provide speedy professional legal advice on consumer issues.

✪ Lobbying the government for changes and improvements to consumer rights legislation.

Financial Services Ombudsman

The **Financial Services Ombudsman** specialises in resolving consumer complaints against banks and other financial institutions such as insurance companies and credit unions. The decision of the ombudsman is binding on the institutions involved. However, if consumers are still dissatisfied they can seek legislative solutions through the courts.

Ombudsman for the Insurance Industry

The **Ombudsman for the Insurance Industry** investigates consumer complaints against insurance companies. The decision of this ombudsman is binding on an insurance company, but not on the individual making the complaint.

The Office of the Ombudsman (for Public Services)

Cannot investigate complaints concerning The President, The Dail, Defence Forces, Garda Siochana, or Prison Service.

The Office of the Ombudsman (for Public Services) specialises in dealing with consumer complaints against State-owned organisations, including all Government departments, the Health Service Executive (HSE) and local authorities. Although financed by the State, the Office of the Ombudsman is independent of the government.

When investigating a complaint, the Office of the Ombudsman has **no power to force its recommendation** to be accepted. Nevertheless, most public bodies comply to avoid bad publicity and damage to their reputation.

Procedure: Before contacting the Office of the Ombudsman, you must first contact the public body involved and make an effort to solve the problem yourself. If this proves unsatisfactory, you can then go to the ombudsman but this must be done within 12 months of the event you are complaining about.

Evaluation: Since 1984 The office ombudsman has helped over 70,000 people with valid complaints and advised and guided many others.

OL Long Q4, 7

HL Short Q8
HL Long Q9

8. How can consumer complaints be resolved in a legislative manner?

> The Small Claims Court is a fast, easy and inexpensive way to use the law to resolve consumer complaints.

If the non-legislative approach of talking and negotiating does not produce a satisfactory result, then a consumer can resort to taking a **legislative approach**. This can be done by using a State conflict resolution agency (such as the **National Consumer Agency** or the **Small Claims Court**) or hiring a solicitor to take the retailer to court for breaking the law.

● Small Claims Court

• It is possible to pursue small claims through this service against product and service providers in any EU State, except Denmark.

The **Small Claims Court** *provides an inexpensive, fast and easy way for consumers to resolve disputes without the need to employ a solicitor.* A consumer with a complaint must first fill in a simple form describing their complaint. This can be done by post or on-line. The court will then invite both parties to come in and present their side of the case before making a recommendation. Unlike other courts, the Small Claims Court **cannot force** an agreement but is very effective at **persuading** sellers to respect consumers' rights.   *NO Solicitor is needed.*

Evaluation: • It's fast and easy way to resolve disputes.
Can be done online • Inexpensive non-refundable fee of €15 payable to a district court when claim lodged
• You will get unbiased and fair Judge.

Fieldwork

The Small Claims Court will only hear complaints up to a certain value. What is the current maximum value of disputes that the Small Claims Court can hear?

The answer is available from **www.smallclaims.ie**

up to a maximum of € 2,000.

● Hire a solicitor

If no agreement is reached in the Small Claims Court, then the consumer can contact a **solicitor** to bring a formal case to the District Court or higher court, depending on the sums of money involved. There will be a full hearing before a judge who will issue a legally binding settlement. All disputes that are too large for the Small Claims Court should be brought to a solicitor.

OL Short Q11
OL Long Q6

HL Short Q9
HL ABQs
HL Long Q8, 10, 11

Advantages of Small Claims Court

1. Faster than going to the District Court or higher court.
2. Low cost – only a small fee and no solicitors involved.

Disadvantages of Small Claims Court

1. Only deals with complaints up to a limited value.
2. Recommendation is not legally binding.
3. If you are not happy with the outcome, you will have to go for a full court hearing in the District Court or higher court.

Case Study

Diabolical Diablo

Eimear's difficulties with Classy Motors were small compared to the problems that an American customer claimed he encountered when he spent €300,000 on a prestigious Lamborghini Diablo. He complained that the roof leaked, the doors regularly got stuck, the battery failed, the horn did not function properly, dashboard lights flickered on and off, the engine stalled and the hydraulic system collapsed.

Dissatisfied, the customer took the manufacturers, Lamborghini, to court. He claimed that there was a clear breach of consumer law as he had to take the car back to the garage ten times for repairs. Lamborghini denied the claim.

'It's very embarrassing,' said the customer. 'You want to get a Lamborghini to be the centre of attention. But now you're the centre of attention because you're some fool locked in a car.'

Recall and Review

1. By going to court, is this consumer pursuing a legislative or non-legislative solution to his consumer problem?

2. If the customer had purchased the car in Ireland, who is legally responsible – the seller or the manufacturer?

3. Identify the Irish legislation that would apply to the above case. Give reasons for your answer.

4. Identify (a) one legislative and (b) one non-legislative way that an Irish consumer could take to try to resolve the issue.

5. Identify one reason why this claim would be unsuitable for the Irish Small Claims Court.

Key Concepts & Business Terms

After studying this chapter the student should be able to explain the following key concepts and business terms:

1. Contract
2. Law of contract
3. Offer
4. Invitation to treat
5. Acceptance
6. Consideration
7. Intention to contract
8. Capacity to contract
9. Legality of form
10. Legality of purpose
11. Termination of a contract
12. Frustration
13. Breach of contract
14. Condition
15. Warranty
16. Specific performance
17. Negotiation
18. Caveat emptor
19. Sale of Goods and Supply of Services Act 1980
20. The Consumer Protection Act 2007
21. National Consumer Agency
22. Consumers' Association of Ireland
23. Office of the Ombudsman for Public Services
24. Financial Services Ombudsman
25. Small Claims Court

 useful websites

www.pixar.com
www.irishstatutebook.ie
www.consumerconnect.ie (National Consumer Agency)
www.consumerassociation.ie

www.financialombudsman.ie
www.ombudsman.gov.ie (Office of the Ombudsman [for the Public Service])
www.courts.ie (Small Claims Court)

Leaving Certificate Practice Questions

Ordinary Level

Ordinary Level – Section 1 – Short Questions (10 marks each)

1. Explain what is meant by a business 'contract'.
2. List **three** elements of a legally valid contract.
3. List **three** reasons why someone may not have the legal right to enter a contract. [LCQ]
4. Explain **two** ways in which a business contract can be terminated.
5. List **two** possible reasons for conflict between a seller and a consumer.
6. Identify **two** pieces of legislation that protect consumer rights
7. Identify the law that protects consumers against false or misleading descriptions.
8. In consumer law, what is meant by 'merchantable quality'?
9. State, giving reasons, whether the following shop signs are legal:
   (a) No refunds will be given
   (b) No credit cards accepted.
   (c) Goods will not be exchanged.
   (d) CCTV in operation.
10. List **two** possible forms of compensation a dissatisfied consumer may request.
11. What is the function of the Small Claims Court? [LCQ]
12. Gerry put a deposit of €50 on a €250 bicycle two weeks ago. Last week he bought a similar model bicycle for €199 in a sale in a different store. The shopkeeper refuses to return his deposit. Is Gerry entitled to his money back? Explain why. [LCQ]

Ordinary Level – Section 2 – Long Questions

1. Describe what is meant by 'capacity to contract'. (20 marks)
2. Outline the remedies for a breach of contract. (20 marks)
3. Outline the main provisions of the Sale of Goods and Supply of Services Act 1980. (20 marks)
4. Ciara bought a ride-on lawnmower from Quality Lawnmowers Ltd. for €2,500. The first time she tried to cut the lawn the blades did not work on the lawnmower. She contacted Quality Lawnmowers Ltd. to complain.
   (a) Name the law that protects the consumer in this case. (10 marks) [LCQ]
   (b) Explain Ciara's legal rights and the duties of Quality Lawnmowers Ltd. (20 marks) [LCQ]
   (c) Outline **one** non-legislative (non-legal) method of solving the above problem. (10 marks) [LCQ]
5. After buying a new pair of jeans, you arrive home and decide that you do not like the colour.
   (a) Explain what legal rights you have in this situation. (10 marks)
   (b) Outline **two** activities prohibited by the Consumer Protection Act 2007. (20 marks)
   (c) Describe the main functions of the National Consumer Agency. (15 marks)
6. Anne Andrews had a new wall built in her garden by a local builder, which cost €500. Within a week a number of bricks had become loose and fallen onto the grass. The bricks had broken into halves when they fell on the ground.
   (a) Illustrate **one** non-legislative (non-legal) method of solving the above problem. (5 marks) [LCQ]
   (b) Outline **three** of Anne's rights under the Sale of Goods and Supply of Services Act 1980 in relation to the service provided by the builder. (15 marks) [LCQ]
   (c) State one reason why Anne could take a case to the Small Claims Court and describe the role of this court. (20 marks) [LCQ]
7. Outline the role of the Office of the Ombudsman. (15 marks)

Higher Level

Higher Level – Section 1 – Short Questions (10 marks each)

1. Explain the term 'invitation to treat'.

2. Give **two** examples of situations where an individual or legal entity does <u>not</u> have capacity to contract. [LCQ]

3. In a contract, what is the difference between 'a condition' and 'a warranty'?

4. Explain the term 'caveat emptor'?

5. In consumer law, distinguish between 'merchantable quality' and 'fit for the purpose intended'.

6. List **two** activities prohibited by the Consumer Protection Act 2007.

7. Explain **two** roles of the National Consumer Agency.

8. Identify **two** non-legislative steps a consumer can take to resolve a consumer complaint.

9. Under what circumstances would you recommend a dissatisfied consumer to bring a case to the Small Claims Court?

Higher Level – Section 2 – Applied Business Question 1

Gourmet Foods

Kevin Ryan is an entrepreneur and founder of Gourmet Foods, a small but growing manufacturer of high-quality ready meals. The business employs very flexible, customer-focused staff and has been putting a big effort into building up a good reputation for its quality products.

Despite being slightly more expensive than its competitors, Gourmet Foods business has been growing. This has mainly been by selling its products through small shops and delicatessens.

Recently the business had a sales breakthrough when a major supermarket chain, Foodland, confirmed by letter that it had decided to place an initial order for €50,000 worth of microwavable dinners. Foodland also paid €1000 deposit for the order. This order was important for Gourmet Foods and Kevin hopes that it will lead to lots of repeat orders and also open up opportunities to distribute the firm's products through other major supermarket chains. Kevin and his staff ordered extra raw materials and got started on making the products for Foodland.

However, one month later Foodland contacted him and informed him that due to a change of company policy, the supermarket no longer wanted to stock Gourmet Foods meals. The supermarket had decided that it wanted to keep costs down by only stocking well-known, low-price international brands. Foodland also asked that the €1000 deposit they handed over with the original order be returned to them.

Kevin was devastated by this development. The order for Foodland had already been produced and was currently being loaded by forklift onto the back of a truck for delivery to the Foodland distribution depot.

1. Identify the different stakeholders in Gourmet Foods. Refer to the case study in your answer. (20 marks)
2. In your opinion, do Gourmet Foods have a contract with Foodland? Refer to the text to support your answer. (30 marks)
3. Explain the legal remedies that are available to Gourmet Foods if they take Foodland to court for breach of contract. (30 marks)

Higher Level – Section 2 – Applied Business Question 2

Global Electrics

Samantha Doyle bought a computer from Global Electrics in the shop's January sale. It had been marked down by 50% to a 'Special Offer' price of €800 and came with a one-year guarantee. At the time, Samantha had happily signed the sales agreement and guarantee without reading the small print carefully.

When she got home Samantha began unpacking her new possession but when she removed the sale sticker she found the original price sticker that read €999. She became even more annoyed when she discovered that when the machine was turned on, it would not connect to the Internet. The computer also began crashing every 30 minutes and was effectively unusable.

Exasperated, Samantha contacted the retailer and explained the problem. Because she had a guarantee, she believed that she would be able to get a replacement. However, Global Electrics told her that it was the manufacturer's responsibility and that the guarantee stated this. The manufacturer of the computer was a Japanese company based in Tokyo. According to the manager, the shop's policy was not to refund, replace or renew faulty goods. Instead he gave her a telephone number and recommended that she call Tokyo.

1. Analyse Samantha's legal rights as a consumer. (30 marks)
2. Explain the legal responsibilities of the Global Electrics retailer in the above case. (20 marks)
3. Recommend a legislative solution that Samantha could pursue to get a refund. (30 marks)

Higher Level – Section 2 – Long Questions

1. Define a 'contract'. Outline why an 'invitation to treat' is not a contract. (20 marks) [LCQ]
2. Describe the elements of a legally binding business contract. (20 marks)
3. Illustrate **four** methods by which a legal contract may be terminated. (20 marks) [LCQ]
4. Demonstrate how the remedies for breach of contract can help solve conflicts between contractual parties. (20 marks) [LCQ]
5. Boris sees a CD on sale for just €2.99 and decides to buy it because he thinks it is a bargain. However, when he goes to the sales desk he is told that the marked price is incorrect and it should have read €22.99. Explain Boris's legal rights in this situation. (20 marks)

6. Evaluate how effective the main provisions of the Sale of Goods and Supply of Services Act 1980 are in protecting consumers. (25 marks) [LCQ]

7. Outline the main provisions of the Consumer Protection Act 2007. Use examples to support your answer. (20 marks)

8. Distinguish between a legislative and a non-legislative approach to resolving a consumer conflict. Use examples to support your answer. (20 marks)

9. Distinguish between the role of the Financial Services Ombudsman and the Office of the Ombudsman (for Public Services). (20 marks)

10. Raymond purchased a second-hand family car described as being 'in perfect condition with only 20,000 kilometres on the clock and a five-year guarantee'. Two weeks later when he, his wife and two children were out shopping in the car, it broke down. He contacted the garage, which agreed to send a tow truck, but insisted that Raymond pay for the call out as they said the guarantee only covered replacement parts. They also said that he probably overloaded the car by having four people in it and that this caused the breakdown.

    (a) Analyse Raymond's legal rights with reference to the relevant consumer legislation. (20 marks)

    (b) Explain the benefits of settling this matter in a non-legislative manner. (20 marks)

    (c) Describe the legal responsibilities of a garage when selling a second-hand car. (20 marks)

11. State **three** advantages of taking a case to the Small Claims Court. (15 marks) [LCQ]

12. 'Consumers are protected against many unfair business practices.' Using examples, explain the main consumer rights set out by law. (20 marks)

Chapter 3
Resolving Conflict in the Workplace

Key Study Questions

Case Study

MEGA DEAL
SUPERMARKETS®

Mega Deal operates a chain of supermarkets. Like most supermarkets, it sells thousands of different types of grocery products. The business currently **employs** over 400 full- and part-time staff in jobs such as checkout assistants, shelf stackers, warehouse staff, delivery drivers, stock control, security guards, accountants and managers.

Many of the staff are members of a **trade union**. The business employs a full-time **human resources manager** who is responsible for looking after **industrial relations** between the company and its employees.

In recent years, more low-price competitors have entered the market and competition among food retailers has become intense. To compete, Mega Deal has had to lower its prices and cut costs. However, this has also meant reduced profitability for the business and the business is under huge financial pressure to survive.

A. Industrial relations and trade unions

1. What are industrial relations?

> Industrial relations refer to the quality of the relationship between the managers and employees in an organisation.

Mega Deal Supermarkets, like all firms, wants to maintain good industrial relations. **Industrial relations** *refer to the quality of the relations that exist between the managers and the employees in an organisation.* A business where managers and employees have a positive partnership approach and get on well with one another is said to have good industrial relations.

Benefits of good industrial relations include:

* It is easier to **recruit and retain** high-quality staff.
* Low levels of **absenteeism** and **labour turnover** (staff resignations).
* Happy staff are more **productive.**
* **Fewer industrial disputes** or strikes disrupting the business.

2. What are the causes of conflict in the workplace?

HL Short Q1

Over the years, there have been a number of industrial disputes in Mega Deal Supermarkets. An **industrial dispute** *is a legal term referring to any conflict between workers and employers.* Industrial disputes can be caused by:

* Conflict over **pay and working conditions**.
* Conflict over **redundancies or dismissals**.
* Conflict over **discrimination of staff**.

Industrial relations conflict can be **made worse** by

* **Poor communications** between employers and employees.
* **Unrealistic employees** who ignore the financial pressures on a business.
* **Excessively demanding employers** who put staff under too much pressure.
* **Aggressive** interpersonal behaviour between employers and employees. For instance, **autocratic managers** who do not listen to their staff or who engage in bullying behaviour.

OL Short Q1
OL Long Q1

* **Lack of trust** between employers and employees. This could arise, for instance, because past agreements were broken.

3. How can good industrial relations be promoted?

Good industrial relations in a business are promoted by:

* Paying **good wages** and providing **good conditions of employment**.
* Having **open communication** between employees and employers.
* **Keeping promises** and building up **trust and respect** between employers and employees.
* **Treating staff fairly**, without discrimination.

✳ **Having a clear grievance procedure** in place for dealing quickly and fairly with any conflicts that may arise between staff and management. **Grievance procedures** *refer to the rules agreed between employers and staff when raising workplace issues.* Effective grievance procedures should provide a **simple**, **fair** and **quick** method for resolving conflicts between employees and management.

✳ Ensuring any **dismissals are fair**.

HL Short Q2

4. What are trade unions?

Many of the staff in Mega Deal are members of a trade union. **Trade unions** *are organisations that represent the views and interests of employees in matters concerning pay and conditions of employment.*

> Example: SIPTU, ASTI. Employees pay an annual subscription to join a union. Typically, trade union members are organised into branches in their place of work. A **shop steward** *is a spokesperson elected by employees in a workplace to act as their local union representative.*

> **Employees join trade unions because it is easier to negotiate pay and conditions and solve industrial relations problems together rather than individually.**

Benefits of union membership to employees

- Seek to **protect employees rights**
- Look for better **pay and conditions**
- **Negotiate** on behalf of employees with employers using skilled negotiators
- Provide **advice** to trade union members on industrial relations and employment issues.
- Provide a **national voice** for workers through the Irish Congress of Trade Unions (ICTU)

Benefits of union membership to employers

- **Simplifies communications** between management and employees on issues concerning pay and conditions, saving time and money.

ICTU

The **Irish Congress of Trade Unions (ICTU)** *is the body that speaks and acts for **all** unions in the Republic of Ireland.* This gives the ICTU a lot of influence with employers and the government. The ICTU:

STRONGER TOGETHER
CONGRESS
Irish Congress of Trade Unions

✳ Acts as a **negotiator** on behalf of all unions in dealings with the government, the EU and national employer organisations such as IBEC.

✳ **Promotes** the benefits of union membership among the general public.

✳ **Resolves disputes** and disagreements between different unions.

✳ Provides **training, education and research** services for unions and their members.

OL Short Q2

OL Long Q2

B. Conflict over pay and working conditions

Example: Mega Deal has had a turbulent industrial relations record, with many industrial disputes between management and workers in the company over the years. When Michelle O'Neill was recruited she was aware of this and decided to join a union. Union members in the supermarket are looking to negotiate a 5% cost-of-living pay rise and have asked their union to start negotiations with the Mega Deal management.

Michelle O'Neill

5. How are employee pay and conditions negotiated?

Pay disputes are a very common cause of conflict in the workplace, and there are different types of pay claims.

* A **cost-of-living claim** *arises where employees want their wages to keep up with inflation.*

    Example: If inflation is 4%, workers may seek a 4% pay increase.

* A **comparability claim** *arises where employees want similar pay and conditions to workers doing comparable work in a different company.*

    Example: Shop assistants in Mega Deal may seek the same pay and conditions as shop assistants in Tesco or Lidl.

* A **relativity claim** *occurs where one group of workers want to maintain higher pay than another group.*

    Example: If the shelf stackers in Mega Deal get a pay rise, then the checkout operators may seek an increase to maintain the relative difference in pay.

* A **productivity claim** *occurs where workers seek improved pay and conditions as a reward for increasing their output and efficiency.*

> **Pay and conditions in a firm can be negotiated by staff individually or collectively.**

Local pay bargaining

When employers or employees want to change the pay or other conditions of employment, a process of negotiation called **local bargaining** can be followed.

❖ **Individual bargaining** *occurs when the employer negotiates individually with an employee.* This can happen in a business where union membership is small.

❖ **Collective bargaining** *occurs when the employer negotiates collectively with a group of employees, usually through a trade union representative.*

National wage agreements

In Ireland national agreements covering pay and other issues are sometimes negotiated between the social partners. The main **social partners** *comprise representatives of the government, employers (through IBEC), and employees (through ICTU).*

Social partnership *refers to the process whereby the government, employers and employees agree pay and conditions nationally.* The purpose of social partnership is to create a more stable and predictable economic environment for business, unions and government to plan and operate within.

| OL Short Q3 |
| OL Long Q3 |

6. What is the Industrial Relations Act 1990?

The **Industrial Relation Act 1990** *is the law that sets out the rules concerning industrial disputes and strikes.* According to this law:

★ **Disputes must be legitimate.** Employees can only take industrial action in a dispute related to their job. This is called a **legitimate trade dispute.** Legitimate disputes and strikes can arise over matters such as **pay, conditions, work duties, dismissals, union recognition** or **employment policies.** However, it is illegal to go on strike over how a business is run (such as factory layout or product marketing) or to strike about political issues.

> The Industrial Relations Act 1990 sets out the law governing the conduct of strikes and industrial disputes.

★ **Unions must hold a secret ballot** of the members involved in the dispute and get majority approval for a strike. A **secret ballot** *means that how a person votes remains confidential.* Voting for a strike by using a show of hands would not be secret and is illegal. All union members entitled to vote must be given a reasonable opportunity to do so and must be fully informed of all ballot details.

★ **Unions must give at least one week's advance notice** to the employer before going on strike.

★ **Official disputes** *are legitimate trade disputes that have received the approval of a majority of workers in a secret ballot, along with trade union and ICTU support.*

> Official disputes have union support.

★ **Immunity:** An employer **cannot sue** unions or employees for loss of earnings arising from an **official dispute.**

★ **Unofficial disputes** *have no union or ICTU approval.* According to the Industrial Relations Act 1990, these disputes are illegal. Organisers of unofficial disputes do not have legal protection against being sued by an employer for compensation due to lost sales or profits arising from the strike. *Workers on strike in an unofficial dispute may receive no support from their union.* A **wildcat strike** *is a type of unofficial dispute where no advance notice or warning is given to management.* Wildcat strikes usually flare up suddenly over some issue, are very short and tend to be resolved quickly.

> Unofficial disputes do not have union support.

* **Picketing** *involves employees and trade union officials walking up and down outside the workplace indicating a strike is in progress.* According to the Industrial Relations Act 1990, **primary picketing** of the employer's workplace is allowed as long as it is peaceful. **Secondary picketing** of another business not involved in the dispute is illegal unless the strikers legitimately believe that the second employer is assisting the first employer to frustrate the strike action.

* **Labour Relations Commission** *was established by The Industrial Relations Act 1990 as a specialist agency to help with resolving industrial disputes.*

OL Short Q4, 5

HL Short Q3

HL Long Q1

7. What types of industrial action can a union undertake?

Example: Mega Deal has refused the union's request for a 5% pay rise on the grounds that the company cannot afford it at present. The union organised a secret ballot of its members who voted by a large majority in favour of strike action in support of their claim.

Employees can take different types of industrial action in a dispute with an employer.

* **Token stoppages** *involve workers stopping work for a short period of time to demonstrate their strength of feeling to the employer.*

Example: Supermarket shop assistants going on strike for two hours.

* A **work-to-rule** *means employees only do their basic job and nothing more.* This inflexibility can be very frustrating for the employer. As they are not yet on full strike, the employees are still entitled to be paid by their employer.

* A **go-slow** *occurs when employees carry out the minimum amount of work they can get away with without jeopardising their basic pay.*

* **Overtime bans** *occur where workers refuse to work extra hours.*

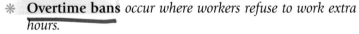

* A **strike** occurs when members of a union in a workplace refuse to do any work. An employer will not pay employees who go on strike. An **all-out strike** *means all union members in an organisation are ordered by the ICTU to stop working and leave the premises.* When this happens it is a sign of the seriousness of the dispute. It is normally accompanied by picketing outside the employer's premises.

8. What are the consequences of strikes for stakeholders?

Strikes and industrial disputes can have **negative consequences for all stakeholders** in a business.

* **Business:** Operations and production are disrupted, sales are lost and profits fall. Meanwhile, competitors can use it as an opportunity to gain market share. The reliability and reputation of a business will be undermined. Recruitment and retention of high-quality staff is made more difficult. Management time and energy is diverted into solving the dispute instead of concentrating on the main work of the business.

* **Employees:** Staff lose wages while on strike and their savings get used up. Their job security may be undermined. If a strike is unsuccessful, they will lose confidence in the union.

* **Customers:** Goods and services are not available which will inconvenience customers. In the case of important goods and services such as electricity, bus services or oil supplies, a strike can undermine the ability of others to make a living.

* **Suppliers:** Strikes can cause a loss of sales and undermine the profitability of suppliers.

* **Investors:** Loss of output, sales and profits will mean a reduction in dividends and undermine a firm's ability to pay the interest on loans.

* **Economy:** Strikes can mean a loss of wages spent and circulated in the economy. Substitute products may have to be imported, undermining Irish jobs.

* **Government:** Strikes mean a loss of tax revenues for the government, including income tax, VAT and corporation tax. Strikes can undermine Ireland's international reputation as a business location and make IDA Ireland's job of attracting foreign investment to the country more difficult.

Case Study

DUNNES STORES

DUNNES STRIKE HITS STAKEHOLDERS

MegaDeal managers are keen to avoid a strike like that which occurred in Dunnes Stores a few years ago. That supermarket lost sales income of more than €5 million a day during an **industrial dispute** when over 5,000 of its workers went on strike, closing 62 of the firm's outlets. Dunnes employees lost out on wages, customers were inconvenienced and the government lost VAT and PAYE tax revenues.

As a result of the strike, Dunnes Stores also had problems paying suppliers because the accounts department in its Dublin headquarters was reduced to only four staff processing the accounts and payments instead of the usual 30. This caused widespread concern in the economy, as suppliers who are not paid on time can suffer serious cashflow problems and could be forced out of business.

9. What is the purpose of the Labour Relations Commission?

Example: The union in Mega Deal have had meetings with managers to request a 5% pay rise for their members. However, management are only willing to consider a 2% rise because of the increased competition and financial pressure on Mega Deal. After three days of negotiations, both the union and management at Mega Deal felt that their negotiations over pay were going nowhere. It was agreed that it was time to consider going outside the organisation and seek the help of a specialist conflict resolution agency – the Labour Relations Commission (LRC).

They used the LRC's Conciliation Service which they found very helpful in understanding each other's position. However, Mega Deal unions and management were still unable to reach a settlement. To prevent a strike, the LRC then decided to refer the dispute to the Labour Court.

The **Labour Relations Commission (LRC)** *is a State agency that helps to resolve industrial disputes.* Set up by the Industrial Relations Act 1990, the LRC provides:

* **Conciliation Service** for disputes involving large numbers of employees. **Conciliation** *means that an Industrial Relations Officer at the LRC assists employers and union representatives to sort out their differences and negotiate a solution themselves. This approach is based on the idea that 'talk-out is better than walk-out'.* However, any suggested solutions are not legally binding and can be rejected by either unions or management.
* **Rights Commissioner Service** *for disputes involving just one or a small group of workers concerning unfair dismissal, maternity leave or disciplinary procedures.* With the agreement of both sides, the Rights Commissioner visits the place of dispute, investigates the issue 'on-site' and makes a recommendation that is not legally binding.
* **Industrial Relations Advisory Service** for firms and employees with queries about employment law and good human resource practices.
* **Codes of practice** *are a set of recommended voluntary rules used in industrial relations to solve disputes.* The LRC prepares and offers guidance to firms in drawing up codes of practice.

Give an evaluation:

LRC Service	Benefits
Conciliation Service	Most disputes between parties that use the LRC Conciliation Service are settled. If not, the dispute may have to be referred to the Labour Court for arbitration, if both sides agree.
Rights Commissioner Service	It is a free service. Recommendations for settling a dispute are not legally binding. Cases are held in private so employees and employers privacy is protected.

Industrial Relations Advisory Service	This service can help firms to prevent disputes by identifying the weaknesses and underlying problems that can cause strikes.
Codes of Practice	These are very useful guides for employers and employees. Codes of practice are not legally enforceable if broken but will be taken into account by the Employment Appeals Tribunal, LRC or Labour Court when settling a dispute.

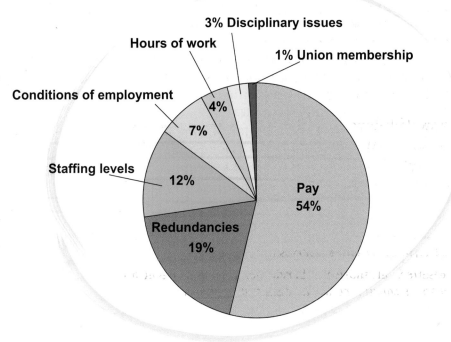

3% Disciplinary issues

Hours of work

1% Union membership

Conditions of employment

4%

7%

Staffing levels

12%

Pay 54%

Redundancies 19%

OL Short Q4

HL Short Q4

HL Long Q2

Fig. 1 Causes of disputes referred to the LRC.

10. What is the purpose of the Labour Court?

Example: The LRC asks the **Labour Court** to help to resolve the pay dispute at Mega Deal. Both unions and management agree to use the Labour Court's **arbitration service** to recommend a solution.

The Labour Court, acting as an arbitrator, listened to both sides, asked questions and then recommended a solution whereby the company gives a 2% pay rise and also provides an extra day's holiday for staff. Mega Deal management and unions accepted this recommendation. The industrial dispute over pay was settled without the need for damaging strike action.

The Labour Court is 'the court of last resort' in industrial disputes.

If the LRC fails to resolve a dispute, then both sides in the dispute may decide to go to the Labour Court. **The Labour Court is 'the court of last resort' in industrial disputes.**

It provides an arbitration service by listening to both sides in a dispute before recommending a solution. The Labour Court:

* **Consists of representatives** from the employers (e.g. a person from IBEC), a representative from the trade unions (e.g. a person from ICTU), and an independent chairperson.

* **Only gets involved** in solving a dispute if asked to by the Labour Relations Commission (LRC) or if the decision of a Rights Commissioner or an Equality Officer has been rejected by employers or employees. It may also get involved if a special request is made by the Minister for Enterprise, Trade and Employment.

* **Provides an arbitration service:** This means that the Labour Court **investigates** a dispute and **recommends a solution**. Usually these recommendations are not legally binding. However, as the Labour Court is the 'court of last resort' for industrial disputes, most recommended solutions are accepted by employers and unions. If both sides agree in advance to accept the decision of the court, then it is called **binding arbitration.** By making recommendations, arbitration makes it clear to employers and employees how to solve a dispute.

* **Registers industrial relations agreements** made between employers and unions. Once registered at the Labour Court, these agreements become legally binding. This reduces the risk of further disputes.

* **Establishes Joint Labour Committees (JLCs)** *as a forum for negotiating minimum pay and conditions in industries where many workers do not have union protection.* These include part-time workers, the fast-food industry and small hotels. They consist of representatives of employers and workers.

OL Short Q5
OL Long Q6, 7, 8
HL Short Q5, 6
HL Long Q3

Evaluation: very effective dispute resolution mechanism. resolves disputes LRC has failed to do. less formal than a court of law.

C. Conflict over redundancies and dismissals

11. What are the Unfair Dismissals Acts 1977 to 2007?

Case Study

MEGA DEAL SUPERMARKETS®

Margaret Whelan was sacked from her job as a checkout operator at a Mega Deal store after she announced that she was pregnant. The company claimed the reason for letting her go was to save money. However, Margaret did not believe this, as a new checkout operator was hired on the same salary to replace her. She believed that she had been unfairly dismissed according to the Unfair Dismissals Acts 1977 to 2007.

She took her case to the **Employment Appeals Tribunal** who agreed that the company had sacked her unfairly. The firm was ordered to pay Margaret compensation amounting to one year's salary.

Dismissal *means to be sacked from a job due to incompetence, dishonesty or breach of company discipline.* **The Unfair Dismissals Acts 1977 to 2007** *are the laws preventing employees from being dismissed from their job for unfair reasons.* It mainly applies to workers employed in a business for more than **one year**.

> Dismissals are fair when an employee's conduct is incompetent or unacceptable, or where the job has become redundant.

- **A dismissal is considered fair if:** *as long as the employer has Proof.*
  - ❖ The employee was **incompetent** or **incapable** of doing a job properly (e.g. due to lateness, absenteeism or a poor work attitude).
  - ❖ The employee's conduct was **unacceptable** (e.g. dishonesty, fighting, or being drunk at work).
  - ❖ The **job had become redundant** (e.g. due to new technology or the need to reduce financial costs to remain competitive). **Redundancy** *occurs when workers are let go from a job because there is no longer enough work for them to do.* By law, workers with more than two years' service are entitled to a minimum lump-sum payment based upon their length of service and pay at the time of redundancy.
    - ✳ **Voluntary redundancy** *is offered to those who wish to apply for it.* Various financial incentives, including cash payments and early pension payments, may be offered to encourage employees to volunteer for redundancy.
    - ✳ **Compulsory redundancies** *arise when employees are not given a choice and must leave.*
  - ❖ The **employer followed proper procedures** before dismissing an employee. This includes giving an employee adequate warning for any breaches of company rules. The responsibility rests with the employer to prove that the dismissal was fair.

- **A dismissal is regarded as unfair if:**
  - ✪ The employer **did not follow proper procedures**.
  - ✪ The **employer cannot prove** that the employee was **incompetent** or incapable.
  - ✪ The **employer cannot prove** that the employee's conduct was **unacceptable**.
  - ✪ The **employer cannot prove** that the job was **redundant**.
  - ✪ The **employer engages in constructive dismissal**. **Constructive dismissal** *means making working conditions for an employee so difficult that the employee is forced to leave his or her job (e.g. giving an excessive workload or harassing the employee).* *The employee terminates the Contract of employment due to conduct of employer.*
  - ✪ The employee has been employed by a business **for any period of time** and is dismissed because:
    - ❖ of their need to take maternity, parental, adoptive or carer's leave.
    - ❖ for joining a trade union or going on strike.
    - ❖ for complaining about breaches of the minimum wage laws.
    - ❖ of their age (except if they are under 16 or have reached retirement age).
    - ❖ of their religious or political opinions.
    - ❖ they are a particular race, colour, gender or sexual orientation.

Employer must have proof e.g Misconduct caught on CCTV.

Counselling / Advice: advice on how to improve is given by supervisors and recorded on the employee's personal record.

Formal verbal warning.
- The evidence for the dismissal must be made known to the employee.

First written warning. If there is no change a formal written warning follows the oral warning.

Before being dismissed, an employee has the right:

* To **know the reason** for his or her dismissal.
* To have a **right of reply** to those reasons.
* To have a **fair hearing** and to be **accompanied by a representative** at any hearing of the dismissal.

The penalties for a company guilty of unfair dismissals: *redress.*

* **Financial compensation** for the employee up to a maximum of two years' pay.
* **Reinstatement** of the employee in his/her job with financial compensation for lost earnings.
* **Re-engagement** of the employee in the same or similar job but with no financial compensation. This may apply where an **employee contributed to his or her own dismissal.**

The Employment Appeals Tribunal

The Employment Appeals Tribunal (EAT) is the State body responsible for ensuring that firms obey the **Unfair Dismissals Acts 1977 to 2007.** The EAT investigates and resolves disputes between workers and employers concerning sackings or redundancies. Its decisions are legally binding. *

Own Evaluation:

OL Short Q6, 7, 8
OL Long Q9, 10, 11

HL Short Q7
HL Long Q4, 5

Dismissals at Mega Deal – fair or unfair?

Examine each of the following cases from one of Mega Deal's Dublin stores and decide, giving reasons, whether the dismissal was fair or unfair.

1. Debbie Collins was dismissed from her job for repeatedly turning up late for work, despite several warnings from her manager. She is now claiming that she was unfairly dismissed and has taken her case to the Employment Appeals Tribunal.

2. Mandy Nolan had an accident stacking shelves and injured her back. She is suing the company for damages. The company has decided to dismiss her because she is suing them, on the grounds that her legal case represents a 'conflict of interest'.

3. Tom Hughes, one of the most efficient and hardworking people in the store, was found to be bullying and harassing another member of staff. He was clearly warned by the company to stop but the bullying continued. The firm dismissed him but he is claiming that he was unfairly dismissed, given his very productive work record.

D. Conflict over discrimination of staff.

12. What is the Employment Equality Act 1998?

The Employment Equality Act 1998 *is the law that says it is illegal to discriminate against anyone at work on the basis of:*

> The Employment Equality Act says when it is illegal to discriminate against an employee.

1. Gender (male, female, transsexual)
2. Marital status (single, married, divorced, widowed)
3. Family status (e.g. being a parent)
4. Age
5. Disability
6. Race
7. Sexual orientation
8. Religious belief (or none)
9. Being a Traveller

Law is binding

 **THE EQUALITY AUTHORITY**
AN tÚDARÁS COMHIONANNAIS

According to the act, **discrimination** *occurs when one person is treated in a less favourable way than another person is, has been or would be treated in a comparable situation.*

The law covers **job applicants**, full-time and part-time **employees** and **customers**.

The act set up the Equality Authority and the Director of Equality Investigations to enforce the law.

The Equality Authority

The **Equality Authority** *is the State agency responsible for ensuring that businesses do not break equality laws.* Its main functions are:

* To **monitor** the operation of all equality legislation.
* To **advise** employers, employees and customers of the legal rights and responsibilities in this area.
* To **assist** people with **equality complaints.** If a complaint appears to be valid, the Equality Authority may refer the case to the Director of Equality Investigations for a full investigation.

The **Director of Equality Investigations** *is responsible for actually investigating complaints concerning discrimination referred by the Equality Authority.*

Dealing with discrimination in the workplace

● Non-legislative

- ✪ **Talk** – raise the issue with the employer.
- ✪ **Seek help** – if the employer's response is unsatisfactory, then **contact your union** if you are a member. Alternatively, you can contact the Equality Authority for advice about how best to resolve the conflict.

● *Legislative*

If a complaint appears to be valid, the Equality Authority may refer the case to the Director of Equality Investigations for a full investigation. The Director of Equality Investigations can investigate complaints in two ways:

RACISM
FREE
ZØNE

www.arww.ie

1. An **equality officer** investigates **serious cases** and provides an **arbitration service**. The officer has the power to enter business premises to obtain any necessary information. If discrimination is proven, compensation and/or back wages may be paid to the victim, or action ordered to correct the discrimination.

2. An **equality mediator** can be appointed for **less serious complaints**. The equality mediator will use **conciliation** to work with both parties to reach a mutually acceptable settlement.

Evaluation:

Case Study

MEGA DEAL

Two Equality complaints at Mega Deal

1. Lorcan Kavanagh, a Mega Deal employee, was warned not to wear an earring to work or else he would be dismissed. Lorcan complained to the Equality Authority that his employer was behaving in a discriminatory manner, as this rule did not apply to female workers. The case was referred to the Director of Equality Investigations. Following an investigation, the company was found to have discriminated against male employees and was ordered to cease this form of discrimination.

Lorcan Kavanagh

2. Bernadette McManus was an unsuccessful applicant for a job with Mega Deal. She claimed that she was discriminated against for being a smoker. The company admitted that for health and safety reasons they have a policy of only hiring non-smokers. The job applicant's complaint was dismissed by the Equality Authority as not valid because under the law it is not illegal to discriminate against people on the grounds that they are smokers. (The Equality Authority would process a claim of discrimination based on one of the nine points listed on page 53).

OL Short Q9, 10
OL Long Q12
HL Short Q8
HL Long Q6, 7, 8

Legislative and non-legislative ways of resolving conflict in the workplace		
Non-legislative ways to resolve conflict in the workplace	1. **Talk:** Employer and employee discuss the issue and try to resolve it themselves. *Seek help from union head or IBEC.* 2. Employee may take the complaint to the **union shop steward**. The union shop steward will follow the **grievance procedure** agreed with the employer. This may involve meeting with the human resources manager. If the shop steward is dissatisfied with the progress being made, the union head office may become directly involved in negotiations with the management.	
Legislative ways to resolve conflict in the workplace	**For disputes involving groups of employees:** With the agreement of both sides, the matter is taken to the **LRC** which provides a **Conciliation Service** for group conflict resolution. ⬇ If conciliation at the LRC is unsuccessful, go to the **Labour Court**, the 'court of last resort' for industrial disputes. It provides an **Arbitration Service**.	**For disputes involving individuals:** LRC provides **Rights Commissioner Service** (for individual conflict resolution) *or* **Employment Appeals Tribunal** for cases involving unfair dismissal *or* **Equality Authority** for **discrimination** issues

3

Independent Third party.
Conciliation will speak to the employer and employee separately and then together highlighting the others point of view.

Key Concepts & Business Terms

After studying this chapter the student should be able to explain the following key concepts and business terms:

1. Industrial relations
2. Causes of industrial conflict
3. Industrial dispute
4. Grievance procedures
5. Trade unions
6. Shop steward
7. Irish Congress of Trade Unions (ICTU)
8. Cost-of-living claim
9. Comparability claim
10. Relativity claim
11. Productivity claim
12. Local pay bargaining
13. Individual bargaining
14. Collective bargaining
15. National wage agreements
16. Social partnership
17. Industrial Relations Act 1990
18. Official disputes
19. Unofficial disputes
20. Wildcat strike
21. Picketing
22. Primary picketing
23. Secondary picketing
24. Token stoppages
25. Work-to-rule

26. Go-slow
27. Overtime bans
28. All-out strike
29. Consequences of strikes
30. Labour Relations Commission
31. Conciliation Service
32. Rights Commissioner Service
33. Codes of practice
34. Labour Court
35. Arbitration service
36. Joint Labour Committees

37. Unfair Dismissals Acts 1977 to 2007
38. Redundancy
39. Voluntary redundancy
40. Compulsory redundancy
41. Constructive dismissal
42. Employment Appeals Tribunal
43. Employment Equality Act 1998
44. Equality Authority
45. Director of Equality Investigations
46. Equality officer
47. Equality mediator

useful websites

www.ictu.ie
www.lrc.ie
www.labourcourt.ie

www.eatribunal.ie
www.equality.ie

Leaving Certificate Practice Questions

Ordinary Level

Ordinary Level – Section 1 – Short Questions (10 marks each)

1. Describe **two** examples of issues that can give rise to a conflict between employers and employees.
2. List **two** benefits of trade union membership to employees.
3. List **three** of the 'social partners'.
4. List **two** functions of the Labour Relations Commission (LRC).
5. Identify **two** functions of the Labour Court.
6. List **two** reasons for <u>unfair</u> dismissal under the Unfair Dismissals Acts 1977 to 2007.
7. List **two** reasons for <u>fair</u> dismissal under the Unfair Dismissals Acts 1977 to 2007.
8. List **two** things an employee is entitled to before being dismissed.
9. Explain the role of the Equality Authority.
10. List **four** grounds on which employment discrimination is outlawed under the Employment Equality Act 1998. [LCQ]

Ordinary Level – Section 2 – Long Questions

1. Identify the main causes of conflict between employers and employees. (20 marks)
2. Kate has just started working in her first full-time job in a factory in her town. The shop steward met with her and discussed the benefits of joining the trade union.
   (a) Describe the benefits to Kate, as an employee, of joining a trade union. (20 marks) [LCQ]
   (b) Describe the relationship that exists between an employer and an employee. (15 marks) [LCQ]

3. Wages can be negotiated through collective and individual pay bargaining.
   (a) Describe the difference between individual bargaining and collective bargaining. (20 marks)
   (b) List **three** of the major stakeholders involved in collective bargaining. (25 marks) [LCQ]
   (c) List **two** advantages and **two** disadvantages of national collective pay bargaining (20 marks)

4. Michael works in a computer factory where there is a dispute concerning pay and conditions of work. Workers are considering picketing the entrance to the factory.
   (a) Illustrate what is meant by a grievance procedure. (15 marks)
   (b) Distinguish between a cost-of-living claim and a productivity claim. (20 marks)
   (c) Explain the term 'picketing'. (15 marks) [LCQ]

5. Mary is the shop steward in a factory. She is holding a secret ballot on whether the workers will take industrial action or not over the dismissal of a colleague.
   (a) Explain the terms 'shop steward' and 'secret ballot'. (20 marks) [LCQ]
   (b) Contrast an official dispute and an unofficial dispute. (20 marks)
   (c) Explain what is meant by a 'token stoppage' and a 'work to rule'. (20 marks)
   (d) Outline the consequences of industrial disputes for stakeholders. (15 marks)

6. The employees of Apricot Ltd have been on a work to rule for six weeks and have now gone on an official strike. The Labour Relations Commission has been called in.
   (a) Explain the terms 'work to rule' and 'official strike'. (20 marks) [LCQ]
   (b) Describe the role of the Labour Relations Commission. (15 marks) [LCQ]
   (c) Explain the terms 'conciliation' and 'arbitration'. (20 marks) [LCQ]

7. Name **two** bodies that help resolve trade disputes and outline **three** functions of **one** of them. (25 marks) [LCQ]

8. Describe the role of the Labour Court. (20 marks) [LCQ]

9. Maple Limited has an employee with whom it is very dissatisfied and wants to dismiss. Outline the procedure that Maple Ltd should follow if it wants to proceed with the dismissal. (15 marks)

10. The Unfair Dismissals Acts 1977 to 2007 protects workers from unfair dismissal.
    (a) List **two** reasons for fair dismissal and **two** reasons for unfair dismissal under this act. (20 marks) [LCQ]
    (b) Describe the role of a Rights Commissioner. (25 marks) [LCQ]

11. George, who worked in a computer firm for two years, has been told that he is no longer wanted. George maintains that he has been dismissed from his position for being involved in a strike. The management of the firm maintain that this strike has lost them a large order and that George's position in the firm is no longer required.
    (a) Describe the relationship that exists between an employer and an employee. (20 marks) [LCQ]
    (b) Name the law that protects George in this case. (10 marks) [LCQ]
    (c) Outline **one** method of solving the above problem and **two** reasons for fair dismissal. (15 marks) [LCQ]

12. List **five** grounds for discrimination as set out under the Employment Equality Act. (25 marks)

Higher Level

Higher Level - Section 1 - Short Questions (10 marks each)

1. Outline what is meant by the term 'industrial relations'.
2. Explain the purpose of a grievance procedure.
3. Distinguish between primary and secondary picketing.

4. Name **four** services provided by the Labour Relations Commission.
5. Name **four** services provided by the Labour Court.
6. Distinguish between 'arbitration' and 'conciliation'. [LCQ]
7. List **three** reasons why a redundancy or sacking may be regarded as fair.
8. Identify **two** functions of the Employment Equality Agency.

Higher Level - Section 2 - Applied Business Question

Crumbs Biscuits Limited

Crumbs Biscuits Limited employs 150 staff in a very busy factory producing a wide range of chocolate biscuits, fingers and wafers. The firm has traditionally had a good industrial relations record and staff turnover has been low. However, recently a number of new managers have taken jobs in the firm and things are beginning to change.

For instance, Bill Walton, a long time factory operative working in the chocolate section, was dismissed for turning up late for work one day. He was shocked as he received no warning and had been delayed because he got a puncture on the way to work. He has contacted the union for advice on what he should do.

Another employee, accountant Sandra Ryan, a wheelchair user, has been passed over by far less experienced junior staff for two recent promotions in the finance department. The successful candidates were both young males who played golf regularly with the new finance manager. Sandra is devastated and deeply disappointed by what has happened as she regards herself as a hard-working employee who has served the company well for many years.

The staff trade union has decided to request a 10% cost-of-living pay rise. Given the high profits that the firm has been making in recent years, many workers are prepared to consider taking industrial action if a suitable increase is not approved by management. However, at the same time, the managers in the company are very concerned about the size of the wage bill. To keep costs under control, they are considering introducing a pay freeze for all staff.

1. Identify the legislation that may apply to Bill Walton's situation and how it could assist in finding a resolution. (30 marks)
2. Analyse the situation facing Sandra Ryan, referring to the text in your answer. Recommend a possible legislative solution to her issue. (30 marks)
3. Describe the mechanisms that could be used by management and unions to find a resolution to the potential conflict over wages. (20 marks)

Higher Level - Section 2 - Long Questions

1. Under the terms of the Industrial Relations Act 1990 explain the reasons for legitimate trade disputes. Illustrate your answer with appropriate examples. (20 marks) [LCQ]

2. Explain the role and main function of the Labour Relations Commission in settling industrial disputes. (20 marks)

3. Describe the purpose of the Labour Court in industrial relations. (25 marks)

4. Explain the function of the Employment Appeals Tribunal. (15 marks)

5. Under the terms of the Unfair Dismissals Acts 1977 to 2007 explain the grounds for dismissal that are deemed to be unfair. Illustrate your answer with appropriate examples. (20 marks) [LCQ]

6. Explain the role of the Equality Authority. (25 marks)

7. Evaluate the role of the Director of Equality Investigations in solving conflicts in business. (20 marks) [LCQ]

8. What is wrong with the following advertisement? How should it be written?

   'Attractive male required to work in local newsagents shop, from 9 am to 5 pm, six days per week. Good pay and conditions for suitable candidate.' (30 marks)

Chapter 4
Entrepreneurs & Enterprise

> *'You see things and say, "Why?" but I dream things that never were and say, "Why not?"'*
> George Bernard Shaw

Key Study Questions

Case Study

ENTERTAINING ENTERPRISE

As a teenager, Moya Doherty loved poetry, literature and drama. During secondary school she took the **initiative** and got involved in school plays and other productions and, after successfully completing the Leaving Certificate, she got a job in RTÉ.

As a **hard worker**, she earned various promotions and got to work in many different parts of the organisation which allowed her to learn all about TV and radio production. One day Moya was given the responsibility for creating a short music and dance interval act during the Eurovision Song Contest. This was a difficult task but she was willing to take on the **challenge**. The result was Riverdance – a fusion of Irish and international music and dance – which received a massively positive reaction from the Europe-wide TV audience. This inspired her to take the **risk** of quitting her job and setting up her own business, Abhann Productions, with her business partner, John McColgan, to bring the show on tour internationally.

The first international show opened in London and the original 10 performances had to be increased to over 150 to meet public demand. Moya's **risk-taking** had paid off and the business thrived. She now has three Riverdance shows touring different parts of the world at the same time and impressing audiences wherever they go. Her business has also expanded into developing other musical and theatre productions

The success of this business inspired Moya to get involved in setting up other enterprises. For example, in partnership with others, she had the **confidence** to set up Radio Ireland to go into competition with RTÉ Radio. However, this venture nearly went out of business but, with persistence and hard work, it was rescued and rebranded Today FM. She has also been involved in setting up Tyrone Productions, an enterprise that makes television programmes.

The winner of an **Entrepreneur of the Year** award, Moya believes that it is fine to make mistakes as long as you learn from them. 'Success and failure go hand in hand. You have to be able to learn from both,' she says.

1. What is enterprise?

Enterprise occurs when an entrepreneur like Moya Doherty identifies a need, problem or an opportunity that is not being satisfied – and then tries to do something about it! **Enterprise** *refers to any attempt to start or do something new.*

An **entrepreneur** *is the person who has the initiative and takes the risk to start an enterprise.*

Enterprise is more than just setting up a business and creating wealth – it involves every attempt to create or shape yourself or the world around you. Without enterprise, nothing new happens.

> **Enterprise is essential to innovation and new developments.**

> **Entrepreneurs are the people who contribute the initiative needed to start new enterprises.**

Example: Moya Doherty was the entrepreneur who had the initiative to turn Riverdance from a four-minute music and dance piece into a globally successful business.

OL Short Q1

2. Where is enterprise relevant?

The entrepreneur's vision and confidence to try something new can be found in all areas of life – households, large and small businesses, schools and government departments. Because enterprise is so central to the business of living, it is important that it is nurtured and encouraged as much as possible.

● Enterprise in Business

Enterprise is the spark that creates all new businesses. Without the risk-taking initiative of the entrepreneur, there would be no new businesses like Riverdance or Today FM.

● Enterprise in the home

❖ Growing your own organic vegetables.
❖ Renovating your home using DIY skills.

● Enterprise in schools

❖ Transition Year students setting up a mini-enterprise.
❖ A group of students getting together to form a Leaving Certificate study group.

● Enterprise in the community

Many community enterprises are set up to meet some need rather than to make a profit. **Not-for-profit enterprises** (*also known as* **social enterprises** *or charities*) *provide services purely for rewards other than making a profit.* Unlike commercial businesses, any income received or surpluses made are reinvested in improving the services provided by the organisation.

Examples:
* Organisations such as the GAA, the Red Cross, Tidy Towns and the St Vincent de Paul.
* Getting involved in politics to help improve your community or country.
* Providing a meals-on-wheels service for the sick or elderly in the locality.
* Fundraising to raise money to build a new community centre.

Case Study

A social entrepreneur helping children

Adi Roche left a well-paid job with Aer Lingus to work on various campaigns that she believed could help to make the world a better place. These included promoting environmental protection and warning of the dangers of nuclear power.

One of the world's worst nuclear accidents occurred when the Chernobyl nuclear reactor exploded in the Ukraine, poisoning a huge area of land with deadly radioactivity that would affect generations to come. Adi decided to do something to help and started the Chernobyl Children's Project, a non-commercial business to help the children who were born years after the disaster but who have been affected by the nuclear radiation that remains in the area. She used her entrepreneurial skills to send dozens of convoys loaded with millions of euro worth of humanitarian supplies to the affected area. Furthermore, thousands of children, who have been diagnosed with terminal cancer from the lingering radioactivity, have been brought to Ireland for holidays, rest and recuperation. It is estimated that every child coming on a holiday has two years added to his/her life.

As a social entrepreneur, Adi Roche's attitude to enterprise is simple: 'If we don't feel that we can make a difference, then I question why we are on the planet.'

Enterprise in the Public Service

Rather than stepping back and waiting for private entrepreneurs to take action, the State has often taken the initiative and set up commercial and non-commercial businesses to provide important goods and services.

Examples of enterprise in the public service:

- **Coillte** is a commercial enterprise set up by the State to develop Ireland's forestry.

- **ESB** was set up by the State to provide electricity.

- **Fáilte Ireland** was set up by the State to market this country as an international tourist destination.

- **The International Financial Services Centre (IFSC)** in Dublin was set up to attract international banks and jobs to Ireland.

- **County enterprise boards** were set up to encourage enterprise and job creation at local level.

- Many **local councils** have taken the initiative to organise community festivals, concerts and other events that improve the local quality of life.

Enterprise at work – intrapreneurship

> Intrapreneurs behave like entrepreneurs inside organisations.

Intrapreneurs *are* **employees** *working within an organisation who use their initiative to act like entrepreneurs. This means coming up with ideas for a new product, ways to reduce costs or some other way in which to improve the business.*

Examples of intrapreneurship:

> OL Short Q2, 3, 4
>
> OL Long Q1, 2
>
> HL Short Q1, 2, 3, 4
>
> HL Long Q1, 2, 6

1. An airline employee who identifies a new way to reduce aircraft boarding queues. This makes customers more likely to want to fly with the airline, thereby increasing customer loyalty and sales.

2. A supermarket employee who identifies ways to use more paper instead of plastic packaging. This reduces costs for the business and is also more environmentally friendly as the paper packaging can be recycled.

Case Study

ESB INTERNATIONAL

A spirit of enterprise at work among ESB staff led them to look for new business opportunities to raise extra revenue for the company. After looking at their skills, they identified an opportunity to provide advice and consultancy services to other electricity generating companies around the world.

They set up ESB International as a subsidiary of the ESB to provide these consultancy services and became so successful that, besides giving advice on electricity generation and supply, the managers also decided to sell their expertise in accountancy, training and management internationally. This spirit of enterprise at work, or intrapreneurship, has been the driving force behind the growth of ESB International into a business with over 1200 employees, sales of nearly a billion euro per annum and customers in over 115 countries worldwide.

3. What are the potential rewards and risks of becoming an entrepreneur?

> Entrepreneurs can be motivated by different rewards.

Setting up a new enterprise is risky as it usually involves the entrepreneur devoting a considerable amount of time, money and effort to trying to make it a success. Despite these risks, people still choose to become entrepreneurs for the following reasons:

● Rewards

❖ **Independence** and freedom to be your own boss. Research has shown that this is an entrepreneur's chief reason for setting up in business.

❖ **Personal satisfaction** of offering goods and services that they themselves enjoy or believe are important. This allows them to meet and work with people who share their interests. Many social entrepreneurs, like Adi Roche, are motivated by a desire to help others.

❖ **Income:** To earn a living and possibly become rich. Entrepreneurs know that few people become rich working for someone else.

❖ **Creativity and new challenges:** Enterprise can provide an outlet for a person's need for creative expression and new challenges. Entrepreneur Richard Branson, founder of the Virgin Group of companies, says: 'I didn't go into business to make money; I went into business because I like the challenge. I was brought up to believe you must be a doer, not someone who watches what other people do.'

● Risks

✪ **Entrepreneurs may lose money** if the enterprise fails.

✪ **Entrepreneurs may waste a lot of time** and effort that could be used elsewhere.

✪ **Stress** and worry (which can cause ill-health) can be a risk for entrepreneurs if not managed carefully.

> OL Short Q5
>
> HL Short Q5

4. What are the personal characteristics of entrepreneurs?

> **Entrepreneurs tend to be naturally:**
> 1. Confident
> 2. Determined
> 3. Innovative
> 4. Realistic risk-takers
> 5. Decisive

Most entrepreneurs tend to have the following personal characteristics:

1. Confident and pro-active

Entrepreneurs believe in themselves and have **confidence** in their own abilities. They are pro-active with a strong 'can-do' attitude. **Proactive** *means being prepared to initiate actions instead of waiting for others to do something.* **Reactive** *people, on the other hand, just wait for somebody else to make the first move.*

> **Example:** Self-confidence is a clear feature of Moya Doherty's personality. She has a very **positive attitude** towards life. This confident and positive attitude allows entrepreneurs like her to stick with their ideas long enough to turn them into a reality.

2. Determined / motivated

Once they set a realistic goal for themselves, entrepreneurs become **very determined** and **motivated.** They are very willing to make sacrifices now for rewards later. Entrepreneurs are also willing to **work very hard** and put in long hours to make the enterprise work. This determination means that entrepreneurs can be very **resilient** when things go wrong.

> **Example:** The entrepreneurs behind Pepsi cola were so determined to succeed that they went bankrupt *three* times before the business finally became a success.

3. Innovative / creative

Entrepreneurs have a constant urge to find a better way to do things and tend to be particularly sensitive to people's needs for products and services. This means that they can be highly innovative and creative as well as quick to identify new business opportunities or new ways of doing things better and more efficiently.

> **Example:** By creating Riverdance, Moya Doherty took traditional Irish dancing and transformed it into something new and dramatic.

4. Realistic risk-takers

Entrepreneurs are **realistic risk-takers**. They are not reckless, but are only willing to take risks (such as giving up a job, investing money, putting in many hours of hard work) if they think the probability of success is reasonably high. They are aware of their skills and limitations and do not get carried away with excessively optimistic plans that are likely to fail.

5. Decisive yet flexible

Starting any new enterprise involves making lots of decisions. In the hurly burly of business, successful entrepreneurs need to be able to make **decisions quickly** and often under pressure. This decisiveness is matched by a **flexibility** to respond to new and changing circumstances by changing plans if necessary so that they do not miss an opportunity.

OL Short Q6
OL Long Q3

HL Short Q7
HL Long Q3

> **Example:** Moya Doherty has a very sharp business mind and is able to make decisions quickly but is also always willing to learn from her mistakes.

5. What are the learned skills of entrepreneurs?

Entrepreneurs learn to:
1. Identify opportunities
2. Set goals and plan
3. Manage their time
4. Manage stress
5. Get along with people

Characteristics may be natural to an entrepreneur, but skills have to be learned and practised.

1. Learn to identify opportunities

To become successful, entrepreneurs learn how to identify new opportunities. They do this by learning to be future-focused, that is, they try to anticipate changes to see what opportunities may arise for them.

2. Learn to set goals and plan

When entrepreneurs see a need or an opportunity, they create a vision of how they will satisfy this need in reality. **Vision** *identifies the goal an entrepreneur wants to move* *towards.* It serves to focus their energy and create self-motivation. Turning a vision into reality requires a **plan.** Successful entrepreneurs learn to break down the overall vision into **steps** and **short-term goals** that must be achieved along the way.

3. Learn effective time management

Successful entrepreneurs need to learn effective **time management**. They need to learn to **prioritise work**, separating the important tasks from the less important and ensure that the most important jobs are done first. They also need to learn to delegate work to others. Successful entrepreneurs work smarter, not harder.

4. Learn to manage stress

Entrepreneurs have strong self-control. They are able to **stay calm** and **not get stressed** when put under pressure by difficulties or deadlines. Good planning and time management skills also help to reduce stress.

5. Learn to get along with people

To get things done, an entrepreneur must be able to establish trust and build good working relationships with all the stakeholders in their enterprise. This requires:

- ❖ **Good social skills** and an ability to get on easily with people.
- ❖ **Good communication skills,** especially speaking, as entrepreneurs need to persuade investors, skilled managers and workers to support his/her vision for the enterprise. Good communication skills are also essential for attracting customers and sales.
- ❖ **Good listening skills**, as successful entrepreneurs are very **open to feedback** from others even if it is negative. This is how they learn where they may be going wrong and how they may need to change.

OL Short Q7, 8
OL Long Q4, 5

HL Short Q6, 8
HL Long Q4

Confident

Able to manage stress

Able to identify opportunities

Determined

Able to set goals and plans

Innovative

Able to get along with people

Realistic risk-takers

Decisive

Able to manage time

Case Study

A Non-stop Entrepreneur

As a boy Richard Branson was always coming up with ideas to earn pocket money, including growing Christmas trees and breeding budgies. Against the wishes of his parents Branson confidently left school at 17 to launch *Student* magazine. He also started a free advisory service for students, displaying a charitable (social entrepreneurial) streak that has stayed with him throughout his business career. *Student* magazine was not a great success, but Branson was determined to use it as a launching pad for his next idea – a mail-order business selling records. He called this business **Virgin Records**, using a public phone box as his first office.

Virgin Records became very successful and the profits allowed Branson to take a calculated risk and start a related recording studio and record label. These also proved very successful. Starting so many enterprises so young allowed him to learn how to identify opportunities, set goals, plan carefully, manage his time, manage stress and get along well with people. He then identified another business opportunity and moved into retailing, starting a chain of **Virgin Megastores** and later expanded into new areas like cinema, video and television. Restless with his entertainment businesses, Branson then changed direction and confidently decided to launch his own airline – **Virgin Atlantic**. He later sold his music business to EMI to allow him to concentrate on running his airline.

As the airline became well established, Richard Branson once again began looking for new and exciting business challenges and decided to set up a personal financial investments service. This was quickly followed by the launch of his own brand of **Virgin Cola** to compete against cola giants Pepsi and Coca Cola.

Richard Branson is a classic entrepreneur. He has strong entrepreneurial characteristics and skills. He is always on the lookout for business ideas that he could turn into reality. Even in his personal life, Branson finds it difficult to stay away from challenges and his ability to manage stress is well demonstrated by his preference for dangerous hobbies such as attempting to break world records by crossing the Atlantic both by high-speed boat and hot air balloon.

Recall and Review

1. Identify the entrepreneurial characteristics displayed by Richard Branson.
2. Identify the entrepreneurial skills displayed by Branson.

6. Why is enterprise important?

For entrepreneurs

❖ The entrepreneur's **personal satisfaction** and sense of achievement is boosted.

For business

❖ **Promotes business profitability** and continued survival and success.

❖ **Intrapreneurship** and initiative is encouraged among employees.

For society

❖ **Jobs** are created and unemployment is reduced.

❖ **Local and national self-confidence** is promoted as people think more positively with a 'can do' attitude.

❖ **Creativity is encouraged** and there is a continuous generation of new and improved goods and services for consumers.

❖ Not-for-profit enterprises provide many valuable **charitable services** to the local community.

❖ Greater enterprise means the government can collect **more taxes** to invest in infrastructure and provide public services.

> **HL ABQ**
> **HL Long Q5, 7**

Key Concepts & Business Terms

After studying this chapter the student should be able to explain the following key concepts and business terms:

1. Enterprise
2. Entrepreneur
3. Relevance of enterprise
4. Social / not-for-profit enterprises
5. Intrapreneurs
6. Rewards and risks of becoming an entrepreneur
7. Characteristics and skills of entrepreneurs

useful websites

www.enterpriseboards.ie
www.esb.ie
www.virgin.com

Leaving Certificate Practice Questions

Ordinary Level

Ordinary Level – Section 1 – Short Questions (10 marks each)

1. What is enterprise?
2. Identify **four** areas of life where you can find enterprise in action.
3. Explain the role of an entrepreneur in business. [LCQ]
4. Explain the term 'intrapreneur'. Give an example of intrapreneurship in action.
5. Describe **two** rewards of becoming an entrepreneur.
6. List **two** personal characteristics or qualities needed to become a successful entrepreneur.
7. List **four** learned skills needed by entrepreneurs.
8. In enterprise, explain what is meant by 'having vision'.

Ordinary Level – Section 2 – Long Questions

1. List **one** example of enterprise in each of the following:
   (a) the home or personal life,
   (b) the community,
   (c) government,
   (d) business. (20 marks)
2. Distinguish between an entrepreneur and an intrapreneur. (20 marks)
3. List **five** characteristics of enterprising people. (15 marks) [LCQ]
4. *Joan Daly has just finished a course on home decorating. She has been decorating friends' houses in the past two years. Her work is very creative and many people want her services. She has been planning for two years and has used her savings to rent a small office to start up her own business. When a local hardware store closed down, she made a quick decision and bought a lot of material at half price.*
   (a) Identify **two** characteristics that Joan possesses that suggest she is an entrepreneur. (20 marks) [LCQ]
   (b) Identify **four** factors that encourage people to become entrepreneurs. (20 marks)
5. *John Molloy has been working in a computer firm for the past twenty years. The firm has now decided to relocate to the Far East and John is being made redundant. He has saved money over the years by doing overtime and his redundancy terms are generous. He is considering setting up his own business in computer maintenance and repairs.*
   (a) Identify **three** enterprising characteristics/skills that John will need. (15 marks) [LCQ]
   (b) Identify **two** risks and **two** rewards of setting up your own business. (20 marks) [LCQ]

Higher Level

Higher Level – Section 1 – Short Questions (10 marks each)

1. Illustrate your understanding of the term 'entrepreneurship'. [LCQ]
2. Identify **two** examples of intrapreneurship in action in a school.
3. List **four** examples of enterprise in action in your own home or personal life.
4. Being an 'intrapreneur' involves . . . [LCQ]
5. List **four** benefits of becoming an entrepreneur.
6. Outline **two** important characteristics of entrepreneurs.

7. Explain what is meant by being a 'realistic risk-taker'.
8. Identify **two** important skills of entrepreneurs.

Higher Level – Section 2 – Applied Business Question

Ruby Byrne

Ruby Byrne always liked a challenge. As a youngster, she earned pocket money by cutting her neighbour's grass and washing cars, and sometimes by selling unwanted items on trading websites like e-Bay.

After her Leaving Certificate, Ruby went to college and qualified as a computer programmer. She has worked for the past five years for a rapidly expanding software company in a growing sector of the economy. A hard-working and determined individual, she recognises that she is probably the most talented and creative computer programmer in the firm, reasonably well paid and responsible for the design of some very innovative software that has proved a major success internationally for the company.

Ruby recently organised a college reunion where she met some old friends who are now self-employed and earning considerably more money than she is. 'You will never become rich working for someone else,' said one of them. They strongly advised Ruby to consider setting up her own software business either on her own or in partnership with some of her colleagues at work. That way, they argued, she could derive the full financial benefits from her creativity.

Since the reunion, Ruby has been calmly and realistically giving the idea considerable thought. She has been involved in setting up a local mini-hockey league and also a local residents' association. But she has never run a business before. Although she finds the idea tempting, especially the challenge and idea of greater independence, she is concerned about a number of points:

- Technology is changing so fast that the technical skills she has today may be obsolete in ten years.
- She has no formal business training and very little cash to invest in a new venture.
- She has financial responsibilities to her family, a mortgage and monthly bills.

1. Identify the enterprising characteristics displayed by Ruby. Refer to the text in your answer. (30 marks)
2. Evaluate the risks and opportunities facing Ruby if she starts up on her own. (30 marks)
3. Discuss the importance of enterprise to the different parts of society. (20 marks)

Higher Level – Section 2 – Long Questions

1. Illustrate how entrepreneurial skills might be used to enhance either
   (a)   the local community, or
   (b)   a government department. (30 marks) [LCQ]

2. Compare and contrast entrepreneurship and intrapreneurship. (20 marks)

3. Identify the personal characteristics normally associated with entrepreneurial business people. (20 marks) [LCQ]

4. Using examples, analyse the importance of **four** different enterprising skills and relate **two** to business and **two** to the community. (20 marks) [LCQ]

5. Discuss how the encouragement of a spirit of enterprise and intrapreneurship can benefit a business. (25 marks)

6. 'Enterprise is more than about having a good idea.' Discuss. (25 marks)

7. 'Enterprise is essential to society.' Discuss this statement using examples. (25 marks)

Chapter 5
Introduction to Management

Key Study Questions

Case Study

From ENTREPRENEUR to MANAGER?

Student Jane Ní Dhulchaointigh realised that many people would prefer to improve, customise or repair something they already own, rather than buy new things. She thought that it would be a great business opportunity if she could develop such a product.

Not having any money, Jane persuaded some retired scientists to help her. Finding a solution was not easy but she was both determined and confident that it could be done. Eventually, after five years of experiments and trial and error, together they invented a simple but highly creative solution: a product Jane called Sugru (from the Irish word for play, súgradh).

Sugru is a bit like plasticine or Play-Doh but with an ingenious twist. When you take it out of the packet, you have 30 minutes to shape it into anything you want before it begins setting into a very durable silicone rubber. The product is designed to stick to as many different things as possible, is highly resistant to extremes of heat and cold, and is also waterproof.

For Jane, this was the business product that she was looking for: a brilliantly simple, low-cost, very user-friendly and durable product. It comes in different colours and can be used by consumers to repair the things they already have and like, or to improve practically anything by making it softer, comfier, stronger, safer or quieter. For example, it has been used by consumers for everything from repairing holes and broken mug handles to providing added impact protection for mobile phones or customising handlebar grips.

With the product developed, Jane began planning to turn Sugru into a business. Using her savings and some business grants, she hired staff and set up production and distribution facilities. Marketing costs were kept to a minimum by generating as much free publicity as possible through social networking sites and blogs on the Internet to promote her company, sugru.com

As an entrepreneur, Jane is energised by the buzz and excitement of starting something new. She is confident that someday Sugru could become as popular as global brands such as Sellotape and Blu Tack. However, turning the business into a profitable success will require more than entrepreneurial flair and talent, it will require strong management skills. Jane must decide whether she is willing to develop these skills or to hire managers to run the business for her.

1. What is management?

> **Enterprise is needed to set up businesses. Management is needed to run them.**
>
> **HL Short Q1**

To be successful, Jane Ní Dhulchaointigh needs to ensure that her business is properly managed. **Management** *refers to the ability to achieve results through people. It involves planning, organising and controlling the work to be done, and requires the skills of leading, motivating and communicating with people.*

Managers *are the people specifically responsible for achieving the objectives set for the business.* In most businesses, the most senior manager is often called the chief executive or managing director. In a school, the top manager is the principal.

2. What are the main management skills?

> **Management means working with people. This requires good leadership, motivation and communication skills.**

❖ **Leading staff:** Effective managers must be able to influence people and get them to work towards the goals of the business. As leaders they should be confident, decisive and capable of inspiring staff and earning their trust and respect. It is important that managers pay special attention to their position as role models in setting an example of the behaviour they expect throughout the business.

❖ **Motivating staff:** Effective managers must be capable of getting their staff to contribute their best by providing suitable incentives and rewards.

❖ **Communicating with staff:** Effective managers are good communicators. In particular, this means being good listeners and clear communicators.

OL Short Q2

HL Long Q2

3. What are the main management activities?

✪ **Planning:** Managers must be capable of setting objectives for a business. This involves being able to identify trends and prepare plans to take advantage of opportunities and to avoid threats to the business. Once objectives are set, they must be broken down into smaller, more achievable steps.

✪ **Organising:** Managers must be able to make the plan happen by putting together the people, finance, equipment and other resources needed. They must decide who does what so that the plan is achieved in an effective and efficient manner.

✪ **Controlling:** Managers must ensure that plans stay on target by regularly monitoring progress and staff performance. However, managers need to be aware of their primary role as facilitators and supporters of staff and avoid smothering their initiative and potential.

OL Short Q1
OL Long Q4

HL Short Q2
HL Long Q1

Management activities	Management skills
Planning the business	Leading staff
Organising the business	Motivating staff
Controlling the business	Communicating with staff

4. Where is management relevant?

Management in the home and personal life

Management is very relevant to home and personal life. Parents are the managers in the home. They need to show **leadership** to their children and **motivate** them to go to school and to study well. They also need to ensure that **communications** are clear and that everyone gets on well together. Family events, holidays and other activities must be **planned.** Household tasks such as cooking, cleaning and financial management must be **organised.** Household finances must be **controlled** to ensure that the household stays within budget.

Management in schools

School principals must show **leadership** to the teachers and students and **motivate** them to do their best. Effective **communications** among staff and students is essential to avoid confusion and misunderstandings. Schools principals must **plan** subject timetables and ensure that facilities such as photocopying are available for staff. Students need to be **organised** into classes and events during the school year, for example sports days and examinations, must also be organised. Students must be supervised to avoid accidents and the school budget **controlled** to ensure money is available for all spending required.

Management in the local community

Running sports activities, community festivals, competitions or campaigns requires **leadership** skills to encourage people to get involved, **motivation** skills to keep them interested and **communications** skills to ensure everyone involved understands what needs to be done. Community events also require proper **planning of** dates and facilities, **organising** people to do the work, and **controlling** the finances and resources that may be involved.

Management in business

Businesses need to set targets, **plan** new or improved products, **organise** production, and **control** finances, quality and the performance of staff. Business managers must provide their staff with **leadership** to give them a clear sense of direction. Staff need to be **motivated** to contribute their best. Managers must also ensure that the business maintains good **communications** with all the stakeholders in the business.

Management in the public service

Politicians need to provide **leadership** to the public that elects them. Government ministers need to **motivate** the staff in their departments. Clear **communications** skills are needed by politicians to inform the public about government policies and decision-making. Money collected in taxes is used by government to provide essential public services such as the army, Gardaí, schools and hospitals for citizens. The delivery and financing of these public services must be **planned** in advance. Government departments and State agencies need to be **organised** with the right staff, organisational structures and resources to do their job. Running the public service costs billions of euro of taxpayers money every year. This spending must be carefully monitored and **controlled** to minimise waste.

OL Short Q4
OL Long Q2, 3
HL Long Q3, 4

5. What are the personal characteristics of effective managers?

* **Problem solvers:** Managers must be able to analyse problems and break them down into smaller, more solvable parts.
* **Decisive:** Managers must be able to set goals for staff, decide how best to organise people, finance, equipment, and act quickly to restore control when things go wrong. They must be willing to take responsibility for their decisions.
* **Good with people:** Managers must be able to **provide leadership and a clear** direction to others. Managers must be prepared to trust their staff and delegate authority.
* **Confident and inspirational:** Managers must be **confident** in their approach to problems. This inspires staff and helps to build effective workplace teams.
* **Good communicators:** Managers must be able to **listen and communicate** effectively (both verbally and written) with staff and all other stakeholders.
* **Good time managers:** Managers must be able to budget time and delegate work where appropriate so that they do not waste time or become overloaded and unable to cope.

OL Short Q3
OL Long Q1

6. What are the similarities and differences between managers and entrepreneurs?

Sugru founder Jane Ní Dhulchaointigh is a successful entrepreneur. But not every successful entrepreneur is a successful manager. Henry Ford was a highly successful entrepreneur who founded the Ford Motor Company. However, as a manager, he was autocratic, ruthless and unpopular with his staff. This led to many strikes and a number of marketing disasters during his time as the top manager of the Ford company.

Entrepreneurs can face difficulties when making the transition from entrepreneurship to management. They need to know when it is time to recruit professional managers to assist in the day-to-day running of their businesses. This will give them more time to concentrate on the creative and entrepreneurial work that they often prefer and are better at.

Comparing Entrepreneurs and Managers		
	Entrepreneurs	**Managers**
Ideas and energy	• Entrepreneurs have the **ideas**, **energy** and initiative to start **new** businesses. • Entrepreneurs tend to put their energy into new projects and enterprises.	• Unless they are intrapreneurs, managers **may have few original ideas or little enthusiasm** for developing new business ideas. • Managers tend to put their energy into **more routine work**
Personal risk-taking	• Entrepreneurs **sacrifice their own time** and **take the personal financial risks** of a business failing. • Entrepreneurs often **operate on their own** or with just a few close business partners.	• Managers **do not take personal financial risks** when running a business. They are employees who are hired by the owners to manage the business on their behalf. • Managers usually have **no personal share in the ownership** of the business.
Managing day-to-day business	• Entrepreneurs **thrive on the excitement of setting up something new** but often get bored with the day-to-day planning, organising and controlling. • Entrepreneurs can be unwilling or unable to delegate decision-making to others.	• The work of managers is **more routine and structured** and concentrates on providing proper planning, organisation and control. • Delegating work to other staff is important for effective time management.

HL Short Q3, 4

HL ABQ

HL Long Q5

Key Concepts & Business Terms

After studying this chapter the student should be able to explain the following key concepts and business terms:

1. Management
2. Managers
3. Management skills
4. Management activities
5. Relevance of management
6. Similarities and differences between managers and entrepreneurs **HL**

useful websites   www.sugru.com

Leaving Certificate Practice Questions

Ordinary Level

Ordinary Level – Section 1 – Short Questions (10 marks each)

1. List **three** management activities.
2. List **three** management skills. [LCQ]
3. List **three** characteristics of managers. [LCQ]
4. Identify **two** reasons why management is important in business.

Ordinary Level – Section 2 – Long Questions

1. Identify and explain **four** personal characteristics a person needs to possess to be an effective manager. (20 marks)
2. Illustrate, using examples, how **three** management activities can apply to managing your personal life. (15 marks)
3. Describe an example of management in action:
   (a) in home and personal life,
   (b) in school,
   (c) in business,
   (d) in the local community. (20 marks)
4. Outline the possible consequences of a lack of management in an organisation. (25 marks)

Higher Level

Higher Level – Section 1 – Short Questions (10 marks each)

1. Define management.
2. List **four** reasons why managers are needed by organisations.
3. Distinguish between an entrepreneur and a manager.
4. Explain how risk-taking differs between managers and entrepreneurs.

Higher Level – Section 2 – Applied Business Question

PARTY PRODUCTS LTD

Entrepreneur Robert Shiels set up a business making party decorations such as banners, balloons, hats and novelty gifts. A hard worker, he admits that one of his best decisions as an entrepreneur was to employ Karen Faye as full-time manager.

Karen is responsible for managing all aspects of the day-to-day management of the Party Products factory and its 25 staff. This leaves Robert free to concentrate on coming up with new toy ideas and increasing sales, the parts of the business that he most enjoys.

As the factory manager, Karen plans the work of the factory, including production quantities and quality control. She has organised the staff into work teams and meets each team first thing in the morning for a short daily planning session. Karen keeps control by supervising the factory staff closely and whenever any problems arise, she is on hand to help sort them out.

To be effective at her job as manager, Karen has to be a good leader whom the staff will respect and listen to. Her attention to detail and focus on quality sets a good example for all the staff. Karen also has to be able to motivate staff to contribute their best to the business. As a manager she is dealing with people all day. This means that she must also be a good communicator who is able to get along well with people and ensure that everyone understands what is going on and what work is required. When business is particularly busy, Karen is always mindful to delegate work where possible to other staff to ensure that she does not get overloaded with work or stressed out.

Karen reports to Robert and has a weekly meeting with him every Monday to discuss the running of the factory over the coming week. These meetings can cover important ongoing issues such as controlling production costs, maintaining quality control as well as occasional issues such as the need to invest in new machinery or to hire new staff.

As an entrepreneur, Robert is very satisfied with Karen's work as manager. Having her in the business means that he does not get bogged down in the day-to-day running of the factory. This leaves him free to concentrate on developing new product ideas and growing the Party Products business.

1. Identify the management characteristics displayed by Karen Faye. Refer to the text in your answer. (20 marks)
2. Contrast the distinct roles of Robert as an entrepreneur and Karen as a manager. (30 marks)
3. Discuss the difficulties that could arise if Robert tried to undertake both roles instead of hiring a manager. (30 marks)

Higher Level – Section 2 – Long Questions

1. Explain the concept of management. (15 marks)
2. Illustrate, using examples, **three** management skills. (15 marks)
3. Illustrate the importance of management skills in **one** of the following areas:
   (a) the home,
   (b) the local community,
   (c) a government department,
   (d) a business start-up. (20 marks) [LCQ]
4. Distinguish between planning, organising and controlling in your personal life. Use examples to support your answer. (15 marks)
5. Differentiate between enterprise and management. Illustrate your answer with examples. (15 marks) [LCQ]

3

Chapter 6
Management Skills of Leadership & Motivation

'Management is doing things right; leadership is doing the right things.'

Peter F Drucker

Key Study Questions

Case Study

Aer Lingus ☘

After completing his Leaving Certificate, Willie Walsh joined Aer Lingus as a trainee pilot. He quickly rose through the ranks and moved into a **management** job.

However, the airline was losing millions and struggling to survive against low-cost competitors such as Ryanair. Banks became very nervous and said that they were unwilling to lend any more money to such a loss-making company. When the airline's top manager left suddenly, nobody else wanted the job. However, Walsh accepted the top job, saying, 'Somebody had to be in charge.'

As **chief executive officer (CEO)** of a company in serious trouble, Walsh realised that Aer Lingus would go out of business unless there was a radical **plan** and quick action. In such a crisis situation, he realised that he needed to provide quick, firm and **decisive leadership** if the airline was to be saved. Walsh saw that the company needed to dramatically slash costs and ticket prices to be able to compete with lower cost rivals. As a result, over 2,000 employees were made redundant, including over half of all the managers in the company.

Walsh's quick **decision-making** worked. Lower costs meant that the airline could charge lower prices and sales began to increase. In just two years and against all predictions, he transformed Aer Lingus from the brink of financial closure into a very efficient and profitable company with rising sales. This success impressed many people including the board of directors of the much larger British Airways who persuaded him to leave Aer Lingus and take over the top management job in that airline.

1. What is leadership?

Leadership involves directing staff, setting an example and delegating work.

As Willie Walsh found out while running Aer Lingus, a key skill for every manager is the ability to provide leadership to people. Employees need managers whom they can trust and be inspired by. **Leadership** *refers to the ability to influence other people to go in a particular direction and achieve a particular goal. It involves* **directing** *staff,* **setting a clear example** *of what is expected of others, and* **delegating** *work to staff.*

- ✪ **Leaders provide direction** by communicating clear instructions to others about the work to be done. This ensures that everyone understands their role and how they need to work together to achieve the goals of the business.

- ✪ **Leaders set an example** and clear direction for others by demonstrating the attitude and behaviour expected in the workplace. By leading by example, managers are far more likely to be respected and trusted by staff. The leadership shown by managers can be very important in creating a positive or negative corporate culture. **Corporate (or organisational) culture** *refers to the general atmosphere and patterns of behaviour within a workplace.* It is mainly created by the attitudes and behaviour of managers towards their work, their staff and their customers.

- ✪ **Leaders delegate work** to other people. **Delegation** *means giving authority for carrying out tasks to others.* Some managers find it easy to delegate work while others find this difficult.

Evaluation: Benefits of delegation

1. Managers who delegate do not have to do all the work themselves. This gives them **more time** to concentrate on other, more important, work.

2. Managers who delegate experience **less stress** from being overloaded with too much work.

3. **Staff gain experience** in handling authority and decision-making. This increases their job satisfaction, motivation and productivity.

4. Staff can become **more skilled** and **flexible**. This increases their ability and willingness to adapt to change.

5. Overall, **work that gets shared gets done faster** and more efficiently.

Why do some managers not delegate?

1. Some managers believe that staff **may not be able to do the work** to the standard required.

2. They **fear** that staff may be able to do the work far better and so undermine the manager's own status, control and position of power.

> **OL Short Q1, 2**
>
> **HL Short Q2**
>
> **HL Long Q1, 2**

2. What are the different types of leader?

> **Leaders can be autocratic, democratic or laissez-faire.**

There are three main types of leadership style: autocratic, democratic and laissez-faire. These leadership styles differ in terms of:

* **Ability to trust** staff and willingness to delegate authority and responsibility.

* **Decision-making style** when making management decisions.

* **Methods of persuasion** used to get people to go along with the leader's views and decisions.

Autocratic leaders

Autocratic (or authoritarian) leaders *do not like sharing their authority with subordinates but prefer to make most of the decisions themselves.* Autocratic managers:

> **Autocratic: 'Do as I say!'**

- Have little **trust** or confidence in the abilities of other staff.
- Are unwilling to **delegate** power and responsibility to subordinates.
- Tend to ignore the views of others during **decision-making**.
- Use their position of **authority** to get their own way.
- May sometimes resort to intimidation and fear to **persuade** others.

Case Study

Autocratic leadership in the army

The Irish Defence Forces includes the army, naval service and air corps. As well as defending the country in times of war, the Defence Forces also provide important services such as **planning** and **organising** participation in UN peacekeeping operations and other humanitarian relief operations, national fishery protection services, search and rescue and air ambulance services. The Defence Forces also deal with natural or other disasters (such as combating oil spillages at sea), and maintain essential services in times of crisis.

It is one of the largest **organisations** in the country with over 10,000 personnel who require strong **leadership** and **motivation** and clear and effective **communications**.

The system of management in the army is based on an **autocratic leadership style**. An autocratic leadership style suits the army as large numbers of soldiers must be managed quickly to deal with crisis situations such as military conflicts or to respond quickly to natural disasters or other emergencies. An army commander uses his/her position of authority to take decisions and expects the soldiers under his/her command to obey them without question. An army officer does not waste time debating or discussing possible options with soldiers about what to do.

OL Short Q5

Evaluation: Advantages of an autocratic style

1. Decisions are made **quickly**.
2. Work gets done the **way** the manager wants.
3. Suits organisations or situations **where discipline is important**, such as the army or responding to an emergency situation.
4. Can be very useful in a **crisis or emergency situation**, such as turning around a business facing bankruptcy.

Evaluation: Disdvantages of an autocratic style

1. Managers who try to plan, organise and control everything can become overloaded with work and **stressed**.
2. Staff get little training or experience in decision-making and may become **de-motivated** or decide to leave.
3. A lack of trust in staff can lead to **industrial relations conflicts**.

Democratic leaders

Democratic leaders *are willing to discuss issues with staff and to delegate power and responsibility where necessary.* Democratic managers:

* Have **trust** in the ability of subordinates to do their work.
* Readily **delegate authority.**
* Take decisions only after **discussion** with others.
* Prefer to **persuade** others through the use of reasonable arguments.

This style of management is common in many businesses.

Case Study

Bob Geldof,
a democratic leader

Entrepreneur Bob Geldof is the founder of many different businesses including a TV and radio production company, an online travel company and a mobile phone company. As a business person, Geldof uses a democratic leadership style. He realises that he is not an expert in many areas so he is happy to listen carefully to the views of others who know more than he does before making any big decisions.

Evaluation: Advantages of a democratic style

1. Shared input into decision-making leads to **better quality decisions**.
2. Delegating work and sharing responsibility, means **more time** and **less stress** for managers.
3. **Staff are more motivated** and loyal to the business when their views are valued. This also helps to maintain **good industrial relations**.
4. Delegation promotes **staff initiative** and **intrapreneurship**.

Evaluation: Disadvantages of a democratic style

1. **Slower decision-making** as managers consult with staff and listens to their views.
2. **Quality of decision-making** may decline if managers try to take too many opinions on board.

Laissez-faire leaders

Laissez-faire: 'Do what you think'

Laissez-faire leadership *(also known as a* **'free rein'** *or* **spectator** *style) involves giving staff general goals and targets to aim for and then giving them the authority to achieve these in whatever way they think best.* Laissez-faire leaders:

- ✪ Have considerable **trust** in the ability of their staff and so **delegate** power and responsibility freely.
- ✪ Are content to **let staff make** most of the **decisions** and only get involved in very important issues.
- ✪ Are very willing to **listen** to the opinions of others before making a **decision**.
- ✪ **Persuade** others primarily through the use of reasonable arguments and their position of authority.

Case Study

RICHARD BRANSON, A LAISSEZ-FAIRE LEADER

Richard Branson, the founder of the Virgin Group of companies, has a laissez-faire leadership style. He delegates most decision-making to his staff and is happy to leave them alone as long as the businesses they are running are successful. He was described by one of his staff as like 'a friendly grandfather who lets you do whatever you like as long as you don't get into trouble'.

Evaluation: Advantages of a laissez-faire style

1. **Speedy decisions** can be made by staff closest to the issues.
2. Delegating considerable authority **challenges** and **motivates staff** to give their best.
3. **Intrapreneurship** is strongly encouraged.

Evaluation: Disadvantages of a laissez-faire style

1. Inexperienced staff may be **unable to handle responsibility** and may find it very stressful.
2. Lack of supervision and control may result in **poor** or reckless **decisions** being made.

OL Short Q4
OL Long Q1, 2, 3, 4

HL Short Q1, 3
HL Long Q3, 4

3. What is motivation?

> **Motivation is the willingness of people to work hard.**

Business leaders like Willie Walsh, Bob Geldof and Richard Branson need to be able to motivate their workers. **Motivation** *is the willingness of people to work hard and to contribute their best effort.* Motivation is important to management as it can lead to:

* **Increased productivity:** motivated staff work harder.
* **Greater intrapreneurship** as staff become more creative and innovative.
* **Improved industrial relations:** motivated staff are less likely to strike.
* **Easier staff recruitment and retention**, which can save money.
* **Repeat business** from customers who pick up on the positive motivation of staff.

> OL Short Q6
> OL Long Q5
>
> HL Short Q4
> HL Long Q5

There are two important theories of motivation used by leaders to motivate people:
* Maslow's Hierarchy of Needs
* McGregor's Theory X and Theory Y

4. What is Maslow's theory of motivation?

> **According to Maslow's Hierarchy of Needs, different people have different needs:**
> * Physical
> * Safety
> * Social
> * Esteem
> * Self-actualisation

Maslow's theory of motivation is known as the hierarchy of needs. **Maslow's Hierarchy of Needs** *says that all human needs can be arranged in a hierarchy (or pyramid) in order of their importance.*

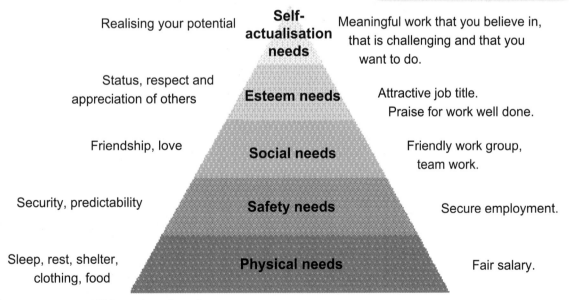

Fig. 1 Maslow's pyramid/hierarchy of needs.

* According to Maslow, human needs begin with the most basic physical needs for food and water and lead up to the most complex psychological needs for self-esteem and self-actualisation.

❖ When one level of need is satisfied, then the next level above it becomes the major motivating factor in a person's behaviour and so on up the pyramid.

❖ According to Maslow's theory, at any one time a person is motivated to satisfy a particular level of need on the hierarchy. To successfully motivate a person, managers must identify what their main level of motivation is and aim to meet this.

❖ If lower/basic needs are not being met, such as staff being poorly paid, then they will remain demotivated even if other higher needs are being met, such as having a pleasant and friendly place to work in or being part of a team.

NEED	DESCRIPTION	SATISFIED BY
Self-Actualisation	Realising your personal potential	Providing meaningful and challenging work; delegating more responsibility to staff; providing training and further education; significant opportunities for promotion; share in ownership of business.
Esteem	Status, respect and appreciation from others	Providing praise for work well done; promotion and other rewards; bigger office; company car; perks.
Social	Friendship, love and relationships	Providing a friendly workplace; staff parties and outings; opportunities for teamwork; company social club.
Safety	Security, predictability and freedom from worries	Providing secure employment; open and honest communications; freedom to join a union; written contract of employment.
Physical	Basic needs such as sleep, shelter, food and clothing	Providing safe working conditions; adequate wages; sufficient holidays.

Evaluation: Advantages of Maslow's theory

1. Recognises that people are motivated by more than money.
2. Recognises that different things motivate different people at different times.
3. Provides leaders and managers with a way to identify the need for different types of motivations for staff.

OL Short Q7
OL Long Q6

HL Short Q5, 6
HL Long Q7

Evaluation: Disadvantages of Maslow's theory

1. People are very complex and the theory may not adequately explain everyone's motivation.
2. In real life people do not just satisfy one need at a time.

Recall and Review

Using Maslow's theory of motivation, what suggestions would you make:
(a) For improving motivation at a company like Aer Lingus?
(b) For motivating students to study?

5. What is McGregor's theory of motivation?

Psychologist Douglas McGregor conducted research which showed that managers could be grouped according to their attitude to motivating staff: having either a Theory X attitude or a Theory Y attitude.

> **McGregor's theory focuses on managers' attitudes to staff.**

● Theory X managers believe employees . . .

- ✪ Are **lazy** and **dislike work.**
- ✪ **Have no ambition** or desire to take part in workplace decision-making and must be given orders by a tough, decisive boss.
- ✪ **Dislike change** and will always resist it.
- ✪ Are only **motivated by money.**

> **Theory X managers have a negative view that people dislike work and must be forced to do it.**

As a result, Theory X managers believe that they should:
- ✳ **Only offer financial incentives** and material rewards to get work done.
- ✳ **Closely supervise** staff to ensure that they are actually working.
- ✳ **Avoid consulting with staff** when deciding what work is to be done or how.
- ✳ **Threaten staff** with sanctions (e.g. loss of bonuses, suspensions, dismissal) to ensure full co-operation.

McGregor called this Theory X the traditional **'controller'** style of management.
- ❖ Managers with this attitude tend to behave in an autocratic manner, distrust their staff and try to control them as much as possible.
- ❖ In turn, their staff will probably resent this approach, become uncooperative, try to do as little work as possible and avoid intrapreneurship. The manager then feels that his original attitude was fully justified.

● Theory Y managers believe employees . . .

- ✳ **Can enjoy work** and can be trusted to work hard and behave responsibly as long as their job is interesting and challenging.
- ✳ **Have ambition,** imagination and intelligence if they are encouraged.
- ✳ **Are open to change** if they are consulted and fully involved in designing how work should be done.
- ✳ Are **motivated by more than money.**

> **Theory Y managers have a positive view that people, given the right conditions, can work hard and enjoy it.**

As a result, Theory Y managers believe that they should:
- ❖ **Provide interesting and challenging work** that staff will find stimulating.
- ❖ **Provide staff with the freedom** to get on with the job without unnecessary interference.
- ❖ **Consult regularly** with staff about what work is to be done and the best way to do it.
- ❖ **Provide plenty of encouragement** and praise for work well done.

This type of manager is often called a **'facilitator'** manager because they facilitate, or allow, staff to get on with the work in the way they think best.

- ✪ Research shows that if a manager adopts a Theory Y attitude, staff are likely to be much more co-operative and morale and motivation will rise.

- ✪ Democratic and laissez faire / spectator managers have a Theory Y attitude to their staff.

- ✪ The global success of Japan in international business is partially attributed to the fact that most Japanese firms adopt a Theory Y approach to motivating their employees.

Evaluation: Disadvantages of McGregor's Theory X (Controller) attitude to management

1. **Reduced motivation.** Staff are demotivated due to lack of trust and encouragement from managers.

2. **Less creativity.** Little enthusiasm and motivation from staff to generate new ideas.

3. **Poor reputation.** Low motivation can lead to lower quality products and services. This can damage the reputation and customer confidence in the business.

4. **Higher staff turnover.** It is more difficult for controller managers to recruit and retain skilled, experienced and enthusiastic staff.

5. **Reduced profitability.** Long-term competitiveness and profitability of the business can be undermined by lack of innovation, poor staff motivation, low quality standards and high staff turnover.

Evaluation: Advantages of McGregor's Theory Y (Facilitator) attitude to management

1. **High motivation.** Staff motivation and enthusiasm are increased.

2. **More creativity.** New ideas and innovation in the business are encouraged.

3. **Better business reputation.** Motivated staff will have greater commitment to quality standards and customer satisfaction.

4. **Lower staff turnover.** It becomes easier to recruit and retain talented staff.

5. **More positive industrial relations** between workers and managers.

6. **Increased profitability** and business competitiveness.

OL Short Q3, 8

OL Long Q7, 8

HL Short Q7, 8

HL ABQ

HL Long Q6, 8, 9, 10

Case Study

Microsoft®

Leadership and Motivation in Microsoft

Microsoft, which has its European base in Ireland, has a reputation for having very highly **motivated** staff. Microsoft managers use a **democratic leadership style**. They believe that work can be enjoyable and that the talent and contribution of all staff should be encouraged and rewarded.

Microsoft is regularly voted as being one of the best companies in the world to work for. All employees are given annual **bonuses** based on their hard work and achievement of work targets. Exceptionally talented and hardworking staff are rewarded with **free shares** in the company. This makes them part owners of the business.

Microsoft organises regular **social and team-building** activities for staff. When staff want to take a break from their work, computer game consoles and free tea and coffee machines are dotted around offices to use. Staff are encouraged to do **further training** and **study**, with the company paying the costs. **Flexible and family-friendly working hours** are available and the company will also release staff to do paid **work for charities** for a few days every year.

Recall and Review

1. Does Microsoft have a Theory X or a Theory Y approach to motivating staff? Refer to the evidence in the case study to support your answer.

2. Identify examples of how Microsoft uses Maslow's Hierarchy of Needs to motivate its staff.

> **Methods of rewarding staff are covered in detail in Chapter 9: Human Resource Management**

Key Concepts & Business Terms

After studying this chapter the student should be able to explain the following key concepts and business terms:

1. Leadership
2. Corporate (organisational) culture
3. Delegation
4. Leadership styles
5. Autocratic leaders
6. Democratic leaders
7. Laissez-faire leaders
8. Motivation
9. Maslow's Hierarchy of Needs
10. McGregor's theory of motivation
11. Theory X managers
12. Theory Y managers

useful websites

www.microsoft.com

Leaving Certificate Practice Questions

Ordinary Level

Ordinary Level – Section 1 – Short Questions (10 marks each)

1. Explain what is meant by 'leadership'.
2. Explain what 'delegation' means. Give an example of delegation. [LCQ]
3. Identify **two** management skills.
4. Identify **three** different styles of leader.
5. List **two** characteristics of an autocratic leadership style.
6. Define motivation. [LCQ]
7. Name the **five** levels in Maslow's Hierarchy of Needs.
8. List **two** ways in which managers can motivate staff.

Ordinary Level – Section 2 – Long Questions

1. Identify **two** types of leadership and explain any **one** of them. (15 marks) [LCQ]
2. Describe the characteristics of **two** leadership styles. (20 marks)
3. Illustrate a democratic style of leadership in action. (15 marks)
4. Outline two characteristics of a laissez-faire style of leadership. (15 marks)
5. Explain what is meant by 'motivation'. Illustrate why it is relevant to business. (20 marks)
6. List the levels of Maslow's Hierarchy of Needs and explain any **two** of them. (20 marks) [LCQ]
7. Describe **either** McGregor's Theory X or Theory Y. (15 marks) [LCQ]
8. Describe how a manager would behave if she had a Theory Y approach to motivation. (20 marks)

Higher Level

Higher Level – Section 1 – Short Questions (10 marks each)

1. Identify **three** different styles of leadership.
2. Explain the term 'delegation'.
3. Distinguish between a democratic and a laissez-faire style of leadership.
4. Define the term 'motivation'.
5. Chart and label Maslow's Hierarchy of Needs. [LCQ]
6. Explain, using an example, what is meant by 'self-actualisation'.
7. Distinguish between a Theory X approach to motivation and a Theory Y approach. (10 marks) [LCQ]
8. Identify **four** alternatives to money as a motivation for staff.

Higher Level – Section 2 – Applied Business Question

Star FM ★ ★

Star FM is an independent commercial radio station employing thirty staff, including ten DJs and presenters. It has been broadcasting for over ten years and has built up a steady listenership. The station manager, William Morris, prides himself on being a 'hands-on' type of manager, involved in all aspects of the station's work. He likes to share his opinions and, as managing director, expects others to agree with him.

While the station's audience ratings are good and it is attracting lots of advertising revenue, staff are not happy. Over recent months William has been telling producers and DJs what music to play and not to play. He has informed the staff that the wearing of casual clothes at work is no longer acceptable, but gave no reason for this decision. There is now a growing sense among staff that William is interfering unnecessarily in their work. Already one DJ has left for another station while another is rumoured to be thinking about following her.

William has become aware of the decline in the level of motivation among staff and has increased staff wages in response. However, this appears to have made little difference. The station's owners are now getting concerned about the way the station is being run.

1. Explain why money alone may not be a sufficient motivation for staff in Star FM. (30 marks)
2. Identify William's leadership style. Recommend, giving reasons, an appropriate style of leadership that you consider suitable for running the radio station. Refer to the text in your answer. (20 marks).
3. Select a theory of motivation and show how William could use it to improve motivation among Star FM's staff. (30 marks).

Higher Level – Section 2 – Long Questions

1. Outline and illustrate what is meant by 'delegation'. (15 marks) [LCQ]

2. Describe the benefits of delegation for a manager (20 marks)

3. Discuss **three** styles of leadership. (30 marks) [LCQ]

4. 'Different leadership styles are appropriate to different circumstances.' Discuss this statement giving reasons for your answer. (30 marks)

5. Explain why the ability to motivate is an important management skill. (20 marks)

6. Describe **one** motivational theory commonly used in management. (10 marks) [LCQ]

7. Illustrate how Maslow's theory of motivation can be used to motivate staff. Use examples to support your answer. (10 marks) [LCQ]

8. Analyse the implications for a business of a manager adopting a Theory X approach to management. (20 marks) [LCQ]

9. Evaluate the motivational theories of Maslow and McGregor. (25 marks) [LCQ]

10. Analyse why leadership and motivation skills are important to managers. (30 marks)

Chapter 7
Management Skill of Communication

Key Study Questions

Case Study

Communications disaster in NASA

NASA is the US government's space agency responsible for space exploration. It employs thousands of staff and has an annual budget of billions of dollars.

The build-up to the launch of a space mission is an extremely busy time for NASA management who, besides dealing with the technical issues, also spend a huge amount of time **communicating** the value and importance of each mission to the public and the government.

After completing a smooth and successful mission, the Space Shuttle Columbia was returning to Earth when suddenly the astronauts' cockpit lit up as emergency lights and the noise of alarms signalled a massive on-board systems failure. The spacecraft then began to shake and tumble out of the sky before blowing apart, scattering debris over a wide part of the southern United States. All seven astronauts on board were killed.

An independent investigation team examined thousands of pieces of recovered debris and eventually identified a specific hardware fault as the cause. However, the investigators also identified a more serious problem.

Apparently, the hardware fault had been known before the launch went ahead. Engineers had tried to warn senior **managers** at Mission Control of the dangers of proceeding with the launch but, afraid of delaying the mission, some managers did not want to listen to these **communications**. Since each Space Shuttle flight costs nearly €200 million, any delay only increases costs more. NASA managers were afraid that after all their communications hype to the government and the public, any delay to the launch of the mission would jeopardise government funding for future space exploration.

The crash investigator's **report** concluded that the real cause of the disaster was a serious **communications failure** by NASA management.

A. Importance of communications

1. What are communications?

> Communication is all about transferring information between people.

In NASA and all organisations, managers need to be able to communicate effectively with other managers, employees, customers, suppliers, government and the general public. **Communications** *refer to the transfer of information between people.* Communications can be verbal (e.g. a face-to-face meeting, telephone or radio), written (e.g. a letter, report, e-mail, websites), visual (e.g. diagrams, advertising) or physical (e.g. personal appearance, body language).

Communications can be formal or informal. **Formal** (or planned) **communications** *pass through the approved channels of communication.*

> Examples: Memos, reports, formal meetings, notice boards, etc.

Informal communications (the 'grapevine') *refer to the informal network of communications that exists within every organisation and industry.*

> Examples: Chats in the company canteen, in a corridor or at social events outside of work and all types of business **gossip.**

Skills needed by managers to communicate effectively include the:

❖ Ability to **speak** clearly.

❖ Ability to **listen** carefully.

❖ Ability to give and receive **feedback.**

❖ Ability to **write clearly** and concisely.

❖ Ability to **read and understand** communications.

❖ Ability to **select the best medium** for the communication.

❖ Ability to use information and communication **technologies (ICT)** effectively.

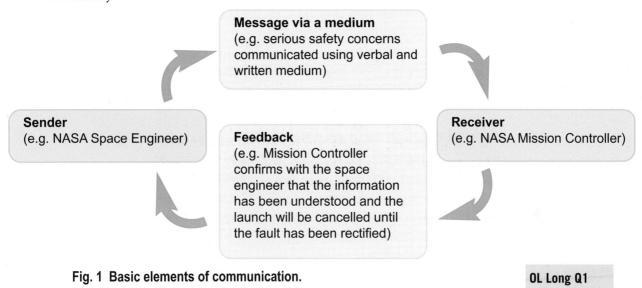

Fig. 1 Basic elements of communication.

OL Long Q1

2. Why is communication important in business?

All stakeholders can be affected by the quality of communications flowing internally and externally about the business.

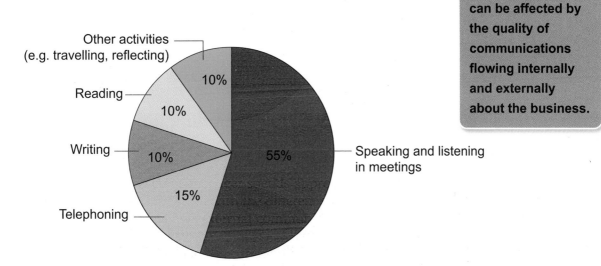

Fig. 2 How managers spend their time

It is estimated that the average manager spends approximately 90% of his or her time communicating in some form with the different **stakeholders** in the business. As a result, effective **internal** and **external** communications are **very important** as breakdowns can lead to misunderstandings and possible conflict with stakeholder groups.

● Communication between internal stakeholders

- ✪ **Employees** and managers must be able to communicate to ensure the correct work is done, on time and to the correct quality standard. Poor communications can cause confusion among staff, reduced morale, possible distrust and industrial relations problems.

- ✪ **Managers** must be able to communicate relevant information with each other to ensure that they have all the information they need to make good decisions. This also will help them to work effectively as a team.

- ✪ **Investors** must be supplied with accurate information about the financial performance of the business. Otherwise, they will not have confidence in management and will be unwilling to invest finance in the business.

● Communication with external stakeholders

- ❖ **Customers** should be kept informed of new product developments, especially if problems arise that will affect customer satisfaction. This way, they are more likely to be forgiving and remain loyal to the company.

- ❖ **Suppliers** need to be kept informed of the firm's supply needs. The business also needs to know from suppliers of any delays or problems that could upset production plans.

- ❖ **Government:** Businesses need to communicate with government agencies when applying for grants, lobbying for changes in the law or reporting breaches of the law, such as pollution incidents.

- ❖ **Society:** The reputation of every business with the general public is very important as it affects the firm's ability to recruit staff, win customers and avoid conflict with vested interest groups. Public relations are particularly important here.

> HL Long Q1

B. Methods of communications

3. What are the methods of communication used by businesses?

> Communications flow upwards, downwards and sideways within organisations. Communications can also be formal or informal, and be directed internally or externally.

The **communications medium** *refers to the actual method used to send the message or data.*

- ✳ **External communications** *are used to communicate with people outside the business, such as customers, suppliers, investors, government and the general public.* Examples include advertising, letters to customers or telephone calls to suppliers.

- ✳ **Internal communications** *are used to communicate between staff in the same business.* Examples include staff meetings, emails, notice boards and mobile text messages sent between staff.

Communications channels *are the routes in an organisation through which information flows between people. They can be upward, downward, horizontal, formal or informal.*

✳ **Upward communications** *refer to staff reporting up the chain of command to their supervisors and managers.*

> **Example:** NASA engineers warning managers about faulty equipment.

✳ **Downward communications** *are messages sent down the chain of command from managers to their subordinates.*

> **Example:** A sales manager sending a message to sales staff.

✳ **Horizontal communications** *travel between people of the same rank and authority in the chain of command.*

> **Example:** A finance manager may have a meeting with the human resource manager about the cost of employing additional staff.

Types of business communications

	Verbal	Written	Visual	Electronic (may be verbal / written / visual)
Internal Communication – sent between people in the same organisation.	• Formal meetings • Telephone • Video conference • Intercom • Informal chats / grapevine	• Letters • E-mails • Internet / Intranet • Text messages • Memos • Notices • Notice board • Signs • Reports • Newsletter	• Posters • Graphs/Charts • Internet websites • Body language • Signs • Physical appearance of staff and premises	• E-mail • Internet / Intranet • Text messages • Video conference
External Communication – sent to or received from people outside of the organisation such as suppliers, customers, investors, the general public.	• Telephone • Meetings • Exhibitions • Video conference • Radio / TV / Cinema advertisements • Internet webcasts (e.g. YouTube) • Press interviews • Conferences • Word of mouth	• Letters • Fax • E-mails • Internet • Text messages • Signs • Reports • Newsletter • Brochures • Advertisements • Press releases	• Posters • Graphs/Charts • Signs • Internet • Brochures • Advertisements • Sponsorship • Product packaging • Merchandising displays • Physical appearance of staff and premises	• E-mail • Internet websites • Text messages • Video conference • Electronic Data Interchange (EDI) **OL Short Q1**

Case Study

Communications in the
Willow Court Hotel

The Willow Court Hotel is a large, 120-bedroom hotel catering for holidaymakers, weddings, banquets and conferences. The managing director is Caroline Lawlor who spends the first two hours of every day 'on the shop floor', monitoring and assisting staff as they serve breakfast and check guests in and out of the hotel. It's an important part of her job as it keeps her in touch with the needs of customers and staff and helps management control by ensuring that everything is running smoothly.

To manage a hotel with 80 employees properly, Caroline must be an effective communicator. 'Nobody can manage without communicating with the business stakeholders inside and outside an organisation. Communications is an essential management skill,' says Caroline. 'For instance, when I walked into the kitchens this morning I was confronted by Ricardo, the head chef, who was fuming with anger. Apparently, the consignment of vegetables delivered was rotten and he had to contact another firm for fresh produce. He wanted me to change suppliers immediately as there have been numerous problems with the current supplier. I agreed and scribbled a note in my diary as a reminder.

'After this it was back to my office to go through the morning post, including any e-mails, faxes and other messages. From this I prepared a detailed "To Do" list for the day.' Today's priority items for Caroline were:

* **Telephoning** the supplier to complain about the poor quality of the supplies and to tell them that if there is not an immediate improvement in quality the hotel would use a different supplier.

* **Meet** with Ed Lyons, the marketing manager, to discuss what to do about the recent drop in room bookings.

* **E-mail** the architects in response to their **letter**, to make an appointment for a **meeting** about the planned new extension. Niall Murphy, the hotel's financial manager, will need to attend as he will be preparing the business plan for the bank if a loan is needed to finance this project.

* Prepare a staff **memo** complimenting them on their quality of work over the busy bank holiday weekend and confirming that the agreed pay rise will come into effect next month.

* **Meet** the chairman of the local Seaside Sailing Club and confirm that the Willow Court Hotel would be willing to provide sponsorship. A letter will also have to be sent to confirm this agreement in writing.

1. Identify the different people Caroline communicated with during her working day.
2. List the different methods of communication Caroline uses in her work.
3. Explain why effective communications is important to a manager like Caroline.

4. What are meetings?

Verbal communications, such as meetings, are the most common means of business communications. **Business meetings** *occur when two or more people get together to communicate with each other.* Business meetings are held to:

❖ **Provide information and pass on instructions to staff,** for instance, to pass on the latest sales results or announce the latest profits to shareholders. Face-to-face meetings help people in business to build up trust and good working relationships.

❖ **Discuss an issue** and share views and ideas, e.g. to discuss how to increase the number of guests staying in a hotel.

❖ **Make a decision.** Holding a meeting to make decisions is particularly important for a democratic style of leadership.

● The main types of meetings

✪ **Formal meetings** *are highly structured because they are planned and run according to agreed procedures. They usually involve a chairperson and a secretary who takes the minutes of the meeting.* Examples include a business staff meeting, a meeting of the board of directors of a limited company, or the AGM of the shareholders of a company.

✪ **AGMs** *(Annual General Meetings) are meetings open to all shareholders of a company.* Issues covered include directors giving reports concerning the previous year's activities, shareholders asking questions and a board of directors for the next year being elected. Clubs and societies also hold AGMs for their members and use it to elect a management committee for the next year.

✪ **EGMs** *(Extraordinary General Meetings) are called to discuss a very important or emergency matter that cannot wait until the next AGM.*

✪ **Ad hoc meetings** *take place at short notice to deal with a problem or issue that has arisen.*

5. How is a formal business meeting organised?

Elements of a formal meeting:
• **Chairperson**
• **Secretary**
• **Agenda**
• **Notice**
• **Quorum**
• **Minutes**

There are two key roles for organising and running a formal business meeting – chairperson and secretary.

A. People

● Chairperson

A **chairperson** *is responsible for the correct running of a meeting.* If a chairperson has not been chosen in advance, the first task of the meeting should be to appoint one, preferably someone with experience.

> **Example:** At the Willow Court's regular management meetings, Caroline normally acts as chairperson. At the hotel's AGM, the role of chairperson is carried out by the chairperson of the board of directors of the Willow Court Hotel Company.

Duties of a chairperson:

❖ **Set an agenda:** Before the meeting, the chairperson must decide on the items to be dealt with at the meeting (see below).

❖ **Open the meeting** and ensure that it was convened (called) in accordance with the rules. The chairperson must also ensure a quorum is present. *A* **quorum** *is the minimum number of people who must attend before an official meeting can begin.*

❖ **Follow the agenda** in the agreed order. Anticipate possible problems with the agenda.

❖ **Standing orders** must be agreed. **Standing orders** *are the agreed rules for running the meeting.* The chairperson must ensure that they are being properly followed. *A* **point of order** *refers to a question to the chairperson regarding how a meeting is being run.*

❖ **Facilitate contributions:** The chairperson must allow everyone who wants to speak reasonable time to express their views. If there is a disagreement, both sides should be given an equal amount of time to put their case.

❖ **Keep order** among the participants.

❖ **Call for votes:** In formal meetings, such as AGMs, the chairperson may put motions to a vote. If a vote is tied, then the chairperson can use their casting vote to break the deadlock.

OL Short Q3
OL Long Q4

● Secretary for a meeting

The **secretary** *is responsible for notifying participants in advance about the meeting. During the meeting, the secretary takes notes of the decisions made during the meeting.*
Minutes *are a written record of what was discussed and decided at a meeting.* They include information on the date, location, and names of attendees, apologies of non-attendees, purpose of the meeting, main views expressed at the meeting, votes taken and decisions made.

Duties of a secretary:

❖ **Before the meeting** a **notice** calling people to the meeting should be sent out to everyone who is supposed to attend, along with copies of the **agenda.** The secretary also arranges a suitable **venue.** **Materials** and resources which may be needed, such as chairs, pens and paper, refreshments, flip charts, markers, overheads and copies of relevant reports should be prepared in advance.

❖ **During the meeting:** Firstly, the secretary **reads out** the minutes of the previous meeting. Those present must approve these minutes as being accurate and they are then signed by the chairperson before the meeting can proceed. Having accurate minutes is important because if a legal dispute arises then the minutes may be used in court as evidence of what was said. The secretary also **takes notes** of the main points made at the present meeting and any decisions taken.

❖ **After the meeting:** The secretary **writes up the minutes** of the previous meeting and circulates them to those who attended. This should be done as soon as possible to ensure accuracy of recall. The secretary **arranges the next meeting** in co-operation with the chairperson.

OL Short Q4

B. Documents for meetings

● Notice of the meeting

Before the meeting, a **notice** calling people to the meeting should be sent out to everyone who is supposed to attend, along with copies of the **agenda.**

● Agenda

An **agenda** *is a summary list of all the items to be dealt with at the meeting.* An agenda should be relevant to all those attending. Important issues should be put near the top of the agenda and less important matters at the end as a precaution against the meeting running out of time.

Sample Notice and Agenda for company AGM

Willow Court Hotel Ltd

NOTICE OF THE ANNUAL GENERAL MEETING

The 15th Annual General Meeting of the shareholders of The Willow Court Hotel will be held in the Willow Court Hotel at 11am on 10 March.

Agenda of the Annual General Meeting (AGM) of the WILLOW COURT Hotel Company.

1. Minutes of the last AGM
2. Matters arising from the minutes
3. Chairperson's report
4. Auditors' report
5. Appointment of auditors for next year
6. Proposed dividend for shareholders
7. Elect a new board of directors
8. A.O.B.

Signed:

Conor Brady

Company Chairperson

OL Short Q2

Minutes of the Meeting

Willow Court Hotel Ltd

MINUTES OF ANNUAL GENERAL MEETING

1. Minutes of the last AGM were read, approved and signed by the company chairperson.
2. There were no matters arising from the minutes.
3. Chairperson presented his report. He presented a review of the year and discussed the plans for the new hotel extension.
4. The auditors presented their financial report and stated that the accounts of the hotel presented a true and accurate picture of the finances. Profits for the past year were €500,000.
5. O'Casey Accountants were appointed as auditors for the following year.
6. A dividend of 20 cent per share was proposed and approved by a majority of shareholders.
7. The following were elected to the company board for next year: B. Brady, C. Casey, D. Duggan, E. Enright.
8. There was no A.O.B.

Signed:

Conor Brady

Chairperson

HL Short Q3
HL Long Q4

Organising a formal meeting of a club

Organising a formal meeting of a club or society is slightly different to organising a company meeting:

* Clubs and societies are **non-profit organisations**.

* Clubs have **members who pay to join** whereas a company has shareholders.

* Clubs have a management committee (instead of a board of directors).

* Club members have to pay annual **subscriptions** (instead of receiving the dividends that are paid to company shareholders).

* **Clubs have slightly different agenda items**, for example a Club AGM will have a treasurer's report (instead of an auditors' report).

● Sample Notice and Agenda for a club AGM

Seaside Sailing Club

NOTICE OF AGM MEETING

The Annual General Meeting of the Seaside Sailing Club will take place in the new clubhouse on 12 June at 8pm.

Seaside Sailing Club

Agenda of Annual General Meeting (AGM)

1. Minutes of last AGM
2. Matters arising from the minutes
3. Club chairperson's report
4. Club treasurer's report
5. Members vote on new membership fees for next year
6. Election of new committee
7. A.O.B

Signed:

Tom Cassidy

Club chairperson

Seaside Sailing Club
MINUTES OF ANNUAL GENERAL MEETING

The Annual General Meeting of the Seaside Sailing Club took place in the clubhouse on 12 June.

The minutes were as follows:

1. The minutes of the last AGM were read and approved.
2. There were no matters arising from the minutes.
3. The club chairperson addressed the meeting. He said that it was a very successful year for the club. The new clubhouse was opened and 50 new members joined during the year.
4. The treasurer addressed the meeting and said that the club finances were healthy and that the Willow Court Hotel had agreed to sponsor the club for the coming year. The loan for the new clubhouse is small and should be paid off in two years.
5. The meeting voted by 200 votes to 150 to increase the membership subscription to €120 per annum.
6. The following were elected to the club committee for the coming year: J. Wilson, B. Murray, H. Delaney, D. Hogan, B. Carroll
7. There was no A.O.B.

Signed

Ashley Whelan

Club secretary

OL Long Q5

HL Short Q2

Evaluation: Advantages of meetings

1. **Clarity:** Verbal communications can be more effective at promoting clear understanding, especially as feelings, tone of voice and body language can be used to add emphasis.
2. **Rapport:** Face-to-face meetings can help to establish a positive relationship between participants.
3. **Speed:** Meetings can deal with issues more quickly than exchanging letters, emails or written correspondence.
4. **Feedback:** Easier to get a response/feedback, especially in small groups.

Evaluation: Disadvantages of meetings

1. **Cost:** Time involved can make them more costly than just exchanging information by e-mail.
2. **Record:** If there is no written record of the meeting, then it can be easy to forget the details of what was discussed and agreed.
3. **Clarity:** Complex and detailed information, such as financial details, can be difficult to transmit verbally. A letter or a report may be more suitable.
4. **Accuracy:** It can be easy to misunderstand something spoken if the speaker is not very clear or precise.

OL Short Q5

OL Long Q2, 3

HL Long Q3

6. What is a memo?

- ❖ **Memos** *(short for memorandum) are short written notes about one particular issue.*
- ❖ Memos are a **very common** method of internal communication, such as a receptionist leaving a telephone message for a manager.
- ❖ Memos provide a **useful written record** of the message to the receiver and are less likely to be forgotten.
- ❖ Memos should be about one topic and **as brief as possible**, in order to be effective.

MEMORANDUM

To: Ricardo Capri, head chef
From: Caroline Lawlor
Subject: Possible change of supplier
Date: 24 October

ABC Foods have apologised for the decline in the quality of food deliveries and have promised that it will not happen again. However, I am concerned about their quality control problems. As head chef, I want you to recommend a possible alternative supplier of high-quality vegetables which the hotel could use.

Signed:

Caroline Lawlor

Managing Director

OL Short Q10

HL Short Q1

7. What are business letters?

Business letters are commonly used in important situations, especially where a written record of the communication is required. They should be clear and to the point in what they are saying. The basic layout of a business letter is given in the following example.

HL Long Q5

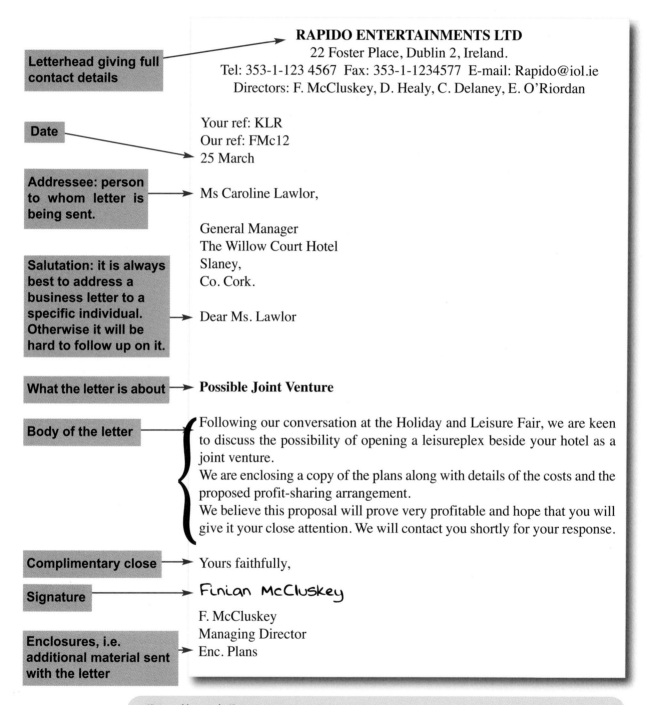

Letterhead giving full contact details

RAPIDO ENTERTAINMENTS LTD
22 Foster Place, Dublin 2, Ireland.
Tel: 353-1-123 4567 Fax: 353-1-1234577 E-mail: Rapido@iol.ie
Directors: F. McCluskey, D. Healy, C. Delaney, E. O'Riordan

Date

Your ref: KLR
Our ref: FMc12
25 March

Addressee: person to whom letter is being sent.

Ms Caroline Lawlor,

General Manager
The Willow Court Hotel
Slaney,
Co. Cork.

Salutation: it is always best to address a business letter to a specific individual. Otherwise it will be hard to follow up on it.

Dear Ms. Lawlor

What the letter is about

Possible Joint Venture

Body of the letter

Following our conversation at the Holiday and Leisure Fair, we are keen to discuss the possibility of opening a leisureplex beside your hotel as a joint venture.
We are enclosing a copy of the plans along with details of the costs and the proposed profit-sharing arrangement.
We believe this proposal will prove very profitable and hope that you will give it your close attention. We will contact you shortly for your response.

Complimentary close

Yours faithfully,

Signature

Finian McCluskey

F. McCluskey
Managing Director

Enclosures, i.e. additional material sent with the letter

Enc. Plans

Recall and Review

Imagine you are Caroline. Draft a business letter to Rapido Entertainments thanking them for contacting you with their proposal but informing them that the Willow Court Hotel is no longer interested in being involved in opening a leisureplex as a joint venture at this time.

Press releaseas are a particular type of business letter sent to the media. **Press releases** *are written communications sent to journalists by organisations or individuals wanting to get publicity for an announcement or to respond to negative publicity.* It may be sent by fax, email or letter to newspapers, radio and television stations or they can be posted on a website.

8. What is a report?

A report *is a written document about a specific topic or issue presenting information, evaluation and recommendations to the specific person or group who requested it.*

Reports can be used for the following reasons:

✳ **To investigate an incident and explain what happened,** for example: 'Report into the cause of the Columbia Space Shuttle Disaster.'

✳ **To solve a problem,** for example: a report recommending a new marketing strategy for the Willow Court Hotel.

✳ **To identify possible courses of action and their implications,** for example: 'A report into the pros and cons of raising prices in the Willow Court Hotel.'

✳ **To monitor progress,** such as sales trends in the Willow Court Hotel for the period January to June.

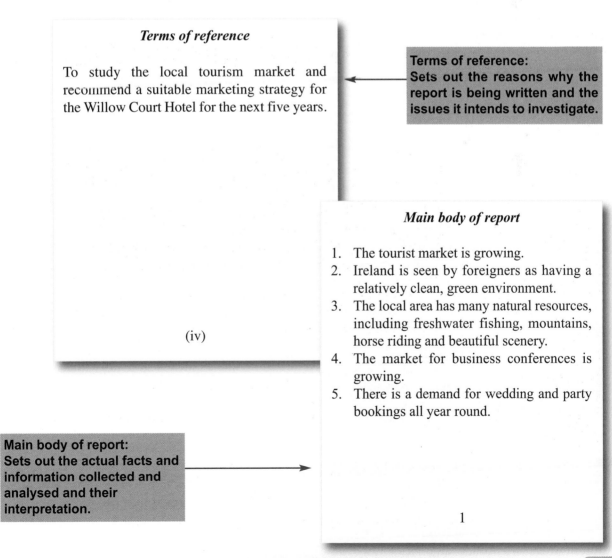

Terms of reference

To study the local tourism market and recommend a suitable marketing strategy for the Willow Court Hotel for the next five years.

Terms of reference:
Sets out the reasons why the report is being written and the issues it intends to investigate.

(iv)

Main body of report

1. The tourist market is growing.
2. Ireland is seen by foreigners as having a relatively clean, green environment.
3. The local area has many natural resources, including freshwater fishing, mountains, horse riding and beautiful scenery.
4. The market for business conferences is growing.
5. There is a demand for wedding and party bookings all year round.

Main body of report:
Sets out the actual facts and information collected and analysed and their interpretation.

1

Conclusions and Recommendations

1. In summer specialise in high-quality 'green tourism' holidays.
2. In winter, when bookings are slack, promote the hotel as a venue for weddings or parties and as a luxury weekend getaway destination.

Conclusions/recommendations: Describes the lessons to be learned from the report and what should be done in the future.

9

Bibliography

*   *Marketing Ireland as a tourist destination*, Bord Fáilte report to the Minister for Tourism.
*   *Report on the future of the tourist industry in the EU*, European Commission
*   *Guide to Marketing Tourist Services*, Business Books.

10

OL Short Q6

HL Short Q4

Bibliography: List of books, magazines, reports and other sources of information used by the writers to compile the report.

● The qualities of a good report

A good report:

*   ❖ **Gathers relevant information** and deals with the issues that were set out in the terms of reference.
*   ❖ **Provides a good analysis** of the subject of the report
*   ❖ **Assists management decision-making** by providing accurate, clear and realistic information and recommendations.

Evaluation: Advantages of business reports
1. Can gather together all **relevant information** on an issue.
2. Can provide **detailed research**, information and analysis.
3. Help managers to make informed **decisions**.
4. Can be compiled by **outside experts** leaving managers more time for other important tasks.

Evaluation: Disadvantages of business reports
1. Can discourage readers if they are too long or badly laid out.
2. Requesting a report can be used as an excuse to postpone dealing with the issues involved.
3. Report recommendations can be ignored by the receivers.

OL Long Q6

9. How can business information be communicated visually?

Visual communications are important both inside and outside a business. Staff can use maps, charts, graphs and other diagrams to communicate business information quickly and accurately. The use of photographs in brochures, on a website and in advertising can also help customers to visualise a business's products or services.

Benefits of visual communications:

* **Improves presentation** by breaking up long sections of written text.
* **Simplifies information**, assists understanding and remembering data.
* **Speeds up the absorption** and understanding of data.

Case Study

Visual Communications in the Willow Court Hotel

As part of his marketing report, the Willow Court's marketing manager explained the different sources of sales revenue for the hotel: 40% of sales come from renting bedrooms, 30% from sales in the bar, 20% from sale of meals in the restaurant and 10% from renting out function rooms for weddings, parties, debs balls, etc. To make the point clearly, quickly and memorably, he wanted to present this information visually. He identified three possible options: using a **pie chart**, a **bar chart** or a **pictogram**.

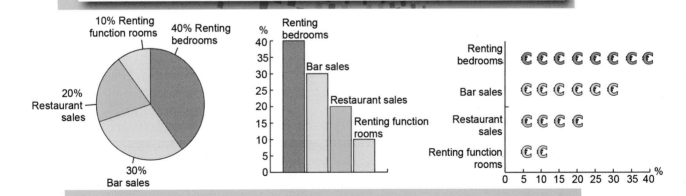

Recall and Review

1. What type of visual communications would you recommend to the marketing manager to use in the report? Give reasons for your answer.
2. Can you identify an alternative way in which the same information could be communicated visually?

● Pie charts

Pie charts *compare different categories as though they were segments of a pie.*

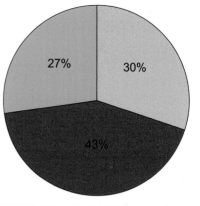

● Pictograms

Pictograms *are diagrams that use small pictures to represent different quantities of people or objects.*

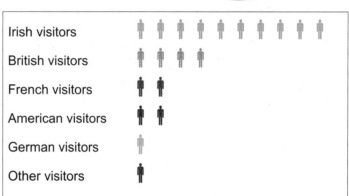

● Line graphs

Line graphs *use the path of a line to show the change in figures over a period of time. They are also known as* **time-trend graphs**.

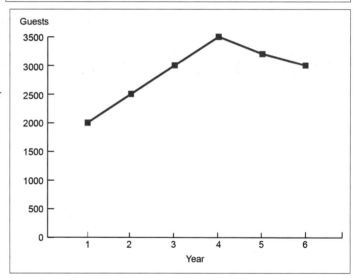

● Bar charts

Bar charts *are used when comparing a large number of different categories.*

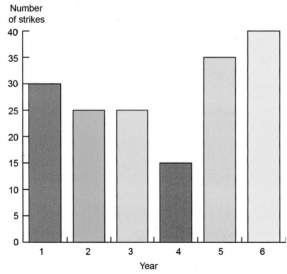

Gantt charts

Gantt charts *are used to visually illustrate the amount of time taken to complete work compared to the amount of time originally planned.* They are very useful for planning projects and scheduling work to be done.

River Court Hotel Renovation Project	Week 1	Week 2	Week 3	Week 4	Week 5
Removal of old furniture and carpets	▓				
Repainting interior		▓	▓		
Laying new carpets				▓	
Delivery and arranging new furniture					▓

Maps

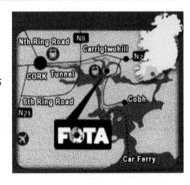

Maps *are useful to illustrate physical locations, such as where a firm's premises are located.*

Organisational charts

Organisational charts *show who does what and how the different people in the organisation are connected.*

> Organisational charts are covered in detail in Chapter 8: Management Activities of Planning, Organising & Controlling.

Break-even charts

Break-even charts *show what level of sales must be achieved before a product will break even (i.e. cover its costs) and begin to make a profit.*

> Break-even charts are covered in detail in Chapter 14: Identifying Business Opportunities.

Graphic design

Graphic design *includes using computer software to make it easier for businesses to communicate information visually.*

OL Long Q8

HL Short Q5

HL Long Q7

C. Effective Communications

10. What are the elements of effective communications?

Effective communications involve:
• Sender
• Message
• Medium used
• Receiver

Effective communications involve:

● Sender

❖ **Timely:** The sender must choose the correct time to send the message. If a notice about a meeting is sent out six months in advance, then it may be forgotten about. If the notice is only sent out the day before, then it may be too late as people may have other appointments.

● Message

❖ **Accurate:** Effective communications must be accurate, as communicating inaccurate information can lead to the wrong decisions being made. A written message or a face-to-face meeting might be preferable if accuracy is important. Numbers, calculations or technical data are best communicated in writing. Telephone conversations, especially on mobile phones, can be subject to bad connections and misunderstandings that undermine accuracy.

❖ **Brief:** Time is valuable so business communications should be as brief and to the point as possible.

> Example: An employee should not send a 10-page report about a telephone message they received when a short note would be perfectly adequate!

❖ **Clear:** The information should be communicated in a way that is easily understood.

> Example: When dealing with complex or large quantities of information such as sales statistics, it is very helpful to use diagrams or illustrations. The recipient should also be able to easily understand the language used.

● Medium used

❖ **Appropriate:** Private or sensitive communications should not be communicated using a medium that may lack privacy. It is also important to respect the feelings of the recipient when communicating messages containing personal information or bad news.

> Example: An employee who is made redundant should be informed privately and in a sensitive manner by their supervisor and not, for instance, through a note stuck on the staff notice board or an announcement over the intercom system.

> **Example:** A business partner may prefer to keep a business idea confidential by discussing it in a private meeting.

❖ **Fast:** If speed is important, such as confirming a valuable conference booking, then a telephone call, fax or courier may be necessary. If speed is not essential, then a letter in the post may be appropriate.

❖ **Low cost:** Methods of communication can vary considerably in terms of time and financial costs involved. Writing a letter will take longer than making a phone call, while posting a letter is far less expensive than sending it by motorcycle courier.

❖ **Provide a record:** To avoid conflicts or misunderstandings with important messages, it is often a good idea to have a written record as proof of what information was actually communicated.

> **Example:** The Willow Court Hotel sends out written confirmation to customers who make telephone or Internet bookings.

❖ **Satisfy any legal requirements:** In some circumstances, special rules may have to be followed.

> **Example:** Legally binding written contracts should not be faxed for signing but should be sent by post.

● Receiver

❖ **Allow feedback:** Ideally, communications should allow for feedback from the receiver. This means that any confusion or potential misunderstandings can be cleared up quickly.

> **Example:** It is much easier to negotiate a sale in a face-to-face meeting where you can monitor verbal and body language reaction rather than sending written messages back and forth.

OL Long Q7, 9, 13

HL Long Q2

11. What are the barriers to effective communication?

Sender	Message	Medium	Receiver
• Choosing an **inappropriate time** to send the message.	• Sending **inaccurate information**. • Sending an unclear, **badly worded** message. • Using unnecessary **jargon** or technical language. • Sending an **inappropriate message**. • Message is **too long** and gets ignored.	• Selecting an **inappropriate method of communication** that does **not get heard**. • Using a medium that is **too slow or unreliable** (e.g. poor mobile phone coverage).	• Message sent to the **wrong receiver**. • **Receiver not listening** or unable to listen to the message. • **Receiver misinterprets** the message. • Receiver **cannot provide feedback** or seek easy clarification. • Receiver **mistrusts the sender** and does not believe the message.

OL Short Q7

OL Long Q10

HL Short Q8, 9

HL Long Q6

Case Study

Wrong message destroys business

Gerald Ratner was a very busy manager. As chief executive of Ratner's Jewellers, he ran a chain of jewellery shops with sales of millions of euro every year. The job involved constant **communications** with staff, suppliers, customers, investors and other **stakeholders** in his business, sometimes in person, often on his **mobile phone** or by **email**.

As a very successful manager, he prided himself on his excellent communication skills. He was invited to speak at a **business conference** about the secrets of his business success. At the conference, he made a joke that the reason his chain of shops was so profitable was because it could sell earrings for less than the price of a sandwich 'but they probably wouldn't last as long'. He then referred to other products sold in his shops as being so cheap because they were 'total crap'.

Unfortunately for Ratner, there was a journalist from a newspaper at the meeting and the next day the story appeared all over the **newspapers**, **television** and **Internet**. Ratner issued a **press release** to try to explain away what he said but it was too late. Members of the public did not like being taken for fools and sales at his stores collapsed as the news of what he said spread. Overnight, his careless verbal communications destroyed the **reputation** of his own business and it was forced to close down.

12. How can ICT help business communications?

Information and communication technology (ICT) *refers to the use of computers, telecommunications and electronics to gather, store, process and distribute information.* ICT has made business communications very fast and accurate.

> **ICT: Information & Communications Technology**

* The **Internet** *is an international network of computers connected through the telephone network.* It can be used to transmit and receive data and information globally at a low cost by anyone with a computer and Internet access. The Internet allows businesses to display websites for communicating information with customers and other stakeholders.

* **E-mail** (electronic mail) allows documents and audio-visual files to be sent instantaneously over the Internet at practically no cost.

> **Example:** The Willow Court Hotel gets regular email enquiries and bookings from people around the world who want to stay in the hotel.

* **Intranets** (*Internal Computer Networks*) *are networks of computers **within** a business.* They allow employees to send files to each other over the computer network thereby speeding up communications within the organisation. Intranets are also known as Local Area Networks (LANs).

* **Electronic Data Interchange** (EDI) *is an automated stock ordering system that allows orders to be placed automatically from a computer in one business to a computer in another business, using the Internet.* An EDI system allows goods to be ordered by firms on time and with a minimum of paperwork or human involvement. EDI has the following benefits:

  * Speeds up stock ordering and reduces human error.
  * Reduces costs by eliminating much of the paperwork and stock management costs.
  * Improves cashflow as invoices (bills) are sent out accurately and on time.
  * Increases customer satisfaction and improves sales as the firm secures regular stock delivery.

Before a firm introduces an EDI stock ordering system, it needs to persuade its suppliers/customers to do likewise, so that orders can be dispatched/received and payments made electronically.

Example: Large supermarkets like Tesco, Dunnes Stores and SuperValu use ICT to link computers in different stores to the head office computer. This allows up-to-date information on each store's sales, stock levels and cash takings to be instantly transferred to head office when the barcodes on goods are scanned as they go through the checkout. Then, using an EDI system linked to their suppliers' computer system, replacement stock can be ordered automatically by a computer when stock dips below a certain level.

∗ **Low-cost communications** using telephone calls, video conferences and digital file transfer can be made using software applications such as Skype.

∗ **Video conferencing** *is a type of virtual meeting where participants can see and hear each other through the use of video cameras, telephone links and monitors.* Video conferences can take place over any distance which means people can be in different cities or countries. This reduces travel time and expense involved in attending conferences and meetings.

∗ **Computer software applications** such as word processors, databases and spreadsheets are powerful information technologies that can assist in the preparation and processing of business communications.

∗ **Word-processing software:** Professional quality reports, letters and other documents can be produced using word-processing software on a computer.

∗ **Database software** allows a business to store huge amounts of data (e.g. customer details,) electronically, which can be quickly accessed, updated or printed out. This reduces the need for storage space for paper and filing and, when used in conjunction with barcode scanners and EDI, can assist in stock control.

Example: In supermarkets, barcode scanners are linked to databases allowing stores to track minute-by-minute which goods are selling and need to be reordered.

∗ **Spreadsheet software** allows users to do complex financial and statistical calculations quickly and present the results in graphical form, saving time and money

∗ **Desk Top Publishing (DTP)** software is used to produce professional quality leaflets, brochures, websites, newsletters and other publications at a very low cost. Like word-processing software, corrections and updates can easily be made on screen.

HL Short Q6, 7

13. What are the benefits and risks of ICT in business?

● Benefits of ICT to business

1. **Faster communications** as very large data files (e.g. documents, audio, video, software) can be sent over the Internet directly from one computer to another.

2. **Advertising** to a global audience becomes easy through the use of websites that can be visited by anyone with an Internet connection regardless of where they are in the world. This greatly assists advertising and generating sales, both domestically and internationally.

3. **Stakeholder relations are enhanced** as websites, emails and video conferencing makes it easier to communicate with customers, suppliers and other stakeholders.

4. **Reduced marketing costs** as more customers are willing to buy online rather than visiting expensive premises or showrooms.

> **Example:** One of the biggest retailers in the world is Amazon.com yet, instead of operating shops, it uses websites to sell to customers. This helps to massively reduce business costs.

5. **Reduced staff travel costs** and expenses as meetings can be replaced by e-mail and video conferencing.

6. **Staff motivation** can be boosted if staff have the option of teleworking from home or other locations.

● Risks of ICT to business

1. **Information security:** computer systems are vulnerable to infection by computer viruses, hackers and other risks that can steal or destroy the information being stored on computers.

2. **E-crime** such as online credit card fraud using fake websites or stolen credit cards is increasing for firms involved in e-commerce. This can reduce customer confidence in dealing with online businesses.

3. **Business disruption risks** are greater if a business relies heavily on ICT. A fault with an ICT system can bring a whole business to a standstill, for example, if the online booking system for a hotel or airline crashes.

4. **Can be expensive** as rapid changes in technology can make expensive equipment obsolete very quickly. Constantly upgrading equipment and staff skills can be expensive. Maintaining proper security and back-up systems can also be expensive.

`OL Short Q8`

`HL Long Q8`

14. What are the Data Protection Acts 1988 & 2003?

The **Data Protection Acts 1988 & 2003** *require that any organisation storing information on other people* **on computer or in manual files** *must ensure that the information is accurate and kept up to date.* Stored information can only be used for lawful purposes. The Acts set out the rights of private individuals (data subjects) and the responsibilities of businesses and other organisations (data controllers).

> **Example:** Data protection is important because incorrect data held by an employer, such as an incorrect start date, could affect someone's pension entitlements. Similarly, if a person's details are incorrect on, say, a bank computer system, they may be unfairly denied a loan.

According to the Acts, a **data subject** *is anyone who has information held about them on someone else's computer.* **Data controllers** *are the people or organisations who keep information about other people on their computers.*

Rights of private individuals (data subjects)

- **Right of access to files:** You have the right to know how much and what type of information is being kept on file about you by an organisation and what it is being used for. You are also entitled to get a full copy of this information within 40 days of asking for it.

- **Right to correction of errors:** You are entitled to have inaccurate data about yourself corrected or deleted. Members of the public also have the right to have their names removed from any direct marketing mailing lists. Data controllers are legally obliged to comply with such written requests within 40 days.

- **Right to compensation where** inaccurate information causes harm, such as denying you a loan or a promotion. Furthermore, you are entitled to make complaints to the Data Protection Commissioner if you are concerned that the law in this area has been broken.

- **Right of individuals not to be subjected to automated decision-making.** Instead, individuals are entitled to have human input into the making of important decisions relating to them.

Responsibilities of business and other organisations (data controllers)

Businesses and other organisations using computers to store personal information about individuals must ensure that:

- The information has been **obtained fairly** and openly.
- The information is used only for the **specific purpose** for which it was given.
- The information is **stored securely** and protected against unauthorised access or theft.
- Subjects have a **right of access to information** about them held on computer files.
- The **information is accurate**, kept up to date and is only held for as long as is necessary.
- Subjects can have incorrect **information corrected** or deleted.

Data Protection Commissioner

The **Data Protection Commissioner** *is responsible for ensuring that the Data Protection Acts 1988 & 2003 are obeyed.* The commissioner is specifically responsible for:

- **Providing information** to the public about the Acts.
- **Maintaining a register** of all organisations such as banks, market researchers, debt collection firms, etc. that may hold sensitive information about members of the public.
- Helping businesses develop **codes of practice** to help them keep within the law.
- **Investigating complaints** from the public about businesses that may be breaking the law.

OL Short Q9
OL Long Q11, 12

HL ABQ
HL Long Q9, 10

Key Concepts & Business Terms

After studying this chapter the student should be able to explain the following key concepts and business terms:

1. Formal communications
2. Informal communications ('the grapevine')
3. Communications medium
4. Internal communications
5. External communications
6. Communications channels
7. Upward communications
8. Downward communications
9. Horizontal communications
10. Business meetings
11. Formal meetings
12. AGMs
13. EGMs
14. Chairperson
15. Agenda
16. Quorum
17. Standing orders
18. Point of order
19. Secretary for a meeting
20. Minutes of a meeting
21. Memorandum (memo)
22. Business letter
23. Press releases
24. Reports
25. Terms of reference
26. Benefits of visual communications
27. Pie chart
28. Pictogram
29. Line graph/time-trend graph
30. Bar chart
31. Gantt chart
32. Elements of effective communications
33. Barriers to effective communication
34. Benefits of ICT to business
35. The Internet
36. E-mail
37. Intranets (LANs)
38. Electronic Data Interchange (EDI)
39. Video conferencing
40. Word processing
41. Computer databases
42. Spreadsheets
43. Benefits and risks of ICT in business
44. Data Protection Acts 1988 & 2003
45. Data subject
46. Data controller
47. Data Protection Commissioner

 useful websites

www.nasa.gov
www.dataprotection.ie

Leaving Certificate Practice Questions

Ordinary Level

Ordinary Level – Section 1 – Short Questions (10 marks each)

1. List **five** types of written communications in business. [LCQ]
2. List **three** items that might appear on an agenda for a meeting. [LCQ]
3. Identify **two** duties of a chairperson at meetings. [LCQ]
4. Outline **two** duties of a secretary at meetings. [LCQ]
5. Outline **two** advantages of a meeting as a method of communication. [LCQ]
6. Explain what 'terms of reference' means. [LCQ]
7. List **three** barriers to effective communication. [LCQ]
8. List **five** ways in which ICT can provide opportunities to a business.
9. Describe **two** functions of the Data Protection Acts 1988 & 2003. [LCQ]
10. Draft the memo from Ann Miller, a marketing manager, to her staff outlining that the monthly staff meeting on 27 June is to be cancelled. [LCQ]

Ordinary Level – Section 2 – Long Questions

1. Describe the elements of the communication process. (15 marks)
2. Describe the purpose of a meeting and outline the merits of a meeting as a method of communication. (15 marks) [LCQ]
3. 'Without proper organisation, meetings can be confused and ineffective.' Describe how a formal meeting should be properly organised. (25 marks)
4. Formal meetings normally require a quorum. Explain the term 'quorum'. (20 marks) [LCQ]
5. The Fairways Golf Club will hold its Annual General Meeting on 1 July at 7.30pm in the clubhouse. The chairperson John O'Dowd has asked the secretary Martin Browne to send the notice and agenda for the AGM to all members.

   Draft the notice and agenda for the AGM. The agenda should include **five** items that you would expect to find on the agenda of Fairways Golf Club. (25 marks) [LCQ]
6. Reports are a very common means of business communication.
   (a) Explain the uses of reports in business. (15 marks)
   (b) Describe the qualities of an effective report in business. (15 marks)
7. Select, giving reasons, which method of communication you would recommend a business to use when:
   (a) ordering new stock from a supplier.
   (b) informing a worker that he is to be made redundant.
   (c) informing staff about the Christmas party.
   (d) reassuring customers about the high quality of the products for sale.
   (e) congratulating a worker on the excellent quality of her work. (15 marks)
8. The following information relates to the number of cars sold by a garage over a six-month period:

Month	Oct	Nov	Dec	Jan	Feb
Number of cars	200	150	50	300	250

Present the above information in the form of (a) a bar chart, (b) a line graph. (20 marks)

9. Outline **three** factors to be considered when deciding on a suitable method of communication. (15 marks)

10. Identify and explain **three** barriers to effective communication. (20 marks) [LCQ]

11. Under the Data Protection Acts 1988 & 2003, people whose personal information is kept on a computer have several rights. Describe **two** of these rights. (20 marks) [LCQ]

12. Draft a letter to a bank requesting a copy of all the data about you that they hold on their computers. Refer to your rights under the Data Protection Acts 1988 & 2003 in your answer.

13. List **three** management skills and explain one of them. (25 marks) [LCQ]

Higher Level

Higher Level – Section 1 – Short Questions (10 marks each)

1. Draft a memorandum (memo), using an appropriate format, to all department managers suggesting **two** topics for an upcoming management training day. [LCQ]

2. Assume you are the secretary of a local youth club. Draft the notice and agenda to be posted to all members of the youth club notifying them of the Annual General Meeting. (The agenda must contain **five** items.) [LCQ]

3. Using an appropriate format, draft a memorandum (memo) to all directors setting out the notice for the AGM of a private limited company. [LCQ]

4. Illustrate what is meant by 'terms of reference'. [LCQ]

5. The following sales information is taken from the books of The Grand Hotel:

   May: Rooms €45,000; Bar €35,000; Restaurant €25,000; Functions €15,000
   December: Rooms €60,000; Bar €40,000; Restaurant €30,000; Functions €95,000

   Illustrate this information in bar chart form. [LCQ]

6. EDI helps a business to . . . [LCQ]

7. What is video conferencing? [LCQ]

8. Outline **three** problems of e-mail in business. [LCQ]

9. List **four** possible barriers to effective business communications.

Higher Level – Section 2 – Applied Business Question

KALAMAZOO CLOTHING

Linda Delaney is the recently appointed chairperson of the board of directors of Kalamazoo Clothing. In recent months sales have been falling even though the firm's products and prices are very competitive and a lot of money has been spent on advertising. Linda asked the chief executive who was employed by the board of directors to run the company why this might be. However, she only got a vague and unsatisfactory answer. Linda decided to find out why by contacting OMD Ltd, one of Kalamazoo's former big customers.

'Kalamazoo's sales staff need to learn some manners,' said the manager of OMD Ltd. 'Whenever we phone up your company, the

people who answer the phone are often rude and impatient. The person we want to speak to never seems to be in, and the people in the office never know where they are or when they will return. Even worse, your staff never phone us back, even if we have asked them to do so. That is simply no way to do business. Your company obviously has little respect for its customers, so why should we do business with Kalamazoo?'

Linda was shocked by this information and decided to raise the matter with the chief executive at the next meeting of the board of directors. However, this turned into a fiasco. Some directors did not receive the notice of the meeting in time and missed it. Those who did turn up found a meeting without any written agenda. The meeting was poorly chaired and Linda was accused of being disorganised and biased in letting some people do a lot of talking while others could barely get a word in. For example, some directors talked at length about the effectiveness of the advertising campaign while other directors who wanted to talk about the threatened strike by staff over rumours of redundancies felt ignored. After five hours, the meeting eventually ended but with no clear decisions. There were also no minutes being taken of the meeting, a fact that further annoyed many of the directors.

1. Identify evidence of poor communications in Kalamazoo and discuss the consequences that this can have for a business. Refer to the text in your answer. (30 marks)
2. Describe how future meetings of the Kalamazoo board of directors should be organised and the important duties of a chairperson. (20 marks)
3. Draft a written agenda for the next meeting of the Kalamazoo board of directors. (30 marks)

Higher Level – Section 2 – Long Questions

1. Illustrate the importance of good communications for the success of a business enterprise. (20 marks) [LCQ]
2. 'On average managers spend over 75% of their time communicating.' Explain the factors that ensure managers communicate effectively. Use examples where appropriate. (25 marks) [LCQ]
3. Discuss the advantages and disadvantages of using meetings as a method of communication. (15 marks)
4. Draft a typical agenda for, and the minutes of, the AGM of a limited company. (25 marks) [LCQ]
5. Using a fictitious name and address, draft a letter to the human resources manager of a business, setting out **four** key characteristics to be looked for when interviewing candidates for management positions. (20 marks) [LCQ]
6. Draft a report to the managing director of a limited company explaining the four main barriers to effective communications in the business. State relevant assumptions where necessary. (20 marks) [LCQ]

7. Draft a bar chart from the following data:

Materials	35%	Labour		20%
General Expenses	10%	Financial Expenses		5%
Transport	25%	Marketing		5%

   (a) Make **two** comments that are relevant to the information in the chart. (10 marks) [LCQ]

   (b) Outline **two** other forms of visual communications that could be used to present the data to a meeting of managers. (10 marks) [LCQ]

8. Draft a business letter to the managing director of an enterprise, outlining the benefits to business of improving its Information and Communications Technology (ICT) systems. Include examples in your answer. (20 marks) [LCQ]

9. The Data Protection Acts 1988 & 2003 set out the following:

   (a) the rights of Data Subjects

   (b) the obligations of Data Controllers

   (c) the functions of the Data Protection Commissioner

   Explain any **two** of the above. (25 marks) [LCQ]

10. Evaluate the management skills of: (a) leading, (b) motivating, (c) communicating. (60 marks) [LCQ]

UNIT 3

'The tragedy in life doesn't lie in not reaching your goal. The tragedy lies in having no goals to reach.'
Benjamin Mays

Chapter 8

Management Activities of Planning, Organising & Controlling

Key Study Questions

Case Study

MANAGING MERCEDES

Mercedes-Benz is the world's oldest automobile manufacturer and has traditionally prided itself on its reputation for quality. The firm, which is owned by Daimler Chrysler, produces automobiles, buses, coaches and trucks.

Mercedes-Benz cars are made in lower volumes and are relatively expensive compared to most other car brands. The company, whose main competitors are Audi, BMW and Lexus, has carefully cultivated an image of superior engineering, quality and service and the cars are

often the vehicles of choice for the rich and famous.

However, poor management **planning**, **organisation** and **control** led Mercedes-Benz to rush out too many new models before they were properly tested. This led to an avalanche of complaints from angry customers that their cars didn't start properly in the morning or kept breaking down. Sales and profits began to slide.

Mercedes-Benz quickly realised that it had a serious **quality control** problem on its hands. It got its engineers to go painstakingly back over all the designs and they identified the problems as being caused by the very complex on-board electronic systems. However, for 1.3 million owners the damage was already done and their cars had to be recalled by the company for emergency repairs. The firm also had to offer 'extended two years free service' guarantees to stop disgruntled owners switching over to rival car brands.

While the problem in the cars was an engineering one, the real cause was poor **management**. Firstly, poor **planning** meant that Mercedes-Benz rushed ahead and launched new models without proper testing. Secondly, managers had made some very poor decisions about how to **organise** the business. This resulted in some very inefficient manufacturing in its factories in Germany. Thirdly, management failure to maintain proper quality control over the production process meant that huge numbers of faulty cars got through the firm's **quality control** system.

The overall effect on the company's reputation was devastating. It slipped from the top to the bottom of automobile reliability ratings. In a competitive global car market, this slip-up was exploited by competitors, especially BMW and Lexus. Today, the once smaller rival BMW now outsells it. For Mercedes-Benz, this fiasco happened because of poor management **planning**, **organisation** and especially **control**. The business has been forced to completely overhaul its **organisational structure** and is now determined never to let poor planning and quality slip-ups happen again.

A. Planning

1. What is planning?

As in all organisations, management in Mercedes-Benz is about planning, organising and controlling the affairs of a business to ensure that results are achieved. **Planning** *means clearly setting out the goals for the organisation and how these are to be achieved.* Planning is important because it means deciding what to do, who will do it, when and how.

> Planning allows a clear direction to be set for the business.

2. What are the stages in the planning process?

		Planning for a business (Mercedes)
Step 1	**Analyse the situation** Where are we now?	Slipping sales.
Step 2	**Identify the goal** Where do we want to go?	Increase sales by 10%.
Step 3	**Draft a plan** How will we get there?	Improve product quality. Launch an advertising campaign.
Step 4	**Implement and review** Break plan into manageable steps. Review progress.	Design and book advertisements for TV, radio and billboard space. Monitor any changes in sales to see if advertising is working.

Planning Step 1: Analyse the situation

Before making any decisions, Mercedes-Benz's managers have to analyse the current situation, including its strengths and weaknesses, and the future threats and opportunities facing the company. This can be done using a SWOT analysis. A **SWOT analysis** *is a management technique used to assess a business in terms of its strengths, weaknesses, opportunities and threats.*

S

Strengths represent the internal strengths of the firm. These are things the firm is good at doing or important assets it possesses that give it an advantage over competitors. A firm should defend and take advantage of its strengths.

> **Example:** Mercedes-Benz had the following strengths:
> • Good reputation. • Loyal customers.
> • Well-known prestigious brand name.

W

Weaknesses are the firm's internal weaknesses. These are the things the business does poorly or lacks and which put it at a competitive disadvantage. Weaknesses should be fixed or remedied as quickly as possible, in order to protect the business.

> **Example:** Mercedes-Benz identified its weaknesses as:
> • Poorly designed cars. • Unreliable electronics.
> • Poorly organised and inefficient factories.

O

Opportunities represent the firm's external opportunities. These offer the possibility of assisting or expanding the business. They should be exploited, where possible.

> **Example:** Mercedes-Benz identified the following opportunities:
> • Growing market for smaller, fuel-efficient cars.
> • Reorganising factories to be more efficient.

T

Threats are the external threats which the firm faces. They undermine its well-being and profitability. Threats should be defended against.

> **Example:** The main threats facing Mercedes-Benz were:
> • Competitors' cars were more reliable.
> • BMW had overtaken them in sales and Audi and Lexus were not far behind.

OL Long Q2

Planning Step 2: Identify the goal

The results of the SWOT analysis are used to help a business decide on the specific goals or objectives it wants to achieve. Goals can be long term, such as launching a new product, or short term and specific such as hiring a new marketing manager within two months.

The most important goal or purpose for every business is set out in the firm's mission statement. **Mission statements** *are short but precise one- or two-sentence statements used by companies to summarise 'who we are, what we do, and where we're headed'.*

> **Example:** Mercedes-Benz's mission is to produce high-quality, luxury cars with state-of-the-art engineering. A national daily newspaper may have a mission 'to establish itself as the biggest selling quality newspaper in Ireland'.

Planning Step 3: Draft a plan to achieve the goal

To be useful, the mission statement must be supported by strategic and tactical plans. **A strategic plan** (or **corporate plan**) *refers to the long-term plan for the whole business. It normally covers five or more years.*

> **Strategic goals are long term.**
> **Tactical goals are short term.**

> **Example: Mercedes-Benz** prepared a strategic plan to enter the small car market by entering into a strategic alliance with Smart Watches to develop Smart Cars. The strategic plan also included investing heavily in quality control to reverse the slide in Mercedes-Benz reputation.
>
> **Example: Fyffes** have a strategy of expanding their banana business by acquisitions and takeovers of existing firms.
>
> **Example: Sony's** strategy is to keep growing by constantly developing new home electronics entertainment products.

Tactical plans *break the general strategic plan down into shorter, more specific and manageable steps, usually of one- or two-year periods.* Most managers must develop specific short-term tactical plans of action for their particular area of responsibility (e.g. marketing, production, human resource management and finance).

> **Example:** At Mercedes-Benz the company's tactical plans included redesigning its cars to reduce the risk of breakdown and reorganising its factories to make them more efficient.

Operational plans *are short-term plans that set targets for weeks or months ahead.* Different areas such as sales, finance or quality control can have their own operational plans.

> Example: Mercedes monthly sales plan for a 6-month cash-flow forecast.

Contingency plans *are special plans prepared to cope with emergencies or unexpected circumstances.* They include:

OL Short Q2, 3

HL Short Q1

HL Long Q1

- A breakdown in production.
- A disruption in supply of essential raw materials.
- A sudden surge of demand from customers.

Case Study

PlayStation Contingency plan to the rescue!

A cargo ship collided with an oil tanker in the Suez Canal while travelling from China to Europe. Unfortunately for the Sony electronics company, the ship was loaded with tens of thousands of PlayStation games consoles for the peak Christmas market. As shops across Europe quickly began running out of game consoles, Sony was facing a massive **sales** disaster. Meanwhile, rivals Microsoft (X-Box) and Nintendo were delighted with Sony's problems.

However, in addition to **strategic and tactical plans**, Sony had prepared a **contingency plan**. The company immediately hired a fleet of large Russian freight jets to fly in replacement **supplies** from China to Europe. Although more expensive than shipping, Sony's contingency plan meant that the company avoided a complete collapse in sales during its busiest sales season.

Planning Step 4: Implement and review the plan

Once the plan has been prepared, it must then be put into action. The manager does this by breaking the plan down into manageable tasks and deciding who is to do what. This must be communicated clearly to all employees involved so everyone knows what they have to do and are committed to achieving the business's goals.

It is also essential that managers review performance at regular intervals so that progress can be assessed and changes made if plans are not on target or if they are slipping out of control. Once the plans are agreed, they are implemented using management organisation and control techniques.

OL Long Q1

3. What are the qualities of a good plan?

	An effective plan is a SMART plan
S – **Specific**	The plan must be clear and precise about its objectives. **Example:** "Mercedes will regain its position as the best-selling luxury car brand in Europe."
M – **Measurable**	The success of the plan should be easily measured. **Example:** Mercedes will sell more cars per year than BMW, Audi, Lexus or Jaguar.
A – **Agreed**	It should have the agreement and support of all the staff in the business. **Example:** All Mercedes managers and staff know about the plan and agree with the goal.
R – **Realistic**	It must be possible to achieve the objectives set, taking into account the people, finances, time and other resources available. **Example:** Mercedes will invest in improved quality control and a new marketing plan to achieve the level of sales it once had.
T – **Timed**	Sufficient time must be allowed for proper implementation, including provision for unexpected events and obstacles. **Example:** Mercedes want to achieve their goal within five years.

OL Long Q3, 4

4. Why is planning important to management?

* **Helps to identify the internal strengths** of the business to be protected and built on.
* **Helps to identify internal weaknesses** in the business that need to be addressed.
* **Helps to identify new opportunities** for the business.
* **Helps to identify threats** that can be anticipated and addressed in advance.
* **Sets out clear targets** and milestones against which the success of the organisation can be measured.
* **Assists leadership and motivation** as they **give direction and purpose** to staff about what work is to be done, by whom, when, how and why.
* **Provides the necessary information to investors** when finance is required.

HL Long Q2

B. Organising

5. What is organising?

> Organising brings people and resources together in an effective way to achieve goals.

Organising *means bringing people and resources together effectively to implement plans.* Organising is important because it allows managers to:

- ❖ **Identify the work to be done**.
- ❖ Create a suitable **organisational structure**.
- ❖ **Identify who** will do what tasks.
- ❖ Maintain a clear **chain of command**.

> Common organisational structures used in business:
> - Functional
> - Product
> - Geographic
> - Matrix/team-based

Organisational (or **management**) **structures** *identify the different departments and management functions in an organisation.* They set out who answers to whom (the chain of command) within an organisation. This helps to reduce confusion in the business.

The traditional types of organisational structure are:

- ✪ Functional
- ✪ Product
- ✪ Geographic

HL Short Q2
- ✪ Matrix / team-based

6. What is a functional organisational structure?

A **functional structure** *divides a business into different departments according to the management functions of* **marketing, production, human resources** and **finance**. It is a very common type of organisational structure.

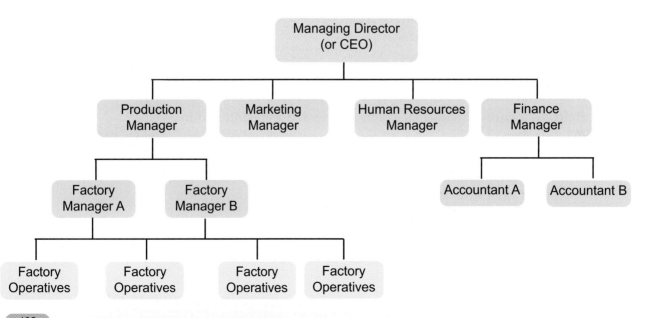

OL Long Q6

Evaluation: Advantages of functional structures

1. **Builds up staff skills** and **expertise** in each of the functions.
2. Provides **clear promotional paths** for staff based on expertise. This can be highly motivating.

Evaluation: Disadvantages of functional structures

1. **Employees** can get focused on their own departmental goals and **lose sight of the overall business mission**.
2. **Communications** between departments **can be slow** and subject to misunderstandings.

7. What is a product organisational structure?

A **product structure** *organises a business on the basis of the products it makes.* Each product division has its own set of specialist management functions.

Example: Mercedes-Benz could organise itself according to its three main product areas – cars, trucks and buses.

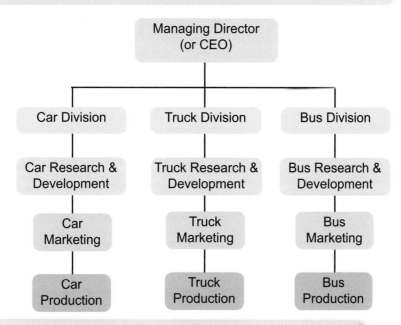

Evaluation: Advantages of product structures

1. **Improves communications** between different functional experts within each product division.
2. Allows a business to **adapt different products** more easily in response to **customer needs**.
3. Allows each division to **focus on its own customers**.

Evaluation: Disadvantages of product structures

1. There can be wasteful duplication of management functions (marketing, finance, etc.) for each product division.
2. There may be **wasteful competition** for the same customers **between different product divisions**.

8. What is a geographic organisational structure?

A **geographic structure** *divides the organisation according to the geographical markets it serves*. Each section of the business may be physically located in a different geographic region.

> **Example:** Mercedes-Benz could structure itself according to the countries or global regions in which it sells its products.

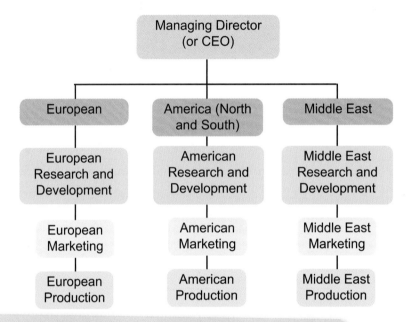

Evaluation: Advantages of geographic structures

1. Staff are better able to **meet local customer needs** and respond to local conditions.
2. Can encourage **healthy competition** between different regions.

Evaluation: Disadvantage of geographic structures

1. It can result in **wasteful duplication** of resources and **lack of co-ordination** between divisions if not properly controlled by management.

HL Long Q5

9. What is a matrix/team-based organisational structure?

Matrix (or team-based) structures *are a type of organisational structure where staff are brought together into teams to achieve a clearly stated team goal, such as launching a new product*. Teams are made up of staff with skills in different specialist areas (e.g. marketing, production). The main characteristics of successful team management are:

* **Self-managing:** Each team is self-managing, which means it is responsible for running its own affairs with as little external input as possible.

* **Responsibilities delegated:** Team members are each delegated particular areas of responsibility.
* **Input into decision-making:** All team members have an input into the decision-making of their own team and are encouraged to contribute to how it can best achieve its goals.

Self-managing project teams empower staff to have a direct input into how different aspects of the business are run, thereby contributing to its success.

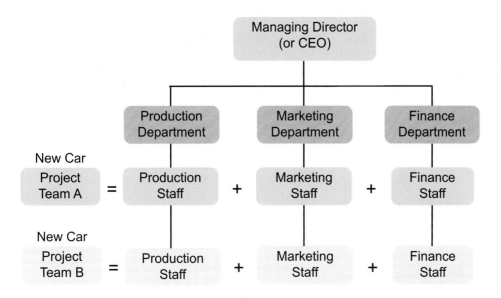

OL Short Q6, 7

HL Short Q4, 5

Evaluation: Advantages of team-based/matrix structures

1. **Synergies:** Combining the strengths of different departments can create synergies, i.e. they can achieve more working together than separately.
2. **Efficiency** can be improved as departments are working closer together with better communications.
3. **Better relationships:** Team members from different departments can gain a better understanding of how other parts of the business work.
4. **Motivation:** Being chosen to work in a team can make employees feel valued and improve their self-esteem and motivation.

Evaluation: Disadvantages of team-based/matrix structures

1. **Two bosses:** Team members have to report to both the team boss and also their regular functional boss. For instance, a marketing person in Team A must report to the team leader and also to the marketing manager. This can slow down decision-making. If there are conflicting orders, employees may become confused and stressed.
2. **Training costs:** Effective matrix structures require well-trained staff with excellent communications and teamwork skills. This can mean increased training costs.

OL Long Q7

10. What is the purpose of an organisational chart?

> **Organisational charts can show:**
> • **Layers of management**
> • **Chain of command**
> • **Span of control**

Organisational charts *are diagrams that visually communicate the type of organisational structure, the chain of command, and the span of control in an organisation.*

● The chain of command

The chain of command *refers to how decisions flow from the top of an organisation down through the layers to the bottom.* The shorter the chain of command through the organisation from senior management level down to front-line workers, the easier and more effective **communications** are through the organisation.

● The span of control

Span of control *refers to the number of people reporting directly to a manager.* A span of control can be described as 'wide' if the manager has many direct subordinates or 'narrow' if there are few. The wider a span of control, the fewer layers required to manage a workforce.

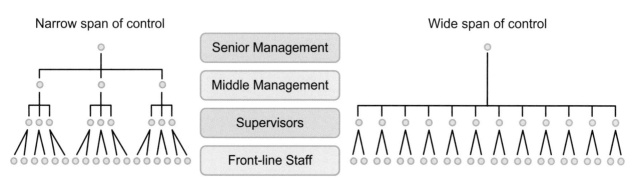

Fig. 1 Some managers have narrow spans of control while others have very wide spans of control.

OL Short Q4, 5
OL Long Q5

HL Short Q3

✳ **Delayering** *refers to reducing the number of layers in the organisational structure of a business.* This has become common among businesses trying to cut costs and to respond more quickly to changing market needs. The spread of information technology has also made it easier to eliminate many office-based administrative jobs.

11. What factors influence the choice of organisational structure?

Every business must choose the structure that is most suitable for achieving its own goals. Companies sometimes change structure from time to time as their needs change.

> Example: When computer sales declined, the Apple Corporation switched from a product structure to a functional structure to save costs. A few years later it switched back again to a product structure when the company began to expand their range of products.

An organisational structure should be:
- ✪ **As simple as possible.**
- ✪ **Allow easy communication.**
- ✪ Use **narrow spans of control** for important jobs that require tight control.
- ✪ Use **wide spans of control** to encourage staff empowerment, intrapreneurship and creativity.
- ✪ Be **cost effective**. Complex organisational structures generally mean more costs and slower decision-making.

HL Short Q6

HL Long Q4

12. Why is organising important to management?

Organising is important to management because it:
- ❖ **Creates a suitable organisational structure** using, for example, functional, product, geographic or matrix structures.
- ❖ Establishes a clear **chain of command** that reduces confusion among staff about who reports to whom in the organisation.
- ❖ **Facilitates** smooth **upward** and **downward flow of communications** in an organisational structure.

OL Long Q10

HL Long Q3, 6

C. Control

13. What is management control?

Case Study

BANK MANAGERS LOSE CONTROL

A disastrous chain of management blunders led to the sudden collapse of Britain's oldest business bank, Barings Bank. A young, inexperienced banker named Nick Leeson was sent to the bank's Singapore branch where, due to too much **delegation** and incompetent **management**, he found himself working completely unsupervised and responsible for managing hundreds of millions of euro worth of investments.

Leeson pretended that his investments were generating good profits and nobody above him in the bank's **chain of command** monitored his investments to see if this was actually the case. His managers began to regard him as the bank's 'golden boy' when, in fact, over a number of months and without his managers' knowledge, he gambled hundreds of millions of euro of the bank's money on the stock markets and lost. There had been warning signs but due to an absence of any **management control** these were ignored. After 232 years in business, Baring's bank suddenly found itself bankrupt, with the debts caused by Leeson amounting to over €1,500 million.

Many people said that this incident was an exception and could never happen again. But it did, this time to AIB. An incompetent employee, John Rusnak, lost over €800 million of the bank's money over a period of a year before managers noticed what was happening. After the fiasco was discovered, AIB **dismissed** the managers who were supposed to be controlling the employee's work and tightened up the bank's **management control**.

> **Control ensures that planning and organising is efficient and effective.**

Management control *refers to the continuous monitoring and checking of results to see if they are in line with the goals and targets set out in the plans.* If there is a divergence, then managers must find out why and make the appropriate changes.

The main types of management control are:

* Stock control
* Quality control
* Credit control
* Financial control

14. What is stock control?

Most businesses, like Mercedes, carry stocks (or inventory) of raw materials and/or finished goods. **Stock control** *ensures that firms have the right quantity and type of goods in stock at the right time, without incurring stockholding costs, such as insurance, security, rent or obsolescence.* **Buffer stock** *refers to the minimum level of stock that should be held. Once stock levels fall below the buffer level, more should be ordered.*

Proper stock control:

* Improves profitability by reducing the amount of money a business has tied up in inventory.
* Improves **cash flow**.
* Allows a business to free up **storage space** for other purposes.

> **Example:** For a large supermarket chain like SuperValu, stock control is very important. They must ensure they have sufficient stock to meet demand without tying up too much cash in stock. In supermarkets, barcodes and scanners are linked to computers to provide an early warning of stocks that are running low.

Just-in-time (JIT) *is a type of stock-control system in which stocks of raw materials, components or finished goods are delivered just when they are needed, no sooner or no later.* JIT stock control systems have very low **buffer stock** levels as JIT aims to minimise the cost of holding stock. It involves very careful planning and the use of weekly or even daily top-up deliveries to maintain production. To be effective, JIT requires a very efficient ordering system and a very reliable delivery service. If the JIT system breaks down and stock runs out, then production and sales can be affected.

> **Example:** JIT stock control is used by Mercedes's main Japanese rival, Lexus.

15. What is quality control?

Quality control *means ensuring that the quality standards expected by customers are properly met.* If properly carried out, quality control can:

- ✪ **Reduce waste and costs** by minimising defective products and minimising the legal costs of being sued by unhappy customers, thereby protecting the name and reputation of the business.
- ✪ **Increase customer satisfaction** and thereby maintain the demand for a firm's products and allow higher prices to be charged.
- ✪ **Help promote a quality image:** Firms who reach sufficiently high quality standards can qualify for awards such as the ISO or the Q Mark (see p140). These can be used in advertising and packaging to reassure potential customers about quality.
- ✪ **Meet legal responsibilities:** According to the **Sale of Goods and Supply of Services Acts**, manufacturers and retailers are legally responsible for ensuring that goods sold are 'of merchantable quality'.

Quality control is also covered in Chapter 10: Managing Change

Quality control can be achieved by:

- ❖ **Regular inspection of the quality of goods** before they leave the factory. This can be either **systematic**, where every item is inspected before it leaves the factory, e.g. testing each car thoroughly before it leaves the Mercedes factory, or **random**, where a sample from each batch is inspected, e.g. testing 10 bars of chocolate from every 1000 bars produced.
- ❖ **Recruiting and training** conscientious, quality-focused employees.
- ❖ Encouraging managers to adopt a **more facilitator management** style that motivates employees to contribute their best to the business.
- ❖ **Facilitating teamwork** among employees with quality and customer satisfaction as their main goal.
- ❖ **Quality circles** *are discussion groups made up of employees who meet regularly to discuss and resolve quality issues.* A wide range of relevant staff attends these meetings, including designers, production staff and customer representatives.

Recognising Quality

Both an **ISO award** and the **Q Mark** can be used by firms in their advertising and promotional activities to reassure customers that the firm operates to very high quality control standards. This can provide a competitive advantage to a firm over its rivals.

✪ **The ISO (International Standards Office)** *provides internationally recognised quality control standards*. To qualify, firms must have very stringent quality control standards and undergo surprise quality inspections.

✪ **The Q Mark** *is a quality standard awarded by Excellence Ireland Quality Association*. It is only recognised in Ireland but is often used by businesses as a stepping stone to a higher ISO standard.

16. What is credit control?

Many businesses sell goods on credit to attract customers and increase sales and profits. **Credit** *means selling goods now but not getting paid until later*. Credit control aims to minimise the risk of bad debts from customers who buy goods on credit. **Credit control** *means monitoring which customers are given credit and for how long and ensuring they pay on time*. Effective credit control reduces the risks of bad debts and protects cash flow.

The Credit Controller *is the person responsible for managing credit given to debtors and collecting payments*.

Bad debts *refer to customers who bought on credit but are now unable to pay what they owe, possibly because they have gone into liquidation (gone out of business)*. A bad or unpaid debt is money lost to the business. The longer a debt is overdue, the greater the likelihood that it will become a bad debt.

Credit control can be improved by:

✳ Offering **discounts** to encourage non-credit sales

✳ Taking out **insurance** against bad debts

OL Long Q8

✳ **Researching** the credit backgrounds of customers

✳ Refusing to **give credit** in the first place.

OL Long Q8

Case Study

No nonsense credit controllers

A Russian electricity company didn't care who its customers were – if you bought on credit but didn't pay your bills on time, then your electricity supply was cut off. One late-paying customer who was cut off turned out to be the Russian Army's Nuclear Missile Command Centre outside Moscow, the nerve centre that controlled all of Russia's nuclear missiles. Power was only restored after an intervention by a furious Russian president who threatened that 'those responsible will be punished!'

17. What is financial control?

Financial control *is used to monitor the financial affairs of the business to ensure it is profitable and always has enough money to pays its bills.* The lack of proper financial control was the reason for the huge losses suffered by Barings Bank and AIB. Financial control can be achieved by using the following:

* **Cash-flow budgets** to plan and monitor expenditure and income.
* **Ratio-analysis** to monitor the financial performance of the business.
* **Cost control** to ensure that costs do not rise beyond planned levels.
* **Break-even analysis** to identify the minimum level of sales needed to make a profit.

> **For more information on financial control see Chapter 12: Managing Business & Household Finance; Chapter 13: Monitoring Business Finances Using Accounts**

> **For more information on break-even analysis see Chapter 14: Identifying Business Opportunities**

Case Study

Swissair management get it all wrong

Swissair was one of the world's most successful airlines. Known as 'the flying bank', for decades it had an excellent reputation as a quality airline that operated a large fleet of aircraft flying to destinations all over the world.

To help the airline to grow, Swissair **managers** put into action a **strategic plan** to increase market share by taking over many smaller airlines. However, poor **planning** meant that most of the airlines that Swissair chose to take over turned out to be very unprofitable.

As the enlarged Swissair **organisation** became very complicated, **communications** between staff in the organisation became increasingly slow and more confusing. Poor communications, in turn, led to increasing **quality control** problems that began to damage Swissair's prestigious reputation.

On top of all these problems, poor **financial control** meant that Swissair found itself paying more for its aviation fuel than most other airlines. This pushed up costs at a time when it was already losing millions from its poorly planned takeovers and also facing intense competition from low-cost rivals like Ryanair.

As a result of these serious mistakes by Swissair managers, one of the world's most prestigious and profitable airlines became a massive loss-making mess and the airline went out of business.

OL Short Q8

HL Short Q7

Recall and Review
1. Explain the terms in bold.
2. Identify how planning, organising and control are all relevant to an airline.

18. Why is control important to management?

Control is important to management because:

○ **Control identifies deviations from plans** that can be investigated and remedied before they become serious. The tighter the control, the less scope there is for serious management errors.

○ **Control reduces waste** of resources. This increases business efficiency and productivity.

○ Stock control can ensure that the **right stock is available at the right time** to meet the needs of the business but with a minimum of wastage.

○ Credit control helps **keep bad debts to a minimum** and helps ensure a healthy cash flow.

○ Quality control helps to **improve product quality**, thereby boosting sales, profitability and customer loyalty.

○ Financial controls, such as cash-flow budgets and ratio analysis, are essential to **monitor the financial health of the business**. They can act as an early warning system of future financial problems. **Break-even analysis** helps a business to identify the minimum sales targets needed to make a profit.

For as long as there is a plan, the control system should be constantly operating to ensure that objectives and targets are achieved.

OL Short Q1
OL Long Q9

HL ABQ
HL Short Q7, 8, 9, 10

Key Concepts & Business Terms

After studying this chapter the student should be able to explain the following key concepts and business terms:

1. Planning
2. Stages in the planning process
3. SWOT analysis
4. Mission statement
5. Strategic plans
6. Tactical plans
7. Operational plans
8. Contingency plans
9. SMART plans
10. Organising
11. Organisational structures
12. Functional structure
13. Product structure
14. Geographic structure
15. Matrix/team-based structure
16. Organisational charts
17. Chain of command
18. Span of control
19. Delayering
20. Management control
21. Stock control
22. Buffer stock
23. JIT
24. Quality control
25. Quality circles
26. Credit control
27. Bad debts
28. Financial control

www.mercedes-benz.com   www.iso.org

www.us.playstation.com   www.qmark.ie

Leaving Certificate Practice Questions

Ordinary Level

Ordinary Level – Section 1 – Short Questions (10 marks each)

1. List the **three** management activities. [LCQ]
2. Distinguish between strategic planning and tactical planning. [LCQ]
3. Explain the difference between a contingency plan and a mission statement.
4. (a)   Explain what is meant by 'chain of command'.
   (b)   Use a diagram to illustrate a simple chain of command.
5. Explain the term 'span of control'. [LCQ]
6. Draft an organisational structure for a private limited company with four departments. [LCQ]
7. Name **four** types of organisational structure.
8. Identify **four** areas of business where management control is required.

Ordinary Level – Section 2 – Long Questions

1. Illustrate **three** steps involved in putting together an effective plan. (15 marks)
2. Explain the term 'SWOT analysis'. (20 marks) [LCQ]
3. 'Good plans are SMART plans.' Explain what this means. (15 marks)
4. Describe the qualities needed for a plan to be effective. (15 marks)
5. Describe, using a diagram, what is meant by a manager having a wide span of control. (20 marks)
6. Using a diagram, illustrate a functional management structure. (20 marks)
7. Outline **three** benefits of teamwork to an organisation. (15 marks) [LCQ]
8. Explain each of the following terms:
   (a)   credit control,
   (b)   quality control. (20 marks)
9. Management activities include planning, organising and controlling. Explain any **one** of the management activities listed. (15 marks) [LCQ]
10. Outline the importance of the management activities of planning and organising in a business. (30 marks) [LCQ]

Higher Level

Higher Level – Section 1 – Short Questions (10 marks each)

1. Explain the purpose of a contingency plan.
2. Define 'organising'.
3. Draft a typical span of control for an organisation of your choice. [LCQ]
4. Draft and label a typical organisational structure for an organisation of your choice. [LCQ]

5. Draft and label a matrix structure for an organisation having two project teams.

6. Identify **three** factors to consider when choosing an organisational structure.

7. Which type of management control do you feel is the most important? Explain your choice. [LCQ]

Higher Level – Section 2 – Applied Business Question

Yamamoto (Ireland) Limited

Yamamoto (Ireland) Limited is a subsidiary of a large Japanese multinational corporation with plants in Japan, Europe and America. Attracted by the generous cash grants available from IDA Ireland and Ireland's low tax rate on business profits, it opened a branch in Cork where it currently employs 500 employees. It pays over €20 million in wages annually and also spends millions more every year on supplies and services from local businesses in the Munster region.

For the first seven years its operations in Ireland were very profitable and most of its output was exported. However, in the past year market changes have led to a sharp drop in sales of its only product, chemical dyes, even though the market for most other chemical products remains strong. The Irish operation is now barely profitable.

Yamamoto allows only one union, SIPTU, in the plant and all employees are members. Staff are highly skilled and motivated. The plant has never experienced any industrial unrest. Employees are organised into departments using a functional management structure.

Last year a meeting of senior managers was held in the Tokyo head office to evaluate the performance of its various plants worldwide. The Cork plant fared badly compared with similar facilities in Poland and India. The parent company has announced that 'the company has to eliminate its less efficient operations or face substantial losses'. Each plant has been given the goal of preparing a strategic plan that will reduce costs and increase efficiency. The managers of the Irish plant must report back to the Tokyo head office in six months' time, when decisions will be made regarding which plants will be kept open and which will be closed.

1. Conduct a SWOT analysis of Yamamoto (Ireland) Limited. Refer to the text in your answer. (30 marks)

2. Recommend, with reasons, a suitable method of communicating the above information to staff in the plant. (20 marks)

3. Draft a short report for Yamamoto (Ireland) managers outlining the role that each of the management activities can play in rescuing the Irish plant from closure. (30 marks)

Higher Level – Section 2 – Long Questions

1. Evaluate how **two** different types of planning contribute to the success of a business or community enterprise. Use examples in your answer. (20 marks) [LCQ]

2. 'Planning is the most important management activity.' Do you agree with this statement? Support your opinion with reasons and examples. (25 marks) [LCQ]

3. 'Organising is the most important management activity.' Do you agree with this statement? Support your opinion with **two** reasons and examples. (20 marks) [LCQ]

4. Discuss the benefits of having a narrow span of control. (15 marks)

5. Distinguish between a functional structure and a geographic structure. Use a diagram to illustrate your answer. Refer to the chain of command in your answer. (20 marks)

6. Illustrate the importance of good organisation for the success of a business enterprise. (15 marks) [LCQ]

7. 'Controlling is the most important management activity.' Do you agree with this statement? Support your opinion with reasons and examples. (30 marks) [LCQ]

8. List **three** types of management control and explain any **two** of them. (25 marks)

9. Evaluate the contribution that stock control and credit control make to the successful management of a business. Use examples in your answer. (20 marks) [LCQ]

10. Discuss how management activities can help improve the performance of a business. (30 marks) [LCQ]

UNIT 4

Chapter 9

Human Resource Management (HRM)

'If you have a happy, highly motivated staff you can achieve anything. If you have a demoralised staff your company will soon disappear.'
Richard Branson

Key Study Questions

HRM in Bus Éireann

Case Study

Bus Éireann provides a wide range of transport services including Expressway coach services to destinations nationwide, international services to UK and continental Europe, local and rural bus services and school bus services.

The company employs more than 2,500 staff in roles ranging from drivers and mechanics to sales and management staff. This large workforce is made up of people of all ages, different ethnic backgrounds, different religions and people with disabilities. With such a large staff, Bus Éireann regards good human resource management as very important to ensuring the success of the business.

Bus Éireann

1. What is human resource management (HRM)?

A business like Bus Éireann is only as good as the people who work in it. **Human resource management (HRM)** *refers to the recruitment, training and retention of motivated staff and includes maintaining good industrial relations.* HRM is important because to grow a successful business, a firm must have excellent staff with the right skills.

> **Human resource management is responsible for managing:**
> * **Recruitment**
> * **Staff training**
> * **Performance appraisals**
> * **Rewarding staff performance**
> * **Promoting good industrial relations**

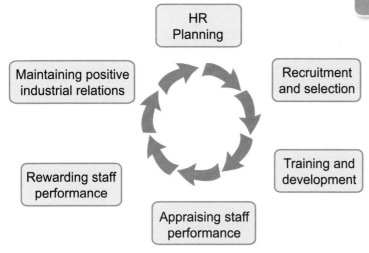

Fig. 1 **The six key elements of human resource management.**

OL Short Q1

HL Short Q1

2. What is human resource (HR) planning?

Bus Éireann is planning to expand its network of bus routes and needs to hire new drivers. The company must plan ahead to ensure it has the right number of drivers before these routes can go into service.

Human resource planning (HRP) *identifies the future staffing needs of the business and plans to have the right number of staff with the right skills at the right time.* It was traditionally known as workforce or manpower planning. To prepare a human resource plan, Bus Éireann must:

1. **Audit the present human resource levels.** A **human resource audit** *is a survey of the skills present in the existing workforce.* This is then compared with future needs to identify possible staff shortages or surpluses.

2. **Forecast future human resource needs of the business.** Staff numbers can rise or fall due to developments such as expansion of the business, mergers and acquisitions or introduction of new technology. These need to be identified and planned for in advance. **Natural wastage** *refers to staff leaving 'naturally' due to retirement or to take up new jobs.* Businesses need to plan their human resources carefully to ensure they will always have the skilled staff needed for the business.

3. **Monitor the level of labour turnover** in the business. **Labour turnover** *refers to the rate at which employees leave a firm.* A certain level of staff turnover is good because it can introduce new blood into an organisation. However, a high labour turnover is undesirable because staff members who leave must be replaced, unless deliberately made redundant. If they are highly skilled staff, then this can

be expensive in terms of recruitment and training. Furthermore, the firm can suffer from a loss of production, sales and profits while the jobs are being filled.

High labour turnover can be caused by:

* **Poor recruitment** procedures resulting in unsuitable staff being taken on.
* **Poor pay** or working conditions.
* **Discrimination,** harassment, unfair treatment, etc.
* **Better opportunities,** jobs and conditions elsewhere.
* **Poor industrial relations,** resulting in low morale.

4. **Prepare a HR plan** to ensure the business has the correct number of staff with the right skills when they are needed. This can be achieved through a combination of:

* **Training** or 'upskilling' existing staff.
* **Promoting** staff to higher positions.
* **Redeploying** unnecessary staff to vacant jobs within the business.
* **Recruiting** new employees from outside the business.
* **Downsizing,** *which means reducing the number of employees in the business.* This can be done through natural wastage or **redundancies.**

OL Short Q8

HL Long Q6

For more information on redundancies see Chapter 3: Resolving Conflict in the Workplace.

3. How does a business recruit and select staff?

Example: Following a **human resource audit,** Bus Éireann has identified a need to hire new bus drivers to replace staff who are retiring. The **job description** of a bus driver includes carrying passengers safely and providing an efficient and effective service to customers. The **person specification** of a driver includes having good bus-driving skills, good interpersonal skills, numeracy and literacy.

When recruiting bus drivers, the company advertises vacancies in local and sometimes national newspapers. Like most companies, they also **advertise vacancies** on the Internet. The selection procedure includes a personality **questionnaire,** an **interview** and a driving test in a bus.

Bus Éireann follows the normal recruitment procedure:

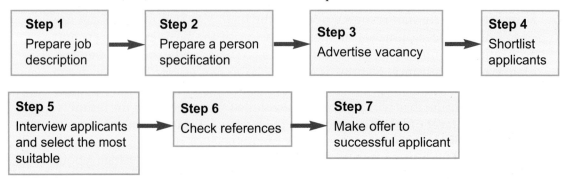

Step 1 Prepare job description → **Step 2** Prepare a person specification → **Step 3** Advertise vacancy → **Step 4** Shortlist applicants

Step 5 Interview applicants and select the most suitable → **Step 6** Check references → **Step 7** Make offer to successful applicant

OL Short Q2

Step 1: Prepare a job description

A **job description** *describes the vacancy that needs to be filled, including the title, conditions, duties and responsibilities involved, the place of work and the supervision and assessment arrangements.* For Bus Éireann, the main role of a bus driver is to carry passengers safely and provide an efficient and effective service to customers.

Job description

Bus Éireann

JOB TITLE:	Bus Driver
SALARY:	Negotiable, depending on experience
HOURS OF EMPLOYMENT:	38 hours per week, 5 days per week
RESPONSIBLE TO:	Depot Manager
DUTIES:	Drive bus
	Carry passengers safely
	Provide an efficient and friendly service to customers.
SUPERVISION & ASSESSMENT:	Induction training under Depot Manager
	Salary review after 6 months
	Job appraisal after 12 months.

Step 2: Prepare a person specification

A **person specification** *describes the qualities required by the person who will fill the job description.* These can include academic qualifications, work experience, level of physical fitness and language skills. Bus Éireann considers the essential requirements of a bus driver to be a clean bus-driving licence, good interpersonal skills, numeracy and literacy.

> OL Short Q3
>
> OL Long Q2
>
> HL Short Q3

Recall and Review

Prepare a job description and person specification for the following positions:
(a) shop assistant
(b) car mechanic
(c) secondary school principal
(d) sports coach in a leisure centre.

Step 3: Advertise vacancy

Many firms look for applicants both internally and externally to get the best selection of candidates. Tesco have a policy of initially advertising vacancies internally on noticeboards in their supermarkets.

Job vacancies can be filled **internally** or **externally**.

1. **Internal recruitment** involves using internal communications such as noticeboards, email, company newsletters or word-of-mouth to advertise the vacancy. Recruiting internally can also mean promoting or redeploying existing staff from within the business. For most jobs in the company, Bus Éireann has a policy of first looking for internal applicants for any vacancies that arise.

2. **External recruitment** involves inviting applications from people outside the firm through:

   * **Personal contacts** with friends or acquaintances.

   * **Internet** websites such as Bus Éireann's own website and specialist recruitment websites.

   * **Newspapers/magazines** likely to be read by people with the desired skills, e.g. local papers or national papers.

   * **Employment agencies** (personnel finders), which will send along suitable candidates for interview and charge the firm a fee if one of their candidates is recruited. FÁS provides this service free to firms.

Evaluation: Benefits of internal recruitment

1. Less risky as the firm **already knows the employee's** strengths and weaknesses, and the employee knows the firm and how it works.

2. Possibility of promotion can **motivate staff** to work harder.

3. It is **low cost** as little advertising is required.

Benefits of external recruitment

1. External candidates can bring new skills and experiences to the business.

2. The firm is likely to get a wide range of applicants from very different backgrounds.

3. External recruits do not bring any internal 'baggage' to the job and are less likely to encounter the jealousy that sometimes occurs when internal candidates are promoted.

OL Short Q4, 5
OL Long Q5

Step 4: Shortlist applicants

After advertising and receiving applications, the human resource manager will draw up a shortlist of the most promising applicants to call for an interview. He/she will usually reject all applications that are sloppy, contain bad spelling or are received without the covering letter requested.

The **covering letter** *is a short letter highlighting why you think you are suitable for the job and requesting an interview.* It should always be included when sending a CV to a potential employer.

A **CV** *(curriculum vitae) is a short document (preferably one page) summarising your education, qualifications, training and experience.* It should be neatly laid out with correct spelling and grammar.

Some large employers like Bus Éireann may ask job applicants to fill in an application form. An **application form** *is a form that may need to be completed when applying for a job. It will ask questions about the applicant's name, address, education, work experience and interests relevant to the job.*

Step 5: Interview applicants

The purpose of the interview is to determine whether the applicant is suited to the job. Questions to be asked should be prepared in advance, concentrating on the applicant's ability to:

- ⚙ **Perform** the job.
- ⚙ Fit in and **get along** with existing staff.
- ⚙ **Develop** their potential and contribute to the business.

Under the Employment Equality Act, candidates cannot be asked about certain personal issues such as age and marital status.

If no candidate stands out as being the obvious choice, then the most promising applicants may be invited for a second interview.

Some employers may also ask applicants to complete a **selection test** *to measure and compare applicants' aptitude, intelligence or personality for the job.*

Step 6: Check references

After completing interviews, the references of the most suitable applicant should be checked for accuracy and honesty before making them a job offer. **A job reference** *is a written or verbal recommendation from a former employer or some other person familiar with the applicant.* Bus Éireann always check the references of all applicants before making a final job offer.

Step 7: Make offer to successful candidate

If the references are satisfactory, then Bus Éireann will offer the job to the successful candidate. Once accepted, a legal contract of employment exists and the employee is entitled to a written copy of the basic terms and conditions of their employment. Unsuccessful applicants should be contacted to inform them that the position has been filled.

When going through the recruitment process, all businesses should behave ethically and comply with equality legislation. The HR manager must ensure that the recruitment process is fair by being free from bias or discrimination, and that the best candidate for the job is selected. **Equal opportunities** *means that all applicants of equal ability for a post have an equal chance of being hired or promoted, regardless of their sex, age, race, religion, sexual orientation, marital or family status.*

> **For more information on equality legislation see Chapter 3: Resolving Conflict in the Workplace.**

> OL Short Q6
> OL Long Q3, 4

4. How do firms train and develop their staff?

> **Example:** After following its recruitment procedures, Bus Éireann has hired five new drivers. They are enthusiastic but need **induction** to familiarise them with the company. More detailed **on-the-job training** will then be given to familiarise them with the different buses, routes and company procedures.

● Induction

Induction (*or orientation*) *refers to the general introduction of new staff into a job and an organisation.* Effective induction should familiarise new staff with issues such as:

OL Short Q7

- ❖ The organisation's policies and rules
- ❖ Staff with whom they will be working
- ❖ Layout of buildings, etc.

● Staff training

Staff training *ensures that employees have the up-to-date skills and knowledge needed to do their present work.* Many businesses like their staff to be multi-skilled. Staff training can be either **on the job** or **off the job.**

- ❖ **On-the-job training** *teaches skills and knowledge through practical work experience. It includes observing more experienced staff performing their jobs,* e.g. trainee bus drivers accompanying fully qualified drivers.
- ❖ **Off-the-job training** *refers to all types of training and education apart from that occurring in the immediate workplace.*

> **Example:** Bus Éireann sending staff away for a week-long training course or paying the fees of staff who want to do relevant part-time college courses.

● Staff development

While training teaches staff to do one job, **staff development** *teaches an employee multiple skills that they can use in many different jobs.* Staff development means staff:

- ❖ are **more flexible** and better able to adapt to change, such as filling in for absent or ill colleagues.
- ❖ are **more suitable for promotion** because they have a wider understanding of the different work done in the business.

OL Long Q6

HL Short Q4

> **Example:** A bus driver receiving training to be a bus station manager.

5. What is performance appraisal?

> Performance appraisals allow managers to provide feedback to staff on their performance.

> **Example:** Bus Éireann needs to identify staff who are working well for possible promotion. It must also identify staff who are under-performing and not doing their job to the standard required.

Performance appraisal *is the process of setting performance standards for each employee and then assessing their performance regularly over a period of time.* Performance appraisals involve:

- ❖ **Agreeing targets:** At the start of the year the employee and their supervisor set agreed targets and goals for the employee to achieve over a stated period (e.g. six months or a year). **Productivity** *is a measure of the efficiency in a business. It is most commonly measured by output per worker (labour productivity).*
- ❖ **Reviewing progress:** The manager and employee meet at regular intervals to review the progress towards the agreed goals.
- ❖ **Discussing outcomes:** At the end of the stated period, the manager and employee meet to evaluate performance and set new targets for the next period.
- ❖ **Identifying any training needs** employees may have.
- ❖ **Identifying employees for promotion** and/or assisting in determining **pay** and bonuses.
- ❖ **Improving communications** between managers and employees.

● Importance of performance appraisals

Performance appraisals can:

- ★ Identify training needs of employers.
- ★ Identify employees who are suitable for promotion.
- ★ Help in deciding pay rises and bonuses.
- ★ Improve communications between managers and employees.

OL Long Q7, 12

HL Short Q5

HL Long Q3

6. What financial rewards can be offered to staff?

Case Study

Managing Intel's human resources

Intel is a global manufacturer of computer chips. It has its European manufacturing and exporting base in Co. Kildare where it employs thousands of staff. This factory is one of the largest employers in Ireland. Most of the full-time staff have third-level education. Financial rewards include relatively **high salaries, bonus payments** for exceeding targets and an **employee share option scheme** that allows workers to purchase shares in the company. Intel also provides **non-financial rewards** such as the use of a subsidised staff canteen and a purpose-built 4,000 square metre factory gymnasium. Annually, the company spends thousands of euros on sports and social programmes to keep staff fit and happy.

In Bus Éireann and most businesses, there are two main types of financial rewards that can be offered to staff: **wages/salaries** and **profit-sharing schemes**.

Staff can be financially rewarded by:
- Wages
- Share in profits

Wages/salaries

Employees must be paid a fair wage for their labour, while high wages can help attract the best employees. Wages/salaries can be paid using **flat rates**, **time rates** or **piece rates** of pay.

- ✳ **Flat-rate pay:** *Employees receive an agreed set rate of pay per week or month based on a standard number of hours worked – for example, €500 per week. This* makes pay predictable and easy to calculate. However, there is no incentive to work harder or longer.

✳ **Time-rate pay:** *Employees are paid a set amount for each hour they work. Overtime work is usually paid at a higher rate.* Time rates are easy to calculate, but there is no reward for improved efficiency and staff may be tempted to work slower so that they will receive payment for working extra hours.

✳ **Piece-rate pay:** *Employees are paid for each item produced that meets the desired quality standard* – for example, €100 for each item produced. Piece-rate pay encourages maximum effort. However, safety rules may be ignored if workers rush their work. Piece rate is not suitable for certain jobs such as teaching and nursing, where the quality of work may be difficult to measure and maintain.

✳ Flat-, time- and piece-rates of pay can be topped up by bonus and commission payments. **Bonus payments** *give employees a share of the profits resulting from their increased effort or efficiency.* **Commission** *is an extra payment based on a percentage of the value of sales achieved.*

✳ **Benefits-in-kind** *are **taxable** non-cash payments to staff.* They include benefits such as free or subsidised meals, company car or reduced prices for company products/services.

✳ **Profit-sharing schemes** *mean firms share part of their profits with employees through payments in addition to wages.* This is often done through **share-ownership schemes** *that offer employees free or low-price shares in the company.* By becoming part-owners of the company, employees are entitled to dividends from company profits. Share-ownership schemes give staff a personal incentive to keep costs down and help to overcome any 'them-and-us' mentality between workers and management. As a result, **industrial relations** and **motivation** can be improved and absenteeism and strikes reduced.

OL Long Q8, 9

HL Short Q6

Example: Over 35% of the shares in telecommunications company Eircom are owned by employees of the company.

Case Study

Rewarding staff in Microsoft

Microsoft pays its staff a **flat-rate of pay** plus **bonuses** based on performance appraisals for exceeding work targets. It also provides subsidised meals and staff discounts on Microsoft products. Since it was founded, Microsoft has also had an **employee share-ownership scheme** designed to share the company's ownership and profits among employees.

Microsoft®

Over the years, as the company has grown from a small business to become a huge global business, the value of the company's shares has risen by over 20,000%. This has made many Microsoft employees into shareholder millionaires. However, the company insists that such employees get no special treatment and have to pitch in with the rest of the staff to get the work done.

7. How is financial remuneration determined?

Some jobs can be better paid than others for the following reasons:

- ✪ **Demand exceeds supply** in the labour market for some jobs. For instance, the supply of highly skilled doctors is smaller than the supply of experienced bus drivers and, as a result, doctors can earn much higher salaries.

- ✪ **The ability and skills** required for some jobs are hard to come by – for example, Premier League soccer players.

- ✪ The **long training periods** required to qualify for some jobs, such as vets and surgeons discourage many people, thereby keeping the supply of specialists down. People in such jobs also look for higher pay as a reward for investing years of their time in gaining their qualifications.

- ✪ The **risk, danger** and **responsibility** involved in some jobs, such as an airline pilot, means that the employee is paid more as compensation.

- ✪ In some firms and industries, **trade unions** have the power to negotiate favourable pay deals for workers.

HL Short Q7

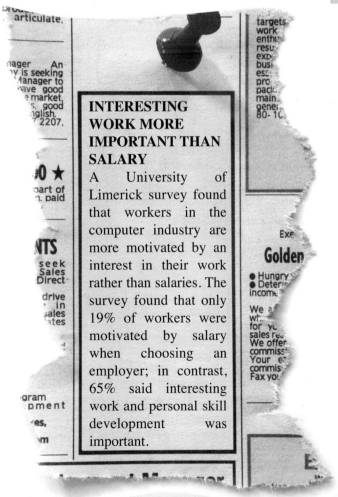

INTERESTING WORK MORE IMPORTANT THAN SALARY

A University of Limerick survey found that workers in the computer industry are more motivated by an interest in their work rather than salaries. The survey found that only 19% of workers were motivated by salary when choosing an employer; in contrast, 65% said interesting work and personal skill development was important.

8. What non-financial rewards can a firm offer its staff?

> Staff can be rewarded non-financially by improved working conditions and job enrichment.

Improved working conditions

Job satisfaction *is the degree to which employees feel positive about their job, enjoy doing it and want to continue working with the firm.* Job satisfaction is very important to workers because without it they can suffer from stress and a decline in morale and **motivation,** while the business can suffer from absenteeism, a rise in **labour turnover** and poor **industrial relations.** Job satisfaction is influenced by the following:

❖ **Shorter working hours and longer holidays**.

❖ **Less stressful work:** It is estimated that over 40% of absenteeism in business in Ireland is attributed to work-related stress, as a result of factors such as overworking, low pay, bullying or harassment, low job satisfaction or job insecurity.

❖ **No discrimination, bullying or harassment** of staff. All workers are entitled to be treated equally in employment matters. Companies like Bus Éireann need to ensure that employees are protected from harassment. **Harassment** *refers to behaviour such as unwelcome comments, looks, jokes, suggestions or physical contact that causes stress or intimidation for staff.* Bullying and harassment in the workplace are **illegal**.

❖ **Safe and pleasant physical surroundings** that are healthy, spacious and clean with access to natural light contribute to job satisfaction.

❖ **Pleasant social working environments** encourage friendships and the growth of a team spirit. Firms can create pleasant social environments by using open plan work areas and shared canteen areas and by organising staff sports or social activities.

❖ **Flexible working arrangements**, such as job sharing, job rotation or flexitime. **Job sharing** *means two people share one job*, either on a week on/week off basis or with each worker working 2.5 days per week. **Job rotation** *means regularly moving staff around from one job to another.* In repetitive jobs, (such as assembly lines) this helps to reduce boredom and increase motivation. **Flexitime** *means allowing employees to choose their own start and finish time as long as a minimum number of hours are worked.*

> OL Long Q10
>
> HL Short Q8, 9
> HL Long Q4, 5, 7

❖ **Job enlargement** *reduces employee boredom by increasing the variety of tasks the employee undertakes.*

❖ **Job enrichment** *means providing employees with work requiring greater responsibility, control and input into decision-making.*

Case Study

German Firm Bans Moaners

Nutzwerk is an IT firm in Germany with an unusual approach to **human resource management**: employees can be fired if they are caught complaining and moaning at work. It may sound absurd, but employees in the business have a clause in their **contract of employment** which states: 'Moaning and whinging at Nutzwerk is forbidden . . . except when accompanied by a constructive suggestion as to how to improve the situation.' Managers claim that moaners depress staff, hamper concentration and reduce productivity.

Since the policy was introduced, three employees have been **dismissed**. However, most staff in the business seem very happy with the policy and **managers** are delighted as profitability has doubled since this unusual policy was introduced.

Recall and Review

1. Identify the reasons why a ban on moaning could increase a firm's profitability.
2. In your opinion, would such a policy conflict with Irish equality legislation? (See Chapter 3: Resolving Conflict in the Workplace).
3. Besides banning moaning, list the different ways in which a firm could increase the job satisfaction of its employees.
4. Rank in order of preference the top five non-financial rewards that would be most important to you in a job.

9. How can HRM maintain positive industrial relations?

Industrial relations *refer to the quality of the relations that exist between the owners and the employees in an organisation.* Maintaining good industrial relations in a business is very important because:

> **Good industrial relations:**
> * **Boosts morale and motivation**
> * **Increases productivity**
> * **Reduces the risk of strikes**
> * **Reduces labour turnover**

* It helps to improve **morale and motivation** among staff.
* **Productivity** is increased.
* There is **less risk of strikes** and other disputes.
* There is a **reduction in labour turnover**.

Actions a HR manager can take to promote positive industrial relations

* **Train managers** to deal with human resource problems so that they can resolve them quickly.
* **Recruit staff** with a positive attitude and **provide proper training and staff development**.
* **Communicate regularly and honestly** with every member of staff about the current state of the business and their role in it.
* **Have clear grievance procedures** for staff and management to follow when conflicts do arise.
* **Provide attractive financial and non-financial rewards** that encourage and recognise employee effort and achievement.

⊗ **Respect staff:** Evidence strongly suggests that employees are far more likely to be committed to an employer who respects them and shows a commitment to their welfare.

⊗ **Create a friendly** and co-operative approach to workplace relations. This helps to promote an organisational culture that encourages good industrial relations.

OL Short Q9
OL Long Q1, 11

HL Short Q2
HL ABQ
HL Long Q1, 2, 8

In large companies, worker directors may be appointed. **Worker directors** *are representatives of the employees elected to sit on the board of directors of their companies.* In Ireland, worker directors sit on the boards of many state-owned companies.

> **For more information on industrial relations see Chapter 3: Resolving Conflict in the Workplace.**

Key Concepts & Business Terms

After studying this chapter the student should be able to explain the following key concepts and business terms:

1. Human resource management (HRM)
2. Human resource (HR) planning
3. Natural wastage
4. Labour turnover
5. Human resource audit
6. Downsizing
7. Recruiting and selecting staff
8. Job description
9. Person specification
10. Covering letter
11. Curriculum vitae (CV)
12. Application form
13. Selection test
14. Job reference
15. Equal opportunities
16. Induction
17. Staff training
18. On-the-job training
19. Off-the-job training
20. Staff development
21. Performance appraisal
22. Productivity
23. Financial rewards for staff
24. Flat-rate pay
25. Time-rate pay
26. Piece-rate pay
27. Bonus payments
28. Commission
29. Benefits-in-kind
30. Profit-sharing schemes
31. Share-ownership schemes
32. Non-financial rewards for staff
33. Job satisfaction
34. Harassment
35. Job sharing
36. Job rotation
37. Flexitime
38. Job enlargement
39. Job enrichment
40. Industrial relations
41. Worker directors

useful websites

www.buseireann.ie
www.intel.com
www.nutzwerk.de

Leaving Certificate Practice Questions

Ordinary Level

Ordinary Level – Section 1 – Short Questions (10 marks each)

1. List **three** functions of a human resource manager. [LCQ]
2. Identify **four** stages in recruiting new staff.
3. List **three** items that should be included in a job description. [LCQ]
4. List **three** places where a firm can advertise for new staff.
5. Identify **two** advantages of internal recruitment. [LCQ]
6. Explain what is meant by 'equal opportunities'. [LCQ]
7. Explain the role of staff induction.
8. List **three** possible reasons why a firm may have a high labour turnover.
9. Identify **two** reasons why good industrial relations are important to a business.

Ordinary Level – Section 2 – Long Questions

1. Describe **two** key functions of a human resource manager. (20 marks) [LCQ]
2. Distinguish between a 'job description' and a 'person specification'. (15 marks) [LCQ]
3. Describe the steps a business should follow before recruiting a new employee. (20 marks)
4. Barry Ronan is the managing director of Ronan Design Ltd, Main Street, Letterkenny, Co. Donegal. He needs to recruit a new employee (a CAD operator with design experience). He decides to advertise the job vacancy in the local newspaper, requesting a letter of application and a curriculum vitae (CV) from each applicant. The closing date for applications is 21 July.
    (a) Draft a suitable newspaper advertisement for the vacancy in Ronan Design Ltd. (20 marks) [LCQ]
    (b) Draft a letter of application to Ronan Design Ltd applying for the position advertised. (20 marks) [LCQ]
    (c) Outline the importance of the recruitment and selection to Ronan Design Ltd. (10 marks) [LCQ]
5. Outline **two** advantages of internal recruitment. (15 marks) [LCQ]
6. Explain the term 'training and development'. (15 marks) [LCQ]
7. Explain the purpose of performance appraisal. (20 marks) [LCQ]
8. Explain the benefits to employees of a profit-sharing scheme. (15 marks) [LCQ]
9. Distinguish between a profit-sharing scheme and benefits-in-kind as rewards for work. (20 marks)
10. Outline **one** financial reward and **one** non-financial reward that a business could give to its staff. (20 marks) [LCQ]
11. Outline the steps a HRM manager can take to promote positive industrial relations in a business. (20 marks)
12. Explain **two** of the following functions of a human resource manager:
    (a) recruitment and selection,
    (b) training/development,
    (c) performance appraisal (25 marks) [LCQ]

Higher Level

Higher Level – Section 1 – Short Questions (10 marks each)

1. List **five** key functions of HRM.
2. Outline **three** areas of responsibility of a human resource manager. [LCQ]
3. Describe the difference between a job description and a person specification.
4. Explain what is meant by 'staff development'.
5. Explain the terms (a) natural wastage and (b) performance appraisal.
6. Distinguish between flat-rate pay and piece-rate pay.
7. List **four** factors that help determine the level of pay for a job.
8. Identify **three** different types of non-financial reward that can be offered to employees.
9. List **three** different sources of job satisfaction for employees.

Higher Level – Section 2 – Applied Business Question

Talamh Energy

Linda Sweeney is the young and newly appointed human resource manager at Talamh Energy, a producer of solar and wind energy products based in Co. Mayo. The firm has been steadily expanding over recent years and currently employs a total of 170 skilled staff. Over 75% of the staff work on the assembly line. The remainder are office based, mainly managers, sales and administrative staff. Talamh has a policy of investing in continuous staff training and development, both on and off the job.

Talamh has recently started selling solar and wind energy products over the Internet and sales have sky-rocketed as a result. To satisfy demand, an extra 30 staff will need to be recruited quickly for a range of customer service and manufacturing jobs. These posts will need to be advertised and filled quickly.

Linda is reviewing the financial and non-financial ways that the firm can attract and retain skilled staff. Up to now, all staff were paid on a flat-rate basis except for the sales staff who were also paid commission. However, Linda is now keen to try to improve productivity in the business and wants to introduce piecework payments and performance appraisal for all the staff working on the assembly line. She feels that these changes will ultimately benefit staff motivation and increase productivity.

However, despite Linda's friendly manner, there is considerable unease and suspicion among factory staff about the proposal and the fact that it will only apply to staff on the assembly line and not other employees.

1. Describe the different methods of payment that could be used to pay staff working on the Talamh assembly line. Recommend, with reasons, the method you consider most appropriate. (20 marks)
2. Draft a short memorandum (memo) for Linda briefly outlining the role of a performance appraisal system and how could it help Talamh. (30 marks)
3. Evaluate the different types of non-financial reward that Talamh could use to attract and retain skilled staff. (30 marks)

Higher Level – Section 2 – Long Questions

1. Outline the functions of a human resource manager. (25 marks) [LCQ]
2. Discuss the advice that you would give to a human resource manager who needs to make a number of workers redundant. (20 marks)
3. Explain the purpose of performance appraisals. Use an example to support your answer. (20 marks) [LCQ]
4. Draft a memo from management to all staff in an enterprise, outlining to them a recently agreed method of staff reward. (15 marks) [LCQ]
5. Explain **five** different methods of reward for employees in a business organisation. (15 marks) [LCQ]
6. 'High labour turnover is often a sign of deeper problems in a company.' Explain labour turnover and its possible causes. (30 marks)
7. Describe **five** initiatives a firm could take to improve job satisfaction for its employees. Use examples to support your answer. (25 marks)
8. Jane Barker runs an estate agency with 25 employees. Jane likes to lead by example and works well with her team. She would like to reward her employees for their ideas and extra work in making the company a success, and she is looking at ways to reward them financially and non-financially.
    (a) Illustrate what is meant by a non-financial reward for an employee. (10 marks) [LCQ]
    (b) Explain the benefits to employees of a profit-sharing scheme. (15 marks) [LCQ]
    (c) Discuss the importance of human resource management to Jane's business. (25 marks)

UNIT 4

Chapter 10
Managing Change

'Times change and we must change with them.'

Anonymous

Key Study Questions

Change management at
TOYOTA

Case Study

A General Motors (GM) factory in California had been producing cars with more defects and at a much higher **cost** than any other car factory in the USA. Daily staff **absenteeism** was very high, staff **morale** was abysmal and **wildcat strikes** were common. Despite many attempts to change this situation, GM management felt that they were getting nowhere and eventually decided to shut down the loss-making factory, making all the staff **redundant**.

The Japanese Toyota Corporation was looking for a location in the US to build cars

5

for the American market. Instead of wasting time building a new factory, they decided to take over the closed GM plant and rehire over 85% of the workers who had been made redundant. Just one year after reopening under new management, the factory was now producing the highest quality cars in the US with the least number of faults and at the lowest costs. Absenteeism was non-existent and staff morale was very high.

Toyota's American competitors were amazed at Toyota's success at introducing dramatic changes so quickly. How did Toyota turn a disaster into a success story?

A. Drivers of change in business

1. What are the main causes of change in business?

For Toyota and all organisations, managing change is an important role of managers. Managers and their staff have to learn new skills to ensure that their firms can constantly adapt to frequent change to survive in the 21st century. The main sources of change in business are:

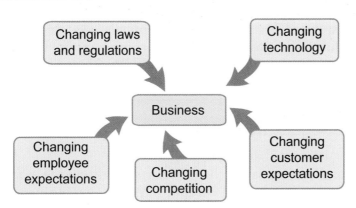

Fig. 1 The five main drivers / causes of change in business.

Changing technology

Technological developments are having a major impact on how and where businesses operate.

❖ New **products and services,** for example hybrid and electric cars and increasingly sophisticated mobile phones.

❖ New and faster **methods of production** such as automated manufacturing using robotics.

❖ New and faster methods of **marketing and selling** using the Internet and mobile phones.

❖ New and faster **methods of communication** internally among staff and externally to customers, suppliers and the public using e-mail, video conferencing and mobile technologies.

Changing laws and regulations

Society has become more complex and citizens more educated and demanding. This has led to new **Irish and EU-wide laws** affecting business, covering issues such as consumer rights, employment law, environmental protection and fair competition.

> See the following chapters for examples of laws and regulations:
> Chapter 2: Resolving Conflict in the Marketplace; Chapter 3: Resolving Conflict in the Workplace; Chapter 21: Ethical, Social & Environmental Responsibilities in Business;
> Chapter 25: Ireland & the European Union.

Changing customers

❂ Consumer **tastes and fashions are constantly changing** due to the impact of mass communications such as the Internet, television and other media.

❂ Rising levels of education are making consumers **increasingly quality conscious.**

❂ Increasing competition and choice is leading to **fewer loyal customers** for many well-known brands.

❂ **Ethical and green issues** are becoming more important to many consumers when making purchasing decisions.

Changing competition

> Constant change requires managers to become experts at change management.

Competitors are changing by:

❖ Constantly **updating** their products or introducing new ones.

❖ Introducing new and **cheaper** ways of doing business, e.g. Internet banking.

❖ **Growing in size** to avail of economies of scale, and forcing less-competitive firms out of business.

Changing employees and labour market

Employees today:

✳ Have **higher levels of education** and skills to bring to their jobs.

✳ Want jobs that are **interesting** and **well paid,** with good working conditions.

✳ Want more **flexible** and **family-friendly working conditions**.

> OL Short Q1

✳ Are becoming more diverse with, for example, more females, immigrants and older people now in paid employment than ever before.

✳ Want to work for organisations with **high ethical standards**.

B. Strategies for managing change

2. How can businesses successfully manage change?

Case Study

TOYOTA prepares to bring in change

Toyota understood the importance of proper change management. The first thing that the Japanese company did was to hold staff meetings to **communicate** with staff to **prepare them** for some major changes in how the factory was to be run. At all of these meetings, **staff were encouraged to share their ideas** about how the factory could be improved. Toyota also began investing millions of dollars in training staff to become skilled in doing more than one job (**multi-skilling**) and to become experts at **teamworking**. The employees were also given **contracts** of employment that emphasised the need for **staff flexibility** and a total **commitment to quality**.

To respond effectively, managers must learn to become effective change managers. **Change management** *is the process of anticipating change and adapting the business to a constantly changing business environment.* Successful change management involves the following elements:

- **Communicating** the need for change with staff.
- Promote a **'facilitator' management** style.
- Promote **employee empowerment.**
- Promote **teamwork** among all staff.
- Promote a **commitment to quality** among all staff.

OL Long Q1

HL Short Q1

1. Communicate the need for change to all staff

+

2. Promote a 'facilitator' management style that believes staff can enjoy work, have ambition and are open to change.

+

3. Promote employee empowerment by giving staff the resources and freedom to decide how best to do their work.

+

4. Promote teamwork by organising staff into flexible and productive work teams.

+

5. Promote a commitment to quality among all staff in every part of the business and in every thing they do.

=

Result
Flexible managers and flexible employees who are willing and able to adapt to the changes needed to constantly improve the business.

Fig. 2 The elements of successful change management

3. How can managers communicate the need for change?

When General Motors tried to make changes to turn the car factory around, they met with huge **resistance** from staff. Such resistance to change can arise because of staff fears such as:

❖ The change will mean taking on an **extra burden** of work.

❖ They are **not sufficiently skilled** or **able to cope** with the new changes.

❖ There will be a **loss of income** or they may even **lose their jobs.**

❖ The **changes will not** work, especially if there are too many changes introduced too quickly.

To avoid resistance, managers should adopt the Toyota approach by preparing staff properly for change by:

✳ **Communicating** openly and honestly about the changes required, the reasons why and the consequences of failing to adapt to change.

✳ **Allowing employee input** into decision-making involving major change. Staff often have good ideas and are also more likely to co-operate with changes on which they have been consulted.

OL Long Q2

HL Short Q2, 3
HL Long Q1

✳ **Negotiating deals** where necessary that provide fair rewards to the employees for any sacrifices that they may have to make to accommodate change – for example, offering longer summer holidays in exchange for taking shorter lunch breaks.

✳ **Providing leadership by example.** Managers need to be seen by staff to be willing to adopt the changes themselves and not just talk about it.

4. How can managers promote a more 'facilitative' management style?

Case Study

After communicating to staff the need for a radical change at the factory, the next element in Toyota's turnaround of the loss-making factory was to completely change the style of management used. Where GM managers had a controlling attitude to staff, Toyota insisted that managers take a more facilitative approach.

See Chapter 6: Management Skills of Leadership & Motivation for more information on McGregor's Theory X and Y.

Successful change management requires that managers become more willing to trust their staff and allow them greater responsibility and a greater say in business decision-making. This means dropping the traditional 'controller' (or autocratic) attitude and becoming a more **'facilitative'** or **democratic** manager. Facilitator managers have a **Theory Y attitude** and a more democratic style. Staff are more likely to co-operate with managers who have a facilitator approach.

Managers can become better facilitators by:

✪ **Providing interesting** and **challenging work** that staff will find stimulating.
✪ **Providing the training** needed for staff to do their jobs well.
✪ **Empowering** staff to get on with the job without unnecessary interference.
✪ **Mentoring** staff by providing plenty of advice and support where necessary, including providing praise, recognition and rewards for work well done.
✪ **Consulting regularly** with staff about what work is to be done and the best way to do it.

OL Short Q2

HL Short Q4
HL Long Q3

5. How can employee empowerment be promoted?

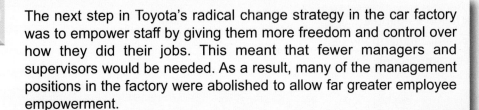

Case Study

The next step in Toyota's radical change strategy in the car factory was to empower staff by giving them more freedom and control over how they did their jobs. This meant that fewer managers and supervisors would be needed. As a result, many of the management positions in the factory were abolished to allow far greater employee empowerment.

> **Employee empowerment provides staff with more power to make their own decisions about how to do their jobs.**

Employee empowerment *means providing staff with a clear goal, deadlines and sufficient resources and freedom to decide how to achieve the goal.* Empowering employees with real power and responsibility boosts self-esteem and self-actualisation. Successful employee empowerment requires:

❖ **Managers to adopt a facilitator attitude** that supports and encourages staff.
❖ **Investing in staff training** if necessary. This is essential if employees are to have the skills to do jobs that have been changed.
❖ **Proper management control** to ensure that any employee errors are quickly identified, rectified and learned from.
❖ **Rewards (financial and non-financial) to encourage staff** to take on the extra decision-making responsibility.
❖ **Teamwork** where staff co-operate closely and support each other.

Benefits of empowerment

If introduced with proper staff training and supervision, empowerment can:

1. Allow businesses to **harness a wide range of staff skill**s, initiative and intelligence.
2. Increase staff creativity and **intrapreneurship**.
3. **Increase staff motivation** and productivity, by meeting **self-esteem** and **self-actualisation** needs.
4. **Reduce absenteeism** and labour turnover.
5. **Increase job satisfaction**, resulting in greater staff loyalty, lower absenteeism and lower staff turnover.
6. **Free up managers' time** for other work.

Possible problems with empowerment

If used at the wrong time in the wrong way, employee empowerment can lead to:

1. **Serious mistakes** being made by staff with inadequate training or supervision.
2. **Unhappy, demotivated staff** who feel inadequately trained or unprepared for the extra responsibility.
3. **Unhappy middle managers** who may feel that their decision-making power is being taken away from them.

OL Long Q4

HL Short Q5, 6

HL Long Q2

6. How can teamwork be promoted?

> Teamwork involves people working together in harmony towards a common goal.

Case Study

Before Toyota took over, the GM factory had suffered from a lack of employee motivation, poor quality control and even sabotage of the assembly line by some bored and disgruntled workers.

Toyota's third step in their turnaround strategy was to organise the workforce into **teams** of workers who would work together to produce each car. Each team was **empowered** to organise its own tasks and switch jobs frequently to avoid boredom. There would be no supervisors, only coordinators chosen on a rotation basis from the workforce.

This initiative proved a major success. Through the stimulation of **teamwork** and **delegation** of authority, Toyota increased **motivation**, quality and productivity among the staff.

Teamwork *occurs when a group of people are working co-operatively towards a common goal.* It empowers staff to have a direct say in how the business is run. **Teams are self-managing,** which means they are responsible for running their own affairs with as little outside input as possible. Characteristics of a successful team are:

* **Clear purpose** about their common goal.
* **Sufficient resources** to do the job that the team is required to do.
* **Team leader** who has good communications and motivation skills, a positive attitude and is also good at planning, organising and controlling.
* **Shared input into decision-making** by all team members.
* **Committed team members** with a positive attitude to the rest of the team and the work to be done.

Becoming a successful team

Successful teams go through four stages: **Forming, Storming, Norming** and **Performing:**

1. **Forming:** The team is formed as team members meet and get to know one another.
2. **Storming:** At first, team members may disagree and argue about how to get the work done and the team leader must ensure that conflicts are minimised and do not damage the work of the team.
3. **Norming:** The team begins to establish ground rules ('norms') for working effectively together in terms of each person's role, responsibilities, behaviour and work methods.
4. **Performing:** Once a team has settled down, it should start to perform well, with all members working together towards the team goals.

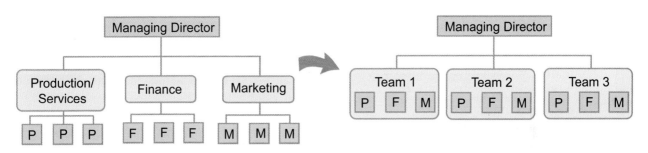

Fig. 3 An example of changing from a functional to a team-based/matrix organisational structure.

Teamwork can be promoted by introducing team-based/matrix organisational structures. **Team-based (matrix) structures** *are a type of organisational structure where staff are brought together into teams to achieve the clearly stated team goals.* Each team is responsible for achieving a **team goal**, such as producing a particular model of car. Depending on the task, each team will include personnel with the different skills needed to achieve the team's aims.

> Matrix organisational structures use teamwork across different departments.

> See Chapter 8: Management Activities of Planning, Organising & Controlling for more information on organisational structures.

Benefits of teamwork

- ✪ **Improves communications** and relationships between staff in a business.
- ✪ **Teams make better decisions** as the level of staff co-operation and consultation rises.
- ✪ **Teams can make faster decisions** as it is no longer necessary for staff to go up through the chain of command for approval before making decisions.
- ✪ **Employee motivation** and **job satisfaction rise** while symptoms of employee unhappiness such as absenteeism, poor quality work and labour turnover are significantly reduced.
- ✪ Committed teams can achieve **better quality products**, thus improving sales and profitability.

> OL Short Q3, 4
> OL Long Q3
>
> HL Long Q4

7. How can a commitment to quality be promoted?

Case Study

The final element in Toyota's strategy of completely changing the operation of their newly acquired American factory was the introduction of a system of **total quality management (TQM)**. This included sending over 600 staff to Toyota's factories in Japan to learn about the importance of quality control and how it is done in practice. These study visits also allowed the American staff to see Japanese teamwork in action.

The introduction of TQM resulted in a completely transformed workforce who were now **empowered** and responsible and who **worked closely in teams** with a **total commitment to producing quality vehicles**. In the words of one worker: 'By making the factory a better place to work, Toyota made us better people and we make better cars.'

> **TQM tries to bring a commitment to quality to all areas of a business.**

Total Quality Management (TQM) *is an approach to management that aims to maximise quality by getting all staff involved in* **continuously** *looking for ways to* **improve the quality** *of a firm's products and services.* Its core principles are:

- ❖ Promoting employee empowerment
- ❖ Promoting teamwork
- ❖ Promoting a commitment to quality among all staff.

All members of staff – from boardroom level right down to workers in the factory, secretaries and sales reps – are encouraged to aim to provide a top-class product and after-sales service to the people they deal with, both work colleagues and customers. TQM is seen by some as the reason why Japanese firms like Toyota have become so successful in international business.

> **Example:** Toyota's engineers treat the firm's own sales staff as valued customers. Similarly, the Toyota Research and Development (R&D) department seeks to provide a top-class service to the marketing and production departments.

OL Short Q5, 6

8. How can a TQM approach be implemented?

> **TQM in practice requires:**
> - Recruiting high-quality staff
> - Empowering employees
> - Encouraging teamwork

- ✳ **Recruit and train** conscientious, quality-focused employees.
- ✳ Managers adopt a more **facilitator management style** that motivates employees to contribute their best to the business.

✳ **Empower and motivate employees** to constantly look for ways to improve customer satisfaction with the business (e.g. by paying bonuses and giving prizes for work of a consistently high quality).

✳ **Facilitate teamwork** among employees with quality and customer satisfaction as the main goal. For TQM this includes setting up quality circles. **Quality circles** *are discussion groups made up of employees who meet regularly to discuss and resolve quality issues.* A wide range of employees from all parts of the business attend these meetings.

✳ **Adopt strict quality control** for all aspects of purchasing, production and delivery of goods. **Quality control** *means checking to ensure that the standard of goods and services produced by a business are to the desired quality.*

✳ Have a **quality assurance system** *that can guarantee customers that a firm's products are of the very highest possible quality standard.* Firms who reach sufficiently high quality standards can qualify for quality awards such as the **ISO** or the **Q Mark**. Such awards can provide a business with a big advantage over competitors.

Benefits of TQM

1. **Better quality** goods and services.
2. **Enhanced business reputation**, which can attract new customers.
3. **Increased customer loyalty** and repeat orders.
4. **Higher prices can be charged** for superior quality products.
5. **Reduced waste** of time and materials and increased profitability. Business gets quality right the first time.

Potential problems with TQM

1. **Implementation can be slow** as the change in staff attitudes and work practices required by TQM can take years to become established.
2. **Stress**: The high standards demanded by TQM can put staff under stress so good HR management is essential.

OL Long Q5, 6

HL Short Q7, 8
HL Long Q5, 6

Successful change at Aughinish Alumina

Case Study

Limerick-based Aughinish Alumina is a large company producing the raw material needed to manufacture aluminium metal used in drinks cans, vehicles and thousands of other products.

The business had a poor **industrial relations** history and some staff members were very resistant to change. Industrial disputes were common and the business was losing over €1 million per week. The company realised that serious **change management** was required if the business was to survive.

- Firstly, managers began communicating to all staff the need for serious change or else the business was finished.

- Secondly, company managers set about adopting a more **facilitative style** in dealing with staff. This helped to create a more positive and constructive working environment.

- Thirdly, the **chain of command** and organisational structure was reduced to just three levels. Jobs were redesigned to allow for greater **employee empowerment**. Full training was also provided to all staff to enable them to take on extra duties and responsibilities. This helped create greater job satisfaction and motivation among staff.

- The company then introduced a **team-based organisational structure**. This gave staff greater input into decision-making, further raised their motivation and also improved the overall quality of decision-making.

- Finally, the firm introduced a **TQM** approach to promoting quality.

Taken together, these three measures had a dramatic impact on Aughinish Alumina. By adopting such a **partnership approach** to employer-employee relations, change management became easier and the Irish plant was transformed from being on the brink of closure to being one of the most efficient and profitable alumina processing plants in the world.

Recall and Review

1. Explain the terms highlighted in bold.
2. Evaluate the possible benefits to Aughinish Alumina of introducing a TQM approach.
3. Outline the steps involved in introducing a TQM approach into a business.

C. New technologies and change

9. How are new technologies changing the role of management?

Case Study

Managing new technologies in Toyota

Toyota is one of the most technologically advanced businesses in the world. It is always looking to use the latest **information and communications technologies (ICT)** wherever it can to improve

quality and reduce **costs** throughout the business. For instance, Toyota uses **electronic data interchange (EDI)** to order and pay suppliers automatically. Using automated technology, it was the first company in the world to use **just-in-time (JIT)** stock control and ordering systems that eliminated the need for – and cost of – holding large stocks of components and raw materials.

In addition to making cars, Toyota also produces the most advanced **robots** in the world and uses them extensively in its highly automated factories to ensure high quality standards are achieved.

The use of new technologies in Toyota and all businesses is changing the role of management in many different areas. Changing technology has implications for key areas of business such as:

- Management communications and decision-making
- Marketing and identifying new business opportunities
- Production
- Human resource management
- Business costs and financial management

> **Changing technology has an impact on each of the main management functions:**
>
> - **Management**
> - **Marketing**
> - **Production**
> - **Human resources**
> - **Finance**

Impact of new technology on management communications

- ❖ Management **decision-making can be speeded up** by sharing information quickly using the Internet and by using technologies such as **databases** (to store files electronically) and **spreadsheets** (for financial calculations) to analyse huge amounts of data.
- ❖ These decisions can then **be communicated** and shared **very quickly** to staff using mobile phones, email and the Internet.

> **See Chapter 7: Management Skill of Communication for more information on management communications and ICT.**

Impact of new technology on marketing

* **Market research** can be conducted using the Internet and the information can be downloaded.

> Example: By using the Internet, Toyota can monitor the activities of other car companies by looking through media reports and online product catalogues. This allows firms to research what similar companies all over the globe are offering their customers. Toyota customers can also fill in online questionnaires and make comments and suggestions to the firm about its products. In this way the Internet provides a relatively fast and inexpensive method of collecting and distributing information.

∗ **Online advertising and sales:** Businesses can use websites to advertise and sell to a global audience at a very low cost, rather than using expensive shops and showrooms.

- **E-commerce,** *also known as B2C (business to consumer), refers to using the Internet to sell to consumers.*

  Example: Toyota sells its cars over the Internet to consumers. Amazon.com is a very successful online retailer.

- **E-business,** *also known as B2B (business to business), refers to using the Internet to conduct all types of business and financial transactions, not just from businesses to consumers.* In particular, it includes buying and selling to other businesses.

  Example: Toyota using the Internet to order components from its suppliers.

- **M-commerce** *refers to using mobile phone technology for business and financial transactions.*

  Example: Sending customised advertisements to mobile phone users.

Impact of new technology on production and stock control

- **Electronic Data Interchange (EDI)** *is an automated stock ordering system that allows orders to be placed automatically from a computer in one business to a computer in another business using the Internet.* An EDI system allows goods to be ordered by firms on time and with a minimum of paperwork or human involvement. This can significantly reduce business costs.

- **Computer Aided Design (CAD) software** *is used to speed up the product design process dramatically.*

  Example: Car companies like Toyota can simulate wind tunnel tests on cars electronically without having to leave their desks. Depending on the product, design processes that previously would have taken years can now be done in a few months.

- **Computer Aided Manufacturing (CAM)** *involves using computers to automate **part** of the work on an assembly line to significantly reduce labour costs and improve quality control.*

  Example: To create a modern car, Toyota has to design, engineer, buy and assemble over 10,000 different parts. This is a very complicated process and the company uses CAM to increase efficiency and to keep its production costs down.

- **Computer Integrated Manufacturing (CIM)** *uses ICT (such as robotics) to control **the entire** production process, from design and stock control to assembly and quality control.* CIM can dramatically reduce labour costs but still needs careful management control to avoid disruptions to the manufacturing process from computer errors.

- **Reduced costs** and **increased efficiency:** Computerisation and automation has reduced the amount of staff and time needed to design and build products. This has pushed down production costs and increased efficiency for most businesses.

Impact of new technology on human resources

- ❖ **Many jobs become redundant**, especially in traditional industries like agriculture and manufacturing as a result of new technologies. Employees need to retrain to keep their skills up to date.
- ❖ **E-working** means work location is becoming less important. **E-working** *means people working from home but linked to an office using ICT such as computers, Internet and telephones*. It reduces the financial and time costs of commuting daily to and from work. It also reduces office administration costs such as rent, light and heat for the business.
- ❖ **Training:** Computer software is now commonly used as a low-cost but effective way of training staff in new skills such as health and safety, foreign languages, design and business skills.
- ❖ **Payroll management** is now far faster, cheaper and more accurate than ever as wages can be paid automatically into employee bank accounts.

Impact of new technology on costs and financial management

- ✳ **New technology can be expensive** to buy and maintain. Further expense may be incurred training staff to use new technologies.

- ✳ **Speed and accuracy of financial accounts** is greatly enhanced. Financial accounts can be quickly and accurately prepared, saved, updated and printed out using spreadsheet software. If the accounts system is linked to the purchasing and payroll systems, then very accurate up-to-date financial data on the business can be maintained.

- ✳ **Reduced costs:** Communications and transport costs are reduced through the use of email and video conferencing. By using **computer networks**, staff in different locations can reduce costs by sharing software and hardware (e.g. printers). Advertising and marketing costs are reduced by using websites, which are cheaper to set up than opening expensive premises.

Challenges of new technology for management

- ✪ **Human resources** and **industrial relations** can face challenges due to the need for staff retraining, redeployment or redundancies. These are sensitive issues that must be carefully managed by the HR manager to avoid industrial relations problems. ICT can also lead to **new jobs** in areas such as software development, web design and network administration.
- ✪ **Business vulnerability:** Computer viruses, sudden power cuts or software errors can corrupt or destroy valuable information stored on computer files. If a business becomes very dependent on new technology, then an equipment failure can bring an entire business to a standstill. Every business needs to have **contingency plans** in place to deal with the risk of technology failures.

> Example: AIB backs up its computer files many times during a single day and stores this data in different locations to protect against data loss or corruption.

See Chapter 7:
Management Skill of Communication for more information on the Data Protection Acts 1988 & 2003.

✪ **Data security:** Data held on computer must be protected against unauthorised access or use. Where businesses hold personal information about people, the Data Protection Acts 1988 & 2003 must be complied with.

OL Short Q7, 8, 9
OL Long Q7, 8

HL ABQ
HL Long Q7, 8, 9, 10

Key Concepts & Business Terms

After studying this chapter the student should be able to explain the following key concepts and business terms:

1. Drivers of change in business
2. Change management
3. Employee empowerment
4. Teamwork
5. Team-based structures/Matrix organisational structures
6. TQM
7. Implementing TQM
8. Quality circles
9. Quality control
10. ISO
11. Q mark
12. E-Commerce
13. E-Business
14. M-Commerce
15. Electronic Data Interchange (EDI)
16. Computer Aided Design (CAD)
17. Computer Aided Manufacturing (CAM)
18. Computer Integrated Manufacturing (CIM)
19. E-working

useful websites

www.toyota.ie

Leaving Certificate Practice Questions

Ordinary Level

Ordinary Level – Section 1 – Short Questions (10 marks each)

1. Identify **four** reasons for the changing role of management.
2. List **two** characteristics of a facilitator approach to management.
3. List the **four** stages that successful teams go through. [LCQ]
4. Outline **two** benefits of teamwork in an organisation. [LCQ]
5. TQM stands for . . .
6. Outline the importance of quality control to a business. [LCQ]
7. What do the following letters stand for: (a) ICT, (b) EDI, (c) CIM?
8. List **two** uses of the World Wide Web (www) for business. [LCQ]
9. Information and Communications Technology provide opportunities to business. Outline **two** of these opportunities. [LCQ]

Ordinary Level – Section 2 – Long Questions

1. Explain what is meant by the term 'change management'. (20 marks)
2. Outline **four** steps a business could undertake to effectively introduce change. (20 marks)
3. Outline **three** benefits of teamwork to an organisation. (15 marks) [LCQ]
4. Describe **two** possible benefits and **two** possible risks of introducing employee empowerment into a business. (20 marks)
5. (a) A business wants to recruit a new secretary. Explain why teamwork is important for the person being selected for this job. (15 marks) [LCQ]
   (b) Describe **two** benefits of total quality management (TQM). (10 marks) [LCQ]
6. Identify **two** benefits for a firm acquiring an ISO award. (20 marks)
7. Explain, using examples, what is meant by the term 'Information and Communications Technology (ICT)'. (20 marks)
8. Outline **four** effects that information technology (IT) has on the role of management. (20 marks) [LCQ]

Higher Level

Higher Level - Section 1 - Short Questions (10 marks each)

1. Change management means . . .
2. List **three** steps managers can take to help a business adapt to change.
3. List **two** reasons for staff resistance to change.
4. Describe **two** characteristics of a 'facilitatory' management style.
5. Empowerment helps a business to . . . [LCQ]
6. Identify **three** benefits of employee empowerment.
7. What do the letters TQM stand for? [LCQ]
8. Total quality management (TQM) helps business because it . . . [LCQ]

Higher Level – Section 2 – Applied Business Question

Venus Chocolates

Alma Hennessy is the chief executive officer (CEO) of Venus Chocolates, a mass-production confectionary company producing chocolate bars and snacks. Despite paying its staff well, the company has a morale and motivation problem that seems to be getting worse. Staff frustration at routine and repetitive work means that the company has a high level of absenteeism and staff turnover. As a result, product quality has started to decline and customer complaints are on the rise. The company is now beginning to lose sales in the very competitive confectionary market.

Alma is described by her staff as having an autocratic and controlling management style. She likes to keep tight control over all staff to ensure that they are working.

Many of the workers have joined a union and their shop steward has contacted Alma using the company grievance procedure to say that staff morale is getting very low.

Venus has a functional organisational structure. Given the current problems, Alma is thinking about changing to a matrix/team-based structure. However, she is worried about how to introduce this kind of change to the staff. She also wants to ensure that quality standards in the company are improved and that the company adopts more modern technologies which are being used by many rival firms in the chocolate industry.

1. Identify the changes facing Venus Chocolates. Refer to the text in your answer. (20 marks)
2. Explain **three** strategies that Alma could introduce into Venus Chocolates to help the business adapt to change. (30 marks)
3. Describe how the use of **four** different types of new technologies could assist the business. (30 marks)

Higher Level – Section 2 – Long Questions

1. Discuss the reasons why people often resist change at work. (15 marks)
2. Explain what employee empowerment means and outline **two** benefits of empowerment. (20 marks) [LCQ]
3. Explain the changing role of a manager from controller to facilitator. Refer to areas such as the empowerment of workers and total quality management in your explanation. (25 marks) [LCQ]
4. Discuss the benefits of teamwork in a business organisation. (20 marks) [LCQ]

5. 'Total quality management (TQM) is important to both the customer and the business.' Discuss. (30 marks)

6. Evaluate the importance of quality control for modern businesses. (25 marks)

7. Illustrate the impact that technology has on an organisation's (a) business costs, (b) personnel and (c) business opportunities. (20 marks) [LCQ]

8. Draft a business letter to the managing director of an enterprise, outlining the benefits to the business of improving its information and communications technology (ICT) systems. Include examples in your answer. (20 marks) [LCQ]

9. Analyse the risks a business may face if it does not adapt to changing technology. (20 marks)

10. Discuss the strategies that can help a manager to persuade staff to support changes which may be necessary for the business to succeed. (20 marks) [LCQ]

UNIT 4

Chapter 11
Managing Business & Household Insurance & Tax

'There is no security in life, only opportunity.'

Mark Twain

Key Study Questions

Case Study

C&D Foods

C&D Foods in County Longford was started by a local entrepreneur with €30,000 of his own money and €60,000 in bank loans. Over time the business grew to become the biggest supplier of own-brand pet foods to supermarket chains in Ireland and the UK, with total sales of over €100 million. As the largest employer in the local area, C&D Foods paid wages of hundreds of thousands of euro per week to local people, as well as purchasing ingredients from local farms and businesses

However, one Sunday morning a fire broke out in the factory and by the following day 80% of the factory was a smouldering ruin. The firm's specially made production equipment that the company used to make 200 million cans of pet food per year was totally destroyed. Although no one was injured, 500 people lost their jobs. The economic impact was also felt by all the shops, garages and restaurants within a fifty-kilometre radius.

Fortunately, C&D Foods had insurance policies that would help to pay to rebuild the premises and purchase replacement equipment. However, the business had no guarantee that its big supermarket customers, who had to switch to other pet food suppliers after the fire, would return if the factory was rebuilt and production resumed. Looking at the ruined factory, the managing director said, 'The situation is about as bad as it can be.' The experience of C&D Foods is a warning to all businesses of the importance of having proper risk control and insurance to cover against fire and other disasters.

A. Business & Household Insurance

1. What is risk management?

> Risk management identifies business risks and puts in place plans to minimise them happening.

Risks such as fire are a fact of life for businesses and households. **Risk management** *means identifying key business risks, their likely effect on the business, and then putting in place a strategy to minimise them occurring and when they do, to resolve them as quickly as possible.* Specifically, risk management involves:

* **Identifying** possible risks (e.g. fire).
* **Reducing the likelihood** of the risk event occurring (e.g. install smoke detectors and sprinklers).
* **Taking out insurance** on the reduced risk (e.g. fire insurance).

> HL Short Q3

Methods of risk reduction

Identifying risks and taking preventative action to minimise or eliminate them can benefit businesses and households, resulting in fewer risks that will cost less to insure against.

Examples of risk reduction/prevention strategies include:

* Using **fireproof materials** in buildings and installing fire alarms and sprinkler systems.
* Installing proper **security devices** such as secure locks and burglar alarms, safes and security cameras.
* Having proper **security systems** in place for handling and transporting cash and valuables such as using a specialist security firm.
* Storing **copies of valuable documents** or computer data in separate locations to minimise potential loss from fire or other events.

❖ Introducing **health and safety programmes** to teach workers to use all equipment and machinery properly.

❖ Having a proper **contingency plan** in place to respond quickly to possible disasters.

> **Example:** Restaurants are particularly at risk from fires starting in the kitchens. They use sprinklers, fire dampers in grease ducts and smoke and heat detectors to reduce fire risks and their insurance costs by as much as 40%.

2. What is insurance?

A key element in successful risk management is having proper insurance cover. **Insurance** *is a contract whereby a person (the insured) pays a fee (a premium) to an insurance company (the insurer) in return for a promise to compensate the insured in the event of a financial loss occurring.* Insurance works on the basis of pooling or sharing risks, as follows:

✪ Insurance companies collect premiums from large numbers of people to cover various risks.

✪ However, over any period of time only a small number of these risks will actually happen and cause financial loss.

✪ This allows the insurance company to pay out compensation when a risk occurs and still have money left over to make a profit.

The importance of insurance to business

✴ **Business survival is protected** in the event of unexpected financial disasters and setbacks. A business does not have to pay for large, unexpected losses out of its own resources.

✴ **Improves cash flow** for the business as it is easier to plan paying regular small premiums than having to pay out one large sum as a result of a disaster.

✴ **Can save money** as paying regular, small insurance premiums may be less expensive than having no insurance if something goes wrong.

✴ **Makes exporting easier** as goods transported over long distances can be insured against damage.

✴ **May be a legal requirement**, such as having third-party motor insurance.

The importance of insurance to households

❖ **Greater financial security** as serious financial risks, such as fire in the home and redundancy can be protected against.

❖ **Greater peace of mind** arises from having insurance protection. In particular, it can provide financial protection for the victims of accidents, theft or redundancies.

❖ **Savings can be enhanced** by the use of life assurance policies that guarantee payment at a future date.

3. What types of insurance should a business have?

Insurance on assets

Every business should have insurance:
- **On assets**
- **On employees**
- **Against possible liabilities**

✪ **Property insurance** for a business premises and contents against risks such as fire, flood, burst pipes and theft.

> **Example:** C&D Foods had property insurance and successfully claimed over €7 million compensation to rebuild its premises and to buy new machinery and equipment.

✪ **Cash and valuables** should be insured while on the premises during working hours and in transit to and from banks.

✪ **Motor insurance:** All motorists, both business and private, must have motor insurance. The main types are:

- **Third-party motor insurance** *covers damage caused by a driver to other people and property.* It is compulsory for all motor vehicles on public roads. In insurance, the first party is the insurance company, the second party is the insured, and the third party is a victim of any accident (caused by the second party). This policy allows drivers to meet their liability for injuries caused to others in any road accidents.
- **Third-party, fire & theft motor insurance** *provides third-party protection plus loss or damage to your own car from fire or theft.*
- **Comprehensive motor insurance** *provides third-party, fire and theft cover plus compensation for any accidental damage that happens to your own vehicle.*

Insurance on employees

✳ **Permanent health insurance** *provides sick pay for workers unable to work due to illness.* This is paid after the first 13 weeks of an illness.

✳ **Key person insurance** *protects a business against loss of valuable staff members.*

> **Example:** If a highly talented scientist, designer, salesperson, finance manager or managing director leaves the business.

✳ **PRSI** (Pay Related Social Insurance) *is a compulsory insurance payment to the State by both employees and employers. It is calculated as a percentage of gross income.* The money raised from PRSI is used for unemployment payments, pensions, maternity benefits, etc.

✳ **Fidelity guarantee insurance** *provides business cover against dishonesty or fraud by an employee against the firm.* This is important for employees who are put in positions of trust, such as those with access to bank accounts, safes, product plans or other valuable information.

> **Example:** General Motors (GM) accused a production manager who left to work for Volkswagen of stealing valuable documents before he left. GM did not have fidelity guarantee insurance and had to sue Volkswagen in the German courts for compensation.

Insurance against liabilities

Public liability insurance *covers a business against claims* if a member of the public is injured in an accident that is considered to be the fault of the business.

Product liability insurance *provides cover against any claims for harm or loss suffered through use of a firm's products.*

> Example: Parents have sued the makers of Ribena drinks for tooth rot caused to their children by the sugar in their drinks. In the USA cigarette companies have paid out compensation to people who have contracted cancer from smoking cigarettes.

Employer's liability insurance *protects a business against claims arising from accidents, injuries and illnesses suffered by employees as a result of their work.* The premium varies depending on the type of work done and the risks involved.

> Example: In Japan some companies have taken out insurance to protect them against being sued by employees for suffering from stress and illness from overwork. Death from overwork, or 'Karoshi', is an officially recognised cause of death in Japan.

OL Short Q1
OL Long Q1

HL Short Q1, 2

Consequential loss insurance (also known as **business interruption insurance**) *provides financial compensation for loss of income in the event of a major risk occurring.*

> Example: C&D Foods had consequential loss insurance and successfully claimed over €5 million compensation for the loss of sales arising from the factory fire.

Case Study

Viking Splash Tours

Viking Splash Tours provides colourful tours around Dublin using World War II amphibious military vehicles. Drivers dressed in Viking costume act as tour captains, telling passengers all about the history and sights of the city. As part of the tour, the vehicles drive off the road and splash into the River Liffey.

Recall and Review
1. Identify the risks involved in running Viking Splash Tours.
2. List and explain the four most important types of business insurance that you would recommend for Viking Splash Tours.
3. What types of insurance polices would you recommend for: (a) C&D Foods, (b) U2, (c) Bus Éireann, (d) a hairdresser and (e) a gym and fitness centre?

4. What types of insurance should a household have?

Households can have insurance to cover their assets, liabilities and personal health.

Assets

❖ **House insurance** *covers both the* **building** *and its* **contents** *(e.g. furniture and appliances) in the event of a wide range of risks, including fire, burglary and accidental damage.*

❖ **Motor insurance** is compulsory for all cars on the road.

Liabilities

⊙ **Mortgage protection insurance** *is now required by all lenders before they will approve a mortgage loan to buy a house.* If the person taking out the mortgage dies before it is fully repaid, the insurance policy will repay the remaining amount.

Personal health

✳ **General health insurance** *covers the cost of private health care in the event of serious illness.* Health insurance premiums can be claimed as a tax-free allowance.

✳ **Permanent health insurance** *pays a percentage of your salary if you have to give up work due to an accident or illness.* The amount paid will depend on the level of risk involved in the work and the size of the premium paid.

✳ **Personal accident insurance** *provides compensation if you have a serious accident.* The amount paid will depend upon the seriousness of the injury.

✳ **Life assurance** *provides compensation to a named beneficiary in the event of the death of the insured person.* While general insurance protects you against some risk that *might* happen, life assurance provides cover for something that *will* happen, i.e. death. There are two main types:

1. **Whole-life assurance** *policies require the insured to pay an annual premium for the rest of his/her life. Compensation will only be paid out after the death of the insured.*

2. **Endowment life assurance** *policies pay out compensation when you reach a certain age, e.g. 60, or if you die before you reach that age, whichever comes first.* It is a combination of savings and risk protection.

3. **Term-life insurance** *provides cover for an agreed period of time, such as twenty years. No lump sum is paid unless death occurs within the stated period.*

OL Long Q5

QUEST

Case Study

COMPUTER GAMES [1]

One Tuesday afternoon after a period of very heavy rain, Ciara O'Loughlin got a call on her mobile phone to say that there was a serious flood at the business park where her computer game business, Quest Computer Games, was located. Fearing the worst, she rushed to the scene to discover that, except for some minor damage, her premises had escaped undamaged. 'I was really lucky, because the ground floor of the business next door, Cosy Carpets Ltd, was completely flooded,' said a relieved Ciara. Besides motor insurance on a van, Quest did not have any other type of insurance. 'Up until now, I have been too busy getting the business up and running – and keeping costs down – to think about it,' says Ciara.

Ciara contacted an insurance broker to help her identify the risks to which the business is exposed and to examine the insurance protection policies which Quest should take out. The main assets of the business are €20,000 worth of computers, software, printers and other ICT equipment, plus furniture and fittings worth a further €3,000. The premises are rented and the firm employs six staff, including two highly talented software programmers. Ciara is also aware that she needs to consider insuring her own home and contents against the risk of fire or burglary.

5. How do you become insured?

Ciara O'Loughlin wants to take out an insurance policy to protect Quest and her home from possible risks. This will involve (a) contacting an insurance company, (b) filling in a proposal form, (c) the insurance company calculating the premium and (d) a policy being issued by the insurance company.

Step 1: Contact an insurance company

Businesses and individuals can contact an insurance company directly or else go through an **insurance broker** or **agent**.

❖ **Insurance brokers** *work independently of insurance companies. They can help you to identify your insurable risks and give you unbiased advice on the best insurance policy to buy and from which firm.*

❖ **Insurance agents** *work for a particular insurance company and only sell that company's policies.*

Step 2: Fill in a proposal form

A proposal form *is an application form completed by the person applying for insurance cover.* The **exposure unit** *is the object being insured, such as premises or a car.*

Step 3: Risk is assessed and a premium is calculated

The insurance company will calculate the premium (fee) to be paid to cover the risk. It will then issue a quotation for that amount.

Factors that influence the size of the premium include:

- **Level of risk** involved. The greater the risk, the higher the insurance premium charged.

> **Example 1:** It is more expensive for an 18-year-old person to get car insurance than a 35-year-old person, even though they may be driving identical cars. From experience, insurance companies know that young males are far more likely to drive fast and recklessly and to be involved in an accident.

- **Value** of the item being insured.

> **Example 2:** A factory worth €25 million will have a higher premium than a house worth €500,000.

- **Loadings** *are extra charges added to motor premiums to take account of the different characteristics, e.g. age of driver, age of car, full or provisional licence, record of previous claims, etc.* **A no claims bonus** *refers to a discount offered on premiums to customers who have made no insurance claims during the previous year.*

OL Long Q6, 7

HL Long Q2

- **Profit targets** set by the insurance company.

Step 4: Policy is issued

If the quotation is accepted, a cover note is issued. A **cover note** *is a temporary document issued by the insurance company as proof of the existence of an insurance contract until the full policy contract is ready.* This will be followed by a full insurance policy. An **insurance policy** *sets out the full contract, including items covered, value of the compensation available and the conditions attached.*

Step 5: Make a claim if insured event occurs

If a risk that is covered by an insurance policy actually happens, the insured must complete a claim form. An **insurance claim form** *is a document that must be completed describing what happened and stating the amount of loss suffered.* The insurance company may send out an **assessor** to inspect the damage and to decide how much compensation, if any, the insurance company will pay.

OL Short Q2

OL Long Q3

6. What principles of insurance will apply when making a claim?

The principles of insurance are:
- **Insurable interest**
- **Utmost good faith**
- **Indemnity**
- **Contribution**
- **Subrogation**

The five principles of insurance *are the basic rules that must be obeyed before an insurance company will agree to pay compensation on an insurance claim.* A breach of any of the principles will invalidate the insurance contract and may result in no compensation being paid out.

Principle 1: Insurable interest

Insurable interest *means that the person seeking insurance must benefit from the continued existence of the item being insured or suffer from its loss.*

> **Example:** Quest Software is entitled to insure its own assets. However, according to the principle of insurable interest it could not insure the assets of Cosy Carpets, the business next door.

Furthermore, Quest can only claim insurance **compensation** on something for which they have taken out insurance. This is known as **proximate cause.** If they insured their equipment against fire but it is then burgled, the business cannot claim insurance for losses caused by the burglary.

Principle 2: Utmost good faith

Utmost good faith *(uberrimae fidei) means the insured must give* **truthful** *information and disclose* **all relevant facts** *when applying for insurance, even if this means they will get a higher premium.* A relevant or material fact is anything that could influence the insurer's decision to take on the risk or what premium to charge.

> **Example:** When Ciara takes out insurance policies to protect Quest she will have to be open and honest in answering all relevant questions. This will include revealing that her premises has a timber frame and does not have a water sprinkler system or a burglar alarm.

> **Example:** A motorist must reveal that they have a provisional licence only; or a person looking for life assurance must reveal that they have a heart condition. Failure to do so means that the insurance contract will be declared null and void.

Principle 3: Indemnity

Indemnity *means the insurer agrees to compensate for the* **actual** *financial loss suffered.* You are **not allowed to profit** from an insurance claim. Insurance companies will

only compensate for the actual financial loss suffered. No compensation is paid for 'sentimental' value. Life assurance is an exception to the principle of indemnity.

> **Example:** Cosy Carpets had insured their premises for €400,000, which they claimed from their insurance company as compensation for the flood. However, the market value of the building before the flood was only €300,000 and therefore the insurance company would only pay €300,000 compensation.

The indemnity rule also affects businesses and households who over- or under-insure items. **Over-insurance** *is when you insure an item for more than it is actually worth.* **Under-insurance** *is where you insure an item for less than it is actually worth.* In the case of under-insurance, the **average clause** rule applies (see p190).

Principle 4: Contribution

The **principle of contribution** *says that where two or more insurers are involved, they will divide the total cost of any claim between them.* It aims to prevent people making a profit (principle of indemnity) by insuring the same risk with a number of companies and hoping to claim compensation from each separately.

> **Example 1:** A truck worth €100,000 is insured with Insurance Company X for €100,000 and with Insurance Company Y for €100,000. A road accident causes €9,000 damage.
>
> | | |
> |---|---|
> | Company X will pay 50% of the compensation | €4,500 |
> | Company Y will pay 50% of the compensation | €4,500 |
> | Total compensation | €9,000 |
>
> **Example 2:** Suppose Cosy Carpets had insured themselves with two different insurance companies. After the flood, Cosy Carpets applied to both companies for full compensation. They were expecting to receive €300,000 from each, giving a total of €600,000. In fact they only receive €150,000 from each, giving a total of €300,000.

Principle 5: Subrogation

The **principle of subrogation** *states that insurers who pay out full compensation for an item insured with them are entitled to* **take possession** *of the item involved and to* **sue a third party** *who caused the loss to occur.*

> **Example:** It was discovered that the flood that badly damaged Cosy Carpets may have been caused by the negligence of builders who had diverted a local river while working on a nearby construction project. However, once the insurance compensation has been paid, Cosy Carpets cannot sue the builders for damages. This right now passes to the insurance company.

The Average Clause Rule

In addition to the five principles of insurance, there is also another important rule – the Average Clause rule. The Average Clause Rule applies to partial loss when you are under-insured. It means you only get compensated for a proportionate amount of the loss suffered. For example, if you insure a house for only 25% of its value (in order to save money on the premium), then the insurance company will only compensate you for 25% of any loss suffered.

Example 1: Delux Cars premises are worth €300,000 and are insured with ABC Insurance Corporation for €150,000. A fire causes €40,000 damage.

Proportion insured is: $\dfrac{€150,000}{€300,000} = \dfrac{1}{2}$

ABC Insurance Corporation will only pay Delux Cars ½ of the €40,000 claim, i.e. €20,000.

Example 2: The equipment and stock owned by Quest Computer Games are worth €10,000. However, they have only been insured for €7,500 (75% of their value). In the event of a fire causing damage, Quest can only claim 75% of the damage done.

OL Short Q3
OL Long Q2, 4, 8, 9

HL Short Q4, 5, 6, 7
HL Long Q3

7. How can an insurance company settle a claim?

Insurance companies can settle compensation claims in the following ways:
* Pay **cash compensation** to the insured. This is the most common method.
* **Replacement of the asset** if the item is completely lost or destroyed.
* **Repair or reinstatement** where a partial loss or damage occurs to an asset.

8. What are the similarities and differences between business and household insurance?

Similarities	Differences
Both businesses and households must: • **Identify** and manage possible risks. • **Insure against** all reasonable risks. • **Fill out** insurance forms, e.g. proposal and claim forms. • **Keep** insurance forms and policy documents safe, up to date and accurate.	• Businesses have **more risks** to insure against than households. • Businesses can suffer **far greater financial losses**. • Households only pay **PRSI on their own income** while businesses must pay PRSI for all of their employees. • Only businesses can treat insurance payments as a **legitimate business expense** to reduce their tax bills.

OL Long Q10

HL Long Q4

CRAZY CLAIMS

Case Study

A man in North Carolina in the USA purchased a case of 24 very expensive cigars and insured them, among others things, against fire. He smoked all the cigars within a month and then made an **insurance claim** on his **insurance policy** claiming that the cigars were lost 'in a series of small fires'. The insurance company refused to pay.

The man decided to sue the insurance company for breach of **contract**. In court, the judge ruled in his favour and ordered the insurance company to pay the man $15,000 compensation. According to the judge, the insurance company had not properly defined what was meant by 'fire' in the insurance policy.

After the man cashed his compensation cheque, the insurance company used the principle of **subrogation** to have the man arrested by the police on a charge of 24 counts of arson. Using the man's sworn testimony from the previous case, he was quickly found guilty of arson as he had deliberately burned his insured property, was sentenced to two years in jail and fined $24,000.

Recall and Review

1. Explain the terms highlighted in bold.

B. Business & Household Taxation

wave (TECHNOLOGIES

Case Study

Wave Technologies Limited is an Irish-owned business developing advanced equipment to harness electricity from ocean waves. The business employs a group of highly skilled engineers and scientists who are world experts in this field. The company has a full range of insurance policies, including key person insurance on its most talented scientists.

As a limited company, Wave Technologies pays **corporation tax** every year on its profits. It must also pay **Value Added Tax (VAT)** on many of its purchases and deducts **PAYE income tax** from its employees' wages.

191

9. What taxes are paid by businesses?

Like all businesses, Wave Technologies must pay the taxes that are required to fund public services such as schools and hospitals, and infrastructure such as roads and waste disposal systems. **The Revenue Commissioners** *is the State agency responsible for collecting taxes on behalf of the government.*

> **Corporation tax is paid by companies on their profits.**
>
> **Irish corporation tax is 12.5%.**

❖ **Corporation Tax** *is the tax paid on the profits earned by companies and co-operatives.* The rate of corporation tax in Ireland is 12.5%, which is relatively low by international standards but considered necessary by the government to attract foreign transnational corporations to set up exporting bases in Ireland. Low corporation taxes also provide a financial incentive for Irish entrepreneurs to take the personal risk of setting up businesses.

❖ **Value Added Tax** *is a percentage tax added to the price of certain goods and services.* Most businesses, except those with very small sales, are required to register as VAT collectors.

> **VAT is a tax added to the price of goods and services.**

> Example: A €10,000 wave turbine will cost €12,100 after adding 21% VAT. Similarly, a €100 jacket becomes a €121 jacket after adding VAT at 21%. The VAT collected by a business must be sent to the Revenue Commissioners every two months.

❖ **Capital Gains Tax** *is paid on profits earned from the sale or disposal of a business asset such as premises.*

❖ **Customs duties** *are taxes levied on imports (e.g. raw materials) coming into the country from outside the EU.*

> Example: Wave Technologies pays customs duties on the specialist equipment it needs to import from Japan and America.

❖ **Commercial rates** *are taxes levied by local authorities on property used for commercial purposes to help finance local government services.* In special 'designated areas' commercial rates may be waived for periods of up to ten years in order to encourage businesses to set up and to promote urban renewal.

OL Short Q4, 10, 11

OL Long Q15

HL Long Q5

❖ **Employers' PRSI** *is levied on firms for every person they employ.* It funds social welfare benefits such as unemployment payments, pensions, maternity benefits, etc. It is calculated as a percentage of the employee's gross income.

10. How does taxation affect business?

> **Taxes reduce the profitability of businesses. They also impact on the management of different business functions.**

✳ **Lower profits:** Taxes reduce the size of final profits. This, in turn, reduces the amount that can be reinvested in a business or paid out in dividends to the owners.

✳ **Higher costs:** Irish businesses collect approximately 95% of all the taxes raised by the government but they are not paid for the time and administrative work involved.

※ **Higher prices:** Taxes such as **VAT** and **customs duties** increase the selling price of goods to customers. Higher prices may mean less sales and reduced profits.

※ **Human resources:** High personal taxation levied on staff can reduce motivation. They may also look for higher wages to compensate.

※ **Incentives:** Firms may locate their business in particular areas or countries to take advantage of tax incentives such as low corporation tax rates.

| HL Long Q8 |

11. What taxes are paid by households?

> **Income tax is paid by individuals.**

★ **Pay As You Earn (PAYE) Income Tax** *is paid by employees on their wages.* All businesses that employ staff must deduct PAYE Income Tax from their employees' wages before they get paid. The money collected is then forwarded to the Revenue Commissioners.

> **Individuals who are self-employed pay income tax under the self-assessment system.**

★ **Self-Assessment Income Tax** *is paid by self-employed people (e.g. a sole trader) on their incomes.* The same rates of tax apply to self-assessment tax payers as for PAYE tax payers but the system of collection is different. Following instructions provided by the Revenue Commissioners, every year self-employed people must calculate their own tax liability (amount of tax due).

Random spot checks are carried out by the Revenue Commissioners on self-assessment tax returns to ensure that full and accurate tax payments are being made. **A tax audit** *is a detailed examination by the Revenue Commissioners of a taxpayer's financial records.*

★ **Employees' Pay-Related Social Insurance (PRSI)** *is a compulsory* **insurance** *payment by employees to the State. It is calculated as a percentage of gross income.*

★ **Universal Social Charge** *is a tax payable on gross income.* It applies to taxpayers regardless of whether they pay income tax under the PAYE or the self-assessment income tax systems.

> **Tax evasion** is when taxpayers illegally evade paying the full amount of tax owed. This can occur by not declaring the full amount of their income or by claiming tax deductions they are not entitled to.
>
> **Tax avoidance** is when taxpayers take advantage of the tax system to legally reduce the amount of tax they owe.

★ **Value Added Tax (VAT)** is added to the price of most goods and services.

> **Example:** Computer games are taxed at 21% so when you buy a game for €30, €5.20 of this price is VAT (€24.80 + €5.20 = €30).

★ **Excise Duties** *are taxes added to the price of certain types of goods such as alcohol, petrol and tobacco.*

★ **Customs Duties** *are taxes levied on imports coming into the country from outside the EU.*

> **Example:** Customs duties are payable on goods purchased over the Internet from the USA or Japan.

★ **Motor Tax** *is a tax that must be paid annually on all roadworthy vehicles. It is collected by local authorities.*

★ **Capital Gains Tax** *is paid on profits earned from the* **sale/disposal of an asset,** *such as property and shares, in Ireland or abroad.* It **does not** apply to profits made on the sale of a person's main private home, lottery prizes, compensation payments or life assurance payments.

★ **Capital Acquisitions Tax** *is paid by those receiving money or assets as a gift or inheritance. Exemptions and different rates apply depending on the circumstances but generally the more you receive, the more you will be taxed.*

OL Short Q5, 12

OL Long Q11

★ **DIRT (Deposit Interest Retention Tax) (at 27%)** *is automatically deducted from all interest paid on bank and building society accounts and passed directly by the banks to the Revenue Commissioners.*

12. How does the PAYE income tax system work?

Every employee must pay tax on their wages under the PAYE system. Currently, PAYE tax is levied at two rates:

✪ A **standard rate of tax** *on all earnings below a certain amount called a* **standard rate cut-off point** *(e.g. 20% tax on all income up to €20,000).*

✪ A **top/higher rate of tax** *applies on all income above the standard rate cut-off point (e.g. 41% tax on all income above €20,000).*

Tax credits available to taxpayers include:

- PAYE Tax Credit
- Single Person's Personal Tax Credit
- Married Person's Personal Tax Credit
- Blind Person's Tax Credit
- Incapacitated Child Tax Credit
- Dependent Relative Tax Credit
- Home Carer's Tax Credit
- Single Parent Tax Credit
- Trade Union Membership Tax Credit

Income tax payers are eligible for different tax credits depending on their circumstances.

✳ A **tax credit** *is an allowance from the government that reduces the amount of tax owed.* To ensure that the full number of tax credits is received, all employees, when starting work for the first time, should fill in a **Form P12A,** *which is used by the Revenue to calculate the rate of tax that will apply and the tax credits that the employee will be entitled to receive.*

✳ A **Notice of Tax Credits** *is a document setting out the tax credits to which a taxpayer is entitled and also the standard tax rate cut-off point that will apply.* A copy is sent to all PAYE taxpayers each year. Employers also get a copy to ensure that they deduct the correct amount of tax from employees' wages.

✳ At the end of each year, all employees receive a Form P60 from their employer. The **Form P60** *shows the amount of pay, income tax and PRSI paid by an employee for the tax year.* A similar form, called a P35, will also be sent to the Revenue Commissioners by the employer, showing the calculations to prove that the correct tax was deducted and passed on to the tax authorities.

✳ **Form P21 (Balancing Statement):** *If an employee thinks that they may have overpaid tax during the year, they send this form to the Revenue Commissioners seeking a rebate of the tax overpaid.*

✳ **Form P45 (Cessation Certificate)** *is given by all employers to staff* **when they leave a job**. It shows how much income tax and PRSI the employee paid in the last year. This form will be needed by the next employer to calculate the correct amount of tax to deduct.

OL Short Q9

13. How is net income after tax calculated?

	Income Tax Calculation
A. Gross Income	**Gross income** *is total pay plus the financial value of any benefits-in-kind.* **Benefits-in-kind** *are free goods and services given by employers to employees, such as the use of a company car for private use.*
B. Calculate Tax	**Gross PAYE Tax** *is the tax due at both standard and higher rates before tax credits are taken into account.* The **standard rate of tax** *is levied on all income up to a certain level called the standard rate cut-off point (e.g. 20% on all earnings below €20,000).* The **higher rate of tax** *is levied on all earnings above the standard rate cut-off point (e.g. 40% on all earnings over €20,000).* **PAYE tax due = Gross PAYE tax *minus* total tax credits** **Tax credits** *are allowances from the government that reduce the amount of tax owed.*
C. Calculate Employee's PRSI	PRSI is calculated as a percentage of total income (e.g. 5% of €40,000).
D. Calculate Universal Social Charge	Universal Social Charge (USC) is levied at different rates at different thresholds. For example: • 2% of first €10,000 of income • 4% on income between €10,000 and €16,000 • 7% on income over €16,000
E. Calculate Net Income	Gross income – minus PAYE income tax due – minus employee's PRSI – minus Universal Social Charge _____ **= Net Income**

OL Short Q8

HL Short Q8

Tax Case Study 1: Jenny O'Connor starts working at Wave Technologies

Jenny O'Connor recently started work as a part-time scientist with Wave Technologies. Her starting salary will be €16,000 per annum. After filling out **Form P12A**, both Jenny and her employer received a **Notice of Tax Credits** from the **Revenue Commissioners**.

Gross Pay	€16,000
PAYE Standard rate of tax	20%
PAYE Higher rate of tax	40%
PAYE Standard rate cut-off point	€20,000
Tax credits	€1,700
PRSI	5%
USC on first €10,000	2%
USC on income between €10,000 and €16,000	4%
USC on income over €16,000	7%

A. Gross Income		**€16,000**

B. Calculate PAYE Income Tax

	€16,000 @ 20%	€3,200
	€0 @ 40%	0
	Gross PAYE Tax =	**€3,200**
	Less Tax Credits	€1,700
	Net PAYE Tax Payable	**€1,500**

C. Calculate Employee's PRSI

	PRSI (5% of €16,000)	**€800**

D. Calculate Universal Social Charge (USC)

	2% of first €10,000	€200
	4% of income between €10,000 and €16,000 (4% of €6,000)	€240
	7% of income over €16,000 (7% of €0)	0
	Total USC Payable	**€440**

E. Calculate Net Income

	Gross Income (A)	**€16,000**
	Minus PAYE Income Tax (B)	- €1,500
	Minus Employee's PRSI (C)	- €800
	Minus Universal Social Charge (D)	- €440
	Total Deductions (B+C+D)	-€2,740
	Net Income	**€13,260**

Tax Case Study 2: Jenny O'Connor gets a pay rise

Jenny has worked hard and secured promotion to a full-time job and a pay increase with Wave Technologies. Her new salary has pushed her over the PAYE standard rate cut off point and a proportion of her extra earnings will now be taxed at the higher rate of tax. The Universal Social Charge thresholds have also been changed by the government.

Gross Pay	€32,000
PAYE Standard rate of tax	20%
PAYE Higher rate of tax	40%
PAYE Standard rate cut-off point	€20,000
Tax Credits	€2,000
PRSI	5%
USC on first €10,000	2%
USC on income between €10,000 and €18,000	4%
USC on income over €18,000	7%

A. Gross Income €32,000

B. Calculate PAYE Income Tax
€20,000 @ 20%	€4,000
€12,000 @ 40%	€4,800
Gross PAYE Tax =	**€8,800**
Less Tax Credits	€2,000
Net PAYE Tax Payable	**€6,800**

C. Calculate Employee's PRSI
PRSI (5% of €32,000) **€1,600**

D. Calculate Universal Social Charge (USC)
2% of first €10,000	€200
4% of income between €10,000 and €18,000 (4% of €8,000)	€320
7% of income over €18,000 (7% of €14,000)	€980
Total USC Payable	**€1,500**

E. Calculate Net Income
Gross Income (A)		**€32,000**
Minus PAYE Income Tax (B)	€6,800	
Minus Employee's PRSI (C)	€1,600	
Minus Universal Social Charge (D)	€1,500	
Total Deductions (B+C+D)		**€9,900**
Net Income		**€22,100**

Tax Case Study 3: Jenny's Manager

Jenny's manager is the head of research and development with Wave Technologies Limited. He is a highly experienced scientist and earns €90,000 per annum.

Gross Pay	€90,000
PAYE Standard rate of tax	20%
PAYE Higher rate of tax	40%
PAYE Standard rate cut-off point	€20,000
Tax Credits	€2,000
PRSI	5%
USC on first €10,000	2%
USC on income between €10,000 and €18,000	4%
USC on income over €18,000	7%

A. Gross Income		**€90,000**

B. Calculate PAYE Income Tax

€20,000 @ 20%	€4,000	
€70,000 @ 40%	€28,000	
Gross PAYE Tax =	**€32,000**	
Less Tax Credits	€2,000	
Net PAYE Tax Payable	**€30,000**	

C. Calculate Employee's PRSI

PRSI (5% of €90,000)	**€4,500**

D. Calculate Universal Social Charge (USC)

2% of first €10,000	€200
4% of income between €10,000 and €18,000 (4% of €8,000)	€320
7% of income over €18,000 (7% of €72,000)	€5,040
Total USC Payable	**€5,560**

E. Calculate Net Income

Gross Income (A)		**€90,000**
Minus PAYE Income Tax (B)	€30,000	
Minus Employee's PRSI (C)	€4,500	
Minus Universal Social Charge (D)	€5,560	
Total Deductions (B+C+D)		€40,060
Net Income		**€49,940**

OL Short Q6, 7
OL Long Q12, 13, 14
HL Long Q6, 7

Recall and Review

1. Establish the following from the most recent government budget:
   (a) Current standard rate of taxation.
   (b) Current standard rate cut-off point.
   (c) Current higher rate of tax.
   (d) Name of a tax credit available to taxpayers.
   (e) Current rate of employee's PRSI.

14. What are the similarities and differences between business and household taxation?

Similarities	Differences
Both businesses and households must: • **Register** for tax with the tax office. • **Keep proper financial records** of incomes earned and taxes paid to ensure correct amount of tax is paid. • **Seek legal ways** of reducing their tax liabilities, such as claiming legitimate tax credits. • **Must co-operate** with the Revenue Commissioners to ensure the correct amount of tax is being paid. • Must consider timing of tax payments when managing their cash flows.	• **Different taxes** can apply to businesses and households. For example, only businesses pay corporation tax, while only households pay capital acquisitions tax. • **Different systems of collection are used.** For instance, self-employed business people pay income tax under the self-assessment system. Employee households pay income tax under the PAYE system. • **There are more tax allowances** (similar to tax credits) available for a business than a household. • **Businesses can claim VAT refunds**, but households cannot. • **Businesses act as unpaid tax collectors** for the government, collecting VAT, PAYE, PRSI and corporation taxes.

HL ABQ
HL Long Q9

Key Concepts & Business Terms

After studying this chapter the student should be able to explain the following key concepts and business terms:

1. Risk management
2. Insurance
3. Types of business insurance
4. Third-party motor insurance
5. Third-party, fire and theft motor insurance
6. Comprehensive motor insurance
7. Permanent health insurance
8. Key person insurance
9. Pay Related Social Insurance (PRSI)
10. Fidelity guarantee insurance
11. Public liability insurance
12. Product liability insurance
13. Employer's liability insurance
14. Consequential loss insurance
15. Types of household insurance
16. Life assurance
17. Insurance brokers
18. Insurance agents
19. Proposal form
20. Exposure unit
21. Loadings

22. No Claims Bonus
23. Cover note
24. Insurance policy
25. Insurance claim form
26. Principles of insurance
27. Insurable interest
28. Utmost good faith
29. Indemnity
30. Over-insurance
31. Under-insurance
32. Average clause rule
33. Contribution
34. Subrogation
35. Revenue Commissioners
36. Corporation tax
37. Value Added Tax (VAT)
38. Capital Gains Tax
39. Customs duties
40. Commercial rates
41. Employers' PRSI
42. Pay As You Earn (PAYE income tax)
43. Self-assessment income tax
44. Tax audit
45. Tax evasion
46. Tax avoidance
47. Employees' PRSI
48. Excise duties
49. Universal Social Charge
50. Capital gains tax
51. Capital Acquisitions Tax
52. DIRT
53. Operation of the PAYE system
54. Standard rate of tax
55. Higher rate of tax
56. Tax credit
57. Form P12A
58. Notice of Tax Credits
59. Form P60
60. Form P21 (Balancing Statement)
61. Form P45
62. Form P35
63. Calculating income tax
64. Gross income
65. Benefits-in-kind
66. Gross tax
67. Net income

useful websites

www.iif.ie (Irish Insurance Federation)
www.cdfoods.com
www.vikingsplash.ie
www.revenue.ie

Leaving Certificate Practice Questions

Ordinary Level

Ordinary Level – Section 1 – Short Questions (10 marks each)

1. List **three** types of insurance relevant to business.
2. Outline the purposes of the following forms used in insurance:
    (a) proposal form,
    (b) claim form and
    (c) policy. [LCQ]
3. Name **three** principles of insurance.
4. Name **three** taxes paid by a business. [LCQ]
5. What do the letters (a) DIRT and (b) PRSI stand for? [LCQ]
6. Distinguish between an employee's gross pay and net pay. (10 marks) [LCQ]
7. Calculate Jim's annual net take-home pay from the following figures. [LCQ]

    Yearly gross pay €14,000   Total tax credits €2,000

    Rate of PAYE 24%   PRSI 6.75%
8. Explain what is meant by 'benefits-in-kind'. [LCQ]
9. Outline what the following taxation forms are for: (a) P45 and (b) P60. [LCQ]
10. What is corporation tax?
11. A limited company has a taxable profit of €68,400. Tax is charged at a rate of 12.5%. Calculate the amount of tax to be paid (show your workings). [LCQ]
12. List **three** types of taxation paid by households.

Ordinary Level – Section 2 – Long Questions

1. Identify the main types of insurance available for a business. (20 marks)
2. State and explain **three** principles of insurance. (20 marks) [LCQ]
3. Describe the steps involved in taking out insurance cover. (15 marks)
4. Patricia Quinlan runs her own hairdressing business, Hair Affair, in a busy town in County Galway. She employs two full-time and two part-time staff. She owns her own premises, which is valued at €250,000 and insured for €200,000. A fire on the premises has caused extensive damage. Patricia submits a claim to the insurance company for €150,000.
    (a) Name the insurance rule that applies in this situation. (5 marks) [LCQ]
    (b) Calculate the amount of compensation that Patricia will receive from the insurance company. Show your workings. (5 marks) [LCQ]
    (c) Apart from fire insurance, name **three** other types of insurance that Patricia should take out for her business. (15 marks) [LCQ]
5. List **four** types of insurance you would recommend a householder to take out. Give reasons for your answer. (20 marks)
6. Describe the factors that would affect the amount of premium to be charged in house insurance. (15 marks) [LCQ]
7. Explain the relationship between premium and risk in insurance. Give an example to illustrate your answer. (15 marks) [LCQ]
8. Explain what is meant by 'utmost good faith'. (25 marks) [LCQ]

9. A house and contents were valued at €100,000 and the owner insured them for €80,000. A fire caused €2,000 of damage to the contents. Calculate the compensation to be paid to the owner. Show your workings. (15 marks) [LCQ]

10. Discuss the similarities and differences between insurance for households and businesses. (20 marks)

11. Outline the main types of taxes that apply to households and private individuals. (20 marks)

12. Lorraine Smith has an annual income of €35,000, is entitled to tax credits of €4,000 and pays PAYE tax at a rate of 25% and PRSI at 7%. Calculate her net income. (15 marks)

13. Calculate Jim's annual net take-home pay from the following figures: Annual gross pay €40,000; Total income tax credits entitlements €5,000; Standard rate of PAYE tax 25%, Higher rate of PAYE tax 45%; Standard cut-off point for PAYE tax is €30,000; PRSI is charged at 8%. (20 marks)

14. Calculate Roisin's annual net take-home pay from the following figures: Annual gross pay €50,000; Total tax credits €4,000; Standard rate of PAYE tax 25%; Higher rate of PAYE tax 45%; Standard cut-off point for PAYE tax of €30,000; PRSI is charged at 8%; Universal Social Charge of 2% on first €10,000; Universal Social Charge of 4% on earnings between €10,000 and €20,000; Universal Social Charge of 7% on earnings over €20,000. (25 marks)

15. Identify **two** taxes that an entrepreneur will have to pay when running a business. Explain **one** of them. (15 marks) [LCQ]

Higher Level – Section 1 – Short Questions (10 marks each)

1. Explain the term 'employer's liability insurance'.
2. Distinguish between the following types of insurance:
   (a) public liability,
   (b) fidelity guarantee,
   (c) consequential loss.
3. Distinguish between 'risk management' and 'time management'. Explain your answer in **one** sentence. [LCQ]
4. Differentiate between indemnity and insurable interest. Illustrate your answer. [LCQ]
5. Distinguish between the insurance principles (a) utmost good faith and (b) indemnity. [LCQ]
6. Which principle of insurance do you feel is the most important one? Explain why. [LCQ]
7. A house worth €400,000 is insured for €300,000. What compensation would the owners receive for water damage to the bathroom amounting to €20,000?
8. Distinguish between gross profit and gross pay. [LCQ]

Taste Budz

Taste Budz is a popular take-away and sit-down fast-food restaurant serving fish and chips, kebabs and burgers. Located in Cork on the banks of the River Lee, the spread of rival large fast-food chain outlets has increased the competitive pressure on the business. However, being located next door to a petrol filling station on a very busy road seems to attract a lot of extra customers to the take-away.

Nevertheless, Sam Keogh, the owner, is thinking of entering the home delivery market, using his two sons as motorbike delivery couriers. He knows he needs to keep costs down to protect his modest profit margins. To save money he does not have any smoke alarms or sprinkler system installed. He currently employs five part-time staff for whom he must pay employer's PRSI.

Sam pays income tax on his earnings from the restaurant under the self-assessment system. He also adds VAT of 13.5% to all his sales, which he passes on to the Revenue Commissioners.

Sam has just received a renewal notice from his insurance company. His premises and contents are valued at €500,000, but to help control his expenses Sam is considering insuring his premises for just €300,000 to reduce his premium and business costs.

1. Identify the risks and types of insurance policies that are relevant to Taste Budz. Refer to the text in your answer. (20 marks)
2. Evaluate the implications for Sam if he goes ahead and reduces the insured value on his premises to €300,000. (30 marks)
3. Analyse the impact that different taxes can have on Taste Budz. (30 marks)

Higher Level – Section 2 – Long Questions

1. Describe what is meant by risk management. Illustrate a method that a business could use to reduce risks to the business. (20 marks) [LCQ]
2. Describe the steps a business can take to reduce its risk exposure and its insurance premiums. (20 marks)
3. Explain **three** important principles of insurance. (20 marks) [LCQ]
4. Distinguish between insurance for a household and for a business. (10 marks) [LCQ]

5. Watertight Ltd is a family-run plumbing and central-heating business. It has a parts outlet that sells to the public and to the trade. It employs three qualified plumbers who work throughout the area using the enterprise's vans. Describe the various types of taxes and types of insurance with which you would expect Watertight Ltd to be familiar. Give reasons for your choice. (20 marks) [LCQ]

6. Simon Blake is single. He has just graduated from college with a certificate in business and has started a job in a hotel. Calculate Simon's net salary from the following information: His current salary will be €25,000; He is entitled to tax credits amounting to €2,100; The first €10,000 of his salary is subject to PAYE tax @ 25%; The remainder of his salary is subject to PAYE tax @ 40%; PRSI is levied @ 6% of total income; Universal Social Charge of 2% on first €10,000 of income; Universal Social Charge of 4% on income between €10,000 and €16,000; Universal Social Charge of 7% on any income over €16,000. (20 marks)

7. Calculate the average net take-home pay per month for Dr. Dervla May from the following figures: Annual gross pay is €60,000; Entitled to total tax credits of €4,000; PAYE income tax is deducted at 20% on the first €38,000 and at 40% on the balance; PRSI is charged at 5%. Universal Social Charge of 2% on first €12,000 of income; Universal Social Charge of 4% on income between €12,000 and €18,000; Universal Social Charge of 7% on any income over €18,000. (20 marks)

8. Analyse the effects that collecting and paying tax can have on a business. (20 marks)

9. 'Managing a household is similar to managing a business enterprise, in the areas of insurance and taxation.' In your opinion, is this statement valid? Explain your answer. (30 marks)

Chapter 12
Managing Business & Household Finance

Key Study Questions

Case Study

The Olive Tree Restaurant

Oliver Ramsey is the owner and head chef in The Olive Tree Restaurant. The restaurant is very successful, not just because of Oliver's reputation as a great cook, but also because he is very good at budgeting and managing the finances of the business. According to Oliver, the most important financial rule of every business should be 'Thou shalt not run out of money!'.

Marie Doyle started work as a trainee chef with The Olive Tree restaurant six months ago. 'At the beginning I thought it was great,' says Marie. 'For the first time in my life I was earning some serious money. The problem was that I was spending the money as fast as I was earning it. I was paid every Friday but by Wednesday of the following week I was often broke. Things had to change or I was not going to be able to afford to go on holidays, buy a house or even open my own restaurant some day.' Now that she is working and earning an income, Marie has learnt the importance of managing her personal finances carefully.

Businesses like The Olive Tree need money to buy stock, equipment and premises. Householders, like Marie Doyle, need money to pay for things like food, transport and clothing. Both businesses and households must manage their money properly so that they can afford to pay for the things they need. To help them manage their finances, both must budget carefully and take out suitable loans when needed.

1. What is budgeting?

> **Cashflow is the amount of money flowing in and out of a business or household over a period of time.**

Both households and businesses need to manage their finances carefully and ensure that they have enough cash flowing in (cash inflows) to meet their spending needs (cash outflows). **Cashflow** *is the difference between the money flowing in and the money flowing out of a business or household.*

A **cashflow forecast (or budget)** *is a document showing the planned flows of money in and out of a business or household over a certain period of time.* It can be used to predict the size of a business's or household's income and expenditure and when they are likely to occur.

2. How do businesses budget?

Businesses like The Olive Tree restaurant use cashflow forecasts to predict the amount and timing of income and expenditure and plan how best to manage their finances. If money flows into the business faster than it goes out, then it has a **positive cashflow.** A positive cashflow is a good thing because it means that a business is generating enough cash to be able to pay all its expenses, survive and grow. A positive cashflow is very important for every business.

However, if cash is flowing out of a business faster than it is coming in, then the firm will run out of cash and will need to borrow (or else it will go bankrupt). This is called **negative cashflow.** When this occurs a business is operating beyond its means. To rectify this, spending needs to be controlled, often by cutting back on non-essential (discretionary) expenditure.

Business cashflow budget for The Olive Tree restaurant (January–March)

		Jan	Feb	Mar	Total
A	Total receipts (e.g. income from sales)	14,500	12,500	15,500	42,500
B	Total payments (e.g. purchasing stock, wages, equipment)	19,000	10,500	12,500	42,000
	Net monthly cashflow (A–B)	(4,500)	2,000	3,000	
	Opening cash (at beginning of every month	3,000	(1,500)	500	
	Closing cash (at end of every month)	(1,500)	500	3,500	

Receipts are the expected sources of finance in the business.

Payments are the uses to which the finance will be put.

Predicted negative monthly cashflow in January of -€4,500.

Predicted closing cash balance at the end of February of €500.

Predicted positive monthly cashflow in February of €2000.

The benefits of cashflow forecasts

✳ **Assists financial planning** by helping to predict the size and timing of future cash flows. Cashflow forecasts can act as an **early warning system** of possible future cash shortages. They can also indicate when cash flow will be positive.

✳ **Financial control:** By predicting cash shortages, cashflow forecasts allow businesses and households to manage their spending. They can identify when and where cutbacks or savings need to be made, when savings need to be dipped into or a loan taken out. By predicting when cash flow will be positive and by how much, it can indicate the most suitable times to plan spending.

✳ **Loan requirements:** For any enterprise, cashflow forecasts can show how much loan finance will be needed to keep a business afloat. Such forecasts will reassure banks and investors that a business is being well managed.

OL Short Q1, 2
OL Long Q7

3. How do households budget?

As for businesses, individuals can also benefit from careful budgeting and cashflow management. Good household financial management aims to have a **positive cashflow,** *with income exceeding payments.* If a household has a negative cashflow and is living beyond its means, it may be necessary to rely on household savings or, as a last resort, take out a loan for the months when there is not enough cash to cover household expenses.

Household cashflow forecast for Marie Doyle (January–June)

		Jan	Feb	Mar	Apr	May	Jun	Total
A	Income (e.g. wages, dividends from investments, social welfare payments, credit union loan)	1,300	1,800	1,300	1,300	1,300	1,300	8,300
B	Payments (e.g. mortgage repayments, car loan repayments, telephone, food, clothing, holidays etc.)	830	1,030	2,065	1,045	1,130	1,030	7,130
C	Net monthly cashflow (A – B)	470	770	(765)	255	170	270	
C	Opening cash	200	670	1,440	675	930	1,100	
E	Closing cash	670	1,440	675	930	1,100	1,370	

Expected sources of finance for the household.

Expected sources of expenditure for the household.

Positive cashflow predicted in January. Income of €1,300 exceeds payments of €830 by €470.

Negative cashflow in March with €765 more money predicted to go out than come in.

OL Short Q3
OL Long Q1

HL Long Q1, 3

4. What are the elements of an effective cashflow forecast?

Seasonal products like mince pies generate uneven cashflow.

When reading cashflow forecasts, it is important to be aware of the following points:

★ **Is it realistic?** Cashflow forecasts should be as realistic as possible. If in doubt, predicted income should be underestimated and predicted expenses should be overestimated. Reserve finances should be available in the form of savings or loan facilities.

★ **Are there seasonal factors?** Does the cashflow forecast take into account any seasonal highs and lows in sales? For example, retailing tends to be very busy around Christmas but dips during the summer. In a household, light and heating bills are usually higher during the winter but fall during the summer months.

★ **Credit?** It is not unusual for businesses to give debtors (customers who owe the business money) a 60-day period of credit before they have to pay up. Cashflow forecasts should take into account possible delays in payment for credit sales. For households, employees need to be prepared for a delay between starting a new job and receiving their first pay packet, which may be a month later.

★ **What about bad debts?** Businesses that allow credit sales should make realistic provision for customers who may 'go bad'. **Bad debts** *are debtors (people who owe you money) who do not pay their bills at all.* This is money that is lost to the business.

★ **Are taxes included?** Business cashflow is also affected by having to collect and pay taxes such as PAYE, PRSI and VAT. Businesses must regularly pay these taxes to the State or else face heavy fines.

HL Short Q1
HL Long Q2

Case Study

A CRUMBY SUCCESS

Bernard Coyle used to work for a bakery, delivering bread to shops. Customers kept asking him if he could supply breadcrumbs as well as bread to use as stuffing and ingredients in other dishes.

Bernard reported this customer feedback to his employers but they were not interested in selling breadcrumbs. After doing some careful **market research**, he decided to leave his job and set up his own business making breadcrumbs.

Running his own business meant that Bernard had to understand the different types of finance available. To get started, he used some **equity finance** in the form of his own savings. He also took out a loan of €157,000 from the bank to set up premises and to buy equipment. He then began trading under the brand name Mr Crumb, supplying plain and mixed varieties of fresh breadcrumbs.

To ensure he had enough finance to meet his monthly **cashflow** needs, Bernard arranged an **overdraft** of €26,000 from the bank.

After a slow start, sales began to take off and he attracted long-term **venture capital** funding from **Enterprise Ireland** of over €1 million in return for shares in the business. This long-term investment was used to expand the business.

As the business grew, **retained earnings** were used to pay off the original **bank loans** that he had used to buy equipment. Bernard was then able to use these **assets** as **security** to get further finance if necessary. He also used **invoice discounting** to raise extra cash from time to time.

The County Westmeath-based business has become so successful that Bernard has now expanded into producing other food products such as gravies, garlic breads and desserts.

5. What are the main sources of finance for households and businesses?

Households need finance to pay their bills. A household, like Marie Doyle's, may need €200 finance to pay an electricity bill while a business, such as the Olive Tree and Mr Crumb, may need €100,000 to purchase new equipment. The right source of finance matches the use for which it is needed. Sources of finance for households and businesses can be:

OL Short Q4, 5

HL Short Q2

Short term:	should be repaid within **one year**
Medium term:	should be repaid within **one to five years**
Long term:	does not need to be repaid for **at least five years**

	Household	Business
Short-term finance	• Credit purchases (credit cards) • Unpaid bills and expenses • Bank overdraft (on current accounts)	• Credit purchases (trade credit) • Accrued expenses • Bank overdraft (on current accounts) • Factoring debts • Invoice discounting
Uses of short-term finance	Regular bills such as food, electricity, telephone, clothing and similar day-to-day household expenses.	Regular bills such as ESB, rent, wages, purchasing stock, etc.
Medium-term finance	• Hire purchase • Leasing • Term loan	• Hire purchase • Leasing • Term loan
Uses of medium-term finance	Expensive items such as furniture, appliances, cars and home improvements.	Expensive assets such as equipment, vans and other machinery.
Long-term finance	• Home mortgages • Savings	• Owner's capital (equity) • Retained earnings • State grants • Debentures/long-term loans • Sale and leaseback
Uses of long-term finance	• Buy a house • Build an extension	• Purchase or build new premises • Take over another business • Business expansion

6. How should a source of finance be selected?

Both businesses and households can use the same criteria when choosing a source of finance:

❖ **Purpose:** The source of finance should match the use for which it is needed. For instance, if finance is needed for a long-term purpose, then a long-term source of finance should be used.

❖ **Amount:** Sources of finance can vary considerably in terms of the amount available. For example, an overdraft may yield just €1,000 while a personal loan could provide €15,000. The source of finance used should be able to provide the amount of finance required. More expensive items may require a medium- or long-term source of finance depending on how long it will take to repay the finance.

❖ **Cost:** Households, like businesses, should try to obtain the cheapest source of finance, i.e. the one with the lowest rate of interest. **APR (Annual Percentage Rate)** *is a standard measure of the interest charges on loans, hire purchase deals and other credit arrangements. It allows households to compare the true cost of credit from different sources.* Lenders are legally required to quote the APR on loans so that potential borrowers can make informed financial decisions. Some sources of finance are tax deductible (e.g. interest on loans) while others are not (e.g. dividends paid on share capital).

❖ **Control:** If loan repayments cannot be kept up, some sources of finance can mean loss of control over personal or household assets which have been used as security. Security refers to an asset that can be sold by the lender to raise the funds to pay back the loan if the borrower is unable to do so.

> **Example:** Failure to keep up hire purchase payments on a car will result in it being repossessed (taken back). Failure to repay a mortgage can mean a home is repossessed by the bank or building society.

❖ **Risk:** The effect of repayments on the size and timing of cash flow is important. A household should ensure that it can spread its repayments over time to avoid wild swings between positive and negative weekly/monthly household cash flows.

7. What are the main sources of short-term finance for households and businesses?

Credit purchases and trade credit (Household and Business)

Both households and businesses can buy goods and services on credit and pay for them later.

> **Example:** Households can buy furniture with a credit card and not have to pay for it until a month or so later. For businesses such as The Olive Tree and Mr Crumb, it is very common to get trade credit for 30 or 60 days from suppliers.

> **Sources of short-term business finance:**
> - **Trade credit and credit cards**
> - **Accrued expenses**
> - **Overdrafts**
> - **Factoring debts**
> - **Invoice discounting**

In business, **trade credit** *means receiving goods from suppliers now but paying for them later.* During this period of time, a business can use the money owed for other purposes, such as paying other bills that are more urgent. However, suppliers usually offer discounts to encourage prompt payment and may charge interest for late payment.

✳ **Amount** available from trade credit can vary depending on the size of the purchases.

✳ **Cost:** Using trade credit can mean missing out on the discounts available for paying cash up front. A firm may be given a poor credit rating if it is frequently late in paying debts. This can make it more difficult to obtain credit in future.

* **Control:** No security is required, but suppliers can retain title (ownership) to the goods until payment is made. Control of the household or business is unaffected unless debts remain unpaid.

* **Risk:** Low risk but the reputation of the business may be damaged with suppliers if it is too slow paying its bills. A bad reputation can mean that suppliers will stop selling on credit to a business.

Unpaid expenses / accrued expenses (Household and Business)

> **When choosing a source of finance consider:**
> - **Purpose/use**
> - **Amount available**
> - **Cost**
> - **Control implications**

Both businesses and households can delay paying some bills, such as electricity, telephone or gas bills, until absolutely necessary. This frees up money to be spent on other items. However, both households and businesses must be careful that they do not delay excessively or the supplier may be forced to cut off supplies until their bills have been paid. **Accrued expenses** *means delaying payment of bills and using the money to pay a more urgent expense.* As a source of finance, accruing expenses can be **unfair** to other businesses.

* **Amounts** available from this source are normally relatively small.

* **Cost:** No interest is paid, but households and businesses may lose out on cash discounts for prompt payment.

* **Control:** Security is not required and control of the household or business is unaffected in the short term.

* **Risk:** A household or business will get a bad reputation for not paying bills or settling debts on time.

Bank overdrafts (Household and Business)

Both households and businesses have current accounts. **Overdrafts** *are short-term bank loans giving a current-account holder permission to pay out sums greater than they actually have in their current account.* The maximum amount of such loans must be agreed in advance with the bank.

❖ **Amount** available varies according to the assets or cashflow of the household or business.

❖ **Cost:** Interest is charged on a daily basis on the amount borrowed, with rates depending on the credit rating of the household or business. A fee may be charged for the overdraft facility.

❖ **Control:** Often security is not required.

❖ **Risk:** The bank can demand repayment at any time.

Factoring debts (Business only)

Factoring *means selling the right to collect payment from your debtors to a factoring (debt-collecting) firm.*

> **Example:** If Mr Crumb is owed €100,000, it might sell the debts to a factoring firm for €80,000. The downside of losing out on €20,000 is offset by avoiding the expense and hassle of trying to collect payment, as well as eliminating the risk of bad debts.

* **Amount:** Depending on the size of your debtors, large sums of finance can be raised quickly. However, factoring firms usually prefer to deal with large firms.
* **Cost:** Factoring can be expensive as factoring firms will only pay you a percentage of the full value of your debts.
* **Control:** No loss of control of the business.
* **Risk:** A firm known to be factoring its debts may be seen as desperate for cash and this could damage their reputation and credit status.

Invoice discounting (Business only)

Another source of finance only available to businesses is invoice discounting. **Invoice discounting** *is when a business gets a loan from a bank to the value of some percentage (e.g. 80%) of the amount owed to the business by its customers (debtors).* When these customers (debtors) settle their bills, the money is used to repay the bank.

* **Amount:** Large amounts may be available depending on the size of a firm's debtors. This can help smooth out a firm's cashflow.
* **Cost:** Banks charge expensive fees for this service.
* **Control:** Unlike factoring, the business retains full ownership of the debts.
* **Risk:** Unlike factoring, there is no risk to the reputation of the business.

> **Example:** Mr Crumb occasionally uses invoice discounting to raise finance for the business.

> OL Short Q7
> OL Long Q4
>
> HL Short Q3, 4, 5
> HL Long Q4

8. What are the main sources of medium-term finance for households and businesses?

Hire purchase (Household and Business)

> **Sources of medium-term business finance:**
> * **Hire purchase**
> * **Leasing**
> * **Term loans**

Hire purchase (HP) *allows a household or a business to buy an asset such as a car or equipment by paying for it in instalments over a period of time.* The asset can be used immediately but full ownership only passes to the purchaser when it is fully paid for.

* **Amount:** Expensive equipment (e.g. delivery trucks) can be purchased on hire purchase.
* **Cost:** The final overall cost of the asset will be higher than if the item was bought for cash. However, for businesses, hire purchase costs are a legitimate business expense and can be offset against tax.
* **Control:** No security is required for purchasing, but the asset cannot be used as security for any loans until fully paid for.
* **Risk:** By the time the item is fully paid for and ownership passes to the firm, it may have become obsolete or depreciated considerably in value.

Leasing (Household and Business)

Leasing *means renting an item, such as a vehicle or a piece of equipment, for an agreed number of years.* When the lease is up, the item is returned to the lessor (leaseholder).

* **Amount:** Expensive assets can be acquired quickly for use by a household or business.

✳ **Cost:** Leasing costs more than a cash purchase but cashflow is improved as money is not tied up in an asset. Businesses can offset leasing costs against tax.

✳ **Control:** No security is required as the leasing company retains ownership of the asset. However, the household or business taking out the lease must sign a contract agreeing to lease the asset for a minimum period of time.

✳ **Risk:** Since you don't own it, you do not have to worry about long-term obsolescence or depreciation in value of the asset.

Term loans (Household and Business)

A **term loan** *is a medium-term loan from a financial institution (e.g. bank, credit union) repaid in monthly instalments over a number of years.* The conditions of the loan are customised to meet the needs of the household or business such as the duration, interest charged, timing of interest payments and security provided. For reliable, low-risk households or well-run businesses with a proven ability to repay, term loans are generally easy to negotiate. Term loans are available from banks, building societies and credit unions.

◆ **Amount:** Large amounts of finance can be borrowed.

◆ **Cost:** Interest paid is usually lower than for overdrafts. The better the borrower's credit status and hence the lower the risk to the lender, the lower the interest charged. While the interest paid on a loan is tax-deductible for businesses, variable interest rates mean that the repayments can go up as well as down.

◆ **Control:** Banks may look for some asset to be used as security (collateral) in the event of non-repayment. Alternatively, a bank may seek personal guarantees from the owners of a business that the sums involved will be repaid.

◆ **Risk:** Failure to repay can damage a firm's credit rating and reputation. However, the duration of the loan can be customised to suit the needs of individual borrowers in terms of repayment times. Since repayments amounts are clearly set out in the beginning, they can be budgeted for in advance.

OL Short Q6, 8

9. What are the main sources of long-term finance for households and businesses?

Sources of long-term business finance:
- **Retained earnings**
- **Owner's capital**
- **Venture capital**
- **Grants**
- **Long-term loans/ debentures**
- **Sale and leaseback**

Mortgages (Household and Business)

Mortgages *are loans used to finance the purchase of a house or other property.* They are available from banks and building societies. Before taking out a mortgage, a household or business will have to calculate the implications of the monthly mortgage repayments on their monthly cashflow.

★ **Amount:** Large amounts of finance can be borrowed.

★ **Cost:** The precise rate of interest charged depends on the borrower's credit status. The lower the risk to the lender, the lower the interest charged.

★ **Control:** The security for a mortgage will usually be the deeds of ownership to a property.

★ **Risk:** Failure to repay can result in repossession of the property by the lender. However, the duration of a mortgage can be customised to suit the needs of individual borrowers.

Savings (Household) and retained earnings (Business)

Savings are a major source of finance for most individuals and households, usually through savings accounts with banks, building societies, An Post or credit unions. **Deposit (savings) accounts** *pay savers interest on the money saved*. The rate of interest is affected by the amount saved and the length of time it is left on deposit. Household savings can be used for large expenditures such as TVs, computers, holidays or new homes.

For profitable businesses like The Olive Tree, the steady accumulation of profits can result in large sums of money being available for investing in long-term development. **Retained earnings** (also known as **reserves**) *refer to profits retained in a business to allow it to expand in the future*. Also known as 'ploughing back profits', they are usually the ideal source of long-term finance for any firm.

- ❖ **Amounts** available can be large if the firm has retained large amounts of profit.
- ❖ **Cost:** No costs involved.
- ❖ **Control:** No loss of control over any part of the business.
- ❖ **Risk:** No risk to the households or businesses.

Owner's capital / equity (Business only)

Owner's capital (equity) *is finance brought into a business by the owner(s)*. Additional equity finance can be brought into the business through an entrepreneur's personal savings, bringing in a new partner or selling shares in a limited company.

- ✳ **Owner(s)' personal savings:** This is a typical source of finance for entrepreneurs starting a new business. It can be obtained from cash savings, redundancy payments or the sale of personal assets such as a car or house.

- ✳ **Bringing a partner** (or partners) with money into a business can contribute finance and additional skills to a business.

- ✳ **Selling shares:** If the business is set up as a limited company, then it can sell shares in the business to outsiders to raise funding.

Example: The Mazda Motor Company needed €1 billion in long-term finance to develop more fuel-efficient, eco-friendly cars. The company did not want to take out a huge loan that would have to be repaid with interest regardless of the firm's profitability. Instead, Mazda decided to raise €750 million by selling shares in the company to investors. The remaining €250 million that was needed was sourced from the company's retained earnings.

- ♦ **Amount:** Personal savings are often insufficient to finance a business but are important to show lenders that the entrepreneur is committed to the new business venture. Bringing in new partners or selling shares in a company may raise large sums of money.

- ♦ **Cost:** If no profits are made, then no interest or dividend payments have to be made to shareholders. If the enterprise is successful, any partners or shareholders in the business are entitled to a share of the profits.

- ◆ **Control:** Control over the business will have to be shared if new partners or shareholders are brought in.
- ◆ **Risk:** No risk to the business but if the business fails, the money may also be lost.

Venture Capital

If it is a potentially high-growth business, then venture capital investors may be interested in buying a stake. **Venture capitalists** *are investors who buy shares in small- and medium-sized enterprises that have strong growth potential.* In exchange for their investment and management expertise, venture capitalists will want a share of the ownership. They will also want to be represented on the board of directors so that they have a say in how the business is run and to protect their investment. *Once the business has become successful, these investors will try to sell their shares at a profit.* The entrepreneur benefits from a source of finance that does not require repayment or interest but must share profits and some control of the business.

> Example: Enterprise Ireland gave financial support to help Mr Crumb expand by making a venture capital investment in the business.

State grants (Business only)

A **grant** *is essentially a free gift of money provided to a business to be used for a specific purpose.* There are **no interest or cash repayments** involved. However, **conditions** are usually attached, such as what the money can be used for and the need to keep proof of expenditure.

> Example: The main providers of grants to entrepreneurs in Ireland are Enterprise Ireland, IDA Ireland and county and city enterprise boards.

- ❖ **Amount:** Depending on the source and the purpose, grants can be quite large.
- ❖ **Cost:** There are no interest charges and usually no **dividend payments.**
- ❖ **Control:** There are usually strict rules concerning what the money may be spent on.
- ❖ **Risk:** There is little risk but, if the conditions of the grant are broken, then the grant may be reclaimed.

Debentures / long-term loans (Business only)

Debentures *are long-term fixed-interest loans secured on a valuable asset, such as premises.* The company must repay the annual interest regardless of the levels of profit or loss. The principal must also be repaid in full at a future date.

> Example: Suppose Mr Crumb takes out a €500,000 debenture loan @ 10% interest rate, dated 31 December 2025. He will pay: Annual interest payment of €50,000 until the year 2025. Principal of €500,000 payable in full in the year 2025.

Ulster Bank head office in Dublin. Like most banks, it provides debenture loans and mortgages to businesses.

* **Amount:** Very large sums are potentially available as long-term loans.
* **Cost:** A fixed-interest amount must be paid annually. Over the life of the debenture, this may prove very expensive if the money has not been put to good use in growing the business.
* **Control:** Security is usually required for a debenture loan from a bank.
* **Risk:** In the event of non-repayment, the asset used as security can be seized and sold off to settle the outstanding debt.

Sale and leaseback (Business only)

If a business owns a valuable property, it could consider raising money through a sale and leaseback arrangement. **Sale and leaseback** *is a contract to raise cash by selling a piece of property and simultaneously leasing it back on a long-term lease.* This provides an immediate lump sum without any disruption to the business premises.

Eircom raised funds from a sale and leaseback deal on its head office.

* **Amount:** Depending on the value of the asset, large sums can be raised.
* **Cost:** The cost involved is the cost of the annual lease.
* **Control:** The business loses the ownership and ultimate control of a valuable asset.
* **Risk:** No direct financial risk to the business.

Example: Eircom raised €180 million from the sale and leaseback deal that it negotiated on its head office. According to the contract, the buyer agreed to lease the building back to Eircom for €8 million per annum.

OL Short Q9, 10
OL Long Q2, 3, 6, 8

HL Short Q6
HL Long Q5, 6

Case Study

Financing The Olive Tree

Reviewing his **cashflow forecast**, Oliver Ramsey has observed that The Olive Tree's **cashflow** is strongest during the summer, autumn and winter months but weakest in springtime. Overall, the restaurant is doing very well and Oliver is thinking of expanding by opening a new branch. However, before he opens a new restaurant, he wants to upgrade the kitchen equipment in the current restaurant. This, he estimates, will cost approximately €30,000.

> ### Recall and Review
> 1. What advice would you give Oliver for managing his cashflow during the spring months?
> 2. What sources of finance would be suitable for opening a new restaurant?
> 3. How could Oliver finance the new kitchen equipment for The Olive Tree?

10. What will a bank look for before agreeing to provide a loan?

● **Amount and purpose of loan**

　★ **Amount required and duration:** The larger the amount and the longer the duration of the loan, the riskier it is for a bank.

　★ **The purpose of the loan:** The more productive and low-risk the purpose, the greater the likelihood of getting approval.

● **Character and creditworthiness of applicant**

　★ **Name, address** and **occupation** of the applicant and/or the **nature** of the business.

　★ **Good character** and **reputation**: For an individual, the bank may want to know how long you have lived at your address and how long you've been in your job. For a business, it will want to know how long it has been established and who owns it.

　★ **Creditworthiness** of applicant, including previous or other loans: An applicant with a good banking history will be viewed more favourably.

● **Capacity of applicant to repay**

　★ **Ability to repay,** by looking for evidence of an applicant's income or the profits of a business. For an individual, this could be a P60 form from the Revenue Commissioners showing a person's income for the past year. For a business, it will be a copy of its accounts certified by an auditor.

　★ **A business plan** if the loan is required for a business. This will need to be well prepared and researched to reassure the bank that the money is likely to be used wisely. If an entrepreneur is looking for the loan, a bank will be reassured if he/she is also prepared to contribute some of his/her own personal funds.

● **Collateral available**

OL Short Q12

HL Long Q7

　★ **Security (collateral)** that can be provided for the loan. The greater the value of the security, the lower the risk for the bank.

11. How can current accounts assist business and household financial management?

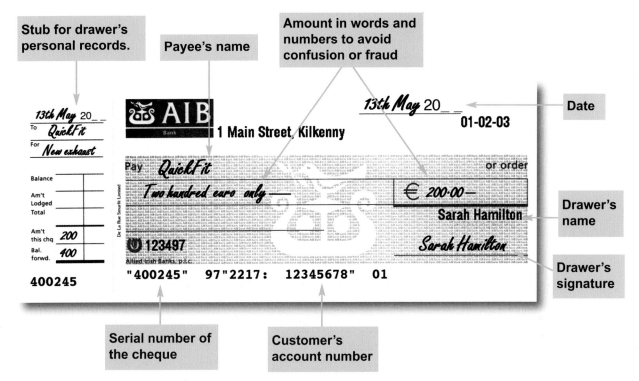

Stub for drawer's personal records.

Payee's name

Amount in words and numbers to avoid confusion or fraud

Date

Drawer's name

Drawer's signature

Serial number of the cheque

Customer's account number

Current accounts *allow households and businesses to withdraw money whenever they want, using chequebooks or ATM machines.* This makes them ideal for managing business or household cashflow. Although money in current accounts normally earns little or no interest, current accounts offer the following benefits:

♦ **Paypath system** for paying wages directly into an employee's current account. It is safer and more convenient than being paid by cash or cheque.

♦ **Chequebooks** allow payments to be made using cheques. **Cheques** *are notes to a bank asking them to pay money from your account to the person whose name is written on the cheque.*

♦ **Standing orders** *are an arrangement with the bank to pay a **fixed amount** out of your account at regular intervals to someone else's account.* They are very useful for regular payments such as car loan repayments.

♦ **Direct debits** *allow the automatic payment of **varying amounts** at regular intervals to someone else's account.* This is very useful for paying variable bills such as electricity and telephone bills.

♦ **ATM cards** *allow the holder to use ATM machines to access bank services such as cash withdrawals, lodgements, bill payments or to order a new chequebook or bank statement.*

♦ **Debit cards** *(also known as laser cards) allow the holder's account to be debited (deducted from) by the bank every time the card is used to purchase something.* The use of debit cards, along with credit cards, are part of the move towards a 'cashless society'. Debit cards have replaced the use of cheques in many shopping situations.

♦ **Overdrafts** *allow current-account holders to spend more money than they actually have in their account up to a pre-set limit.* This allows the account holder to borrow and repay in a flexible manner. However, interest is charged on all overdrawn amounts.

♦ A **bank statement** *is issued by a bank to a customer and lists all the transactions that have occurred in an account since the last statement was issued.* Anything that reduces the amount in an account (e.g. cheques written, withdrawals, bank charges, etc.) is listed as 'Debits'. Anything that increases the amount in the account (e.g. lodgements, interest added, etc.) is listed as 'Credits'.

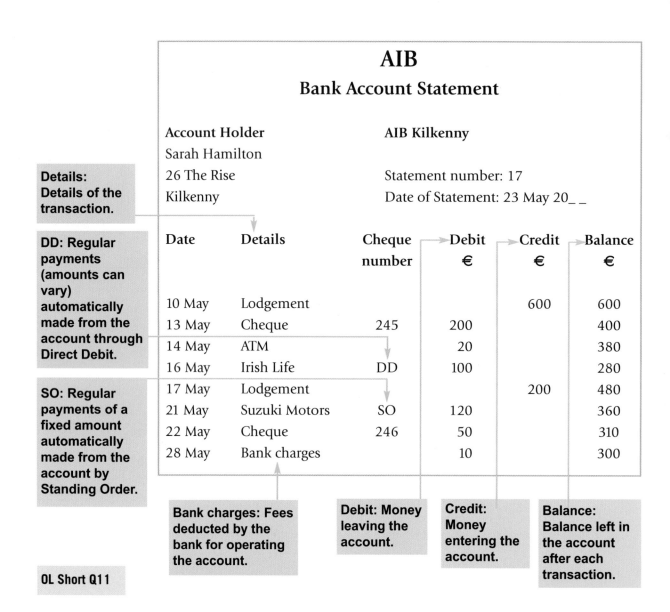

Details: Details of the transaction.

DD: Regular payments (amounts can vary) automatically made from the account through Direct Debit.

SO: Regular payments of a fixed amount automatically made from the account by Standing Order.

AIB
Bank Account Statement

Account Holder			AIB Kilkenny		
Sarah Hamilton					
26 The Rise			Statement number: 17		
Kilkenny			Date of Statement: 23 May 20_ _		

Date	Details	Cheque number	Debit €	Credit €	Balance €
10 May	Lodgement			600	600
13 May	Cheque	245	200		400
14 May	ATM		20		380
16 May	Irish Life	DD	100		280
17 May	Lodgement			200	480
21 May	Suzuki Motors	SO	120		360
22 May	Cheque	246	50		310
28 May	Bank charges		10		300

Bank charges: Fees deducted by the bank for operating the account.

Debit: Money leaving the account.

Credit: Money entering the account.

Balance: Balance left in the account after each transaction.

OL Short Q11

12. What are the similarities and differences between managing household and business finance?

Similarities	Differences
• Both businesses and households can budget using **cashflow forecasts**. • Both should take action to **deal with projected surpluses** (e.g. make investments) **or deficits** (e.g. take out a loan).	• Business **cashflow forecasts** can be **more complex** with potentially many different sources of income and payments. • Businesses finances usually deal in much **larger amounts** than households.

- They both need to **keep accurate financial records** and ensure correct amounts of taxes are paid.
- Businesses and households can **raise finance** from similar sources such as credit purchases, overdrafts, loans, hire purchase and leasing.
- Both can use financial services such as **current accounts**.

- Business cashflow forecasts should include regular payment of **VAT and other taxes** collected on behalf of the Revenue Commissioners.
- Businesses can access **additional sources of finance** not available to households (e.g. invoice discounting, debenture loans).

OL Long Q5, 9, 10

HL Short Q7, 8
HL ABQ
HL Long Q8

Key Concepts & Business Terms

After studying this chapter the student should be able to explain the following key concepts and business terms:

1. Cashflow
2. Cashflow forecast/budget
3. Positive cashflow
4. Negative cashflow
5. Bad debts
6. Selecting a source of finance
7. APR (Annual Percentage Rate)
8. Short-term sources of finance
9. Credit purchases
10. Trade credit
11. Accrued expenses
12. Overdraft
13. Factoring
14. Invoice discounting
15. Medium-term sources of finance
16. Hire purchase
17. Leasing
18. Term loan
19. Long-term sources of finance
20. Mortgages
21. Deposit (savings) accounts
22. Retained earnings
23. Owner's capital/equity
24. Venture capital
25. State grants
26. Long-term loans/debentures
27. Security
28. Sale and leaseback
29. Current accounts
30. Cheques
31. Standing orders
32. Direct debits
33. ATM cards
34. Laser cards
35. Bank statement

www.mabs.ie (Money Advice and Budgeting Service)
www.ibf.ie (Irish Banking Federation)
www.mrcrumb.co.uk

Leaving Certificate Practice Questions

Ordinary Level

Ordinary Level – Section 1 – Short Questions (10 Marks each)

1. Outline **two** reasons why a cashflow statement would be prepared. [LCQ]
2. If a business cashflow forecast predicts a negative cashflow in the future, identify **two** ways in which this problem could be solved.
3. Identify **two** items that could be included in the 'Receipts' section of a cashflow forecast.
4. Identify **two** sources of medium-term finance available to businesses.
5. List **two** sources of long-term finance available to businesses.
6. Explain the term 'leasing' and give **one** advantage of leasing. [LCQ]
7. List **two** sources of short-term finance available to households.
8. Identify **two** sources of medium-term finance available to households.
9. List **two** sources of long-term finance available to households.
10. Identify a suitable source of business finance for the following:
    (a) A truck costing €90,000 (b) a new factory costing €1.5 million.
11. Identify **three** services that are provided with current accounts.
12. List **four** pieces of information a business must supply when applying for a bank loan.

Ordinary Level – Section 2 – Long Questions

1. Identify **three** items that could be included in the 'Payments' section of a cashflow forecast. (15 marks)
2. Scandeck Ltd. has prepared the following cashflow forecast:

	July	Aug	Sept	Oct	Nov	Dec	Jan
	€	€	€	€	€	€	€
Total income	1,500	800	1,000	1,500	2,000	2,000	1,800
Total expenditure	1,400	1,400	1,400	1,400	1,500	1,500	1,400
Net monthly cashflow	100	(600)	(400)	100	500	500	400

   (a) According to the cashflow forecast, during what months will the business be facing a deficit? (15 marks)
   (b) Name and briefly outline **three** sources of finance the company could consider using to cover these deficits? (15 marks)
3. Outline the main sources of long-term finance for businesses. (20 marks)
4. Identify and explain **three** short-term sources of finance for a household. (20 marks)
5. Outline **two** sources of finance common to a business and a household and explain either of them. (15 marks) [LCQ]
6. When choosing a short-, medium- or long-term source of finance, an entrepreneur has been advised that she should always match the source of finance with the purpose for which the finance is to be used. Explain, using examples from each type of finance source, why this is so. (20 marks)
7. Describe the effects a rise in petrol prices would have on both a household and a business. (20 marks) [LCQ]

8. Identify and explain **three** sources of business finance that do not require interest payments. (15 marks)

9. Outline **two** sources of finance common to a household and a business and explain any **one** of them. (15 marks) [LCQ]

10. Outline some similarities in managing a household and managing a business. (15 marks) [LCQ]

Higher Level

Higher Level – Section 1 – Short Questions (10 Marks each)

1. List **three** questions that should be asked when interpreting a cashflow forecast.

2. Define short-term finance. [LCQ]

3. Identify **three** short-term sources of business finance.

4. Outline **two** short-term finance options available to an established manufacturing business. [LCQ]

5. Explain what is meant by 'invoice discounting'.

6. Identify **four** long-term sources of finance available to a business.

7. List **four** activities that are similar when managing a household and managing a business. [LCQ]

8. List **four** contrasting activities in managing a household and managing a business. [LCQ]

Higher Level – Section 2 – Applied Business Question

Elizabeth Fitzgerald, Solicitor

Elizabeth Fitzgerald is employed by a large firm of solicitors and is required to travel quite a lot getting to and from work. 'Running a car can be expensive and I'd like to buy a more fuel-efficient model than I have at the moment,' says Elizabeth. She has seen a suitable second-hand car for €14,000 with very low mileage which she reckons is a good deal 'as long as I can work out how I will pay for it!'

Elizabeth is also planning to open her own solicitors practice next year. She has produced a cashflow budget for the planned business and is confident that after just six months her monthly income will begin to exceed her expenditure.

The start-up expenses that Elizabeth has identified include the cost of buying a suitable premises (approximately €300,000), hiring a secretary (wages will be approximately €2,000 per month), and the purchase of office furniture and computer equipment (approximately €10,000). She expects that most of her sales will be on credit and that it will take up to three months to convert her debtors into cash. The business will also need monthly supplies of stationery, while telephone and electricity bills will arrive every two months.

1. Evaluate each of the following as a suitable source of personal finance for Elizabeth's new car: (a) overdraft, (b) savings, (c) personal loan and (d) mortgage. (40 marks)
2. List the financial needs of Elizabeth's new business under the headings of (a) short term, (b) medium term and (c) long term. (15 marks)
3. Analyse how preparing regular cashflow forecasts can assist Elizabeth to manage the finances of her new business. (25 marks)

Higher Level – Section 2 – Long Questions

1. Business cashflow forecast of Momentum Ltd.

	January	February	March	Total
Receipts	€40,000	€50,000	€55,000	€145,000
Payments	€38,000	€53,000	€57,500	€148,500
Net cashflow	€2,000	(€3,000)	(€2,500)	(€3,500)
Opening cash	€2,500	€4,500	€1,500	
Closing cash	€4,500	€1,500	(€1,000)	

   (a) Explain why a business would prepare a cashflow forecast. (10 marks)
   (b) In which month(s) has Momentum got a cashflow problem? Outline two possible reasons why. (15 marks)
   (c) Suggest **two** things which Momentum can do to improve the cashflow of the business. (20 marks)
2. Outline the factors which should be considered when reading a cashflow forecast for a business. (20 marks)
3. Contrast the contents of the cashflow forecast that would be prepared for a household with the one that would be prepared for a business. (20 marks) [LCQ]
4. Evaluate the benefits of **three** short-term sources of finance for a business. (20 marks)
5. Discuss the factors that should influence a firm's choice of long-term finance. (20 marks)
6. Distinguish between equity finance and debentures as long-term sources of finance for a business. (20 marks)
7. Analyse the factors a bank will consider before deciding whether or not to approve a household loan application. (25 marks)
8. Outline **two** activities that are common and **two** activities that are different when managing a business as opposed to managing a household. (20 marks) [LCQ]

Chapter 13
Monitoring Business Finances Using Accounts

'We are prone to judge success by the index of our salaries or the size or our automobiles rather than by the quality of our service and relationship to mankind.'
Martin Luther King

Key Study Questions

Case Study

FIT FOR BUSINESS

Sportz Clothing Limited is a producer of sports and outdoor clothing. Set up by sports enthusiast and entrepreneur Jack O'Reilly, its products are targeted mainly at skiers, surfers, hikers, campers and rock climbers. The company has recently launched a range of specialist clothing for the growing personal fitness and yoga markets.

Like all businesses, proper **financial monitoring** and control is essential for Sportz Clothing. The clothing market is very

sportz clothing TM

competitive with a lot of low-cost competition from China and the Far East. Many firms in the industry have gone out of business because of poor financial control. As a result, Jack monitors the finances of his business very carefully to ensure that money is not wasted and that there is always enough to pay the bills.

Every year, Sportz Clothing's accountants draw up financial accounts including a **profit and loss account** and a **balance sheet**. These accounts are used to measure the financial performance of the business. In particular, managers will want to ensure that the business has enough financial **liquidity** to pay its bills, is generating enough **profit** for its owners, and does not owe too much **debt**.

1. What financial accounts do businesses use to monitor their finances?

All organisations, whether commercial (such as Sportz Clothing) or non-commercial (such as a school), need to keep financial records of their transactions to ensure that they have enough money to pay their expenses. At the end of the year, most businesses will summarise their financial performance in two very important financial statements: (a) **a profit and loss account** and (b) a **balance sheet.**

OL Short Q1

2. What is a profit and loss account?

A **profit and loss (P & L) account** *shows the amount of income earned, expenses incurred and* **profit** *made by the business.* It also shows how much of the profit was paid out in tax, how much was paid out in dividends and how much was retained in the business for future use.

Basic Profit and Loss Account	
Sales	100
Less cost of sales (e.g. raw materials)	40
Gross profit	60
Less expenses (e.g. advertising)	50
Net profit	10

Profit and Loss Account for Sportz Clothing Ltd.

Cost of sales: The direct cost of purchasing or making the goods, including raw materials and direct labour.

	Year 1	Year 2	Year 3
Sales	1,000,000	1,400,000	2,000,000
Less cost of sales	400,000	600,000	1,200,000
Gross profit	**600,000**	**800,000**	**800,000**
Less expenses	450,000	550,000	760,000
Net profit	**150,000**	**250,000**	**40,000**
Less corporation tax @ 10%	15,000	25,000	4,000
Less dividends	100,000	150,000	30,000
Retained earnings for the year	**35,000**	**75,000**	**6,000**

Gross profit: Profit before expenses and any interest on loans are deducted. **Low gross profit** can indicate that the cost of raw materials may be too high or that selling prices are not high enough to cover costs.

Expenses: Include items such as salaries, insurance, market research, advertising, transport, administration, electricity and bills.

Net profit: This is the final profit after all costs and expenses are deducted. **Low net profits** can indicate that a business's expenses may be too high and need to be cut back.

Dividends: Share of the profits distributed to shareholders.

Retained earnings: Profit left over after all costs, overheads, tax and dividend payments are deducted. This is an important source of long-term finance available to businesses.

Corporation tax is paid by companies on their profits.

OL Short Q2, 3
OL Long Q1, 5

3. What is a balance sheet?

Where do company profits go?
- **Corporation tax**
- **Dividends to shareholders**
- **Retained earnings for future use**

A **balance sheet** *is a statement of the wealth of a business. It shows all the assets owned and all the liabilities (or debts) owed by the business on a specific date.*

Fixed assets: These are the permanent items owned by the business. They can be tangible (e.g. buildings) or intangible (e.g. valuable brand names). The value of **fixed assets** shows how much security the business will have to offer a bank when applying for a loan.

Current assets: These are not permanent, which means that they are always changing into and out of cash throughout the year. **Debtors** *are the people who owe the business money. They are an asset.*

Current liabilities are debts that are likely to be paid within 12 months, e.g creditors and unpaid taxes. **Creditors** *are the people to whom the business owes money.* They are a liability.

Working capital *refers to the finance being used to pay for day-to-day running expenses, e.g. buying stock, paying wages, bills, etc.* This figure shows if the business has enough money to pay its short-term debts. Working Capital = Current Assets – Current Liabilities.

Financed by: This section shows the sources of long-term finance raised by the business. It can include ordinary shares, preference shares, debenture loans and reserves. It also indicates the current level of borrowings in the business and if there is scope for further borrowings.

Ordinary shares refers to the value of shares issued to shareholders in the business.

Equity capital: This refers to the total value of the funds in the business that is owned by the shareholders.

Capital employed: This is the total finance used by a firm in the current year.

Balance Sheet of Sportz Clothing Ltd.

	Year 1	Year 2	Year 3
Fixed Assets Section			
[A] Total fixed assets (e.g. land, buldings, equipment)	1,500,000	1,700,000	1,900,000
Current Assets Section			
Closing stocks	200,000	400,000	700,000
Other current assets (e.g. debtors, money in bank, cash)	460,000	740,000	985,000
[B] Total current assets	660,000	1,140,000	1,685,000
[C] Total current liabilities (e.g. creditors, unpaid expenses)	260,000	510,000	800,000
[D] Working capital (B – C)	400,000	630,000	885,000
Total Net Assets (A + D)	1,900,000	2,330,000	2,785,000
Capital Employed Section (how the business is financed)			
[E] Loans and debentures	400,000	350,000	300,000
[F] Ordinary shares	1,465,000	1,870,000	2,369,000
[G] Retained earnings	35,000	110,000	116,000
[H] Equity capital (F+G)	1,500,000	1,980,000	2,485,000
Total Capital Employed (E+F+G)	1,900,000	2,330,000	2,785,000

OL Short Q4

HL Short Q4

4. How can accounts be interpreted using ratios?

The profit and loss account and the balance sheet of a business like Sportz Clothing can be interpreted using ratio analysis. **Ratio analysis** *refers to the study of one piece of accounting data in relation to another piece of accounting data.* It allows users to do a financial health check on a business by analysing its accounts. Comparisons can be made between different years to observe trends. There are three main types of ratios:

> **Ratio analysis reveals:**
> - **Profitability**
> - **Liquidity**
> - **Debt/equity structure**

- ◆ **Profitability ratios** *show the effectiveness of a business in using its resources to generate profits.*
- ◆ **Liquidity ratios** *show the ability of a business to pay its **short-term** debts as they fall due.*
- ◆ **Debt/equity (gearing) ratios** *show the capital structure of the business (including equity and loans) and its ability to pay its **long-term** debts.*

The Key Business Ratios

A. Profitability Ratios

Gross Profit Margin *(also known as Gross Margin or Gross Profit Percentage)* This shows the percentage gross profit earned on every item sold. The higher the gross profit margin, the easier it is to pay the expenses of running the business.

$$\frac{\text{Gross Profit}}{\text{Sales}} \times 100 = \%$$

Net Profit Margin *(also known as Net Margin or Net Profit Percentage)* This shows the percentage net profit earned on every item sold. The higher this is, the higher the profitability of the business.

$$\frac{\text{Net Profit}}{\text{Sales}} \times 100 = \%$$

Return on Investment (ROI) *(also known as Return on Capital Employed)* Return on investment measures the firm's ability to generate profits from the money invested in the business. The higher the percentage, the better.

$$\frac{\text{Net Profit}}{\text{Capital Employed}} \times 100 = \%$$

B. Liquidity Ratios

Current Ratio *(also known as Working Capital Ratio)* The current ratio measures a firm's ability to pay its current liabilities. Ideally, this should be at least 2 or, as a ratio, 2:1.

$$\frac{\text{Current Assets}}{\text{Current Liabilities}}$$

Acid Test Ratio *(also known as Quick Ratio)* This ratio measures a firm's ability to raise cash quickly to pay current liabilities but without having to sell off stock. Ideally, this should be at least 1 or, as a ratio, 1:1.

$$\frac{\text{Current Assets} - \text{Closing Stock}}{\text{Current Liabilities}}$$

C. Debt–Equity Ratios (Gearing)

Debt–Equity Ratio *(also known as Gearing or Leverage)* This measures the balance between fixed-interest loan capital and equity capital. The lower a firm can keep its gearing, the less fixed-interest debt it will have to repay.

$$\frac{\text{Fixed-interest Capital}}{\text{Equity Capital}} \times 100 = \%$$

5. What can profitability ratios tell us about a business?

Profitability ratios:
• **Gross profit margin**
• **Net profit margin**
• **Return on investment**

Gross profit margin

Gross Profit Margin (Percentage)		
Formula	**Sportz Clothing Ltd – Year 1**	**Year 2**
$\dfrac{\text{Gross Profit}}{\text{Sales}} \times 100 = \%$	$\dfrac{600{,}000}{1{,}000{,}000} \times 100 = 60\%$	$\dfrac{800{,}000}{1{,}400{,}000} \times 100 = 57\%$

The **gross profit margin** *measures gross profit as a percentage of sales. The higher a firm's gross profit margin, the easier it is to pay the expenses of running the business.* Ideally, every business should be aiming for a steady or rising gross profit margin.

> **Example:** Sportz Clothing's gross profit margin has slipped slightly from 60% in Year 1 to 57% in Year 2.

A decline in the gross profit margin percentage can be due to:

✳ **Increased cost of sales** due to higher material or production costs, or greater wastage of stock.

✳ **Lower profit margins** on each item sold due to charging lower prices.

✳ An increase in sales of a firm's **less profitable** products.

OL Short Q9

HL Short Q3

> **Recall and Review**
>
> Calculate the gross profit margin for Sportz Clothing Ltd. in Year 3 and comment on your findings.

Net profit margin

Net Profit Margin (Percentage)		
Formula	**Sportz Clothing Ltd – Year 1**	**Year 2**
$\dfrac{\text{Net Profit}}{\text{Sales}} \times 100 = \%$	$\dfrac{150{,}000}{1{,}000{,}000} \times 100 = 15\%$	$\dfrac{250{,}000}{1{,}400{,}000} \times 100 = 17.9\%$

The **net profit margin** *measures net profit as a percentage of sales. It indicates how effective a firm is at minimising expenses and generating profits.* Ideally, every business should aim for a steady or rising net profit margin. The higher this margin, the better.

> **Example:** Sportz Clothing's net margin has risen from 15% to 17.9%. This indicates that the business is very profitable and that the trend is improving. A rise in this margin can be due to sales rising far faster than expenses or the business becoming more efficient, e.g. running expenses are falling.

> ### Recall and Review
> 1. Calculate the net profit margin for Sportz Clothing Ltd. in Year 3. Comment on your findings.

Return on investment ratio

<table>
<tr><td colspan="4" align="center">**Return on Investment Ratio**</td></tr>
<tr><td align="center">**Formula**</td><td align="center">**Sportz Clothing Ltd – Year 1**</td><td align="center">**Year 2**</td></tr>
<tr>
<td align="center">$\dfrac{\text{Net Profit}}{\text{Capital Employed}} \times 100 = \%$</td>
<td align="center">$\dfrac{150{,}000}{1{,}900{,}000} \times 100 = 7.9\%$</td>
<td align="center">$\dfrac{250{,}000}{2{,}330{,}000} \times 100 = 10.7\%$</td>
</tr>
</table>

The **return on investment ratio** *measures the percentage return (profit) that a business is generating on the capital employed.* **Capital employed** *is the total finance used by a firm in the current year.* The figure for return on investment indicates the overall profitability of the business compared to the money invested in it. It should be compared to that of rivals and also to the interest rate available on a deposit account in a bank. If the return on investment is lower than the bank desposit rate then it could be argued that the owners would do better financially by selling off the business and depositing the proceeds in the bank. This ratio is also known as *return on capital employed.*

> Example: Sportz Clothing Ltd. had a return on investment of 7.9% in Year 1, which rose to 10.7% in Year 2. For most businesses, these are very good figures. A rising return on investment is a particularly good sign as it shows that the firm is becoming more efficient at generating profits from the money invested in it.

OL Long Q4

> ### Recall and Review
> Calculate the return on investment for Sportz Clothing Ltd. in Year 3. Comment on your findings.

6. What can liquidity ratios tell us about a business?

Liquidity

Liquidity (solvency) *refers to the ease with which a business can pay its short-term bills. It is achieved by having assets that can be easily converted into cash to meet short-term debts.* If liquidity falls too low then a business may no longer be able to pay its bills on time.

> **Liquidity ratios:**
> - **Current/working capital ratio**
> - **Acid test ratio**

HL Short Q1

Insolvency *occurs when total liabilities (debts) exceed total assets. This means that the business is unable to pay all its debts.* Insolvency is a very serious matter and can lead to the liquidation of the business. **Liquidation** *occurs when a business is closed down and its assets sold off.* The money raised from the liquidation sale is used to pay creditors as much as possible from the money raised.

Current ratio (working capital ratio)

Current Ratio (Working Capital Ratio)		
Formula	Sportz Clothing Ltd – Year 1	Year 2
$\dfrac{\text{Current Assets}}{\text{Current Liabilities}}$	$\dfrac{660{,}000}{260{,}000} = 2.5 : 1$	$\dfrac{1{,}140{,}000}{510{,}000} = 2.2 : 1$

The **current ratio (working capital ratio)** *measures a firm's ability to pay its current liabilities.*
❖ The ratio calculation is shown as $x : 1$
❖ A healthy ratio for a business is at least $2 : 1$, i.e. a business has twice as much money in current assets as it owes in current liabilities and is regarded as being **liquid (solvent).**
❖ As a firm's current ratio increases, it becomes easier to meet its current liabilities – assuming all current assets can be easily turned into cash.

OL Short Q6, 10
OL Long Q2

HL Short Q5, 6

Example: Sportz Clothing had a current ratio of 2.5 : 1 in Year 1. This was well above the recommended level and shows that the firm was well able to pay its current liabilities. In Year 2 the ratio slipped slightly to 2.2 : 1, but it was still above the recommended level. Sportz Clothing needs to monitor this trend closely and manage its cashflow carefully to ensure that this ratio does not slip further in future years.

Recall and Review
Calculate the current ratio for Sportz Clothing Ltd. in Year 3. Comment on your findings.

Acid test ratio

Acid Test Ratio		
Formula	Sportz Clothing Ltd – Year 1	Year 2
$\dfrac{\text{Current Assets – Closing Stock}}{\text{Current Liabilities}}$	$\dfrac{660{,}000 - 200{,}000}{260{,}000} = 1.8 : 1$	$\dfrac{1{,}140{,}000 - 400{,}000}{510{,}000} = 1.5 : 1$

The **Acid Test Ratio** *measures a firm's ability to raise cash quickly to meet its current liability debts.* Stock is deducted from current liabilities because it is considered the most difficult current asset to convert rapidly into cash.

* ★ To ensure that all bills can be paid as they fall due, a firm should have an acid test ratio of at least 1:1.

* ★ If the acid test ratio falls below this level a firm may have difficulty paying its bills and become **illiquid**.

> Example: Sportz Clothing had an acid test ratio of 1.8 : 1 in Year 1 that declined to 1.5 : 1 in Year 2. While these ratios are still well above the recommended minimum level, the downward trend is a concern.

HL Short Q2
HL Long Q4

> ### Recall and Review
> Calculate the acid test ratio for Sportz Clothing Ltd in Year 3. Comment on your findings.

7. How can a business manage its working capital?

It is essential for all businesses to manage their working capital to ensure there is sufficient cash to meet their debts. Steps that can be taken to improve a firm's cashflow liquidity include:

* **Selling off slow-moving stocks** to convert them into cash.

* **Proper stock control** will improve cashflow by reducing the amount of money a business has tied up in inventory. It also allows a business to free up storage space for other purposes.

* **Credit control.** Many businesses sell goods on credit to attract customers and increase sales and profits. **Credit** *means selling goods now but not getting paid until later.* However, to avoid cashflow and working capital problems, businesses must plan in advance how they will meet their cash requirements while they are waiting to be paid for goods sold on credit. **Credit control** *means monitoring which customers are given credit and for how long, and ensuring they pay up on time.* Effective credit control reduces the risk of bad debts and protects cashflow.

* **Increase prices** and profit margins to raise more money.

* **Raise more finance** by selling shares or getting a long-term loan. Alternatively, sell off some assets to raise money.

* **Prepare proper cashflow forecasts** to identify likely future flows of money in and out of a business over a certain period of time. It can help a firm predict and avoid liquidity problems.

OL Short Q7
OL Long Q3

HL Long Q5, 6

8. What can the debt-equity ratio (gearing) tell us about a business?

Debt-Equity Ratio (Gearing)		
Formula	**Sportz Clothing Ltd – Year 1**	**Year 2**
$\dfrac{\text{Debt Capital (or Fixed Interest Capital)}}{\text{Equity Capital}} \times 100 = \%$	$\dfrac{400{,}000}{1{,}500{,}000} \times 100 = 26.7\%$	$\dfrac{350{,}000}{1{,}980{,}000} \times 100 = 17.7\%$

Equity capital *is the total value of issued ordinary share capital plus retained earnings.* **Debt (fixed-interest) capital** *is the total value of the long-term debt owed by the business. It includes any preference shares issued plus long-term loans (debentures).* **Preference shares** *are shares whose owners are paid dividends before the owners of ordinary shares.* **The debt/equity ratio** *shows how much long-term debt has been borrowed compared to how much equity finance has been invested by the owners.* It is also known as **gearing** or **leverage.** The calculation is shown as *x* : 1 or as a percentage.

> **Low gearing indicates a low level of long-term debt in the business.**
> **High gearing indicates a high level of long-term debt finance in the business.**

♦ **A low debt/equity ratio (also known as low gearing)** *refers to having a ratio of debt to equity capital of considerably less than 1:1 or, in percentages, considerably less than 100%.* A company with low gearing will find it easier to pay dividends and/or reinvest profits in the business. The lower the gearing, the lower the risk to the business.

♦ **Neutral gearing** *refers to having a debt/equity ratio of 1:1 or, in percentages, of 100%.*

♦ **A high debt/equity ratio (also known as high gearing)** *refers to having a debt/equity ratio considerably greater than 1:1 or, in percentages, considerably greater than 100%. This means a business has a level of long-term debt greater than its equity capital.* A high level of debt capital means that a business will be incurring considerable interest payments on its borrowings. This will reduce the amount of cash available to pay dividends to shareholders or to reinvest in the business.

High gearing may be suitable for a business during times of high profitability when debt repayments can be easily afforded. However, high gearing is risky as it can cause the following problems:

❖ **Greater pressure on management** to sustain or increase profits to pay debenture interest, preference share dividends and ordinary share dividends.

❖ **Reduced dividends** for ordinary shareholders as payments to lenders of debenture loans and preference shareholders receive priority.

❖ **Greater difficulty raising finance** from selling ordinary shares as the business is seen as less able to pay high dividend returns and therefore a more risky investment.

❖ **Difficulties in raising additional loan finance** as potential lenders have doubts about the firm's ability to meet its fixed-interest commitments.

❖ **Risk of liquidation** if interest payments are not made in full and on time, as the business may be forced to close and sell off all its assets to clear its debts.

Example: Sportz Clothing Ltd. had gearing of 26.7% in Year 1 and 17.7% in Year 2. This means that the firm is low geared. Sportz Clothing's combination of low gearing and high profitability means that lenders are likely to be willing to lend further finance to the business if needed. Similarly, investors are likely to be interested in purchasing ordinary shares in a highly profitable business.

OL Short Q8
OL Long Q6

HL Short Q7
HL Long Q2, 3, 7

Recall and Review
Calculate the debt/equity ratio for Sportz Clothing Ltd in Year 3. Comment on your findings.

Case Study

High gearing trips up fitness business

While Jackie Skelly was a student at university, she started attending a gym and developed a huge passion for personal fitness because, according to her, 'It didn't feel like work.' This gave her an idea for a **business** running her own gym. As someone who was 'always very independent' and was captain of the hockey team at secondary school, she felt she had what it would take to become a fitness entrepreneur.

After completing her degree, Jackie got a part-time job as an employee in a gym. This helped her learn more about the fitness market and she set about planning for her business idea. To raise the finance that she needed, she sold her VW Beetle car and **invested** the money into starting the business. However, this was not enough money to rent suitable premises or to buy the equipment she needed, so she **borrowed** €19,000 from a bank.

Jackie's gym proved to be very successful and she quickly built up a loyal **customer** base. As the business thrived, she decided she needed to expand but needed more **long-term finance** to do so. She approached a number of potential **investors** and persuaded them to invest finance in expanding the business in exchange for receiving 35% of the ownership. This allowed her to begin expanding the enterprise into a nationwide chain of gyms and fitness centres employing hundreds of staff.

Like all businesses, proper **financial monitoring** and control was essential for the business. Every year, Jackie's accountants drew up its financial accounts including a **profit and loss account** and a **balance sheet**. These accounts were used to measure the financial performance of the business. In particular,

Jackie had to ensure that the business had enough financial **liquidity** to pay its bills as well as being profitable enough for her and her investors.

However, over time the business was also accumulating an increasing amount of **debt** that eventually rose to over €12 million, most of which was owed to Ulster Bank using the business as security. This significantly increased the **debt/equity (gearing) ratio** of the business.

As long as the business was sufficiently profitable, this high debt/equity ratio could be managed. However, when gym membership **sales** suddenly dropped sharply by 30% in the space of a single year from €20 million to €14 million the business ran into serious trouble. Using accounts to monitor her finances, Jackie Skelly realised that her once-profitable business had become **unprofitable**, was rapidly losing financial **liquidity**, and was **too highly geared** to be able to repay all its debts.

The risk of failure is a risk that all entrepreneurs take. After an exciting and profitable career as an **entrepreneur**, Jackie lost control of the entire business as it had been used as security for the loans that she could no longer repay.

9. Why are stakeholders interested in monitoring the finances of a business?

Different stakeholders are interested in monitoring the financial performance of a business. So too are competitors.

STAKEHOLDER	INTERESTED IN . . .
Managers	Managers want to know how well they are **managing the finances** of the business compared to previous years and how the business is performing compared to **rival firms**. **The key business ratios** can assist in management decision-making.
Owners and investors	Owners such as shareholders want to know how well the business is performing financially, especially the ability of the business to **generate profits** and **pay dividends**, or **interest on long-term loans**. **Example: Net profit percentage** reveals to owners what size of **dividend** the business can afford to pay out, if any. Looking at the **return on investment** (ROI) can reveal if putting money on deposit in a bank might be a better option for potential investors. The **debt/equity ratio** reveals how risky investing in the business might be if there is a fall in profitability.
Employees	Employees want to know how **profitable** the firm is and its **financial stability**, as this can affect their job security and the prospects of receiving wage increases. **Example:** Employees will look at **profitability ratios** to see if the business can afford to maintain employment or pay higher wages.

Banks	Banks are interested in the ability of the business to repay loans and also the value of any assets used as **security**. Banks will look at **liquidity ratios** to see if a business is likely to be able to repay a loan. The debt-equity (gearing) ratio can reveal if a business has borrowed too much long-term debt. **Example:** A company can be put into **receivership** by a bank if it defaults on repayments on a fixed interest loan like a debenture. The **receiver** then takes legal ownership of the asset used as security for the loan. This security could be a piece of property or even an entire company.
Suppliers	Suppliers are interested in gaining information about a firm's **ability to pay** for goods supplied on credit. Suppliers will not want to sell on credit to any business where there is a real risk of non-payment. **Example:** If a firm is unable to pay its bills it may be forced into **liquidation**. Liquidators are appointed to companies which are unable to pay all their debts. The **liquidator**'s job is to sell off all the assets of the business and use the money raised to pay creditors as much as possible of what they are owed.
Government	The Revenue Commissioners can use a firm's accounts to calculate **how much tax** has to be paid. Other State agencies will be interested to know if **grants** or venture capital provided have assisted the firm to grow and expand.
Competitors	Competitors can identify the financial **strengths** and **weaknesses** of a business. Such information can reveal whether a business is doing well and likely to expand, or struggling to survive.

OL Long Q7

HL Short Q8
HL ABQ
HL Long Q1, 8

Answers to Recall and Review Questions – Sportz Clothing Ltd – Year 3

Gross margin	40%	Big concern. Despite strong rise in sales, cost of sales has risen too fast. Urgent attention is needed here.
Net margin	2%	Too small. Business is now barely breaking even. Expenses have increased too much and need to be cut.
Return on investment	1.4%	Extremely disappointing. The firm is now barely generating any profit from all the money invested in it.
Current ratio	2.1 : 1	Still good, but there is a downward trend that is a cause for concern.
Acid test ratio	1.2 : 1	Ok, but the continued downward trend must be a cause for concern.
Gearing	12.1%	Very good. The firm has very little debt capital and could seek extra debt or equity finance to invest in improving efficiencies needed to return the firm to the strong profitability of previous years.

Jack O'Reilly of Sportz Clothing uses spreadsheets to prepare and analyse his financial accounts.

Key Concepts & Business Terms

After studying this chapter the student should be able to explain the following key concepts and business terms:

1. Profit & Loss account
2. Gross profit
3. Net profit
4. Balance sheet
5. Fixed assets
6. Current assets
7. Debtors
8. Current liabilities
9. Creditors
10. Working capital
11. Ordinary shares
12. Ratio analysis
13. Profitability ratios
14. Liquidity ratios
15. Debt-equity ratio / gearing
16. Gross profit margin
17. Net profit margin
18. Return on investment
19. Capital employed
20. Liquidity
21. Insolvency
22. Liquidation
23. Current (working capital) ratio
24. Acid test (quick) ratio
25. Stock control
26. Credit
27. Credit control
28. Equity capital
29. Debt (fixed-interest) capital
30. Low gearing
31. High gearing
32. Receivership
33. Liquidator

Leaving Certificate Practice Questions

Ordinary Level

Ordinary Level - Section 1 - Short Questions (10 marks each)

1. List **two** important financial statements used by businesses.
2. Explain what is meant by a firm's gross profit.
3. Explain what is meant by the term 'retained earnings'.
4. List **two** current assets that can appear in a balance sheet.
5. Outline the formula for calculating a firm's net profit percentage. [LCQ]
6. The following information is available from the final accounts of GF Ltd: current liabilities of €100,000, current assets of €300,000. Calculate (a) the working capital and (b) the working capital ratio. [LCQ]
7. Define the term 'credit control'. [LCQ]
8. Explain what the debt/equity ratio is and why it is important to a business. [LCQ]
9. If sales for firm X Ltd are: €200,000, gross profit is €100,000 and net profit is €35,000,
   (a) Calculate the gross margin %
   (b) Calculate the net margin %. [LCQ]
10. Identify **one** consequence of poor financial liquidity.

Ordinary Level – Section 2 – Long Questions

1. (a) Explain the purpose of a profit & loss account. (10 marks).
   (b) Identify **three** expenses that can appear in a profit & loss account. (15 marks)
2. The following financial information is available from the accountant of Brady Furniture and Carpets Ltd.

	Year 1	Year 2
Balance Sheet – Extract	€	€
Current Assets	200,000	180,000
Current Liabilities	100,000	120,000
Capital Employed	500,000	500,000
Profit & Loss Accounts – Extract		
Net Profit	50,000	40,000

   (a) Calculate the working capital ratio for Year 1 and Year 2 and comment on the trend. (Show the formulas and all your workings.) (25 marks) [LCQ]
   (b) Calculate the return on capital employed for Year 1 and Year 2. (Show the formulas and all your workings.) (15 marks) [LCQ]

3. Gerard O'Mahoney is an accountant with Allied Electronics. He is preparing a financial report for Ms Jane Coughlan, managing director. Gerard prepared a P & L account and a balance sheet. He found that the net profit percentage of the company was 15% and the ROI was 25%. The following is an extract from the balance sheet.

	Year 2	Year 1
Balance Sheet – Extract	€	€
Current Assets	80,000	120,000
Current Liabilities	160,000	80,000
Closing Stock	40,000	20,000

(a) What do the letters ROI and P & L mean? (10 marks) [LCQ]

(b) Calculate the working capital ratio for Year 1 and Year 2. (20 marks) [LCQ]

(c) Calculate the acid test ratio for Year 1 and Year 2. (20 marks) [LCQ]

(d) Draft the financial report outlining the profitability and liquidity position of the firm. (20 marks) [LCQ]

(e) Distinguish between a debtor and a creditor. (5 marks) [LCQ]

4. Would you be willing to invest in a firm that is making a return on investment of 20% per annum? Explain your answer. (20 marks)

5. Café sales for the year:

Menu item	Price of item	Items sold		Sales revenue
Irish breakfast	€5.00	4,000	=	€20,000
Coffee and sandwich	€2.50	1,600	=	€4,000
Fish and chips	€3.00	4,000	=	€12,000
Apple pie and cream	€2.00	2,000	=	€4,000
Minerals	€1.00	20,000	=	€20.000
Total Sales Revenue			=	

Cost of Sales   =   €24,000 pa
Expenses: General Expenses   =   €12,000 pa
                   Loan interest   =   €4,000 pa

(a) Calculate the total sales revenue and the gross profit generated by the café for the year. (10 marks) [LCQ].

(b) Calculate the net profit generated by the café. (10 marks) [LCQ]

6. Murray Ltd. has a bank loan of €30,000 and equity of €10,000. Calculate the gearing ratio and comment on your result. (15 marks)

7. Identify **five** stakeholders and the reasons they may be interested in the accounts of a business. (15 marks)

Higher Level

Higher Level – Section 1 – Short Questions (10 marks each)

1. Explain what is meant by a firm's liquidity.
2. The following are figures relating to Laser Ltd:

	Year 2	Year 1
Balance Sheet – Extract	€	€
Current Assets	90,000	85,000
Current Liabilities	60,000	40,000
Closing Stock	20,000	25,000

   Calculate the acid test ratio for Year 1 and Year 2. [LCQ]
3. Calculate the gross margin if a business has sales of €160,000 and a gross profit of €40,000.
4. Explain the purpose of a firm's balance sheet.
5. Outline **two** reasons why a business would calculate the working capital ratio. [LCQ]
6. Differentiate between working capital and equity capital.
7. The following figures relate to a company for the past two years:

	Year 2	Year 1
Balance Sheet – Extract	€	€
Ordinary Share Capital	420,000	320,000
Long-Term Loans	140,000	270,000
Retained Earnings	30,000	40,000

   Calculate the debt/equity ratio for Year 1 and Year 2.
8. List two types of financial problem that a firm can encounter.

Higher Level – Section 2 – Applied Business Question

Logistix Transport

Judith Hannaway has been appointed managing director of Logistix, a family-owned transport company that specialises in making deliveries to supermarkets on behalf of small producers. She has just come out of her first meeting with Darren Healy, the company accountant, who presented her with the following financial figures for the business for the past two years:

	Year 2 €	Year 1 €
Sales	160,000	120,000
Gross Profit	30,000	25,000
Net Profit	20,000	20,000
Current Assets	85,000	75,000
Closing Stock	40,000	35,000
Current Liabilities	50,000	45,000
Loans	210,000	160,000
Equity Capital	250,000	240,000

Judith has a background in human resource management but little experience in finance or interpreting financial accounts. She has looked over the figures and is happy with them as they show sales rising sharply.

However, Darren seems more concerned by the figures. He pointed out to Judith that 75% of the firm's business is on credit but that the company is also experiencing a growing level of bad debts. He emphasised that one of Judith's priority tasks will be to sort out the amount of credit that Logistix will allow its customers.

1. Apply ratio analysis to the above data to assess the profitability, liquidity and gearing of Logistix. Comment on the trends identified. (40 marks)

2. Identify the main users of financial reports about Logistix and explain the possible reasons for their interest. (20 marks)

3. Evaluate the importance of preparing (a) a profit & loss account and (b) a balance sheet for Logistix. (20 marks)

Higher Level – Section 2 – Long Questions

1. Discuss the importance of the following financial statements to the management of a business enterprise: (a) The profit and loss account and (b) The balance sheet. (30 marks) [LCQ]

2. Examine the following figures from Savin Ltd.

	Year 2 €	Year 1 €
Current Assets	91,500	80,450
Current Liabilities	62,400	43,200
Closing Stock	49,000	40,100
Equity Share Capital	250,000	250,000
Long-Term Debt	253,000	120,000
Retained Earnings	20,000	18,000

(a) Calculate for Year 2 and Year 1: (i) Working capital ratios, (ii) Acid test ratios and (iii) Debt/equity ratios. (15 marks)

(b) Applying your knowledge, comment on **two** trends that you notice developing in the business. Suggest what you would do about them. (25 marks)

3. Examine the following figures from Brick Construction Ltd.

	Year 1 €	Year 2 €
Current Assets	15,900	16,800
Net Profit	15,100	7,400
Equity Share Capital	100,000	105,000
Current Liabilities	8,100	7,400
Closing Stock	9,100	12,400
Gross Profit	45,150	40,950
Retained Earnings	20,000	21,000
Sales	169,500	157,500

(a) Using two ratios in each case, analyse the profitability and liquidity trends in Brick Construction Ltd, from the above figures for Year 1 and Year 2. (20 marks) [LCQ]

(b) Recommend how the trends might be improved. (20 marks) [LCQ]

4. Analyse the profitability and liquidity trends in Gracey and Co. Ltd from the following figures for Year 1 and Year 2. (40 marks) [LCQ]

	Year 1 €	Year 2 €
Current Liabilities	9,400	8,200
Closing Stock	8,200	10,100
Equity Share Capital	85,000	85,000
Gross Profit	58,250	42,560
Retained Earnings	7,100	16,450
Current Assets	13,500	15,450
Net Profit	13,500	13,255
Sales	141,500	121,500

5. Explain why working capital management is so important for businesses. (20 marks)

6. Outline the steps a firm can take to protect its liquidity and effectively manage its working capital. (25 marks)

7. Explain what is meant by the term 'highly geared'. Discuss the implications of high gearing for a business. (20 marks)

8. Explain the importance of good financial information (e.g. financial ratios) to the management team of a business. Use examples to illustrate your answer. (20 marks) [LCQ]

Chapter 14
Identifying Business Opportunities

> 'Most people don't recognise opportunity when it comes, because it's usually dressed in overalls and looks a lot like work.'
> Thomas Edison

Key Study Questions

Case Study

CULLY & SULLY

Friends Cullen Allen ('Cully') and Colum O'Sullivan ('Sully') originally met in Cork when Cully was studying sculpture and Sully was studying food science. After college they became interested in setting up their own business. As Sully's mother owned a food store and Cully's parents ran a hotel and a farm, they were interested in starting some sort of food-related business. However, before they could go any further with their aspirations to become entrepreneurs, they needed to come up with a clear business idea.

All new enterprises must start with an idea. Established businesses also need to identify new ideas and business opportunities if they want to expand or to replace older products that are approaching the end of their life cycle.

Individuals and existing businesses can look for new business ideas from two sources – **internally,** by examining their own strengths and weaknesses, and **externally,** by looking at the opportunities and threats in the marketplace.

1. What are the internal sources of business opportunities?

Internal Sources of Business Ideas

For aspiring entrepreneurs:

- **Hobbies and interests**
- **Skills**
- **Personality**
- **Frustrating experiences**
- **Inventions and unexpected occurrences**
- **Brainstorming ideas**
- **Management buy-outs**

For existing business:

All those above plus

- **Customer feedback**
- **Market trends**
- **Staff suggestions**
- **Research and development (R&D)**
- **Supply substitution**

Internal sources of ideas for aspiring entrepreneurs

It is said that our strengths offer us our only true opportunities. If we can identify them, then we can go a long way towards identifying what kind of business we are most suited for. The best place to begin looking for business ideas is our own interests, skills and experiences.

★ **Hobbies and interests:** Entrepreneurs look at their interests or hobbies.

> **Example:** An interest in sports, animals, mechanics or music can often be turned into a business. Because of their shared interest in food, Cully and Sully went looking for an idea in the food business.

★ **Skills and knowledge:** What are you good at? What skills do you have – for example, drawing, entertaining people, designing clothes?

> **Example:** Sully had expertise in food science and Cully had learned a lot from his family's hotel and farm business.

★ **Personality:** What type of person is the entrepreneur? What type of work do they like – physical work, paperwork, working with people or working on their own?

★ **Frustrating experiences:** Personal frustration with not being able to find a particular product or service.

> **Example:** Richard Brierley set up Fiacla Toothpaste when he was unable to find an Irish-made toothpaste in the shops.

★ **Inventions and unexpected occurrences.**

> **Example:** While searching for a cure for deafness, Alexander Graham Bell invented the telephone.

★ **Brainstorming** *is a creativity technique for coming up with new ideas. It can be done individually or as a group to generate ideas.* Brainstorming involves:

☐ Setting yourself a **time limit**, such as ten minutes.

- ◻ **Quickly writing down** as many possible business ideas as you can think of. Try to be as creative as possible, no matter how silly some of the ideas may seem. It is important to **be positive** and **not to criticise** or evaluate any of the ideas while still generating them.

- ◻ When the time is up and you think you have exhausted generating ideas, **review all the ideas** carefully, considering the pros and cons of each one.

- ◻ **Select the best** or most promising for further research.

OL Long Q1, 2

Internal sources of ideas for existing businesses

An existing business can use most of the internal sources that an aspiring entrepreneur can use but also has some extra sources of ideas not available to entrepreneurs.

- ✳ **Customer feedback** through market research, and complaints or compliments picked up by a firm's **sales staff** are very useful sources of new product ideas.

  > **Example:** Customer feedack gave Pizza Hut the idea to launch a '4 for All' pizza with four sections each with a different topping.

- ✳ **Market trends:** Feedback from customers and sales staff assists the marketing manager in identifying market trends and competitor innovations. These trends can then be used to identify product improvements or new product ideas likely to appeal to customers.

  > **Example:** Coca-Cola introducing Diet Coke.

- ✳ **Staff suggestions** can be very useful and many firms offer incentives and rewards to staff to come up with new ideas, even if not ultimately used by the business. Such incentives encourage a spirit of intrapreneurship.

- ✳ **Research and development (R & D)** *refers to firms investing in the development of new and improved products.* Sometimes, when trying to develop one product, research and development may accidentally discover a different and more profitable innovation.

  > **Example:** When trying to develop a new superglue, one firm accidentally discovered a glue that only remained sticky for a few days, which led to the invention of the Post-It sticky notepads.

- ✳ **Supply substitution:** If a firm's supplies of raw materials are of poor quality, unreliable or too expensive, this may prompt them to produce the goods themselves and sell them to other Irish firms.

HL Short Q1
HL Long Q3

2. What are the external sources of business opportunities?

External Sources of Business Ideas
For aspiring entrepreneurs:
• **Friends and family**
• **Publications, television**
• **Internet and other media**
• **Networking**
• **Copying an existing idea**
• **Foreign holidays and travel**
• **State agencies**
• **Franchising**
• **Management buy-outs**
For existing businesses:
All those above plus
• **International trends**
• **Import substitution**
• **Market-research companies**
• **University and third-level linkages**

Many new ideas are actually just copies, variations or improvements of existing ones.

External sources of ideas for aspiring entrepreneurs

✤ **Friends and family** can also have frustrating experiences that can spark an idea.

Example: Cully and Sully noticed that many of the ready meals available in shops were of poor quality, were not very tasty and came in wasteful plastic packaging. Their friends agreed and said that they thought that there was a gap in the market for a quality alternative.

✤ **The media:** Magazines, newspapers, TV, the Internet and other media are often good indicators of changing fashions and interests. Successful entrepreneurs are sensitive to changing market trends and can identify business opportunities that are opening up. They look out for subjects that people are becoming interested in and talking about more, such as green energy, fitness, mobile phone applications, etc.

Example: Cully and Sully noticed an increasing demand for high-quality ready meals such as soups and pies but that there were few quality competitors in the market.

✤ **Networking** *means deliberately making useful business contacts through socialising, attending meetings of professional associations (e.g. the Marketing Institute) or joining useful clubs (e.g. golf clubs).* It works on the assumption that finding a business opportunity is often the result not of 'what you know' but rather 'who you know'.

Example: By networking with people in the food business, Cully and Sully became convinced that there was a gap in the market for their idea for a business producing high-quality ready meals.

✤ **Copying** an existing successful business. This is a very common occurrence and sometimes the copycat business improves on the original. **Foreign holidays and travel** can often inspire ideas for a business that could be copied or adapted for the Irish market.

Example: Geoff Read got the idea for Ballygowan Spring Water after noticing that, at the time, there was no Irish mineral water on the market.

✤ **State agencies** such as Enterprise Ireland and county enterprise boards provide assistance to aspiring entrepreneurs and existing businesses looking for new opportunities. They can provide market research information and technical assistance in developing a new product.

Example: Edward McCluskey was looking for a business idea. He contacted Enterprise Ireland who told him that all the cotton wool sold in Ireland was imported and that the market was worth millions in sales every year. Gerry set about researching how cotton wool is made and its many uses. With advice and financial assistance from Enterprise Ireland, he then set up his own manufacturing business, Irish Breeze, which has become a very successful producer of cotton wool products.

❖ **Franchising:** This means renting a complete business idea, name, logo and expertise from an existing business. It particularly suits service businesses.

Example: Supermacs, Snap Printing and PHQ are available as franchise business ideas.

❖ **Management buy-outs** *occur where managers in a business buy it from the owners and earn the profits for themselves.*

Example: Lifestyle Sports used to be owned by Tesco before they decided to sell it, as sports did not fit with the supermarket business on which they wanted to concentrate. Managers in Lifestyle seized the opportunity and purchased the business from Tesco for themselves.

See Chapter 17: Business Expansion for more information on franchising.

OL Short Q1, 2

HL Short Q10
HL Long Q1

PHQ is available as a franchise

Case Study

Ballygowan – A very simple idea

Geoff Read noticed that sales of mineral water in Ireland were increasing but that all of the brands on the market were imported and overpriced. He **researched the market** in more detail and reckoned that there was an opportunity for an Irish firm in the market. Quitting his job as a male model, he established the Ballygowan bottled water company.

Geoff Read started Ballygowan by **copying imported products** and became so successful that other Irish enterprises copied his idea and successfully entered the market with their own versions, such as Tipperary, Kerry and Carlow Castle mineral waters. Even Coca-Cola copied the idea by launching the River Rock brand of mineral water.

Bottled water was not a new idea, but an Irish mineral water was. Like Ballygowan Spring Water, many 'new' ideas are actually just copies, variations or improvements of existing ones.

External sources of ideas for existing businesses

An existing business can use all of the sources available to an aspiring entrepreneur plus the following:

✪ **International business trends** and foreign visits can be a rich source of ideas. Companies frequently send representatives to trade shows abroad to search for new ideas or products currently unavailable in Ireland.

✪ **Import substitution** occurs where a business decides to produce a product in Ireland that up until now has been imported. **State agencies** such as Enterprise Ireland can provide information to budding entrepreneurs on thousands of different products that could be made in Ireland but are currently being imported.

✪ **Market-research companies** that specialise in researching markets for new and existing products can provide reports that identify new trends and gaps in the market that could be filled by a new product.

✪ **University and third-level linkages** with business can generate many new products and ideas. As a result, many firms sponsor college research in areas in which they are interested.

HL Long Q2, 4

Example: Elan Pharmaceutical in Athlone linked up with TCD to develop anti-smoking nicotine patch products.

3. How can new business ideas be researched?

To increase their chances of success, entrepreneurs need to carry out proper market research into their business idea. **Market research** *is the process of gathering and analysing information about the potential market for a product.* The benefits of market research include:

❖ **Indicates the size of the market** and whether it is growing, shrinking or static. It can provide information on the consumers in terms of age, gender, income, tastes, lifestyles and spending patterns.

❖ **Identifies competitors:** Market research identifies competitors in the market and how well they are doing, their strengths and weaknesses and how they are likely to react to a new competitor.

❖ **Tests consumer reaction** to product samples, packaging and prices to ensure that the business has got its strategy right. It can identify important influences on customers such as product features, name, image, packaging, price and distribution outlets. It can also find out what customers want and what they don't want.

❖ **Predicts sales:** Market research can estimate the likely level of sales for a product and thus the optimum amount to produce.

❖ **Reduces risk and saves money:** Proper market research reduces the risk of product or business failure.

OL Short Q3
HL Short Q2

Case Study

Coke's Market Research disaster

Coca-Cola is the best-selling cola **brand** in the world despite fierce competition from rival **brands** such as Pepsi. To help expand sales and stay ahead of their rivals, Coca-Cola decided to replace the traditional drink and launch 'New Coke' with a 'New Improved Flavour' that the company felt would be even more popular. It developed samples of the new drink and tested it on a very small group of consumers.

Market research reaction to the new taste was very positive and Coke went ahead with a multimillion euro **product launch** and massive world-wide **advertising** confident that the new replacement drink would be a huge global success and significantly boost Coca-Cola's sales.

Instead, the new drink flopped and Coca-Cola had to bring back the old flavour, losing millions in a wasted investment. The reason was simply that Coke's managers had failed to conduct proper market research.

---

4. What types of market research can be carried out?

The two main types of market research are **desk research** and **field research**. The type of research chosen will depend on:

- what **information** is required
- the amount of **detail** and accuracy needed
- the **costs** involved in collecting it
- the **time** and **money available** to do the research.

Sources of Market Research	
Desk Research	**Field Research**
• Internal company reports	• Observation
• Reports and statistics from State agencies	• Customer surveys
• The Internet	• Talking to people already in the market
• Newspapers and magazines	• Getting relevant work experience
• Trade associations	
• Experts	
• Commercial market-research companies	

Desk research

Desk research *(also known as secondary research) means accessing information that has already been gathered by others.* Most of this research can be gathered by sitting at a desk using books, reports and statistics, hence the name. The main sources of desk research are:

* **Reports** and **statistics** compiled by government agencies such as the Central Statistics Office and Enterprise Ireland and also by **trade associations,** such as the Society of the Irish Motor Industry, which often have information on the size and value of their markets.

* **The Internet:** The global computer network can provide access to a huge range of often free information about businesses in Ireland and around the world.

> **Example:** Cully and Sully made extensive use of the Internet to look for ideas for a food business that could work for them.

* **Newspapers** and **magazine articles** can be useful sources of general information.

> **Example:** Geoff Read got his idea while reading a newspaper article about sales of mineral water rising but that all the brands on sale at the time were imported and overpriced.

* **Experts:** If you can find an expert in the area you are interested in, they can be a useful source of information and advice.

Bord Bia
Irish Food Board

> **Example:** Cully & Sully sought advice from An Bord Bia, an organisation that specialises in assisting in the development of new food-related businesses.

* **Feedback** from sales staff and previous market-research reports can be very useful to an existing business researching a new idea.

> **Example:** Coca-Cola's internal reports showed that sales of traditional coke were stagnant.

* **Commercial market-research companies:** Some firms specialise in collecting information about different markets, which they then sell to firms.

> **Example:** Ipsos MRBI, Red C Marker Research.

Advantages of desk research
1. Large quantities of useful information are **available quickly** and at a relatively **low cost.**

Disadvantages of desk research
1. The data may be too general or out of date.

Field research

Field research *involves going into the market place (the field) to gather the business information directly from customers and competitors.* Although more expensive than desk research, field research can yield very detailed information.

Types of field research

❖ **Observation research** *involves watching (observing) the behaviour of consumers.* For instance, observing how shoppers in a supermarket choose between different brands. This can reveal the most popular products and indicate market share. However, observation research only reveals what people do, not why they do it. Observation research can also be used to study competitors and observe how they run their businesses. This can be useful when planning a new business.

❖ **Customer surveys** *involve using a questionnaire and asking consumers about their attitudes towards new product ideas or to existing goods and services.* Surveys can be done **face to face,** over the **phone,** over the **Internet or by post**. Since it is usually not possible to survey every potential customer in the target market, a sample of the target market should be selected instead. **Sampling** *refers to interviewing a small group of people who are representative of the larger target market.*

| OL Short Q4 |
| OL Long Q3, 4 |
| HL Short Q3, 14 |
| HL Long Q8 |

> **Advantages of field research**
> 1. **More accurate and detailed** information can usually be obtained, especially about people's attitudes and behaviour.

> **Disadvantages of field research**
> 1. Face-to-face interviews and surveys can be a **time-consuming** and **costly** way of obtaining large amounts of information.

5. What are the stages in developing a new product or service?

New product development process

To maximise chances of success, new business opportunities should go through a development process before any decision is made to launch a new product on the market.

Stage 1	Stage 2	Stage 3	Stage 4	Stage 5	Stage 6	Stage 7
Idea Generation	Product Screening	Concept Development	Feasability Study	Prototype Development	Test Marketing	Production and Launch

Fig. 1 New product development process

Stage 1 – Idea generation

As discussed earlier, idea generation can come from internal or external sources of new ideas.

> **Example:** Cully had expertise in food while Sully had a business qualification from UCC. Using media reports, brainstorming and networking, they decided to look for possible business ideas related to food.

Stage 2 – Product screening

After identifying a number of potential business ideas, the next step is to select the most promising for detailed investigation and market research. **Product screening** *means sorting the promising product/service ideas from the weak ones.* These ideas can be classified as: (a) unrealistic, (b) marginal but with some potential or (c) definitely worth further investigation. By carefully selecting the most promising ideas, you will reduce the risk of wasting time and money researching unrealistic ideas.

> **Example:** After generating a number of possible food-related ideas, Cully and Sully carefully examined each one to assess how risky or promising it looked. This included doing some basic market research to screen out the least promising ideas and led them to drop all their ideas except for one targeting the ready-made meals market.

Stage 3 – Concept development

The next step involves turning the idea into a precise product concept or description that will appeal to customers and also be different from rivals' products. This is known as your unique selling point (USP). **A unique selling point (USP)** *is a feature of a product/service that makes it attractive and distinctively different from its rivals.*

> **Example:** Cully and Sully's idea to produce ready-made meals was refined and the concept was developed into a detailed idea with a USP of producing a high-quality range of meals using reusable ceramic dishes instead of plastic packaging.

> **Example:** In the car market, Mercedes-Benz's USP is luxury, while Toyota's is reliability.

Stage 4 – Feasibility study

A feasibility study *is a preliminary investigation into how realistic it will be to produce a product, how much it will cost, how many it is likely to sell and how much profit could be generated.* Feasibility studies are carried out to determine:

* **Production feasibility:** Can we make it? Do we have or can we get the necessary raw materials, equipment, skills, etc.?
* **Costs:** How much will it cost to make the product/provide the service?
* **Profit:** How much profit are we likely to make from this business idea? This is where a break-even analysis is very useful.

Example: With a clear idea of what their business would produce, Cully and Sully conducted a detailed feasibility study that showed the business idea could be profitable. This included doing detailed desk research into the market, competitors, costs and likely profitability.

Stage 5 – Prototype development

For manufactured products, a working prototype or test samples should be produced. *A prototype is a sample product manufactured on an experimental basis to see if the design idea works in practice and appeals to customers.* It helps an entrepreneur to identify what raw materials to use and how the product will be manufactured and also to calculate production costs and profits.

Example: Energised by the positive feasibility study results, budding entrepreneurs Cully and Sully set about experimenting with a prototype range of ready-made meals. Some recipes worked very well, while others were not so successful. For example, the recipe for the vegetarian pie had to go back to the drawing board because the sweet potatoes kept coming out 'too mushy'.

Stage 6 – Test marketing

Test marketing *involves launching the product on a small scale to evaluate consumer reaction to it.* Positive and negative reactions are then used to refine the design, price and promotion of the product. Test marketing is very important, as launching a new product can be very expensive and risky due to the large production, advertising and opportunity costs involved.

Example: When they were satisfied with their prototype recipes, Cully and Sully moved into field research by test-marketing their recipes, business name and packaging on potential customers. Feedback on the taste and price of their products was very positive, while the packaging was successful in creating a quality, wholesome image.

Stage 7 – Production and launch

If a product idea successfully passes the test marketing stage, then full-scale production can begin. The choice of target market will determine what price should be charged, where it should be sold and the best promotional strategy to use to persuade potential customers to buy the new product.

Example: Once test marketing had identified the most appealing product design, Cully and Sully set about setting up their business with proper finance, production facilities, staff and marketing. Using 'Cully & Sully' as their brand name, they were then ready to launch their range of ready-made meals and were confident that it would be successful.

OL Short Q5, 6
OL Long Q5, 6, 7
HL Short Q5, 6, 7
HL Long Q5, 6, 7

6. How can break-even analysis help to assess the likely profitability of a business idea?

Case Study

Bolsa Bags needs to break even

Sophie Cashell is considering setting up Bolsa Bags, a business producing stylish, upmarket, leather bags. Her market research has shown that there is a gap in the market for such a product. Sophie is writing her business plan and needs to know how many leather bags she needs to sell per week in order to break even.

Fixed costs   =   €4,000

Variable costs   =   €20 per bag

Sales price per unit =   €100 per bag

Sales price per unit is the price customers pay for a single item, i.e. the cost of a single Bolsa Bag.

To be profitable, a proposed new business such as Bolsa Bags must generate enough sales income (revenue) to cover all of the costs involved in the business.

❖ **Fixed costs** *are the costs that remain the same, regardless of the number of products produced.* For Bolsa Bags, this includes the cost of factory rental, wages, electricity and insurance. Even if the factory makes nothing, these costs will still be incurred.

❖ **Variable costs** *are costs that vary depending on how many units are produced.* If nothing is produced, no variable costs are incurred. For Bolsa Bags, this includes such things as the cost of leather, stitching and buckles.

❖ **The break-even point** *shows the amount of sales that must be achieved at a particular price in order to cover costs and break even.* If sales are below the break-even point, then losses will be made. If sales exceed the break-even point, then profits will be made. The break-even point for a product can be found by using a simple formula or by drawing a break-even chart.

OL Long Q8

Finding the break-even point using a simple formula

$$\text{Break-even formula} \ = \ \frac{\text{Fixed costs}}{\text{Sales price per unit } \textit{less } \text{Variable cost per unit}} \ = \ \frac{4,000}{100-20} \ = \ 50$$

Using the break-even formula, Sarah needs to sell 50 bags to break even.

✪ If sales are greater than 50, then the business will make a profit.

✪ If sales are less than 50, then the business will make a loss.

✪ If sales are, say, 80 units, then the company has a break-even margin of safety of 30 units.

The **margin of safety** *refers to the amount by which a firm's sales can drop before reaching break-even point.*

Recall and Review

Calculate the break-even point for Bolsa Bags for each of the following scenarios:

(a) Fixed costs = €4,000; Variable costs = €20; Price is set at €150
(b) Fixed costs = €4,000; Variable costs = €20; Price is set at €80
(c) Fixed costs = €4,000; Variable costs = €20; Price is set at €50
(d) Fixed costs = €5,000; Variable costs = €30; Price is set at €100
(e) Fixed costs = €5,000; Variable costs = €50; Price is set at €100

The expected **total revenue** and **total costs** for Bolsa Bags can be calculated at different levels of sales. For instance:

* If weekly sales are 0, then the business will make a loss of –€4,000.
* If sales are 50 bags per week, the business will break even.
* If sales are 100 bags per week, the business will make a profit of €4,000.

These figures are shown in the break-even calculations table below.

Sales (number of bags sold)	0	50	100
Price (average per bag)	€100	€100	€100
Total Revenue (TR) = Sales x Price	€0	€5,000	€10,000
Fixed Costs (FC)	€4,000	€4,000	€4,000
Variable Costs of €20 each (VC)	€0	€1,000	€2,000
Total Costs (TC) FC + VC	€4,000	€5,000	€6,000
Profit (TR – TC)	–€4,000	€0	€4,000

Finding the break-even point using a break-even chart

Using the figures set out in the break-even calculations table above, the break-even point can be presented using a break-even chart. A **break-even chart** *visually illustrates if a product will make a profit or loss depending on the quantity of sales achieved.*

● Step 1

Draw a **horizontal axis** to show output. This axis is labelled '**Quantity of Units Sold**'. The Bolsa Bag factory can produce a maximum of 100 bags per week. Mark the different quantities of output that can be produced by the business.

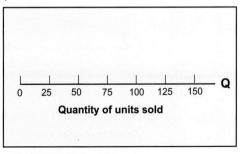

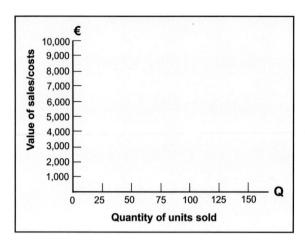

Step 2

Draw a **vertical axis** and label it 'Value of Sales/Costs'. Mark this line with the different amounts of revenue that the business may earn from sales, up to the maximum possible revenue of €10,000. This shows that if Bolsa produces 100 bags per week and sells them for €100 each, then it will make sales of €10,000.

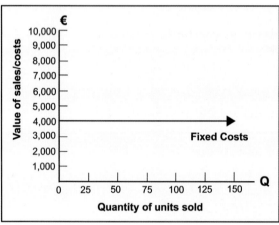

Step 3

Draw a **Fixed Costs line** straight across from €4,000 parallel to the horizontal axis.

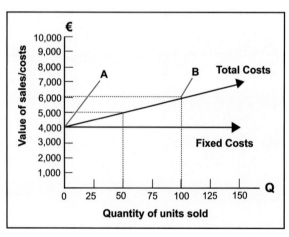

Step 4

Draw a **Total Costs line** starting at point A because Total Costs are €4,000 even when output is at zero. This line will go out to point B where total costs are €6,000 if 100 units are sold.

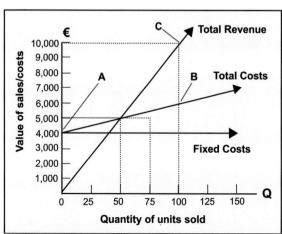

Step 5

Draw a **Total Revenue line** starting at 0 because if units produced are zero, sales revenue will also be zero. It will travel out to finish at point C, which indicates the revenue that will be generated (€10,000) if 100 units are sold.

Step 6

The point on the chart where the Total Revenue line crosses the Total Costs line is the **Break-even point.** This is where Total Revenue = Total Costs. The actual break-even amount can be read off the horizontal 'Quantity of Units Sold' axis. If sales fall below this quantity then Bolsa Bags will make a loss. Above this point, Bolsa Bags will make a profit.

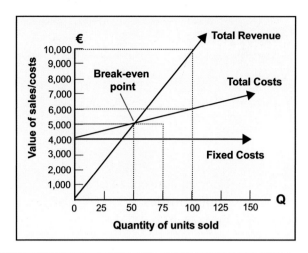

Step 7

Using the break-even diagram, it is easy to see the firm's margin of safety. The **margin of safety** is the difference between the actual level of sales and the break-even point. It shows the amount by which sales can drop before the firm reaches its break-even point. In this example, when Bolsa Bag's sales are 75, the margin of safety is 25 units (or bags).

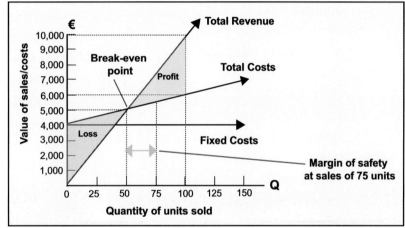

OL Short Q7

HL Short Q8

HL Long Q9, 10

Advantages of using break-even analysis

1. **Calculates the break-even point** for a product using a simple formula.
2. **Shows** how far sales could drop before making a loss.
3. **Shows** the possible **effect of price changes** on the break-even point and so helps marketing managers to **decide what prices** to charge.
4. **Shows** how the possible **effect of changes in fixed or variable costs** on the break-even point can be easily calculated.
5. Assists entrepreneurs and managers in assessing the financial **feasibility** of a new product.
6. Break-even charts can **communicate information** clearly about costs, revenue, break-even point and margin of safety in graph form.

Disadvantages of using break-even analysis

1. **It is simplistic** because it assumes that all units produced will be sold at the same price. In reality, firms often produce more than they can sell and have to sell the remaining stock at a discount.
2. **It ignores the effect that a change in price** will normally have on the level of sales. For instance, if prices are increased, then sales are likely to fall and vice versa but break-even analysis ignores this.

OL Short Q8

HL Short Q9

HL ABQ

Key Concepts & Business Terms

After studying this chapter the student should be able to explain the following key concepts and business terms:

1. Internal sources of business opportunities
2. Brainstorming
3. External sources of business opportunities
4. Networking
5. Management buy-outs
6. Market research
7. Desk research
8. Field research
9. Observation research
10. Customer surveys
11. Sampling
12. Stages in developing a new product
13. Product screening
14. Unique selling point (USP)
15. Feasibility study
16. Prototype
17. Test marketing
18. Break-even analysis
19. Break-even point
20. Fixed costs
21. Variable costs
22. Sales price per unit
23. Margin of safety
24. Break-even chart

useful websites

www.cullyandsully.com
www.ballygowan.ie

Leaving Certificate Practice Questions

Ordinary Level

Ordinary Level – Section 1 – Short Questions (10 marks each)

1. Identify **three** external sources of business opportunities for entrepreneurs.
2. List **two** agencies that can assist an entrepreneur to identify opportunities and get started in business.
3. Define 'market research'. [LCQ]
4. List **two** sources of information from field research.
5. List **five** of the seven stages of the new product/service development process.
6. Explain the term 'prototype development'.
7. Sketch and label a break-even chart. [LCQ]
8. List **one** reason why a break-even chart is important to business. [LCQ]

Ordinary Level – Section 2 – Long Questions

1. Explain **five** areas where an entrepreneur can look for a business idea. (25 marks)
2. Describe how an entrepreneur could use brainstorming to generate business ideas. (15 marks)

3. (a) Give **three** reasons why businesses carry out market research. (15 marks) [LCQ]

   (b) Explain the terms 'field research' and 'desk research' and use an example to illustrate each. (20 marks) [LCQ]

4. Distinguish between observational research and a customer survey. (20 marks).

5. Outline **five** steps involved in developing a new product. (25 marks)

6. Product screening, concept development and prototype development are some of the stages in the new product/service development process. Explain any **two** of the stages listed. (20 marks) [LCQ]

7. Discuss the importance of test marketing a product. (20 marks)

8. Distinguish between a fixed cost and a variable cost. (20 marks)

Higher Level

Higher Level – Section 1 – Short Questions (10 marks each)

1. Identify **three** sources of internal business opportunities for an existing business.

2. Define 'market research'. [LCQ]

3. Demonstrate a method of carrying out market research. [LCQ]

4. Distinguish briefly between desk research and field research.

5. What is meant by the term 'product screening'?

6. Define the term 'feasibility study'. [LCQ]

7. Prototype development involves . . . [LCQ]

8. Draw a break-even chart clearly indicating the following: (a) total cost line, (b) revenue line, (c) margin of safety, (d) fixed cost line and (e) break-even point.

9. List **three** uses for a break-even chart.

10. List **two** agencies that can assist an entrepreneur to identify business opportunities.

Higher Level – Section 2 – Applied Business Question

Rosewood Perfume

Rosewood Perfume was founded ten years ago and has established itself as a small but successful player in the international perfume market. The business was originally established by an entrepreneur who has since sold all his shares to ABC Investments Limited. These new owners have employed Sorcha Hanratty as the new chief executive to run the business.

As manager, Sorcha's first challenge was to get the business growing again. At present, the firm's sales are beginning to decline as larger competitors are now promoting their products with very expensive advertising campaigns. The business is now barely breaking even and Sorcha believes that Rosewood cannot compete in the mass market against such larger competitors. Instead she wants to concentrate on selling products for smaller niche markets.

> Sorcha has been looking for new ideas in magazines and on the Internet. One idea that caught her attention is to launch a range of pet perfumes for cats and dogs. 'Many people have pet cats and dogs. If just 5% of them bought Rosewood Pet Perfume, we would have a very successful product on our hands' she thinks.
>
> Sorcha is also aware that Rosewood Perfume is a relatively small business and cannot afford to risk investing large amounts of time and money launching a new product unless it is very confident of success.

1. Describe the sources of new business ideas that are available to Rosewood Perfume. (20 marks)
2. Explain how following the stages in the new product development process could help Sorcha minimise the risk of failure. (30 marks)
3. Evaluate the benefits of break-even analysis to Sorcha when considering launching a new perfume. (30 marks)

Higher Level – Section 2 – Long Questions

1. Outline **three** sources from which an enterprising person might identify new business ideas. (20 marks) [LCQ]
2. Discuss **four** external sources of new product or service ideas. (25 marks) [LCQ]
3. List and explain **four** sources of internal business opportunities. (20 marks)
4. Discuss why it is easier for an established business to identify and develop new business opportunities than for entrepreneurs starting out. (20 marks)
5. Outline the stages involved in the development process of a new product or service. (20 marks) [LCQ]
6. Deirdre Moloney hopes to start up her own cosmetics and personal beauty products business aimed at the consumer market. She has approached you as a marketing consultant for some marketing advice. In one single report, explain to her the stages in the development of a new product/service. (20 marks) [LCQ]
7. Evaluate the advisability of omitting the feasibility study stage from the product development process. (20 marks)
8. Illustrate how successful market research can be achieved through (a) field studies and (b) desk research. (20 marks) [LCQ]
9. A business supplies the following figures about its activities:

   Forecast output (sales) 20,000 units   Selling price €50 per unit

   Fixed costs €300,000   Variable cost per unit €20

   (a) Illustrate by means of a break-even chart: (i) the break-even point, (ii) the profit at forecast output, (iii) the margin of safety. (25 marks) [LCQ]

   (b) Outline the effect on the break-even point if variable costs increased to €25 per unit. Illustrate your answer on the break-even chart. (10 marks) [LCQ]

10. Seatsoft Ltd. manufactures office chairs. To survive it must cover its costs. Using the information below, illustrate by means of a break-even chart (a) the break-even point, (b) the profit at full capacity, and (c) the margin of safety. (40 marks) [LCQ]

Forecast output (sales)	70,000 units	Selling price	€40 per unit
Fixed costs	1 million	Variable costs per unit	€20

Chapter 15
Marketing

Key Study Questions

Case Study

The Gleeson Group

Irish drinks company, the Gleeson Group, produces brands such as Tipperary Spring Water, Cadet Lemonade and Boost Energy Drinks. It competes in an Irish soft drinks market that is highly competitive and dominated by big names such as Club Orange, Coca-Cola, Pepsi, 7-Up, Fanta and Lucozade.

The Gleeson Group decided to launch a new soft drink but understood that to be successful they would have to get the marketing right. The company was very aware that many internationally successful brands like Canada Dry, Sunkist and Tango entered the Irish market but due to poor marketing failed and ended up losing millions of euro instead.

As a first step, Gleesons carried out extensive **market research** to reduce the risk of failure. **Desk research** revealed that the soft drinks market in Ireland has sales of hundreds of million of euro per annum and that the average Irish person is estimated to consume over 100 litres of soft drinks every year. The desk research also showed that 70% of soft drinks in Ireland are sold through vending machines and

small independent retailers, 20% through multiple supermarkets and the remaining 10% through pubs. Furthermore, desk research revealed that consumer tastes are changing, moving away from traditional sugar-based soft drinks towards lighter, more natural drinks with refreshing flavours. This has led to a strong growth in sales of diet, herbal, energy and mineral water drinks. Many new **brands** have been launched on the market to satisfy these new consumer tastes.

Using **field research**, the marketing manager learned that people, especially young adults, were prepared to pay a higher price (premium) for many of these new drinks.

Overall, market research revealed a niche in **the market** for a high-quality soft drink with natural ingredients and a fresher taste that would appeal to the young **female adult segment** of the market. This led the Gleeson Group to devise a marketing strategy to create such a soft drink with a high-quality image to win over these customers.

Before launching their drink, a **marketing mix** had to be designed, covering the product design, packaging, price, distribution and promotion. The company was aware that they had to get the mix right from the very beginning as they would only have one shot at getting the formula right for the very competitive soft drinks market.

1. What is marketing?

> **Marketing is about identifying and satisfying consumer needs.**

In the past, businesses often produced what they were good at and then tried to find buyers for those products. Today, however, successful businesses usually do the opposite, operating on the basis of the marketing concept. The essence of the **marketing concept** is to firstly identify the market needs and then develop products to profitably meet those needs. It focuses the firm on **customers' needs** at all times. This means that **marketing is not the same as selling.** Selling is concerned with trying to persuade customers to buy a good or service after it has been developed.

Marketing starts **before** the product or service has been developed, by trying to find out what customers want, and then getting it to the market. **Marketing** *means identifying the needs of consumers and then producing and selling products and services to satisfy those needs profitably.* When done effectively, marketing means producing goods that customers will buy if sold at the right price and available in the right place.

OL Short Q1

2. What is a marketing strategy?

A **marketing strategy** *is a plan setting out how a business will identify and satisfy the customer needs identified by market research.* Developing an effective marketing strategy involves:

- ✳ **Researching** the market to identify new business **opportunities**
- ✳ **Segmenting** the market to identify suitable **target markets**
- ✳ **Positioning** the product in the market.
- ✳ **Devising** a suitable **marketing mix** before launching the product

> A marketing strategy is a plan for how the needs of the target market will be identified and satisfied.

> See Chapter 14: Identifying Business Opportunities for more information on market research.

Segmenting the market

Businesses use market research to identify different types of consumers and those whose needs may have been overlooked. **Market segmentation** *divides consumers into different categories, e.g. young females, high-income males, sports enthusiasts, etc.* The two most common methods of segmenting a market are **demographic** and **psychological**:

- ✪ **Demographic segmentation** *analyses consumers in terms of age, income, sex, social class, geographic area, etc.*

> **Example:** Pepsi Max drinkers are young males under 25 spread across all geographic areas. Finches' consumers are young, health-conscious females.

- ✪ **Psychological segmentation** *analyses consumers on the basis of their attitudes and tastes, for example, yuppies, hippies, conservatives or impulsive shoppers.*

> **Example:** The Gleeson Group segmented the soft drinks market into various segments including high-quality and low-quality drinks, fruit drinks, colas, health-conscious consumers and those who didn't care, budget brands and high-price brands.

> **Example:** Volkswagen uses psychological segmentation to analyse the car market.

Case Study

How Volkswagen segment the car market

Audi, SEAT, Volkswagen and Skoda cars are all designed and built by the Volkswagen company with similar parts and quality standards. Volkswagen used **psychological segmentation** to analyse the car buyer market and identified four basic distinct groups: prestige, adventurous, conservative and economy. Using careful design and promotion, each of these car brands is then **positioned** to target consumers in each of these distinct **market segments**.

❖ Audi is targeted at the prestige segment of the market

❖ Skoda is targeted at the economy segment of the market.

❖ SEAT is targeted at the adventurous segment of the market

❖ Volkswagen is targeted at the conservative segment of the market

OL Short Q2

Target a market niche

Targeting a specific group of consumers is likely to be more effective than wasting time trying to make a product appeal to everyone. A **market niche** *is a specific gap in the market for a new* **product** *or service.* Successful entrepreneurs and businesses are quick to identify and satisfy market niches for new products or services. Once a niche has been identified, the customers who will buy such a product will become the **target market**. The target market is a precise description of the customers to whom a product will be aimed. Normally, this will only be decided after careful market research.

> Example: The Gleeson Group identified a niche for a high-quality soft drink that would appeal to health-conscious young consumers.

Position the product

Product positioning *means creating an image for a product in the mind of consumers in the target market.*

> Example: Gleesons decided to position their new product as a superior quality soft drink aimed at young consumers. Club Orange, on the other hand, is positioned as a more fun product.

HL Long Q1, 2

Case Study

Pepsi Max & Coca Cola Zero

One of the Gleeson Group's largest rivals, Pepsi Cola, conducted their own **desk research** and **field research** to find out who bought their cola drinks. After analysing their **market research** findings, they discovered that both males and females liked the taste of Diet Pepsi and were concerned about their sugar intake.

However, the market research also showed that males

were unwilling to buy Diet Pepsi because they were afraid of being seen as enjoying a 'girlie' diet drink. According to Pepsi's **marketing manager**, 'Diet drinks in Ireland have been traditionally perceived as having an inferior taste and a feminine image. We knew that if we overcame these two obstacles we could have a winner.'

Pepsi used their market research to divide the cola market into two distinct **segments** with different needs. For females they would continue to sell traditional Diet Pepsi. For the male segment they created a new product with a 'cool', macho image and called it Pepsi Max. Same product but different **branding**.

Coca-Cola then copied Pepsi's strategy and launched the Coca-Cola Zero brand for young males who were put off by the idea of being seen buying Diet Coke.

Recall and Review

Who do you think are the target markets for the following?

(a) Organic Fanatic Drinks
(b) Lyons Tea
(c) *The Simpsons*
(d) Nissan Micra
(e) RTÉ Radio 1

(f) Finches Orange
(g) *The Irish Times*
(h) Rolls Royce cars
(i) MTV
(j) 2FM

OL Long Q1

HL Short Q1

3. What is the marketing mix?

Once the target market and product positioning have been determined, all the elements of the marketing mix are put together to achieve the marketing goal. **The marketing mix** *consists of four elements (the 4 Ps) used to turn the marketing strategy and product positioning into reality – Product, Price, Place and Promotion.*

The marketing mix breaks the marketing strategy down into four key areas:
* **Product**
* **Price**
* **Place**
* **Promotion**

4. In the marketing mix, what is 'product'?

In the marketing mix, product focuses on:
* Design
* Quality
* Branding
* Packaging
* Product life cycle

The **product** *is the good or service produced to meet a consumer need.* Designing a suitable product is the most important part of the marketing mix. If the product does not satisfy customer needs, then the other **Ps** of the marketing mix will not work. The **product portfolio/range** *describes the range of products produced by a business.*

**Fig. 1 The key elements involved in designing
a product for the market.**

Product design and quality

> **Example:** Gleesons carefully designed their product to ensure that customers would agree that it tasted better than the competition. The company used outside experts to help them get the flavour and ingredients just right.

Product design and quality must consider function and form:

Function: The product must **do what consumers expect it to do**. According to the law, this means that the product must be of **merchantable quality** and **fit for the purpose intended**.

Form: The product must also be **practical** and **appealing** to the target market in terms of shape, style, colour and image.

Product branding

> **Example:** Coming up with a **brand name** for the new product was an important part of designing an attractive **product**. Gleesons wanted a name for their new product that suggested the brand had an old, established Irish heritage. They came up with 'Finches'. The marketing manager liked the name but, just to be sure, used field **research** to test reaction among potential customers. Reaction was very positive and the name became part of the 'product'.

Top-selling grocery brands in Ireland
- **Coca-Cola**
- **Avonmore Milk**
- **Brennan's Bread**
- **Danone Yogurt**
- **Tayto Crisps**
- **Lyons Tea**
- **Cadbury Dairy Milk**
- **Denny sausages**
- **Jacob's Biscuits**

Branding means creating an identity for a product that clearly distinguishes it from competitors. It consists of a brand name and logo.
A **brand name** *is the distinctive name given to a product, such as Finches or Pepsi Max.* A **brand logo** *is a distinctive visual image that will help the product stand out from competitors. It can be the way a brand name is written, a separate image, or both.*

> **Example:** Finches' brand logo is a combination of how the name is written and a picture of a bird. Pepsi chose the Pepsi Max name because they felt it was catchy and conveyed the idea of maximum taste. Coca-Cola was originally called Yum Yum but that brand name failed to catch on and had to be changed.

A **brand leader** *is the brand with the highest percentage share of a particular market.*

> **Example:** Coca-Cola is the brand leader in the Irish soft drinks market, while Tayto is the brand leader in the Irish crisp market.

Own-label brands *are products sold by retailers under their own brand name.* The goods are produced by manufacturers to the retailers' precise specifications and are usually sold at a lower price than similar leading private brands.

> **Example:** Tesco's own-label brand is called Tesco Finest.

Benefits of product branding to a firm

- ✪ **Recognition:** Branding improves recognition of the product and the business name and **differentiates** them from competitors. This makes it easier to advertise a particular product. It is cheaper and easier to launch new products if they are associated with an existing well-known brand name.

- ✪ **Desire:** Branding helps to promote a desired image of a product to the target market.

- ✪ **Loyalty:** Easy recognition and familiarity to consumers increases sales and promotes long-term customer loyalty. **Brand loyalty** *occurs when customers repeat-purchase a particular branded product on a regular basis.* Coca-Cola has a high level of brand loyalty in the soft drinks market.

- ✪ **Higher Price:** A high-quality brand image can allow a firm to charge a higher price and earn extra profits.

OL Long Q3

HL Short Q3

> *Recall and Review*
>
> 1. Marketing managers frequently talk about their brands as having different brand images or 'personalities'. Analyse the brand images that you think each of the following brands have:
>   (a) Diet Coke
>   (b) Finches Orange
>   (c) Cidona
>   (d) Tesco Finest Cola
>   (e) Club Orange
>   (f) Sunny D
> 2. Have a class brainstorm to identify suitable brand names for the following products:
>   (a) a new brand of breakfast cereal,
>   (b) a new brand of sports car,
>   (c) a new brand of chocolate bar.

Product packaging

Product packaging should address the following:

❖ **Provide protection** from damage on the way from manufacturer to consumer. Ideally, packaging should also be designed for easy storage and display.

> **Example:** The Finches' range of drinks was designed to be sold in a range of different size packages, including returnable bottles for pubs and 1.5 litre plastic bottles for the independent shops and supermarket retailers.

❖ **Look good** to encourage consumers to purchase them. Design and packaging have been described as the 'silent salesperson' because an eye-catching design, conveying the right **image** and product information, can strongly influence sales.

> **Example:** Pepsi carefully researched the taste and packaging for Pepsi Max before launching it. Field research showed that the red, blue and silver design was the most appealing look for the young male target market.
>
> Besides protecting the drink, Finches bottles were designed to appeal to the target market.

❖ **Provide information** regarding the ingredients, specifications, manufacturer, use of the products, etc.

Protecting product design and branding

Depending on the business, valuable product designs, packaging and logos can be protected using **patents** and **trademarks**.

✳ **A patent** *provides legal protection of an invention or a design of a product to the inventor or designer.* Copying a patented invention or design is illegal.

> **Example:** Like many firms, Coca-Cola aggressively protects its trademark logo and this has meant frequently going to court to protect the highly successful logo from infringement.

✳ **Trademarks** *are logos that are legally registered by businesses to distinguish them and their products from competitors.* Like patents, registered trademarks are legally protected and it is illegal for anyone to copy them.

To get patent or trademark protection, a fee must be paid to the Patents and Trademarks Office.

Product life cycle

The **product life cycle** *refers to the theory that most products pass through distinct life stages: product development, launch, growth, maturity, saturation and eventual decline.*

Product development: Market research identifies a market niche. A product, such as Finches Orange, is designed and test marketed. A marketing strategy and mix is planned. Due to research costs and initial low sales, the product will generate a negative cashflow during this stage.

Growth: The product becomes known and accepted and sales begin to rise rapidly, generating a positive cashflow. Money may have to be invested in expanding production to keep up with demand while also ensuring that quality is maintained.

Saturation: Sales flatten out. Radical changes may be necessary in the marketing mix to hold or increase sales. Competitive advertising and sales promotions often become common to prevent sales going into decline. This is the stage for Coca-Cola in Ireland at present.

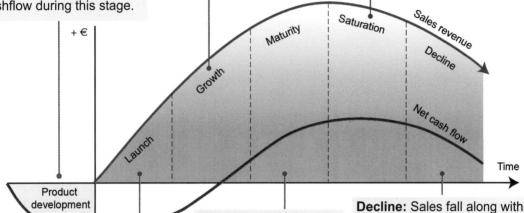

Launch: The product is launched onto the market. Typically there is a high expenditure on distribution and product promotion to build customer awareness.

Maturity: Sales start to level off. Product is generating strong profits that justify the heavy expenditure in the earlier stages. Rival 'copy-cat' products may enter the market. Firms often use special offers to keep consumers interested and so increase sales.

Decline: Sales fall along with profitability. The marketing manager needs to determine whether to stop producing the product, let sales die out 'naturally' or try to rescue the product by redesigning the marketing mix. When sales of Cidona and Club Orange began to decline, a decision was taken to increase advertising and change the brand image to appeal to younger customers.

Fig. 2 The stages of the product life cycle.

The product life-cycle theory says that every product will eventually decline and die. A business should therefore be constantly developing new products to bring to the market to replace those going into decline. Ideally, new product development should be financed from the positive cash flow generated by profitable brands in the maturity/saturation phase.

Factors that influence the length of a product life cycle

- ☼ **Durability:** Goods that are relatively durable, such as cookers, will not have to be replaced for many years. This can result in market saturation very quickly. The situation is similar with high-quality goods such as expensive cars.

Short fad product life cycle

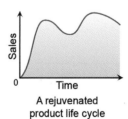

A rejuvenated product life cycle

A partially rejuvenated product life cycle

○ **Fashion:** Highly fashionable items, such as very trendy clothing, are likely to go into decline very quickly.

○ **Technological innovation:** New inventions and products can make relatively new products obsolete very quickly.

> Example: The development of new microchips can make existing computer models go out of date in only a few years.

○ **Marketing:** Some firms successfully redesign the entire marketing mix for products in decline to give them a new lease of life. This was done with Club Orange and Skoda cars.

> Example: Over time, Gleesons have expanded the Finches **product range** to include Finches Orange, Finches Lemon, Finches Orange Light and Finches Rock Shandy. This has extended the product life cycle of the Finches brand.

OL Short Q4
OL Long Q2

HL Short Q2
HL Long Q3, 4

5. In the marketing mix, what is 'price'?

Prices must be set at a level that will allow the business to earn a profit. The price set will also influence the level of sales and may affect the image and positioning of the product in the eyes of the target market.

Pricing Strategies

In the marketing mix, pricing strategies can be:
- **General**
- **High price**
- **Low price**

Pricing strategies *aim to set a price that will help the firm to achieve its long-term marketing objectives.* Whatever the price, it must generate sufficient **sales** to earn a **profit** for the business.

● General pricing strategies

❖ **Mark-up (cost-plus pricing)** *means adding a standard profit percentage to the direct costs of production (cost of sales) of the item to arrive at the final selling price.*

> Example: A retailer may add 40% to the cost price of soft drinks before selling it to customers.

❖ **Psychological pricing** *means setting a price based on the expectations of the customers in the target market.* Many companies, such as perfume and car producers charge a high price for their product in order to create a luxurious, exclusive image for it that will attract higher sales. Setting prices below psychological barriers is also very common, e.g. €1.99 instead of €2.

Sadolin use psychological pricing

High price strategies

* **Price leadership/premium pricing** *occurs when a firm deliberately charges a higher price than competitors to create an impression of superior quality.* This is reinforced by the other elements of the marketing mix such as expensive packaging and stylish promotion.

Example: Finches' marketing mix was originally designed to convey an image of quality and to ensure profitability. This meant that a suitable pricing strategy had to be carefully selected. For the launch it was decided that prices would be set roughly 10–20% higher than those of competitors.

* **Price skimming:** *This is where firms charge a very high price at the launch of a new product with the intention of recovering the high development costs as quickly as possible.*

Example: Price skimming is very commonly used by businesses launching new consumer electronic products.

* **Profit-maximising pricing** *means setting a price that will generate the largest amount of profit as quickly as possible.*

Example: Profit maximisation is often used when setting ticket prices for major music concerts.

Low price strategies

* **Penetration pricing:** *This is when an initial low price is charged in order to capture as much market share as quickly as possible.* This allows the business to generate economies of scale rapidly.

Example: Penetration pricing has been used to promote the sale of mobile phones in Ireland.

* **Discriminatory pricing** *means charging different prices to different customers for the same product or service.* This is usually done to accommodate the different incomes of different segments of the market.

Example: Bus Éireann charge different prices for students than for other customers.

* **Predatory pricing** *means setting prices below cost in order to drive a competitor out of the market.* A **price war** *occurs when competing firms retaliate against price cuts with further reductions.* This creates a downward cycle in prices as firms compete to attract customers.

Example: When Dunnes Stores and Virgin launched their own-brand colas, a soft-drinks price war broke out. Coke, 7-Up, Fanta and Club Orange all dropped their prices to retain customers. However, Gleesons did not cut the price of their Finches product for fear of damaging the brand's quality image. The strategy worked as customers remained loyal.

* A **loss leader** *is a product sold at or below cost price in the hope of generating other, more profitable sales.*

Example: This tactic is commonly used by retailers to attract customers into a store.

OL Short Q5, 6
OL Long Q4

HL Short Q4
HL Long Q5, 6

Factors that influence price

OL Long Q5

> The price selected should cover all costs and make a profit.

Before deciding on the final price, the marketing manager will consider the following:

❖ **Costs** of production and the need to make a **profit**. This means looking closely at the **break-even point** for the product.

❖ **Level of demand** for the product. The higher the demand, the higher the price that can be charged.

❖ **Competitors' prices** and desired **product positioning**, e.g. exclusive image or mass market appeal?

❖ Stage in the **product life cycle.** Products in the final stages cannot support a high price.

❖ **Government taxes** such as VAT that will be added to the final price need to be considered.

❖ **Legal restrictions** on freedom to set prices for certain products or services (e.g. taxi fares) or to prevent illegal price-fixing among competitors.

6. In the marketing mix, what is 'place'?

In the marketing mix, **place** focuses on where customers will be able to access the goods or services. This means selecting a suitable channel of distribution. **Channels of distribution** *describe the various paths that goods may follow from producer to consumer.*

> **Example:** Finches' marketing mix was designed with the intention of distributing the drink through small retailers, supermarkets and pubs. This ensured that it would be available to most consumers at their point of purchase and was essential in securing a share of the soft drinks market.

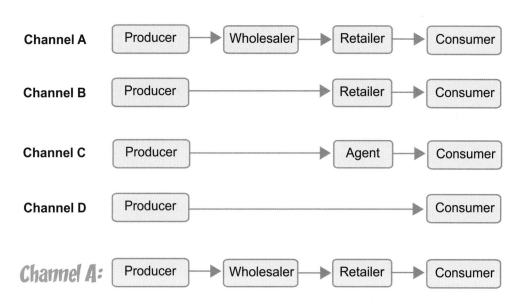

Channel A: Producer → Wholesaler → Retailer → Consumer

Wholesalers *are businesses that buy in very large quantities from producers and sell in smaller quantities to retailers.* This method of distributing consumer goods is known as 'breaking bulk'. Traditionally, this was the main route for distributing consumer goods in the past and is still very important for distributing goods to small, independent retailers who need to stock a wide variety of goods from different manufacturers. **Retailers** *are outlets at the end of the chain of distribution that sell goods and services to consumers.*

> **Example:** Finches Orange is distributed to small retailers using this channel of distribution.

Benefits of Channel A

1. **Distribution** is simplified as wholesalers take responsibility for 'breaking bulk'.
2. **Costs** are reduced by selling to a smaller number of large wholesalers who, along with retailers, are also responsible for transport and storage costs.
3. **Market** reached is potentially **very large**.

Possible problems of Channel A

1. End product may be **more expensive for consumers** as separate profit mark-ups are usually added at each stage.

OL Short Q7
OL Long Q6

Channel B:

Producer ⟶ Retailer → Consumer

The growth of large retail chains like Dunnes Stores, Aldi, Lidl and Tesco has meant that they can now bypass wholesalers and purchase large quantities of goods directly from manufacturers at a discount. This allows them to sell the goods to consumers more cheaply than smaller retailers that have to buy through wholesalers.

> **Example:** When supplying Finches drinks to supermarkets, the Gleeson Group are using this channel of distribution.

Own-brand products are produced specially for many of these large retail chains. This channel also includes mail-order businesses and online retailers that buy directly from producers.

Benefits of Channel B

1. **Distribution** is simplified by cutting out the wholesalers.
2. **Costs** are reduced by selling to a smaller number of large retailers.
3. A **mass market** can potentially be reached by producers.

Possible problems of Channel B

1. Producers' **profitability** can be undermined by the very large discounts expected by large retailers.

Channel C:

Producer → Agent → Consumer

Some manufacturers distribute their goods through agents. **Agents** *are businesses contracted to sell goods on behalf of a producer in a particular area.* In return, the agents earn a commission on every sale they make. This is not a common channel of distribution, but is used by some producers such as travel agents, Tupperware and Avon Cosmetics.

Benefits of Channel C

1. Larger **profit** margin as both wholesalers and retailers are cut out.

Possible problems of Channel C

1. Good **selling agents** can be difficult to find, motivate and retain.
2. It can be difficult to reach a **mass market**.

Channel D:

Producer → Consumer

Some producers sell directly to their customers. This channel of distribution particularly suits perishable products (e.g. farmers markets) or specialised products (e.g. craft jewellery). It is becoming more popular as many producers now use the Internet to sell directly to consumers without having to distribute through retail outlets (e.g. Dell, Apple).

Benefits of Channel D

1. **Profit** is maximised for producers as there are no middlemen.
2. Valuable **feedback** can be obtained by producers from customers.

Possible problems of Channel D

1. All the **responsibility for sales** lies with the producers, not all of whom may have the marketing skills or time required.

Choosing a distribution channel

Producers want to make as much profit as possible by reaching as many target consumers as possible. They need to consider:

* **Target market:** Will the chosen channel of distribution allow the goods to reach the target market?

* **Product image:** How will the channel affect the desired brand image? For example, French cosmetics company Chanel refuses to allow its perfume products to be sold in supermarkets.

* **How easy will it be to transport** supplies through this channel?

* **Cost:** The more stages there are in a channel of distribution the more expensive it will become for the end consumer. Each of the 'middlemen' will add a mark-up to the price before selling it on.

* **Impact on cashflow:** Small retailers may pay cash on delivery for their stock, while larger retailers may look for two months' credit before paying.

* **Special conditions:** Some retailers or wholesalers may attach special conditions before agreeing to distribute a manufacturer's goods, such as the manufacturer not being allowed to supply goods through rival channels or retailers.

> OL Short Q8, 9
> OL Long Q7
> HL Short Q5

Ease of transport is important for product distribtion

Case Study

Marketing Goodfella's Pizzas

Goodfella's pizzas are manufactured in Ireland by Green Isle Foods. Before Goodfella's American-style pizzas was launched, careful desk **market research** was carried out to determine whether there was a big enough market in Ireland for a new brand of pizza. The research was very positive and indicated that the new pizza brand should be targeted at young adults and households with young children.

A suitable **marketing mix** was put together including a €6 million advertising campaign to launch the product in the first year, a very large sum by Irish standards. The advertising and other **marketing** promotions were carefully designed to show pizzas as a fun food and good for sharing with people of all ages. The result was a quadrupling of the overall pizza market, with the Goodfella's **brand** capturing a 75% share.

Since the original product launch, the brand has been supported by ongoing sales promotion and advertising to protect Goodfella's **product positioning** in the Irish market. Additionally, owners Green Isle Foods are constantly conducting **desk research** such as examining market statistics and other data that may identify problems and new opportunities for pizza products. One result of this ongoing desk research has been the successful exporting of pizzas from Ireland to other countries, including Italy.

Recall and Review

1. Explain the terms highlighted in bold.

2. Design a marketing mix for a new pizza brand that could compete against Goodfella's.

3. List **one** example of a product distributed through each of the different channels of distribution.

1. In the marketing mix, what is 'promotion'?

In the marketing mix, *promotion* focuses on making the target market aware of – and favourably disposed towards – the product.

Promotion *refers to all the efforts (excluding price) made by the seller to communicate and influence the target market to buy a product.* Promotion is often used when:

- ✪ A new product is being introduced to the market.
- ✪ An existing product is at maturity, saturation or decline and sales may need to be boosted.

Example: The final element of the marketing mix for the Finches soft drinks range was to design a **promotional campaign** to launch the product. Suitable promotional activities and media had to be selected. Advertising campaigns were designed that had to be effective in communicating persuasively with the young target audience.

Finches' **advertising** for the original launch was done mainly through cinema and television advertising because they were considered to be very effective at reaching this target market. Public relations and sponsorship has also been used to promote the brand.

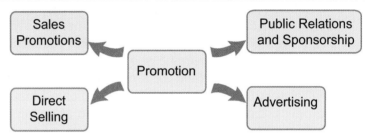

Fig. 3 The key elements in promoting a product.

Advertising

- ❖ **Advertising** *consists of messages designed to* **inform, persuade or remind** *people to buy a product or service.*
- ❖ The **advertising media** *refers to the communication channels available to a business for its advertising.* Each differs in terms of cost and how effectively it reaches the target market.
- ❖ **Point-of-sale advertising** *uses promotional displays at the place of purchase.* The intention is for them to be eye-catching and attractive enough to stimulate impulse buying. This is regularly used to promote the Finches brand.
- ❖ **Merchandising** *refers to point-of-sale promotional displays designed to attract attention to a product and increase sales.* They include using window displays, cardboard displays, giving free samples or attractively positioning goods on shelves. Merchandising is important for many businesses because many supermarket purchases are impulse purchases. **Impulse purchases** *are unplanned decisions to buy a particular product or brand.* Many goods such as books and sweets are very prone to impulse purchasing by consumers.

OL Long Q12

Choosing an advertising media depends on:

* **The target market** the business is trying to reach. A mass market needs a mass media such as national radio or television. A specialist market, such as farmers, could be better reached through a specialist publication like the *Irish Farmers' Journal*. A local business should use a local media, while a national business should use a national media.

* **Cost** of buying advertising and the size of the **advertising budget** available. TV advertising is the most expensive, but it reaches the largest audiences.

> **Common advertising media include:**
> * Point-of-sale displays
> * TV
> * Radio
> * Internet
> * Magazines
> * Newspapers
> * Cinema
> * Posters
> * Buses
> * Word of mouth

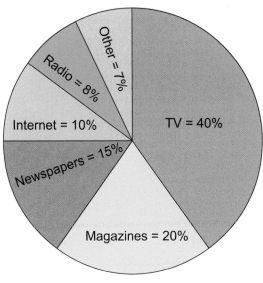

Fig. 4 Where most spending on advertising goes.

Energizer batteries have used poster advertising

> OL Short Q12
> OL Long Q9, 11, 13
> HL Short Q7, 8

Sales promotions

✪ **Sales promotions** *refer to specific incentives offered to customers to attract their attention, increase sales and encourage customer loyalty.* Techniques used include special offers, giving out free samples, money-off coupons, loyalty cards and competitions, and merchandising.

> Sales promotions provide incentives to the target market.

> HL Short Q10

279

Direct selling

Personal selling contacts target customers directly in person or by telephone.

There are three main types of direct selling:

❖ **Personal selling** *refers to contacting existing and potential customers in person to generate sales.* This job is normally carried out by sales representatives (reps) of the business. Sales reps must have good communications skills and product knowledge to convince customers to buy.

❖ **Telemarketing** *means communicating with customers by telephone to generate sales and deal with customer queries and complaints.* It can involve calls to targeted consumers, for example, encouraging consumers to make enquiries using a free phone number and to place orders. Telemarketing reduces the need for sales reps to travel, thus saving on travel costs. It can also provide **instant customer feedback** and is convenient for customers.

❖ **Direct mail** *involves sending promotional messages directly to target customers, most commonly by post, door-to-door leafleting or e-mail.* It is also known as 'junk mail' because advertisers know that a very high proportion of the material will be thrown away. However, even a small percentage of responses could be sufficient to justify the financial cost of the mail-out to the advertiser. **Spam** *refers to electronic junk mail.*

Public Relations (PR)

Public relations means using media such as TV, radio, Internet, newspapers and magazines to attract favourable coverage.

Public relations (PR) *means communicating with the media using news stories to create good publicity for a firm or its products or to respond to negative publicity.* PR tries to protect and enhance the reputation of a business to boost sales. Some companies employ their own public relations officer (PRO) while others hire PR agencies to provide this service.

> Example: When the Finches Orange brand became a success despite fierce competition from the giants of the drinks industry, the marketing manager issued press releases and encouraged journalists to report this success.

Sometimes, PR can mean defending the reputation of the business from criticism in times of crisis. A business does this by trying to put across the firm's side of a story to the public.

> Example: When the launch of 'New Coke' flopped, Coca-Cola had to hold interviews with the press to reassure the public that the original flavour would still be available.

● PR Methods

❖ **Sponsorship** *is a type of PR where a company pays money towards the cost of a sporting or other charitable cause.* In return, the business gets the benefit of being associated with exciting sporting events or good causes.

Example: Firms providing sponsorship to the top GAA county teams spend hundreds of thousands of euros to have their brand name and logo appear on the team jerseys. The money is used by the teams to cover expenses, such as equipment, travel and meals.

❖ **Contacting the press** to attract media attention to some aspect of the business such as the launch of a new product, the official opening of new premises or positive achievements of the business or its staff.
❖ **Paying celebrities** to be associated with (to '**endorse**') a firm's products.
❖ **All contact with the public** is designed to create a good public impression. These include the courtesy shown by staff towards the public when answering the **phone,** dealing with enquiries, and handling complaints, as well as the **appearance** of staff, premises, websites, etc.

OL Short Q10, 11
OL Long Q8, 10
HL Short Q6
HL Long Q7, 8, 9

Case Study — Jacob Fruitfield

Every year hundreds of millions of euro worth of biscuits are sold in Ireland. Companies competing in this market include Cadbury, McVitie's and the **market leader** Irish firm Jacob Fruitfield who have over 50% market share with products such as Fig Rolls, Cream Crackers, Club Milk, Afternoon Tea and Kimberly biscuits.

Jacob Fruitfield's marketing is aimed at retaining its high **market share** despite intense foreign competition. It regularly reviews the **marketing mix** for its biscuit brands to ensure that they appeal to their target market.

In recent years, **product design** has changed as biscuit recipes have been improved, including adding more chocolate. **Prices** are constantly monitored to ensure they remain very competitive.

Packaging, including wrappers and tins, have been redesigned to appear more attractive. New advertising campaigns using TV and poster advertising campaigns are used to promote the Jacob Fruitfield **product range**. The business also regularly uses merchandising displays in supermarkets to promote impulse purchasing in shops and supermarkets.

Recall and Review
1. Analyse how the marketing mix is used to ensure success for the Jacob's range of biscuits.
2. Recommend changes you would make to the marketing mix for Jacob's Club Milk bars to make them more attractive to teenagers.

Putting together a promotional campaign

> Marketing promotions need to be carefully planned, implemented and evaluated.

There are three key stages in the development of a successful marketing promotion campaign: planning, implementation and evaluation.

1. Plan

* **Identify the target audience** at which the marketing promotions will be aimed and decide the purpose of the campaign.
* **Set a budget:** Decide how much will be spent on the campaign.
* **Create a promotional message.** Effective promotional messages should focus on a product USP.
* **Choose an appropriate medium** to ensure the promotional message reaches the target audience as cost-effectively as possible.

2. Implement

Put the promotional campaign plan into action and ensure there is sufficient stock and sales staff to deal with the anticipated increased demand. **Businesses** should also be prepared to react quickly to any negative feedback or controversy that the campaign might produce in order to protect the firm's reputation and the image of a brand.

3. Evaluate

OL Long Q14, 16, 17

Compare the results of the campaign with the original objectives and identify the reasons for any unexpected success or failure.

8. What is the role of ethics in marketing promotions?

Case Study

Schoolgirls Rumble Ribena

Two schoolgirls in New Zealand caught out one of the largest companies in the world after results of their school science experiment suggested that ready-to-drink Ribena contained almost no trace of vitamin C, while the orange juice they tested contained almost four times as much. The girls were puzzled as Ribena's advertising claimed that 'the blackcurrants in Ribena have four times the vitamin C of oranges'.

Astonished, they wrote to Ribena's manufacturers, transnational Glaxo Smith Klein (GSK). The company did not respond to their letters and their phone calls were not returned. The girls' findings were then brought to the attention of advertising watchdogs in New Zealand who took the company to court on charges of misleading advertising.

Under the **Consumer Protection Act 2007**, it is illegal for advertisements and other marketing promotions in Ireland to make obviously false statements. However, they can still mislead through the use of suggestion and by the use of subtle or indirect claims. Complaints against advertising in Ireland can be made to the:

> **Advertising should obey consumer rights laws and voluntary regulations.**

✪ **National Consumer Agency,** a State agency with the power to ban any form of marketing promotion that breaks laws such as the Consumer Protection Act 2007. The agency can prosecute businesses which make legally false or misleading claims. It is also responsible for enforcing the ban on advertising products such as cigarettes.

> **Example:** Irish bakeries were banned from advertising 'light bread' products as being 'cholesterol free' and 'low fat'. What the bakery advertisements did not tell the consumer was that all bread is cholesterol-free and very low fat anyway. The advertisements were clearly aimed at a health-conscious segment of the market and tried to create the misleading impression that 'light bread' is in some way different from ordinary bread.

✪ **Advertising Standards Authority of Ireland (ASAI),** a body set up and financed by the advertising industry in Ireland to ensure that advertisements are socially acceptable. They operate a **voluntary code of conduct** whereby advertisements are requested to be 'legal, decent, honest and truthful'. The public are invited to complain about advertisements which they think break the code. However, the ASAI can only request that the advertiser remove the advertisement; it has **no legal power** to stop advertisements.

> **OL Long Q15**
>
> **HL Short Q9**

Case Study

DASANI disaster

Coca-Cola is one of the largest corporations worldwide and the producer of the best-selling soft drink in the world. However, the company became concerned that sales of Coca-Cola had flattened out and that the product is now in the **saturation stage** of the **product life cycle**.

In response, the company tried to boost sales by increasing the **product range** and introducing new varieties such as Diet Coke and Cherry Coke. Some of the new flavours worked, while others like Vanilla Coke and 'New Coke' did not and had to be withdrawn due to poor sales. However, overall sales of Coke remained flat.

The company's **desk research** revealed that sales of bottled water were going through a growth phase and the company saw an opportunity to launch its own **brand** of bottled water called Dasani to compete against brands like Ballygowan and Volvic.

Coca-Cola is a hugely experienced company and has one of the biggest **marketing** departments of any company in the world. It expected this **new product development** and launch to go very smoothly and, at first, it did, with customers liking the bottle's distinctive blue label. Sales began to rise.

Then an inquisitive journalist discovered that Coca-Cola's expensive bottled water was not from a natural spring or a mountain glacier, but actually from an ordinary tap. Newspaper headlines all over Europe suddenly appeared with headlines such as 'Coke sells tap water', 'Are they taking us for plonkers?' and 'The Real Sting' (a play on Coke's slogan 'The Real Thing').

Customers were not impressed and the growing European sales of Dasani quickly began to slide. A few weeks later Coke also admitted that the product had become contaminated at the bottling plant with a potentially lethal chemical and all bottles had to be withdrawn from retailers.

In just five weeks, and at huge expense, Coca-Cola's new drinks' brand had come and gone from the European market, providing more entertainment than refreshment. The company lost millions in wasted marketing and production expenditure.

The marketing lesson is clear: even though Coca-Cola had identified a market opportunity, conducted detailed market research and spent millions on putting together an expensive **marketing mix**, a product simply will not sell if it is not what it pretends to be and consumers think they are being conned.

Source: *The Irish Times* and *BBC News*.

Recall and Review

1. Describe how Coca-Cola could use public relations to defend its reputation in the above situation.
2. Identify ways in which a company like Coca-Cola could try to prevent its cola drinks going into the decline stage of the product life cycle.
3. Design a marketing mix for a new brand of mineral water that does come from a pure mountain source.

OL Short Q3

HL ABQ
HL Long Q10, 11, 12

Key Concepts & Business Terms

After studying this chapter the student should be able to explain the following key concepts and business terms:

1. Marketing
2. Marketing strategy
3. Market segmentation
4. Demographic segmenting
5. Psychological segmentation
6. Market niche
7. Target market
8. Product positioning
9. Marketing mix
10. Product
11. Product portfolio/product range
12. Branding
13. Brand name
14. Brand logo
15. Brand leader
16. Own-label brands
17. Brand loyalty
18. Patent protection
19. Trademarks
20. Product life cycle
21. Pricing strategies
22. Mark-up (cost-plus pricing)
23. Psychological pricing
24. Price leadership/premium pricing
25. Price skimming
26. Profit-maximising pricing
27. Penetration pricing
28. Discriminatory pricing
29. Predatory pricing
30. Price war
31. Loss leaders
32. Channels of distribution
33. Wholesalers
34. Retailers
35. Agents
36. Selecting a suitable distribution channel
37. Promotion
38. Advertising
39. Advertising media
40. Point-of-sale advertising
41. Merchandising
42. Impulse purchases
43. Sales promotions
44. Personal selling
45. Telemarketing
46. Direct mail
47. Public relations (PR)
48. Sponsorship
49. National Consumer Agency
50. Advertising Standards Authority of Ireland

useful websites

www.gleesongroup.ie
www.volkswagenag.com
www.goodfellaspizzas.com
www.jacobfruitfield.com

Leaving Certificate Practice Questions

Ordinary Level

Ordinary Level – Section 1 – Short Questions (10 marks each)

1. Define 'marketing'. [LCQ]
2. Explain, using an example, the term 'market segmentation'. [LCQ]
3. List the 4 Ps of the marketing mix and explain any **one** of them. [LCQ]
4. Draw a labelled diagram of the product life cycle.
5. What is the purpose of a loss leader?
6. List **three** pricing strategies that could be used by a business.
7. Distinguish between a wholesaler and a retailer. [LCQ]
8. List **four** stages in the channel of distribution available for getting a product to the customer. Name **one** product suitable for the channel that you have listed. [LCQ]
9. List **two** factors that influence the choice of distribution outlet.
10. List **three** types of sales promotion.
11. Outline **two** examples of public relations (PR) methods used in business. [LCQ]
12. List **three** advertising media.

Ordinary Level – Section 2 – Long Questions

1. Describe the steps involved in developing a marketing strategy. (20 marks)
2. Explain, using a diagram, the main stages in the product life cycle. (30 marks)
3. (a) Explain the role of branding in business. (20 marks)
   (b) Outline **three** benefits a brand name can give to a business. (15 marks)
4. Distinguish between psychological pricing and predatory pricing strategies. (20 marks)
5. Identify four factors that a business should consider when deciding the price of its products. (20 marks) [LCQ]
6. Explain the terms 'retailer' and 'wholesaler'. (20 marks) [LCQ]
7. Illustrate **two** channels of distribution that could be used by a computer manufacturer. (20 marks)
8. Explain **four** types of advertising media and illustrate your answer with an example of each. (25 marks) [LCQ]
9. Describe **three** methods of advertising that a DIY and hardware shop might use to promote its business. (15 marks) [LCQ]
10. Explain PR as a method of promotion. Give **two** examples of PR that the business might use. (25 marks) [LCQ]
11. List **three** different types (media) of advertising a firm can use and give an advantage of each one. (15 marks) [LCQ]
12. Explain **three** main functions of advertising. (15 marks) [LCQ]
13. Gerard Morgan owns a small café. He has been running the business for three years and before that was a manager of a restaurant for five years. The café is situated on a busy street on the centre of town alongside a large hospital.

    Describe **three** appropriate types of advertising media in which Gerard could promote his café. (15 marks) [LCQ]
14. Describe the steps involved in putting together an advertising campaign. (25 marks)

15. Outline the role of the Advertising Standards Authority of Ireland. (15 marks)
16. Select a product or service of your choice and use it to describe the various elements of the marketing mix. (20 marks)
17. Contrast the duties of a human resource manager with the duties of a marketing manager in a company. (20 marks) [LCQ]

Higher Level

Higher Level – Section 1 – Short Questions (10 marks each)

1. Define the term 'target market'. Give an example.
2. List **three** factors that should be considered when designing a product.
3. Explain the term 'brand leader'.
4. Outline **one** high pricing strategy and **one** low pricing strategy.
5. List **three** factors that influence the choice of retail outlet.
6. Sales promotion is a popular promotion technique. List **three** other promotion techniques used by business. Outline any **one** of them. [LCQ]
7. List **four** advertising channels used in marketing.
8. Explain what is meant by a media mix.
9. Identify **two** bodies that regulate advertising in Ireland.
10. Draft a memorandum (memo) using an appropriate format, to all sales executives in the organisation listing **two** methods of sales promotion to be used in the business. [LCQ]

Higher Level – Section 2 – Applied Business Question

Country Crunch Cereal Bars

Paula Prendergast had been looking for a new product idea for some time so that she could start her own business. She had investigated many potential new product opportunities but did not find one that she was happy with, until now that is.

She has identified a very promising possibility for a new range of natural, cereal-based snack bars targeted at young, health-conscious consumers. Her feasibility studies, prototype development and market testing have all produced very promising results. Furthermore, as the Irish and international markets for snack foods is expanding, desk and field market research suggests that such a product has a very high profit potential if she can get the marketing mix correct.

Encouraged by her market research, Paula has decided to go ahead with the idea and to call her product Country Crunch Cereal Bars. As there are many other competitors in the market, she is aware that she will be entering a very competitive market. To be successful, her new product will have to be properly designed to ensure the taste, packaging and brand image are all correct. The new product range will also have to be sold at the right price and be supported by a high-profile advertising campaign in order to build brand awareness and, ultimately, brand loyalty.

1. Describe a suitable imaginary marketing mix for Country Crunch Cereal Bars. (40 marks)
2. Illustrate, using a diagram, two suitable distribution strategies for Paula's product. (20 marks)
3. Evaluate **two** different pricing strategies that Paula could adopt when launching her new product. (20 marks)

Higher Level – Section 2 – Long Questions

1. Distinguish between the marketing concept and the marketing strategy. (20 marks) [LCQ]
2. Evaluate the benefits of market segmentation to a business. (20 marks)
3. Analyse the issues a marketing manager must address when designing a new product. (20 marks)
4. Explain how the product life cycle model can assist a marketing manager. (30 marks)
5. Describe the important factors that a marketing manager would consider when deciding on the price of a new product or service. (20 marks) [LCQ]
6. Distinguish between (a) penetration pricing and (b) predatory pricing. (20 marks)
7. Evaluate **three** promotional methods for a product or service of your choice. (30 marks) [LCQ]
8. The marketing manager of a firm producing soaps and deodorants has been asked to sponsor a local rugby team. Evaluate the potential risks and benefits of this arrangement. (30 marks)
9. In the case of a particular product/service of your choice, evaluate the role of (a) advertising, (b) public relations and (c) personal selling in the promotion of the product/service. (30 marks) [LCQ]
10. Evaluate the elements of the marketing mix using a product or service of your choice. (30 marks) [LCQ]
11. You are the marketing manager for a new luxury hotel that is to open shortly. Draft a short report recommending a suitable marketing mix for the hotel. (40 marks)
12. 'Marketing is essential to business success.' Discuss. (30 marks)

Chapter 16

Getting Started

> 'A journey of a thousand miles must begin with a single step.'
>
> Chinese proverb

Key Study Questions

THE BLISS BAKERY

Case Study

Elaine Cleary set up The Bliss Bakery after she saw a **business opportunity** for a speciality cake business, producing birthday and wedding cakes. After **researching** the local market, she was confident that there was a large potential market for the business.

Elaine decided to leave her job and invest €8,000 in **savings** in the project. After drafting a well-researched **business plan**, she persuaded her local **county enterprise board** to give her a €6,000 **grant** which she used to buy equipment and **lease** suitable small premises just outside her town. The Bliss Bakery was now in business.

Elaine's wedding cakes were in high demand. However, the business proved to be highly seasonal, with large fluctuations in sales during the year. This meant she had to endure some rough patches when

there was very little **cashflow** coming in. 'I refused to become discouraged because I knew the idea had the potential to become a very successful business,' she says.

Elaine then hit on the idea of diversifying into miniature cakes 'because they can be made with exactly the same ingredients as the wedding and birthday cakes but are popular all year round'. The cakes can be personalised and, so far, popular designs include 'Get Well' and 'Happy Birthday' versions. She **advertised** her mini-cakes to businesses and, according to Elaine, the response was 'huge'.

Miniature cakes with company logos have become very popular with business customers who often place an order when they are celebrating some event. 'For example, last week I made 100 miniature cakes for a Galway firm celebrating the opening of their new premises,' says Elaine. The Bliss Bakery now employs four full-time staff and she is confident that it will continue to grow.

Once a business idea has been identified and a suitable marketing strategy prepared, there are three important issues to be addressed so that the business can get started:
1. Legal structure
2. Sources of finance
3. Production options

1. What are the main ownership options for a business start-up?

Case Study

When preparing her business plan, Elaine Cleary had to decide what type of legal business structure to choose for her business: sole trader, partnership or limited company. 'After careful consideration, I decided to start off as a sole trader but I expect to change later to a partnership or limited company as the business grows and I need to raise more money for expansion,' she says.

Legally, entrepreneurs can set up:
- **As sole traders**
- **In partnership with others**
- **As a limited company**

* **Sole traders** *own and manage their own businesses.*
* **Partnerships** *are where two or more people (but not more than twenty) are in business together in order to make a profit.*
* **Private limited companies (Ltd.)** *are businesses registered with the Companies Registration Office that are owned by investors called* **shareholders.**

✳ **Co-operatives** *are businesses that are democratically owned and controlled by their members who may be the firm's workers, suppliers or customers.*

See Chapter 19: Types of Business Organisation for more detail on legal structures for business.

Summary of the main forms of legal structures available to entrepreneurs

	Sole Trader	Partnership	Private Limited Company	Co-operative
Formation	• Register for tax with Revenue Commissioners. • May have to register business name.	• Register to pay tax with Revenue Commissioners. • May have to register business name.	• Register with Revenue Commissioners. • Register with Companies Registration Office.	• Register with Revenue Commissioners. • Register with Companies Registration Office.
Ownership & Control	• Owned and controlled by sole trader.	• Owned and controlled by partners.	• Owned by shareholders who elect board of directors to make decisions.	• Owned by members who elect management committee.
Management & Finance	• Decisions made by sole trader. • Without partners, members or shareholders, raising extra finance for expansion can be difficult.	• Decisions made by partners. • Can raise equity finance by bringing in new partners but this dilutes ownership.	• Decisions made by board of directors. • Equity finance can be raised by selling shares.	• Decisions made by management committee.
Profits & Risk	• Sole trader keeps all the profits but pays income tax on earnings. • Sole trader has **unlimited liability**.	• Partners share all the profits and pay income tax on their earnings. • Partners have **unlimited liability**.	• Profits are shared among shareholders according to number of shares held. • Company pays corporation tax. Shareholders pay income tax on dividends. • Shareholders benefit from protection of **limited liability**.	• Profits are shared among members equally. • Co-op pays corporation tax. Members pay income tax on dividends. • Members benefit from protection of **limited liability**.

OL Short Q2, 3   HL Short Q3
OL Long Q3   HL Long Q2

2. What factors should an entrepreneur consider when choosing a source of finance?

An entrepreneur should use the following criteria when selecting the most appropriate source, or combination of sources, of start-up finance.

Every entrepreneur must choose a suitable legal structure.

HL Short Q6
HL Long Q3

❖ **Purpose:** Types of finance should match the purpose for which they will be used.

❖ **Amount:** Sources of finance can vary considerably in terms of the amount available. For example, an overdraft will yield far less than a term loan.

❖ **Cost:** How much will the source of finance cost in interest repayments? How will this affect production costs and the profitability of the business?

❖ **Control:** Some types of finance involve giving away some control over the business, such as share ownership, seats on the board of directors or assets to be used as security.

❖ **Risk:** Entrepreneurs need to be aware of the **potential risks of a source of finance**. Inability to repay a bank loan secured on an asset means losing the asset and possibly the business. A business should also be aware of the implications of a source of finance on its cashflow, particularly on the firm's ability to meet regular payments such as staff wages, tax returns, etc. Some loans only require immediate repayment of interest, with the loan itself being repayable at a future fixed date. Whatever the source of finance, it is essential to consider its effects on the business's cashflow.

3. What are the main sources of finance for a new enterprise?

Case Study
THE BLISS BAKERY

Before setting up The Bliss Bakery, Elaine identified what premises, equipment and other resources she would need. She reckoned that she needed to rent workspace and buy food mixers, oven, trolleys and other equipment, along with a second-hand van. Elaine had only €8,000 in savings to invest in the project. Her local county enterprise board was willing to provide The Bliss Bakery with a grant of €25,000. The remainder had to be found elsewhere.

Every start-up business must have suitable sources of finance to start up and keep operating. These can be classed as short term, medium term or long term, depending on how long the finance will be used for.

Summary of the types, sources and uses of finance needed by a start-up enterprise		
Duration	**Sources**	**Uses**
Long term (Used for 5+ years)	• Equity capital • Grants • Debentures	Long-term development of the new business, e.g. purchasing premises, developing new products, etc.
Medium term (Used for 1–5 years)	• Leasing • Hire purchase • Term loan	Purchase of expensive assets, such as equipment, vans and other machinery.
Short term (Used for 0–1 years)	• Trade credit • Bank overdraft • Accrued expenses	Payment of regular bills, such as electricity, rent, wages, stock, creditors, etc.

OL Short Q4, 5, 6
OL Long Q4, 5

HL Short Q4, 5
HL Long Q4

See Chapter 12: Managing Business and Household Finance for more details on sources of business finance.

Case Study

A wise investment

Shortly after opening her first store using her own savings, Body Shop entrepreneur Anita Roddick decided to expand her business. The banks regarded Roddick's business idea as too risky and refused to provide a loan. However, a friend offered to give her €4,000 in return for 50% ownership of the business. Anita accepted, as she had no other choice. As the business grew her friend's initial investment grew to be worth hundreds of millions.

4. What are the main production options for a new enterprise?

When organising production, a business like The Bliss Bakery needs to determine the most suitable production process. A **production process** describes how the work is done. There are three basic types of production process options available for a manufacturing enterprise:

1. Job production
2. Batch production
3. Mass production

Production can be set up as
• Job
• Batch
• Mass

A business may use a combination of all three at different times depending on the product or customer needs. Alternatively, an entrepreneur could decide to **subcontract** production.

Job production

Job production *means producing a single product at a time, usually customised to meet the needs of a particular customer. When work on one job is finished, then production of another can begin.* Job production is typically used when making relatively expensive or highly skilled items such as ships, designer clothing or customised cakes. It can also be used to customise products like handmade clothing or sandwiches to customers' precise requirements.

> Example: When making one-off customised wedding and birthday cakes, Elaine Cleary is using a job production process.

The Bliss Bakery's wedding cakes are job produced

> **Advantages of job production**
> 1. Easier to **customise** an item for each individual customer.
> 2. A problem making one product does not necessarily mean that it will disrupt the production of other items.
> 3. The greater degree of employee involvement can increase their job satisfaction.

> **Disadvantages of job production**
> 1. Workers need to be **highly skilled** to be able to handle the customised orders in job production.
> 2. Requires a **flexible** workforce able and willing to carry out a wide range of tasks on one product.
> 3. One-off, individually made products tend to be more expensive for customers than those produced in large quantities.

Batch production

Batch production *involves manufacturing a limited number of identical goods at the same time, such as cakes, bread or books. Each stage of production will be completed for all goods in a batch before all the goods move onto the next stage.* Some small enterprises use a combination of batch and job production methods.

> Example: When The Bliss Bakery receives an order from a business, it is often for a large number of mini-cakes (e.g. 100), depending on the size of the business and the occasion it is celebrating. To satisfy such orders, Elaine Cleary uses a batch production method.

Advantages of batch production

1. Workers do not need to be as skilled as they would be making the same goods in job production.
2. Tends to be more efficient and involve less waste than job production.
3. The average costs of production are a lot less than for job production.

Disadvantages of batch production

1. Requires more equipment.
2. Compared to job production, batch production requires better **management skills** to ensure the efficient **planning** and production control of larger amounts of goods.

Small cakes are produced in batches

Mass production

Mass production *is the continuous production of large quantities of identical goods. This process is usually very highly automated. Examples include cornflakes, pens and paperclips.* Because of the long production runs involved, product design usually remains the same over long periods, unlike job or batch production. Mass production suits businesses that need to produce very large quantities of goods for a very **large market.** It is unsuitable for firms producing goods in **small quantities.**

> Example: According to Elaine, if The Bliss Bakery ever decides to expand into supplying very large quantities of standardised, identical cakes to large supermarkets such as Tesco, Dunnes Stores or Lidl, the business would have to adopt a mass production system.

Advantages of mass production

1. The use of highly automated machinery and long production runs means **significantly reduced costs and selling price** of each product produced. Lower average costs increase competitiveness and profitability.

Disadvantages of mass production

1. **Heavy financial investment** is required to set up an automated assembly line and to keep machinery functioning and the production line flowing.
2. **Breakdowns** in one part of the assembly line can cause delays and hold-ups elsewhere along the line.
3. **Staff morale** can decline if they feel their work is repetitive and over-specialised with little meaning.

Large bakeries use mass production.

OL Short Q1

OL Long Q1

HL Short Q1

Case Study

Mass, batch and job production in BMW

A business may use a combination of all three types of production at different times depending on the product or customer needs. For example, BMW **mass produces** most of its cars but the company's most expensive, top-of-the-range sports models are produced in **batches**.

BMW have also used **job production** to produce unique custom-made cars full of unusual gadgets for use in the James Bond films.

Recall and Review

1. Identify three products that are job produced.
2. Identify three products that are batch produced.
3. Identify three products that are mass produced.

5. What is subcontracting/outsourcing?

Instead of making their own products, some businesses subcontract production to outside producers. **Subcontracting** *(or outsourcing/contracting-out) means finding a supplier to manufacture part of or the entire product for you.* Price, quality standards and delivery dates are all agreed in advance. This leaves the entrepreneur free to concentrate on other areas of the business such as marketing and finance.

> **Example:** Production of Jacob's Fig Rolls is subcontracted to producers in the UK and Portugal. The Nike sportswear company owns just one small factory, yet every year the firm sells huge quantities of sports goods to markets all over the world. This is because virtually all of its production is subcontracted out to suppliers in Taiwan, South Korea and other Asian countries.

Evaluation
Advantages of subcontracting

1. **Simplifies management**: The management team can be kept small and focus on marketing the product and identifying new opportunities.
2. Sometimes it can be a lot **cheaper to subcontract** production to specialist producers.
3. **Extra production staff** not needed.
4. **Can suit** businesses with significant **seasonal dips** in demand for their products (e.g. Christmas crackers) and can avoid the waste of having equipment lying idle for long periods of time. It can also helps businesses that are already producing at maximum capacity.

Disadvantages of subcontracting

1. There is **less control over the quality** and delivery times of the goods.
2. Sometimes it can be **more expensive** as subcontractors will charge a price that includes a profit margin for themselves.
3. The subcontractor may decide to market the product itself and become a **competitor**.

OL Long Q2

HL Short Q2
HL Long Q1

6. What is a business plan?

Proper planning is essential to business success and every new enterprise should draw up a business plan. A **business plan** *is a document setting out* **who** *is setting up the enterprise,* **what** *is the product or service,* **how** *it is going to be produced and promoted,* **where** *it is going to be sold, where the* **finance** *is expected to come from and* **how much** *profit is expected to be generated.* A business plan is important because it:

A business plan is an essential document for every new enterprise.

- ✪ **Sets targets** for a business and provides a benchmark against which to measure the actual performance of the business. This is very useful for business control.
- ✪ **Is needed to raise finance from** investors, banks or grand aiding bodies.
- ✪ **Reduces risk by** helping an entrepreneur to think through their ideas and anticipate possible problems and how to overcome them.

7. What information does a business plan contain?

A business plan should clearly describe the proposed enterprise under the following headings:

- ✳ **A description of the entrepreneur/owners** and any key staff, including their relevant skills, experience and personal investment in the enterprise. Financiers and investors often judge a business proposal on the ability of the entrepreneurs or management to run a successful business.
- ✳ **Market description and analysis,** including its size, competitors and the target market.
- ✳ **A description of the product or service** clearly emphasising the advantages (unique selling points) that it has over existing products in the market.
- ✳ **Production:** The premises and equipment required, type of production processes to be used and the labour skills and raw materials required.
- ✳ **Marketing:** Describe the marketing strategy and marketing mix that will be used to appeal to the target market.
- ✳ **Management:** How the business will be organised and controlled.
- ✳ **Costs,** including the cost of premises, equipment and raw materials.
- ✳ **Sources of finance** the business is expected to use (e.g. savings, grants, loans, etc.). It is very important to show realistic estimates of the likely level of sales.

See Chapter 13:
Monitoring Business
Finances Using Accounts
for more detail on Profit
& Loss and Balance
Sheets.

* **Profitability forecasts** for the business. This can include a break-even chart, a cashflow budget and an estimate of the likely profit & loss accounts and balance sheets. Potential investors will want to be assured that the entrepreneur has examined the financial side of the business carefully and that the business will generate sufficient cashflow to meet all the daily expenses without running short.

BUSINESS PLAN FOR THE BLISS BAKERY

Description of the entrepreneur

Ms Elaine Cleary (entrepreneur) has a Leaving Certificate with four honours and two passes and a certificate in catering studies from the local Institute of Technology. She has five years' experience working in The Tasty Bakery.

Description of the market (market analysis)

All the local supermarkets and food shops stock cakes that sell well. There are no cake producers in the local area. The nearest competitor is 30 miles away and produces mainly breads and very few cakes.

Description of the product

The Bliss Bakery will produce cakes that are made entirely from natural ingredients, are sugar-free and feature a range of unusual flavours (e.g. banana, mango and almond cake).

Marketing plan

To position The Bliss Bakery as an affordable, wholesome brand, the following marketing mix will be applied:

- *Product:* The cakes will contain no artificial ingredients and will be baked to the highest quality standards. They will be packaged in an eye-catching cardboard box.
- *Price:* The Bliss Bakery cakes will be sold at a slightly higher price than competitors' products.
- *Place:* Cakes will be distributed through delicatessens, supermarkets and health food stores. Cakes will also be delivered directly to individual customers placing Internet orders.
- *Promotion:* Advertisements will be placed in the local papers and on the side of the delivery van.

Production plan The business will require premises that are convenient for making and receiving deliveries, two large ovens for baking, four mixers and a delivery van. The necessary raw materials (flour, fruit, eggs, etc.) can be sourced easily from local wholesalers or farmers. For customised orders, a job production method will be used. For orders of two or more identical cakes, a batch method will be used. Quality will be maintained through proper staff training and regular inspections throughout the production process.

Management plan The business will be set up as a limited company. Overall responsibility for production, finance and marketing management will rest with Ms Cleary. As the business grows, full-time production staff will be hired.

Financial plan

Expected start-up costs

3-year rent of premises	€30,000
Purchase of van and equipment	€50,000
Working capital (to pay wages, electricity and other expenses until sales take off)	€40,000
	_____
Total start-up finance required	€120,000

Sources of finance

Personal savings	€8,000
Grant	€25,000
Bank loan	€87,000

Profitability forecasts

It is expected that The Bliss Bakery will make a loss for the first two years before becoming profitable.

Projected yearly profits

	Year 1	Year 2	Year 3	Year 4
Sales income	10,000	40,000	85,000	150,000
Running expenses	50,000	60,000	70,000	80,000
	_____	_____	_____	_____
Projected yearly profit	(40,000)	(20,000)	15,000	70,000

OL Short Q7
OL Long Q6, 7

HL Short Q7
HL Long Q5, 6

Case Study

A BUSINESS CRASH LANDING

Jet Magic was an airline founded by a group of Irish **entrepreneurs** to offer VIP flight treatment, including plush leather seats and a gourmet in-flight menu. Their vision was to create a 'hip' airline and they advertised its flights as 'hip-hops'.

The entrepreneurs drew up a detailed **business plan** to attract **investors** to buy **shares** or lend money to the venture. To differentiate the new airline from the mainly no-frills, low-cost competitors, Jet Magic designed its marketing strategy and **marketing mix** to emphasise a high-quality in-flight service that they thought would appeal to high-income customers.

The airline initially started flying from Cork to Brussels, Nice, Barcelona and Belfast but soon flew into difficulties. For a start, the founders had not properly researched the full costs involved in running an airline. According to one observer, the money they spent getting started 'was barely enough to open a sweet

shop, let alone an airline'.

The level of estimated sales in their business plan and **cashflow forecast** was also wildly optimistic and did not happen in reality. Part of the reason for this was the airline used propeller aircraft rather than jet aircraft on some routes and these were very unpopular with customers.

As the airline struggled to get off the ground financially, investors had to be approached again to invest more money to keep the airline going. New routes were then introduced but there was little **market research** to see if there was sufficient customer demand to generate the level of sales needed to **break even** and make a profit.

As a result, the airline's cashflow began to get tighter and tighter and as cash began to run out the airline owners decided it was time to call it a day and close the airline. When it ceased trading, Jet Magic had debts of nearly €4 million, and made 110 people redundant. Investors lost over €11 million and 400 passengers were left stranded abroad.

Recall and Review

1. Explain the terms highlighted in bold.
2. Identify the possible sources of finance available to entrepreneurs wanting to start an airline.
3. Draft an imaginary business plan for a proposed new airline.

Common mistakes when getting started in business

1. Poor **market research** and product development.
2. Underestimating the **costs** involved.
3. Not having enough **finance** to fund the business during the difficult start-up stage when sales are still low.
4. Entrepreneur cannot keep proper **financial accounts** or financial control.
5. Getting the **marketing mix** all wrong
6. Over-optimistic **sales predictions**.
7. Not having a well thought out **business plan**.
8. Entrepreneur turns out to have **poor management skills**, struggles with planning, organising and control, unwilling to delegate work, and suffers from stress and burnout.

Key Concepts & Business Terms

After studying this chapter the student should be able to explain the following key concepts and business terms:

1. Sole trader
2. Partnership
3. Private limited company
4. Co-operative
5. Job production
6. Batch production
7. Mass production
8. Subcontracting/outsourcing
9. Business plan

Leaving Certificate Practice Questions

Ordinary Level

Ordinary Level – Section 1 – Short Questions (10 marks each)

1. List **three** types of production options available to a business. [LCQ]
2. List **three** different types of business organisation.
3. Outline **two** benefits of a sole trader as a type of business organisation. [LCQ]
4. Explain the term 'equity capital'. [LCQ]
5. List **two** sources of short-term finance available to business.
6. Identify **two** examples of the use to which medium-term finance can be put.
7. Outline **four** key headings in a business plan. [LCQ]

Ordinary Level – Section 2 – Long Questions

1. Distinguish, using examples, between job, batch and mass production methods. (15 marks)
2. Explain the benefits to an entrepreneur of subcontracting production. (20 marks)
3. (a) Explain what is meant by a 'sole trader'. (10 marks) [LCQ]
   (b) Distinguish between (i) a partnership and (ii) a limited company. (10 marks)
4. Identify **two** sources of medium-term finance available to a sole trader and explain one of them. (15 marks) [LCQ]
5. List **three** finance options available to a new business enterprise under each of the following headings: (a) short-term, (b) medium-term and (c) long-term. (30 marks)
6. Outline **three** benefits of writing a business plan. (15 marks)
7. Explain **four** main sections that a business plan should contain. (20 marks)

Higher Level

Higher Level – Section 1 – Short Questions (10 marks each)

1. Name and illustrate three types of production. [LCQ]
2. What is subcontracting?
3. Distinguish between a sole trader and a private limited company.
4. List **two** short-term and three long-term sources of finance suitable for a new business enterprise. [LCQ]
5. Define 'equity finance'.
6. List **four** factors that should be considered before choosing a source of finance.
7. Name **three** sections normally found in a business plan.

Higher Level – Section 2 – Applied Business Question

Lunch Bites

While working part time in her local supermarket, Susan Kearns noticed the large number of sandwiches and rolls sold each day. She also noticed how basic and plain they were; yet they still sold well because of their convenience to students and workers from nearby schools and businesses.

Susan went home, produced twenty sample sandwiches and rolls with different fillings, such as carrot and apple, cheese and beetroot, and took them to the supermarket. When she spoke to the manager she got a very favourable response and was told they could be put on sale to test customer response. She was also told that the contents, weight and price would have to be clearly labelled on the packaging.

The next day the supermarket asked Susan to supply fifty as they had sold out the previous day. These also sold out and the supermarket offered her a contract to supply 200 sandwiches daily. She was also delighted to hear that other branches in the supermarket chain would be interested in stocking her range of sandwiches.

However, there was a problem. Susan was told that under hygiene regulations, she could not use an ordinary domestic kitchen to supply the supermarket. She would need to use professional catering facilities. 'What seemed like a promising but small business idea is now beginning to look like a more substantial enterprise,' says Susan. Despite this obstacle, Susan remains undeterred and is now determined to take advantage of this clear business opportunity to start up her own business, which she has already named Lunch Bites.

1. Identify **three** types of legal business ownership that Susan can use to set up in business. (15 marks)
2. Recommend **one** method of production Susan should adopt. Give reasons for your answer. (15 marks)
3. Draft a business plan that Susan could present to her bank to help her negotiate a loan. (30 marks)
4. Evaluate the risks and benefits to Susan of seizing this enterprise opportunity. (20 marks)

Higher Level – Section 2 – Long Questions

1. Discuss the **three** basic production options a business must choose from. (30 marks)
2. Distinguish between a sole trader and a partnership as a form of business organisation. Use an example of each in your answer. (15 marks) [LCQ]
3. Discuss the questions an entrepreneur should ask before choosing a method of finance. (20 marks)
4. Describe **four** sources of start-up finance that can be used by entrepreneurs. (20 marks)
5. What is a business plan? Explain its role in business start-ups. (20 marks) [LCQ]
6. Paula and Thomas have recently returned to Ireland having worked with transnational companies for ten years. They wish to set up in business together in Ireland manufacturing a range of new organic breakfast cereals. Paula has particular expertise in production and finance and Thomas in marketing and human resources.

   Draft a business plan for this proposed new business using **five** main headings, outlining the contents under each heading. (40 marks) [LCQ]

Chapter 17
Business Expansion

'Being good is not good enough when you dream of being great'
Anonymous

Key Study Questions

Case Study

Expansion at Ryanair

Ryanair was founded by entrepreneur Tony Ryan who saw an opportunity in the airline market. He felt that other airlines were inefficient and charging excessive prices. Ryan thought he could attract customers by running a more efficient airline with slightly lower prices.

He set up Ryanair with just one 15-seat propeller aircraft flying from Waterford to London. For the first few years, the business was unable to **break even** and was running at a loss. Then the airline changed its **marketing strategy** and redesigned its **marketing mix** to become a very low-price airline with absolutely no frills. It began flying to smaller airports with cheaper landing fees and adopted a very simple

organisational structure with as few layers of management as possible.

The new marketing mix worked and Ryanair finally became profitable. **Management** then decided that the airline should generate further **economies of scale** by expanding to become a European-wide airline, which meant raising large amounts of finance to purchase a new fleet of jet aircraft. The company chose to raise **equity finance** to buy the aircraft by selling shares on the stock market. However, by placing a large order for aircraft, Ryanair was also able to negotiate very favourable discounts from aircraft manufacturers Boeing on the normal cost of the jet aircraft.

To save money and keep costs to a minimum, Ryanair aircraft are without reclining seats or seat back pockets. This alone cuts hundreds of thousands of euro off the cost of an aircraft. It also means reduced cleaning and repair costs later. Staff must pay for their own uniforms and to reduce the airline's electricity bill they are banned from charging their own mobile phones at work. The company does not employ an advertising agency, but designs all its own marketing promotional material.

Using a low-cost, **low-price strategy**, Ryanair has expanded rapidly to become one of the largest low-cost airlines in the world and, along the way, forced less competitive rival airlines out of business. One of the tactics the company uses is **predatory pricing**, by reducing its fares to ridiculously low levels until smaller rival airlines are no longer able to compete and are forced to pull out of the market.

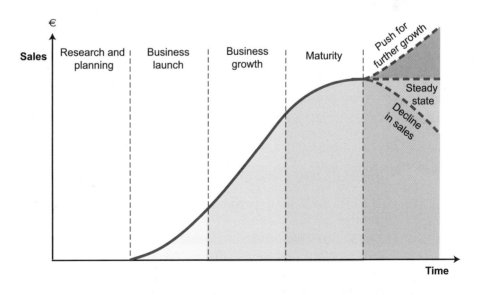

Fig. 1 Like products, businesses can be described as going through a life cycle.

1. What are the reasons for expanding a business?

| Business expansion can arise for:
- **Defensive reasons**
- **Aggressive reasons** |

Defensive ('have to') reasons

Sometimes a business may **have to** expand to ensure its continued survival, as this can enable it to:

★ **Reduce costs:** Business expansion can generate economies of scale that can create a competitive advantage. **Economies of scale** *are benefits that arise in a business as it becomes larger and more efficient.* Such economies help to reduce the average cost of each item produced and thus more competitive prices can be charged, leading to increased sales and higher profits.

Example: As a large airline, Ryanair is able to negotiate higher discounts on bulk purchases of new aircraft and take out loans at more favourable rates of interest. In a manufacturing business, it can mean being able to use mass production methods.

★ **Survive economic shocks:** Bigger can mean stronger as large firms are often better able 'to ride the storm' and survive upsets in the business environment, such as economic downturns, new government legislation or rises in interest rates.

★ **Reduce risk:** A firm may produce new products or enter new markets to spread its business risks by avoiding having 'too many eggs in one basket'. This is also known as **diversification**.

Example: Toyota has diversified its product range to include cars, trucks, forklifts, robots, textile machinery and financial services.

★ **Protect raw material supplies:** Businesses may expand to secure their sources of raw materials by taking over a supplier of raw materials. This is known as **reverse integration**.

Example: Fruit importers, Fyffes, has expanded by purchasing its own banana plantations to ensure continuity of supplies.

★ **Protect labour supplies:** Larger firms can afford to recruit more qualified and experienced staff by offering better pay, conditions and promotion prospects.

★ **Eliminate competition:** Firms like Ryanair will often try to merge with or take over rival firms to eliminate competition that is threatening their market share.

Aggressive ('want to') reasons

If a firm does not have to expand for defensive reasons, it may still **choose to** expand for the following reasons:

❋ **Increase profits:** A simple desire to increase profits for the owners is often the main fuel for expansion. As a firm grows, it can make more efficient use of resources, lower its costs and generate higher profits. If it grows large enough, it may achieve a dominant or monopoly position in the market where it can get away with increasing prices without fear of losing sales. Irish and EU **competition law** can prevent deals between firms or business activities that significantly reduce competition or cause unfair business practices in the Irish marketplace.

✳ **Acquire new products:** If a rival business develops a new product it can be quicker and cheaper to take over that firm rather than spend time trying to develop a similar product. It may also expand to acquire **new technology** or inventions that have been developed by another company.

Example: When the Unilever Corporation decided to enter the ice cream market, it decided that the quickest and lowest risk means of doing so was to takeover the existing and very successful Ben and Jerry's ice cream company.

✳ **'Empire building':** Many business people are motivated by the desire to be 'empire builders', creating the largest business in their area, industry, country or globally. According to Maslow's theory of the hierarchy of needs, this helps business people to earn the admiration of others which can satisfy their **esteem** needs.

✳ **New challenges:** Many business people constantly need new projects and challenges, such as developing new products or masterminding takeovers, to avoid becoming bored and restless.

> OL Short Q1
> OL Long Q1, 2
>
> HL Long Q1

Example: The excitement of new challenges is a strong motivator for Richard Branson's expansion of the Virgin Group of companies.

2. What are the methods of business expansion?

A business that wants to grow can choose **organic** or **inorganic** methods of expansion.

❖ **Organic growth** *is where a firm expands **gradually** through the use of its **existing products** or by **developing new products***.

❖ **Inorganic growth** *involves forming strategic alliances with, or by engaging in mergers and acquisitions of, other businesses*.

> **When choosing a method of expansion, a business should consider:**
> * **The costs involved**
> * **The speed of expansion**
> * **The effect on profits**
> * **The effect on control of the business**
> * **The risks involved**

Organic methods of expanding a business

Organic growth is also known as **internally driven growth** as it does not involve any outside firms. This type of expansion tends to be more gradual as any additional profits generated are reinvested in selling more products or developing new ones. There are two main types of organic growth:
1. Using existing products
2. Developing new products

● Organic growth – strategy 1: Use existing products

Using existing products, a firm can expand through **increasing domestic sales**, **exporting**, **licensing** or **franchising**.

✪ **Increasing sales domestically** on the Irish market can be relatively low risk as the product may already be well known and there are no extra R&D costs or staff skills needed. However, as Ireland is a relatively small country, growth opportunities may be limited and the speed of expansion can be slow.

Example: Food producers Cully & Sully initially expanded by increasing their sales in Ireland.

✪ **Exporting:** Exporting to foreign markets many times larger than Ireland's can be very profitable and does not affect the ownership or control of the business. However, exporting can take years to generate profits due to the need to invest in staff language training, adapting the marketing mix, making changes to products and production methods to adapt the goods to foreign needs, and setting up distribution facilities. The risk is also greater when entering unknown markets, than when competing domestically on familiar 'home ground'.

Examples: Ryanair expanded by opening air routes all over Europe (not just to and from Ireland). Cully & Sully expanded into the UK and French markets when they felt that they had grown as far as they could in Ireland.

✪ **Licensing** *means allowing other firms to use or sell an invention or design in return for payment of a licence fee or royalty.* For the firm selling the licence (licensor), licensing can be a fast, low-cost and low-risk expansion method. However, licensing involves some loss of profits and control over the use of patents and trademarks. For the firm acquiring the licence (licensee), it can be a low-risk expansion method but a licence fee must be paid.

Example: Manchester United football club earns millions every year from licensing the club name and logo to firms producing a massive range of products ranging from pillow and duvet covers to wallpaper and slippers.

✪ **Franchising** *means the renting (by a franchiser) of a complete business idea, including name, logo and products to someone else (known as a franchisee).* It is a sophisticated form of licensing that is growing in popularity as a method of business expansion, particularly in retailing and service industries.

Examples: Supermac's, McDonalds, Snap Printing.

- **For the franchiser** it is a fast, low-cost and low-risk expansion method. However, there is a loss of both potential profits and control over the day-to-day management of franchise outlets. There is also the risk of damage to the reputation of the whole business if unsuitable franchisees are selected.

- **Franchisees** benefit from a proven business idea with an existing brand image and reputation as well as supports such as training and advice from the franchiser. However, they bear the risk and financial burden of the new outlet, with little real control over how they manage it. They must also pay the royalty fee usually based on the sales of the franchised outlet.

● *Organic growth – strategy 2: Develop new products/diversification*

It makes sense for a business to constantly seek to develop new products to replace those that may be coming to the end of their product life cycle. This can be done through diversification. **Diversification** *refers to increasing the range of products or services offered by the business.*

Examples: Xtra-vision diversified from just renting movies to selling movies and video games, confectionary, music products, mobile phones and entertainment-related electronic goods. Ready-made meal producers Cully & Sully expanded by increasing their range of meals. Kelloggs have expanded by constantly developing new cereal-based products.

Diversification is a **very popular** method of expansion as there are potentially very **high profits** from developing successful new products. However, diversification is also **high cost** and **high risk**, as many new products fail. It can also take a **long time** to get from the new product development stage to launching on the market.

Inorganic methods of expanding a business

Inorganic growth involves linking up with other firms either through 1. strategic alliances or 2. mergers and acquisitions. Also known as externally driven growth, this can be a method of achieving rapid business growth.

Kelloggs have grown by developing new products

● Inorganic growth – strategy 1: Form a strategic alliance

Strategic business alliances (joint ventures) *occur when two or more firms agree to co-operate in the establishment of a project or business together.* The firms involved remain separate but agree to come together to share their skills and resources to maximise the possibility of success. It can be a faster, lower risk method of expansion as costs, technology and other resources are shared between the firms involved.

> **Strategic business alliances allow firms to grow by sharing expertise.**

However, profits and control must also be shared. The need for greater communications and shared decision-making between the firms involved can also slow down the expansion.

> **Example:** Food company Glanbia has expanded by forming strategic alliances with other companies. Its first strategic alliance was with a French company to produce and market the Yoplait brand of products in Ireland. More recently, Glanbia formed a strategic alliance with an American company to share the cost of building and operating a €150 million cheese factory in the USA. This reduced the cost to Glanbia and also gave it an American partner with good knowledge of the American cheese market. The strategic alliance made Glanbia the biggest supplier of cheddar cheese in the USA.

Yoplait is sold in Ireland as a result of a strategic alliance.

● Inorganic growth – strategy 2: Acquire/merge with another business

Acquisitions/takeovers *occur when one firm buys at least 50% of the voting shares of another firm and gains majority control.* Takeovers are 'hostile' if they take place against the wishes of the management of the company being taken over. **Subsidiaries** *are companies where another company owns 50% or more of their shares.*

> **Acquisitions/takeovers can help a firm to expand rapidly. However, it is a very expensive way of expanding.**

> **Example:** Ryanair used acquisitions as part of its expansion strategy when it took over rival UK budget airline Buzz.

Mergers *occur when the managers and shareholders of two companies of roughly equal size agree to voluntarily join together to form a single firm.* The State's Competition Authority or the EU Commission may investigate proposed takeovers and mergers if they think it would result in a dominant or monopoly situation that would be against the interests of the consumer.

> **Example:** In Ireland, AIB was formed through the successful merger of a number of smaller banks.

Acquisitions and mergers allow a business **to spread** the business **risk by diversifying** into new products and markets. The firm can also quickly gain access to new products, technology, patents or well-known brand names owned by the firm taken over/merged with.

OL Short Q2, 3, 4, 5
OL Long Q3, 4, 5, 6

HL Short Q1, 2
HL Long Q2, 3, 4, 5, 6

However, buying another business can be **expensive** and usually requires large amounts of long-term finance. In addition, **industrial relations' problems** may arise if redundancies are necessary to reduce staff duplication in the companies being merged or taken over.

3. What are the main sources of finance for business expansion?

Sources of finance for expansion:
- **Grants**
- **Equity**
- **Debt**
- **Sale and leaseback**

Any business that wants to expand must identify where it will raise the money needed to fund the growth. The main sources of finance for expansion are **grants**, **equity**, **loans** and **sale and leaseback**.

> **Example:** Expansion that occurs without proper finance in place to pay for the larger business will cause **cashflow** problems that could lead to the business over-trading and collapsing. This happened to Xtra-Vision a number of years ago when it **expanded too quickly** and accumulated more **debts** than it could afford to pay back. This forced the founder, entrepreneur Richard Murphy, to sell his share of the business to pay off the debts.

Grants

Grants are an ideal source of finance for expansion as there is no loss of ownership or control of the business. There are also no dividends, interest or repayments to be made (unless conditions of the grant are broken). The main sources of grants in Ireland are government agencies such as **county** and **city enterprise boards** (for small firms), **Enterprise Ireland** (for exporting firms), and **IDA Ireland** (for foreign-owned firms in Ireland). **The European Union** also provides grants to assist the growth of firms in important developing industries such as waste recycling and renewable energy technologies.

Equity

Equity *refers to finance provided by the owners of a business.* Equity can be raised by:

★ **Retained earnings** *where profits are retained in the business to finance future developments.*

★ **Entrepreneur investing more** of his/her own money into the business.

★ **Bringing a new partner** into the business, who will also invest money to finance expansion.

★ **Issuing (selling) shares** if the business is legally set up as a limited company. The shares can be sold to existing or new shareholders.

Case Study

Enterprise Ireland finances expansion

In recent years Enterprise Ireland has moved away from just giving **grants** to businesses that want to expand. Increasingly it prefers to invest taxpayers' money in providing **equity finance** by  buying shares in such companies. In this way, if the company is successful, Enterprise Ireland can sell its shares at a later date and re-use the money to assist other firms to expand. This approach provides better value for taxpayers' money rather than just giving out free grants. Enterprise Ireland is now the largest provider of venture capital for business expansion in Ireland.

Example: Enterprise Ireland provided €320,000 in equity finance to Kingspan to assist the growth of the Cavan-based manufacturer of building products and then sold this equity share in the business a number of years later for a profit of €11 million.

Debt finance – loans and debentures

Before a business takes out a long-term loan to finance expansion, it must be confident that it can generate sufficient income to pay back the loan plus annual interest. **Debentures** *are long-term fixed-interest loans secured on a valuable asset, such as premises.* There is no loss of ownership or control and interest payments are tax-deductible.

However, security is usually required for most long-term loans and loan repayments must be made on time. Also, if profits turn out to be less than repayment costs, the business will be left with extra debts but no extra income with which to pay them.

See Chapter 12: Managing Business & Household Finance and Chapter 16: Getting Started for more details on business finance.

When choosing finance for expansion consider:
- Amount
- Cost
- Control
- Risk

Example: Largo Foods, the producers of Hunky Dory and King Crisps, spent over €62 million taking over rival Tayto Crisps. The company financed the takeover by taking out a debenture loan.

Sale and leaseback

Sale and leaseback *is a contract to raise cash by selling a piece of property and simultaneously leasing it back on a long-term lease.* This allows your business to continue trading in the same office, shop, factory or business premises as if nothing happened.

OL Short Q6, 7, 8

OL Long Q7, 8

HL Short Q3, 4

HL Long Q7

Example: Celtic Helicopters raised millions of euro to expand the business by selling an aircraft hangar that had proven more expensive to run than anticipated. They sold the hanger to a Russian company on the understanding that they could lease it back after the sale. The managing director described it as 'a good deal on our behalf; it made commercial sense. We're in the helicopter business, not in property.'

HL

4. What are the implications of using equity or debt financing as a method of business expansion?

Case Study

Gary Chooses equity, Jackie chooses debt

Gary Lavin, the founder of the Vit Hit and Organic Fanatic brands of soft drinks, **favours equity over debt** as a method of financing his business expansion. When he needed finance to expand, rather than take out a large **loan** he decided to sell a 17% share of the business to an **investor** in return for €250,000 in cash.

However, fitness entrepreneur Jackie Skelly chose a combination of equity and increasingly large loans to finance the expansion of her chain of fitness centres. For many years this strategy worked well as sales increased. But when her sales dropped suddenly, she found herself unable to continue repaying the loans. Jackie then lost control of the entire business as it had been used as security for the loans that she could no longer repay.

Comparing and contrasting the use of equity and loan finance for expansion

	Equity Finance	Debt Finance
Amount	Potentially **large amounts** are **available**, depending on how attractive the business is to investors.	Potentially **large amounts** are **available** if the risk is low enough and sufficient security is available.
Cost	Equity financing is **cheap** as dividend payments to ordinary shareholders are optional. However, if no/little dividend is paid, the share price will fall and the directors may be voted off the board by dissatisfied shareholders.	Debt financing can be **expensive**. Interest and principal must be repaid on schedule and in full. Interest rates may be high.
Ownership and control	Existing owners' **control is diluted** as new partners or shareholders are brought into the business.	There is **no loss of ownership or control** although there will be restrictions on the use of any assets being used as collateral (security).
Risk	Equity finance is **low risk**. If the firm makes little or no profit, only the providers of the equity will lose out. However, the assets of the business remain untouched. A firm mainly financed by equity is said to be **low geared**.	Debt financing is **high risk**. The loan and the interest must be repaid regardless of the level of profits. If the firm cannot afford to make the repayments, then it may be liquidated and the assets sold off to fund the debt repayments. A firm with a high level of long-term debt finance is **highly geared**.

HL Long Q8, 9

5. What are the implications of expansion for a business?

Many businesses expand because they think it will make them more profitable. However, this does not always happen as expansion can also bring many negative changes that a business must avoid to ensure growth is successful.

* **Profitability:** In the short term, profits may fall because of the possible costs of expansion such as larger premises and more staff. In the long term, larger businesses can benefit from **economies of scale** such as buying supplies in bulk and being able to use more efficient technology and greater automation.

* **Organisational structure:** Business may need to change its organisational structure. For example, changing from a functional structure to a geographic one. Additional managers may be needed. Communications with staff can become more difficult. The larger a business becomes, the more complicated it can become to manage it. This can require greater management delegation and adopting new methods of communication and control.

* **Human Resource Management:** Expansion usually means **recruiting more**

staff although expansion by merger or acquisition may mean some redundancies to eliminate wasteful duplication. A **human resource manager** may be needed in the business to recruit and retain the right staff and to maintain good industrial relations.

* **Marketing:** Expanding businesses can offer a wider range of products to customers. Large businesses can spend more on market research and developing new products. Marketing becomes more complex as different marketing mixes may have to be put in place for a wider range of products.

* **Legal:** Business may have to change its legal structure, for instance changing from a sole trader to a partnership or a limited company. Limited companies may need to change their legal structure to public limited companies listed on the stock market to raise large sums of equity finance. A **public limited company (PLC)** *is a company whose shares can be bought and sold on the stock market.* This option is mainly used by businesses that need to raise very large sums of money to finance their expansion.

* **Finance:** Business may need to raise finance to pay for the expansion by raising equity finance or taking out loans. Larger businesses generally will find it easier to raise finance for further growth.

* **Ownership:** New owners may come into the business as partners or shareholders. The original owners may become unhappy with the approach of the new owners/investors.

> **Example:** Anita Roddick, the founder of the Body Shop regretted expanding her business by selling shares on the stock market because the new shareholders who invested in the company were not interested in the original ethical values of the business, only in making a profit. This ultimately led Roddick to resign from the company.

Case Study

Mercedes goes too far too fast

As part of their **strategic planning**, management at Mercedes–Benz conducted a **SWOT analysis**. This led them to decide that the company's car, truck and bus **product range** was too narrow and that it should **diversify** to reduce the potential business risk of just making vehicles. They wanted to create a large, **diversified business** that could compete in many different markets. Through **expansion by acquisition**, they took over dozens of existing businesses in industries such as aerospace, industrial electronics, consumer goods and financial services.

However, the senior managers in Mercedes were soon spending all their time trying to **plan, organise** and **control** the vast new empire of completely unrelated businesses and product areas that they did not properly understand. Despite their best efforts, the managers were not able to properly control their new and enlarged business empire which soon started to lose hundreds of millions of euro.

Realising that they had bitten off more than they could chew,

Mercedes managers changed their **strategy**. They decided to sell off all the new businesses and in future to stick to an internal **organic growth** strategy by doing what they knew best – making cars, trucks and buses.

HL Short Q5, 6

HL Long Q10

Recall and Review

1. Explain the terms highlighted in bold.
2. Identify the sources of finance that could be used to expand a business.

6. What are the reasons for staying small?

Not every business wants to grow and expand and there are many owners who prefer to keep their business at a relatively small size.

Aer Arann is content to stay a small niche airline.

Advantages of staying small

1. **Easier to manage** and **keep control over** a small business than a large one. For sole traders or partnerships, growth can mean extra work and responsibility that they may not want.
2. **Less stress** for the entrepreneur managing a small but profitable business. Once the business has reached a certain size, they may prefer to spend more time taking holidays, playing golf or pursuing other leisure activities.
3. **Staff relations** and **communications are easier** when the business is small enough for all staff to know each other.
4. **A stronger sense of team spirit** and **motivation** is common in many small businesses where staff can feel more noticed and valued than in a larger, more impersonal organisation.
5. **A better personal service** to customers can often be provided by small businesses with loyal staff than many larger organisations.
6. **Many businesses can remain competitive** in a small niche market without economies of scale if they offer a high-quality product and flexible service that appeals to customers.

Disadvantages of staying small

1. **Costs tend to be higher** for a small business than for larger firms who can use methods of mass production.
2. **Profits tend to be smaller** in small businesses.
3. **Less opportunity for investing in the business** such as recruiting highly skilled staff, acquiring new technology or conducting new product research and development.
4. **Small firms have to struggle more** to compete against larger firms that have more financial muscle.

OL Long Q9, 10

HL ABQ

Key Concepts & Business Terms

After studying this chapter the student should be able to explain the following key concepts and business terms:

1. Reasons for business expansion
2. Economies of scale
3. Methods of business expansion
4. Licensing
5. Franchising
6. Diversification
7. Strategic business alliances/joint ventures
8. Mergers
9. Acquisitions/takeovers
10. Subsidiaries
11. Finance for business expansion
12. Grants
13. Equity
14. Enterprise Ireland
15. Debentures
16. Sale and leaseback
17. Implications of using debt/equity for expansion **HL**
18. Public limited company (PLC)
19. Reasons for staying small

useful websites

www.ryanair.com
www.enterprise-ireland.com

Leaving Certificate Practice Questions

Ordinary Level

Ordinary Level – Section 1 – Short Questions (10 marks each)

1. Outline **three** reasons for expansion of a business. [LCQ]
2. Explain what is meant by franchising and illustrate your answer with an example. [LCQ]
3. What is a strategic alliance?
4. Explain what is meant by a merger.
5. In business, what is an acquisition?
6. List **two** sources of finance suitable to fund business expansion.
7. Explain the term 'equity capital'. [LCQ]
8. Define the term 'retained earnings'. [LCQ]

Ordinary Level – Section 2 – Long Questions

1. Describe **four** reasons why a business might want to expand. (20 marks) [LCQ]
2. Explain what is meant by economies of scale. (15 marks)

3. (a) Describe **two** methods of expansion that a business could use. (10 marks) [LCQ]

   (b) Illustrate what is meant by organic growth. (5 marks) [LCQ]

4. (a) Why might a firm enter into a strategic alliance? (10 marks)

   (b) Distinguish between a strategic alliance and a takeover. (20 marks)

5. Outline the implications of licensing as a method of expansion. (20 marks)

6. Explain franchising and outline its advantages as a method for business expansion. (20 marks)

7. Name **three** sources of long-term finance that can be used for business expansion and explain **one** of them. (20 marks) [LCQ]

8. Explain what is meant by the term 'sale and leaseback'. (15 marks)

9. Discuss the effect that a business expansion may have on three different stakeholder groups. (30 marks)

10. Identify and explain **three** potential negative effects of business expansion. (15 marks)

Higher Level

Higher Level – Section 1 – Short Questions (10 marks each)

1. List **two** methods of expansion using existing products.

2. Outline **one** advantage and **one** disadvantage of using a strategic alliance to expand a business.

3. Identify **two** advantages of equity as a source of finance for business expansion.

4. What is a debenture?

5. List **four** possible implications for stakeholders of business expansion.

6. Identify **two** possible implications for staff if a business expands.

Higher Level – Section 2 – Applied Business Question

Jupiter Software Limited

Irish firm Jupiter Software is a start-up software company based in Kerry specialising in producing educational software such as maths and language teaching programmes. They have been very successful in the Irish market, where sales have increased to €10 million and the number of staff employed has risen to nearly forty. However, after just a few years, sales have now begun to flatten out and the owner, Eoin Connolly, feels that the domestic market has now reached saturation and that it is time to look for other ways to expand.

From holiday experience he is aware that major sales opportunities exist in many foreign countries for the firm's maths and language training products. As a first step, he is investigating the UK market because of its large size and proximity to Ireland. He has identified three possible expansion routes into the UK.

The first is to export their goods directly for sale in large UK retail outlets.

The second option is through entering a licencing agreement with British firm Bulldog Software. This firm has already contacted Jupiter and offered to sell the software in the UK under its own Bulldog software brand. In return it is offering a 5% share of the price of each item it sells.

The third option is to set up a joint venture with Liberty Training Limited. This large American company has recently approached Jupiter about setting up a separate subsidiary together to jointly develop and market software tailored specifically for the UK market. If it goes ahead, the subsidiary would be owned 50:50 by Jupiter Software and Liberty Training. Eoin has done some research which has revealed that the Welsh government would provide generous business grants if the subsidiary were to locate in Wales and employ local people.

1. Analyse the risks and benefits to Jupiter Software Limited of expanding. (20 marks)
2. Evaluate the **three** different expansion options Eoin has identified for Jupiter Software. State, giving reasons, which option you would recommend. (30 marks)
3. Draft a short memo to Eoin outlining, with reasons, the sources of finance that you would recommend for a business looking to expand. (30 marks)

Higher Level – Section 2 – Long Questions

1. Describe **three** reasons for business expansion other than to increase profit. (20 marks) [LCQ]
2. Describe **three** expansion paths that a business may follow if it wishes to grow. (30 marks)
3. Distinguish between a diversification and a merger. (20 marks)
4. Discuss the importance of exporting as a method of expansion for Irish firms. (20 marks)
5. Explain **one** advantage and **one** disadvantage of expansion through acquisition. (20 marks)
6. Evaluate the potential benefits and risks involved for a business considering using franchising as a method of business expansion. (20 marks)
7. Identify and explain **two** possible sources of finance a firm can use to fund its expansion. (20 marks)
8. Contrast equity and loan capital as sources of finance for expansion. (30 marks) [LCQ]
9. Discuss the importance of choosing the correct source of long-term finance for the expansion of a business. Refer to **two** long-term sources of finance in your answer. (20 marks) [LCQ]
10. Describe how the development of a good marketing strategy (plan) would aid business expansion. (15 marks) [LCQ]

Chapter 18
Industries and Sectors in the Economy

'The earth provides enough to satisfy man's need but not every man's greed.'

Mahatma Gandhi

Key Study Questions

Supermac's

Case Study

Pat McDonagh gave up his teaching job for business after he identified a lucrative **niche** in the Irish fast-food market. He noticed that **service industry** firms such as McDonald's and Burger King were expanding rapidly in large urban centres in Ireland but had not yet expanded into smaller towns.

Seeing a business opportunity, he decided to open his first fast-food restaurant in Ballinasloe, County Galway. Although he had no previous experience of the food industry, he hired a chef 'to manage the place and train the rest of us in'. This was the beginning of the highly successful Supermac's fast-food chain.

As an advantage over his foreign rivals, Pat decided to use only fully traceable Irish ingredients and supplies. This meant he could closely control the quality of the **raw materials** used.

Pat McDonagh expanded Supermac's rapidly across the country, partially through **franchising** the successful formula in return for a fee and an annual royalty. He grew the business to employ over 2,500 staff in over ninety outlets and planned further **expansion** in the future. As part of its marketing promotions, the business has engaged heavily in **sponsorship**, particularly with the GAA teams.

Despite intense competition, Pat McDonagh demonstrated how an Irish entrepreneur can successfully take on larger multinational rivals and win. The company has made a significant impact on the economy by directly creating jobs in his business, while the firm's policy of buying all its food ingredients from Irish suppliers has supported **employment** in the **primary sector** of the economy.

1. In business, what are the factors of production?

The factors of production are:
• **Land**
• **Labour**
• **Capital**
• **Enterprise**

Supermac's, like every business, requires four basic ingredients known as **the factors of production** to be brought together before anything can be produced. These **factors of production** *are the four essential resources that entrepreneurs combine to make a product or service.*

Land

Land *refers to the natural resources that give us the raw materials and energy needed for all business activities.* It includes **land, water, rivers, lakes** and **seas, materials** taken from the land and sea (such as gas, oil, iron, animals, timber and other crops), **air** and **climate.**

Many natural resources are **non-renewable,** *meaning that they are in limited supply and therefore need to be used sparingly and wisely, e.g. oil and copper.* Other resources provided by nature are **renewable,** *meaning that if they are carefully managed they have the potential to last indefinitely, e.g. wood, water supplies, wind and solar power.* However, some resources like forests can only be renewed and replenished at a very slow rate and need to be used in a sustainable manner.

Labour

Labour *refers to the human work and effort needed for a business to operate.* Like Supermac's, every firm needs to employ staff with the appropriate range of skills. The availability of labour (human effort) is limited by the number of fit and healthy people willing and available to work as employees in a business.

Capital

In the factors of production, **capital** *refers to anything man-made used in running a business.* It includes equipment, buildings, vehicles and power stations used in production as well as the money needed to pay for things such as staff, heating, marketing, etc. As a factor of production, capital is also limited in supply.

Enterprise

Enterprise *as a factor of production refers to the human creativity and initiative required to pull together the three other factors of production and start a business to provide goods and services.* Pat McDonagh provided the enterprise needed to start Supermac's. However, enterprise is in limited supply because people do not have equal amounts of entrepreneurial ability.

OL Short Q1

2. What are the main sectors (or categories of industry) in the Irish economy?

Businesses in the economy are often classified according to the industry they are in. An **industry** *is a group of businesses engaged in producing similar goods and services.* Examples are the tourism, computer and fashion design industries. Industries can be grouped into three basic sectors of the economy:

> **The main sectors of the economy are:**
> * **The primary sector**
> * **The secondary sector**
> * **The tertiary sector**

* The **primary sector** *refers to agriculture and other extractive industries, such as fishing, drilling and mining.*

Example: The primary sector produces the beef, chicken, milk and vegetable raw materials used by Supermac's.

* The **secondary sector** *refers to construction and manufacturing industries, such as chemicals and computers.*

Example: The secondary sector manufactures the premises, uniforms, packaging and restaurant furnishings used by Supermac's.

* The **tertiary sector** *refers to service industries, such as retailing, financial services, tourism and transport.*

Example: Supermac's is a service business. It also buys insurance, security and legal services from other firms in the tertiary sector.

OL Short Q2

3. What is the primary sector?

The main industries in the primary sector are agriculture, forestry, fishing, drilling, quarrying and mining.

● Importance of the primary sector to the Irish economy

* ❖ **Agriculture's** share of economic activity has declined rapidly in importance in recent decades. However, it is still high compared to other developed countries and it provides important raw materials and ingredients for the food processing industry.
* ❖ **Forestry** in Ireland is small compared to other countries but is growing as more farmers diversify out of traditional agriculture.

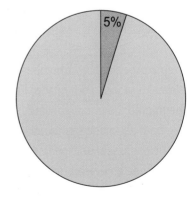

Primary sector provides approximately 5% of all jobs in the economy. Despite the relatively low numbers employed, it is a very important sector as it supplies raw materials for the manufacturing, construction and services sectors.

❖ **Fishing** provides valuable employment for many coastal communities who depend on it for local jobs and incomes.

❖ Ireland is very dependent on foreign **energy supplies** of oil and gas. Mining for lead and zinc has been an important business activity in the primary sector. Quarrying provides essential products such as sand, gravel and limestone for use in the construction industry.

Trends and challenges facing the primary sector

✪ **Declining EU payments:** As part of its policy of making Europe self-sufficient in food, the EU has traditionally provided very generous support for Irish farmers through its Common Agricultural Policy. However, this policy has changed, with farmers now receiving just one single farm payment regardless of how much output they produce in a year.

✪ **Small farm sizes:** Many Irish farms are too small to be economically viable. Many small farmers are selling out, leading to fewer but larger farms that can better achieve the economies of scale needed to survive.

✪ **Diversification:** As incomes from traditional agricultural activities such as tillage and livestock decline, many farmers, especially smaller ones, are being forced to **diversify** into specialist activities, such as organic farming, forestry, production of biofuels and farmhouse holidays.

✪ **Consumer concerns:** Growing consumer concern over food issues such as mad cow disease, excessive use of antibiotics in meat products and genetically engineered foods has led to a growth in the market for foods produced organically (without the use of chemicals or pesticides).

✪ **Climate change:** Farming is particularly vulnerable to extreme weather conditions such as flooding, droughts and storms. The effects of climate change on Ireland will become a big issue for the industry in the future.

✪ **Depletion of fishing stock:** As a result of over-fishing, the European Union has imposed limits (called quotas) on the amount of fish that can be caught at sea.

✪ **Need for greater energy independence:** Ireland spends billions of euro every year importing non-renewable oil and gas. The country needs to develop greater energy independence by developing its own independent sources of power such as wind, wave, solar and possibly nuclear.

OL Long Q1, 2, 3

HL Long Q2

23%

4. What is the secondary sector?

The secondary sector of the Irish economy consists of two main industries: 1. construction and 2. manufacturing

The secondary sector provides approximately 23% of jobs in the economy. It pumps billions of euro per annum into the economy in the form of wages and also by purchasing raw materials and services from other sectors of the economy. The secondary sector also contributes a disproportionately large amount of corporation tax to the government.

1. The construction industry in Ireland

The construction industry *is involved in building houses, factories, offices and infrastructure, such as roads, tunnels, bridges and pipelines.* Fast-food chains like Supermac's need the construction sector to build their premises.

● Importance of the construction industry to the Irish economy

★ **Use of Irish resources:** The construction industry uses mainly Irish raw materials, such as sand, gravel and wood which reduces imports and helps to keep money in the economy.

★ **Employment:** Construction is also a very labour-intensive industry and can provide employment to large numbers of people.

● Trends and challenges facing Irish construction

★ **Economic fluctuations:** The construction industry is very sensitive to the general level of economic activity in the economy. When the economy is doing well, construction does well but when the economy is doing poorly, construction activity and employment can drop dramatically.

2. The manufacturing industry in Ireland

The manufacturing industry *converts raw materials into finished goods, such as computers, furniture, soft drinks and machinery.* Today most manufacturing in Ireland is concentrated in:

✳ **Food and drink production.** This area is dominated by indigenous agribusiness firms such as the Kerry Group and Glanbia.

✳ **Chemicals and pharmaceuticals.** This sector is dominated by foreign-owned transnational companies (TNCs).

✳ **Electronic and computer products.** This area is composed of a mix of small indigenous and larger transnational companies such as Microsoft and Intel.

✳ **Other manufacturing** covering an extremely wide range of activities mainly carried out by indigenous Irish firms.

● Importance of the manufacturing industry to the Irish economy

❖ **Employment:** Manufacturing creates direct employment in factories and also many indirect jobs in firms producing raw materials and supplying services such as transport and legal advice.

❖ **Exports:** Manufacturing produces value-added goods that can be exported and bring money into the country.

● Trends and challenges facing Irish manufacturing

✪ **Employment** in manufacturing is declining but output is increasing (i.e. more output is being produced by fewer people). This is due to increasing productivity arising from the use of new technologies such as automation, robotics and ICT.

✪ **High labour and other costs** have made Irish firms less competitive compared to many competitors in countries with lower costs.

✪ **Relocation of operations:** Declining employment in the secondary sector is being caused by firms relocating their manufacturing operations to lower cost countries and to be nearer expanding foreign markets.

> **What is agribusiness?**
> **Agribusiness** *refers to those manufacturing firms that use agricultural produce such as dairy, meat, fish, cereals, fruits and vegetables as their main source of raw materials.* One third of Ireland's top 100 firms are involved in agribusiness.

Importance of agribusiness to the Irish economy

★ Agribusiness is a key industry in the Irish economy as it buys most of its raw materials from Irish agriculture and also exports over 50% of its output. Well-known agribusiness firms such as the Kerry Group and Glanbia are major suppliers of raw materials such as beef and cheese to firms like Supermac's.

Trends and challenges facing Irish agribusiness

✳ **Mergers/takeovers** are becoming more frequent as Irish agribusinesses look for the economies of scale needed to compete against large transnational firms (especially in the area of new product research and development). This has led to concentration of production in a few very large companies.

✳ A number of agricultural co-ops have converted into **public limited companies** (PLCs) in order to raise equity finance on the stock market for expansion.

✳ **Foreign retailers:** The spread of foreign food retailers such as Tesco, Aldi and Lidl in Ireland presents a further challenge as they traditionally buy much of their food stock from foreign suppliers, not local agribusiness firms, and also have the power to force suppliers to accept low prices for their products.

✳ The agribusiness industry is affected by increasing **consumer concerns** over food safety.

✳ **Research and development:** Increased spending in new product research and development (R&D) has become a necessity for firms in the agribusiness industry if they are to develop the new products needed to compete against foreign competition.

OL Long Q4, 5, 6

HL Short Q1

HL Long Q3, 4

5. What is the tertiary sector?

The tertiary (or service) sector refers to all businesses that provide services. **Service industries** *do not manufacture physical products but provide services to other businesses and consumers.* Service activities include tourism, financial services, telecommunications, advertising, education and health. Supermac's is operating in the service sector of the economy. Demand for services expands as an economy grows.

Tertiary sector businesses include:
- **Financial services**
- **Advertising**
- **Telecommunications**
- **Tourism**
- **Music**
- **Civil service**
- **Pubs and hotels**
- **Restaurants**
- **Insurance**
- **Legal services**

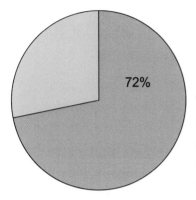

Tertiary services provide over 72% of all jobs in the economy. As a source of employment, this sector has grown rapidly in recent decades.

Hertz car hire is a service business.

Importance of the service sector

❖ **Employment:** Service businesses tend to be very labour intensive and this sector has become by far the largest sector of the economy in terms of employment.

❖ **Tourism** is one of the most important service industries, with millions of visitors attracted to Ireland every year by our culture, green image and friendly people. These visitors spend billions of euro here, thereby supporting a huge number of jobs in transport, restaurants, hotels and the entertainment businesses.

❖ **Exports:** Ireland exports valuable financial and software services, thus bringing large amounts of money into the country and improving our balance of payments.

❖ **Loyalty:** In Ireland, most service firms are also indigenous firms, which means their profits are kept in the country for the benefit of the wider economy.

❖ A well-developed service sector is essential to **attract transnational corporations (TNCs)** to Ireland. In particular, TNCs look for good transport and telecommunications services.

❖ **Growth of TNC service businesses** locating their European bases in Ireland. Many foreign TNCs specialising in financial services, software and customer services have been attracted to set up in Ireland by IDA Ireland.

Trends and challenges facing the service sector

✪ **Globalisation of services:** Future growth for Irish service-based industries lies in developing more international markets for their services. This is already happening in telecommunications, financial services, software development and advertising and is being made possible through the use of ICT such as the Internet.

OL Short Q3
OL Long Q8
HL Short Q7
HL Long Q1, 8

✪ **Information and communications technology (ICT)** is changing what and how services are provided. People can buy goods, take out loans and look for information or place orders using the Internet or telephone. Many businesses have realised that it is cheaper to have people working from the end of a telephone line in an out-of-the-way location than in expensive, high-rent offices in the centre of a town or city.

6. What is the role of indigenous firms in the economy?

Case Study

TOUGH Technology

Timoney Technology based in Navan, County Meath is an indigenous Irish company that has become a world leader in developing heavy duty and specialist vehicles with rugged design and construction.

Products include airport crash rescue vehicles, fire trucks, dumper trucks, military vehicles and components for the European Ariane space rocket programme. The company also has a contract with the US military to develop an unmanned robotic six-wheeled vehicle called 'The Crusher'.

Indigenous firms *are Irish-owned and locally based firms.* Indigenous firms like Timoney Technology are encouraged by the State because it is recognised that it is too risky for Ireland to be so dependent on foreign-owned firms for jobs and wealth creation. **Enterprise Ireland** *is the State agency specifically responsible for supporting the development and growth of indigenous Irish firms. In particular, it concentrates on firms that produce goods and services which can be exported.*

● Importance of indigenous firms

★ **They can export** their goods and services and bring money and employment into the country. Unlike foreign-owned firms, the wealth generated by indigenous firms is mainly spent within the economy and not repatriated to other countries.

★ **Linkages:** Indigenous firms are far more likely to get their raw materials and supplies from other Irish businesses.

★ **Growth potential:** Indigenous firms can grow and become international businesses with Ireland as their base, e.g. the Kerry Group. They are also less likely to relocate abroad, even during an economic downturn. This creates more economic stability for the Irish economy.

● Trends and challenges facing indigenous firms

✳ **Decline of traditional manufacturing:** Traditional indigenous manufacturing, including footwear and clothing, has suffered continuous decline in the face of intense low-cost competition from eastern Europe and Asia.

✳ **Emergence of indigenous Irish high-tech firms** in areas such as software, engineering and biotechnology, often as a result of people leaving foreign-owned firms to set up their own businesses.

✳ **European market:** Open competition within the EU has made it easier for foreign-owned firms to take over indigenous Irish firms and vice versa. For example, HB Ice Cream is now owned by Unilever, a giant multinational.

✳ **Niche marketing:** The only way for many Irish firms to survive against larger, low-cost global competitors is to identify a niche market where low prices are not as important to customers as factors such as quality of product design, style, taste, image, innovation or customer service. This strategy has been used by Timoney Technology.

> OL Short Q4
> OL Long Q7
>
> HL Short Q4, 5, 8
> HL Long Q6

7. What is the role of transnational firms in the Irish economy?

Case Study

Intel chooses Ireland

Intel is a massive American TNC that produces the microchips for computers. It is one of over 1,000 transnational companies that have chosen Ireland as their European base. It was persuaded to set up in this country by IDA Ireland and has invested over €7 billion in developing manufacturing and research and development facilities in its factory at Leixlip, County Kildare. The firm provides direct employment to thousands of Irish staff while thousands more are employed in businesses providing raw materials and services. Intel is very clear about why it decided to build its European manufacturing and exporting base in Ireland: low corporation taxes, a highly educated workforce, and easy access to the massive EU market.

Transnational companies (TNCs) *are firms that produce and market goods and services in more than one country.* Also known as **multinationals,** businesses such as Microsoft and Intel have a global perspective which means they see the world as one giant market. TNCs do not have strong ties to any particular country; instead, they carry out research, raise

> Foreign transnational firms dominate Irish manufacturing.

finance, source raw materials and manufacture in whatever country is most profitable for them to do so.

Foreign direct investment (FDI) *refers to transnational firms setting up facilities in Ireland to produce goods and services for export.* To promote economic development, Ireland has deliberately sought to attract FDI into Ireland. This strategy has proved to be very successful and today Irish manufacturing industry is dominated by foreign transnationals.

> **Examples:** Intel, Microsoft, Coca-Cola and Pfizer. Most of these firms are located in industrial parks in the east and south of the country and this 'cluster effect' has encouraged similar firms to locate here.

Importance of TNCs

- ❖ **Exports:** 90% of Irish exports are from non-Irish TNCs that have based their European manufacturing in Ireland. Exports bring money into the Irish economy.
- ❖ **TNCs directly employ** thousands of people, especially in high-skilled jobs that tend to pay more than other jobs. They also **indirectly** support hundreds of thousands of additional jobs among Irish suppliers and service firms.
- ❖ **Local communities benefit** from the spending power of the employees. **Local businesses benefit** from local linkages whereby transnationals buy raw materials and services from local firms, further boosting the local economy.
- ❖ **TNCs contribute a huge amount of taxes** to the government through corporation tax, PAYE and PRSI on staff wages. This pays for investment in infrastructure and public services.
- ❖ **TNCs make up for the traditional weakness of indigenous Irish manufacturing.** A huge proportion of manufacturing in Ireland, especially chemicals, electrical engineering, computer hardware, software and internationally traded services, is dominated by high-tech, foreign transnational firms. Without the TNCs, the manufacturing sector in Ireland would be very small and mainly based on agribusiness.
- ❖ **TNCs raise labour skills levels** by exposing Irish employees to world-class advanced scientific, management and work practices. As employees change jobs, these valuable skills are spread around the economy.

Where TNCs in Ireland come from:		Major transnationals based in Ireland:
USA	47%	Microsoft
Germany	14%	Pfizer
UK	11%	Siemens
Rest of Europe	20%	Oracle
Asia Pacific	5%	Intel
Rest of world	3%	eBay
		EA Games
		Analog Devices
		Google
		Bayer
		Boston Scientific

Why do TNCs locate in Ireland?

The reasons TNCs choose Ireland as a base from which to manufacture and export are:

- **Low rates of corporation tax** compared to other countries.
- Free access to the **EU market,** without government-imposed trade barriers such as tariffs (import taxes).
- Availability of **grants** from IDA Ireland and other State agencies to pay for premises, staff training etc.
- Availability of a highly educated and **skilled labour force.**
- A traditionally **low level of strikes** and industrial unrest.
- A **stable economic and political environment** that makes business less risky and planning easier.

● *Trends and challenges of TNCs for the economy*

> **Global competition for FDI is increasing from countries offering far lower costs and/or attractive tax rates.**

- ❂ **Labour and other costs** are higher in Ireland than in many other countries. Ireland has become a more expensive and a less profitable production base for many TNCs.

- ❂ **Global competition for FDI** is increasing from other countries that are now offering lower corporation tax rates than Ireland in order to tempt TNCs to relocate from Ireland.

- ❂ Ireland has **poor infrastructure** in terms of transport links (roads, rail, public transport) and often poor national telecommunications coverage.

- ❂ **Energy supply risks:** Ireland has a very high dependency on imported energy. In the long term, as oil and gas become scarcer and more expensive, it is risky for energy-hungry firms to be based in Ireland in the event of an international energy crisis.

- ❂ **Highly skilled labour** must be available in sufficient quantities to attract transnational companies to set up exporting bases in Ireland.

- ❂ **Investment in R&D** by TNCs located in Ireland is being encouraged by the State as a means of getting them to put down long-term roots in this country.

- ❂ **No loyalty:** TNCs have little loyalty to the countries in which they set up operations. They are far more likely than indigenous firms to close down and relocate to another country if economic circumstances change.

- ❂ **Local economic shocks:** The closure of a large local TNC plant will usually have a strong negative effect on the local economy, which may have been very dependent on the TNC for jobs and linkages.

- ❂ **Poor linkages:** Many TNCs have a poor record of purchasing supplies from local businesses. Instead, components and supplies are shipped in from the parent company overseas. Many TNCs are also reluctant to share their technological know-how with local Irish employees, preferring to keep most of their well-paid high-tech jobs and R&D facilities in their home country. IDA Ireland and Enterprise Ireland are trying to change this.

- ❂ **Profit repatriation:** The large profits most TNCs generate from their Irish exports are usually repatriated to their head office in another country. It is estimated that up to 20% of all the income generated in the Irish economy in a given year is transferred to other countries.

- ❂ **Political power:** Many TNCs are growing so large that they have more economic power than many governments, a trend that is likely to continue. TNCs can threaten to pull out of a country if they do not get their way on

For more information on transnational companies, see Chapter 25: Global Business

issues such as planning permission, extra grants, low taxes, etc.

- **Divert grants:** TNCs often look for very generous grants or other assistance before deciding where to locate. These grants divert money away from helping indigenous firms to grow.

Case Study

Donnelly Mirrors - from Irish success to TNC pullout

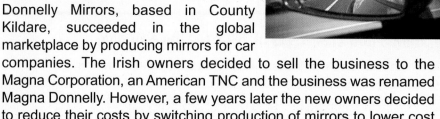

Donnelly Mirrors, based in County Kildare, succeeded in the global marketplace by producing mirrors for car companies. The Irish owners decided to sell the business to the Magna Corporation, an American TNC and the business was renamed Magna Donnelly. However, a few years later the new owners decided to reduce their costs by switching production of mirrors to lower cost locations in eastern Europe. The Irish factory was shut down and over 200 staff were made redundant.

OL Short Q5, 6
OL Long Q9, 10

HL Short Q2, 3, 6
HL ABQ
HL Long Q5, 7, 9

Key Concepts & Business Terms

After studying this chapter the student should be able to explain the following key concepts and business terms:

1. Factors of production
2. Renewable and non-renewable resources
3. Natural resource-based businesses
4. Labour
5. Capital
6. Enterprise
7. Industry
8. Primary sector
9. Trends and challenges facing the primary sector
10. Secondary sector
11. Construction industry
12. Manufacturing industry
13. Agribusiness
14. Trends and challenges facing the secondary sector
15. Tertiary sector
16. Service industries
17. Trends and challenges facing the tertiary sector
18. Indigenous firms
19. Transnational firms (TNCs)
20. Foreign direct investment (FDI)
21. Factors that attract TNCs to Ireland

useful websites

www.supermacs.ie
www.cso.ie

Leaving Certificate Practice Questions

Ordinary Level

Ordinary Level – Section 1 – Short Question (10 marks each)

1. There are **four** factors of production. List the **four** and explain any **one** of them. [LCQ]
2. Name the **three** categories (sectors) of industry and give an example of each one. [LCQ]
3. Explain, using **two** examples, what is meant by the services sector. [LCQ]
4. Explain what is meant by an indigenous firm. [LCQ]
5. Explain the term 'transnational company'. [LCQ]
6. Identify **two** incentives for a transnational company to locate their exporting base in Ireland.

Ordinary Level – Section 2 – Long Questions

1. Explain with examples what is meant by the primary sector of the economy. (15 marks) [LCQ
2. Outline the importance of the primary sector to the Irish economy. (15 marks) [LCQ]
3. Explain **two** important issues facing Irish agriculture. (20 marks)
4. Outline the importance of the secondary sector to the Irish economy. (15 marks) [LCQ]
5. Explain **two** challenges faced by manufacturing industries In Ireland. (15 marks) [LCQ]
6. Describe how the manufacturing industry in the Irish economy has changed in recent years. (20 marks)
7. Describe **two** benefits of indigenous firms to the economy. (20 marks)
8. Explain what is meant by the tertiary sector of the economy and outline its contribution to the economy. (15 marks) [LCQ]
9. Outline **two** possible reasons why transnational companies might relocate from Ireland to eastern Europe. (15 marks) [LCQ]
10. (a) Explain **two** benefits of transnational companies for Ireland. [LCQ] (10 marks)
    (b) Outline **two** disadvantages of transnational companies to the Irish economy. (10 marks)

Higher Level

Higher Level – Section 1 – Short Questions (10 marks each)

1. Identify **two** major issues facing manufacturing industry in Ireland.
2. Explain what is meant by foreign direct investment.
3. Distinguish between an indigenous firm and a transnational firm.
4. List **two** benefits of promoting indigenous firms to the Irish economy. [LCQ]
5. Identify **two** issues facing indigenous firms in Ireland.
6. Identify **three** benefits of transnational firms to the Irish economy.
7. Explain the term 'service industry'. [LCQ]
8. Illustrate your understanding of the term 'indigenous firm'. [LCQ]

Higher Level – Section 2 – Applied Business Question

Ballymore

Colette Turner lives in Ballymore, a small town that has experienced a lot of unemployment over the years. Today she read in her local newspaper about three potential new businesses considering locating in her town. If they choose to locate in the community, each firm expects to employ approximately 100 staff.

The first business is GameX, an American transnational corporation producing electronic components for computer games consoles. It is looking for mainly low-skilled staff to work on assembly lines manufacturing the components for export to other EU countries. Most of the raw materials for the production will be imported from outside Ireland.

The second firm is Fidelity Insurances, a financial services company that specialises in selling insurance products to customers globally. It will be looking mainly to employ highly skilled third-level graduates for its operation. As an international services company, access to high quality information and communications technologies is essential to its choice of business location.

The third firm is Green Dinners, a well-established Irish firm that produces a wide range of frozen vegetable and other foods for the domestic and international markets. It is considering opening a factory in the town as it needs to increase its production capacity to meet steadily increasing demand for its products. It expects to employ a mixture of high- and low- skilled staff. It will also be sourcing most of its raw materials from local farmers.

1. Assess the possible impact on the local economy of each of the above firms if they choose to locate in Ballymore. (30 marks)

2. Discuss the reasons why a firm such as GameX may consider Ireland as a manufacturing location. Refer to the text in your answer. (30 marks)

3. Evaluate the importance to the Irish economy of indigenous agribusiness firms such as Green Dinners. (20 marks)

Higher Level – Section 2 – Long Questions

1. (a) Identify and give an example of each of the main sectors (categories of industry) in the economy.

   (b) In the case of **one** of these, describe its contribution to the economy. (20 marks) [LCQ]

2. Discuss the contribution of the primary sector to the development of the Irish economy. (20 marks)

3. Evaluate the important role of agribusiness to the economy. (15 marks)

4. Identify and explain four trends affecting manufacturing in Ireland. (20 marks)

5. Contrast the contributions of indigenous and transnational firms to the Irish economy. (30 marks)

6. Discuss the important issues facing indigenous manufacturing in Ireland. (25 marks)

7. Analyse the attractiveness of Ireland as a global location for transnational companies. (25 marks)

8. Evaluate how the services sector contributes to the Irish economy. (20 marks)

9. Analyse the impact of transnational companies on Ireland. [LCQ] (15 marks)

Chapter 19
Types of Business Organisation

'The only place where success comes before work is in the dictionary.'
Vidal Sassoon

Key Study Questions

Case Study

Same entrepreneur, different legal structures

After working as a music journalist, Bob Geldof's first serious enterprise was as lead singer with the punk band The Boomtown Rats. Like all music groups, the band was also a **business**, providing a musical service to those willing to buy their music or attend their live performances. The band was run as a business **partnership** with **profits** shared among the band members.

The Boomtown Rats eventually broke up and Bob Geldof used his experience of working with radio, TV and music companies to set up a **limited company** called Planet 24 Productions

Limited, to make TV programmes.

Geldof discovered that he was good at business and the company became very successful. He then sold it for €8 million and used some of the money to set up another **enterprise**, Deckchair.com Ltd., a travel website selling cheap flights. This was followed by more new business ideas including Ten Alps Broadcasting Ltd., again making TV programmes, and Atomic TV Ltd., a specialist music channel.

Despite all this business activity, Geldof still has the music bug and has released a number of albums as a solo artist. This music initiative was conducted as a **sole trader**.

In his role as an **entrepreneur**, Geldof admits that he hates boredom. 'It's the idea that gets me. It's boredom avoidance because I get bored so easily.' His **motivation** in business is not to make profits: 'I don't like it when it's just about money,' he says. 'I'm there for the ideas; that is what really interests me.' He gets enjoyment from the creative and development side of business, by taking a seed of an idea and developing a successful product or service based on it.

The Boomtown Rats
Live at Middlesex Polytechnic, Hendon, UK. 22nd September 1978

A. Structures used by new businesses

The five basic legal structures for new businesses:

- Sole trader
- Partnership
- Private limited company
- Co-operative
- State-owned enterprise

When an entrepreneur like Bob Geldof is starting up in business, he or she must choose from four main types of different legal structures: **sole trader**, **partnership**, **limited company** or **co-operative**. A fifth type, known as a State enterprise, is sometimes used by the government when setting up a business.

These different legal structures of a business can be compared using the following headings:

* **Formation and dissolution** – how they are set up and how they can be dissolved.

* **Ownership and control** – who owns them and how much control they have over the business.

* **Management and finance** – how they are managed and their ability to raise finance for expansion.

* **Profits and risk** – what happens to profits and the degree of risk involved for the owners.

1. What is a sole trader?

Sole traders *own and manage their own business.* They are the **most common** type of legal business structure in Ireland and are frequently found among businesses such as small shopkeepers, farmers, family businesses, musicians and tradespeople such as plumbers and electricians.

> Sole traders own and control all aspects of their business and have unlimited liability.

- ❖ **Formation** is very easy for a sole trader. If you are using your own name then you can **start trading immediately.**
- ❖ However, if you want to use a different business name from your own (e.g. Village News & Sweets), then you must register it with the Companies Registration Office (CRO). This allows the real identity of the owner to be established if there is a legal dispute.
- ❖ For some types of business, such as a pub, you must get a **licence** from the courts.
- ❖ Like all new businesses, sole traders must be registered with the **Revenue Commissioners** for tax collection purposes.

Advantages of setting up as a sole trader

1. **Formation & dissolution:** Very easy to form.
2. **Ownership & control:** The business is owned and controlled by a single person.
3. **Management & finance:** Speedy decision-making means you can respond quickly to competitors and the needs of customers. Privacy is protected as the accounts and financial records of the business only have to be revealed to the tax authorities. Sole traders have the least amount of paperwork to deal with and lower overhead costs.
4. **Profits & risk:** As the sole owner, the sole trader keeps all the profits after taxes are paid.

Disadvantages of setting up as a sole trader

1. **Formation & dissolution:** Since the sole trader is the owner, if he/she dies, then so does the business.
2. **Management & finance:** Long working hours are common and there is no help or advice from a business partner with decision-making. It is difficult for sole traders to raise all the finance themselves for start-up or expansion, and loans are often more expensive for small businesses.
3. **Profits & risk:** Sole traders have unlimited liability. **Unlimited liability** *means the owner bears full responsibility for all the debts of the business.* This means he/she can lose personal belongings such as home, car and savings to pay the debts owed.

OL Short Q1

2. What is a partnership?

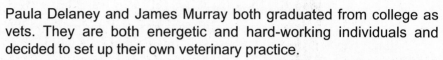

Case Study — PET CLINIC

Paula Delaney and James Murray both graduated from college as vets. They are both energetic and hard-working individuals and decided to set up their own veterinary practice.

After locating suitable premises on the edge of a large town, they used a combination of equity and loan finance to install pet consulting rooms, an X-ray facility, an operating theatre, recovery rooms and kennels. Their friendly, professional and caring approach to treating pets has led to the business growing quickly.

As a business, Paula and James are currently operating as a partnership although they have not agreed anything in writing. For now, they have agreed to split the income from the business 50:50. However, Paula is concerned that disagreements may arise in the future. 'What will happen if one of us wants to take longer holidays?' she asks. 'Should we still be sharing all the profits equally?'

Recall and Review

1. Identify the problems that you think might occur in a partnership but not in a sole trader.
2. Draw up a list of points that you think the vets should put into their partnership agreement.

> **Partnerships involve the sharing of ownership and control with others and have unlimited liability.**

A partnership *is two or more people (but not more than twenty) who are in business together in order to make a profit.* In Ireland, partnerships are commonly found among businesses such as accountants, solicitors, architects and rock bands.

⭐ **Formation** of a partnership is simple. Partnerships can start in business immediately but must register with the Revenue Commissioners for tax. If the business name of the partnership is different from the partners' names, it will also have to be registered with the Companies' Registration Office.

⭐ Partnerships are often formed through verbal agreements. However, it is advisable to have a written partnership agreement, known as a deed of partnership. A **deed of partnership** *is a written agreement containing the rules and conditions for running a business as a partnership. It is used to avoid future disagreements.*

Advantages of setting up as a partnership

1. **Formation & dissolution:** Partnerships are easy to form (the deed of partnership agreement is optional).
2. **Management & finance:** Work and responsibilities can be shared, leading to less stress/pressure. Partners can bring different talents, skills and expertise into a business which should mean better decision-making. New partners can bring in extra finance or expertise needed to expand the business. Like sole traders, the financial affairs of the business are confidential.
3. **Profits & risk:** Two or more people working together can often achieve more than working alone. This can significantly boost profitability and reduce the business risk.

Disadvantages of setting up as a partnership

1. **Formation & dissolution:** If a partner dies or leaves, the partnership ends and a new partnership must be agreed.
2. **Management & finance:** Partners may have disagreements, making the business difficult or even impossible to run. It can also be more difficult for partnerships to borrow finance than for a company.
3. **Profits & risks:** Profits are shared between the partners. Each partner usually has unlimited liability meaning that each can be sued individually by any creditors (people who are owed money by the business) for all of the money owed by the partnership.

> OL Short Q2, 3, 4
> OL Long Q1
>
> HL Short Q1

3. What is a private limited company?

Case Study

Alchemy Productions Limited

After studying video and media production in college, Gina Curley decided to set up her own business making radio and television advertisements and programmes. As a legal structure, she chose to set up her business as a private limited company called Alchemy Productions Limited. Gina sold 45% of the shares to other investors to raise finance, but kept 55% of the shares and control of the business for herself. Setting up as a limited company also made it easier for her to persuade banks and State agencies to give her the loans and grants she needed to get the business established.

337

> **Private limited companies are owned by shareholders who have limited liability.**

Private limited companies *are businesses registered with the Companies Registration Office that are owned by a maximum of fifty investors called shareholders.* The money raised from the sale of shares to these shareholder investors is used to finance the business. Any profits made are divided among shareholders in the form of dividends. However, if there are losses, shareholders have the protection of limited liability.

Limited liability *means that the owners are not personally liable for any of the business's debts. They only lose the value of their investment in the business if the business goes bankrupt.*

Formation: The rules for setting up and running a private limited company are set out in the Companies Acts 1963–1999. These include rules about how many shareholders and directors are required, how to run Annual General Meetings (AGMs) and elect directors. The law also states that a company must have the word Limited (or Ltd.) or its Irish equivalent, Teoranta (Teo.), after the company name. To form a private limited company requires:

1. At least one **shareholder** and two **directors.** A director can also be a shareholder.
2. Preparation of a **Memorandum of Association.** *This is a document for the* **public** *setting out details such as the name of the company, its purpose and the number of shares held by each founder shareholder.* This has to be made available for public inspection at the Companies Registration Office.
3. Preparation of the **Articles of Association** *which is a document for* **shareholders** *setting out the internal rules for the company, such as the way meetings are to be conducted and the procedure for electing and replacing directors.*
4. Registration with the **Companies Registration Office (CRO)** using an **A1 form** and paying a registration fee. The CRO then issues a 'birth certificate' for the company called a **Certificate of Incorporation.**

5. The first **AGM** of shareholders is held to issue the share certificates to the shareholders and appoint the **board of directors** to oversee the management of the company. **The board of directors** *are elected by shareholders to oversee the running of the company on their behalf.* The enterprise can now commence trading as a limited company and is treated as a separate entity in the eyes of the law. This means that it can enter into contracts and can sue, and be sued, in its own right.

The Companies Registration Office (CRO)

All companies and co-operatives set up in Ireland must register with the Companies Registration Office (CRO). The **CRO** *is the State agency responsible for ensuring that businesses operating under company and co-operative law comply fully with their legal obligations.* If a firm is found to be in breach of the rules for running a company or co-operative, then it may be 'struck off' the CRO's list. This means that the owners of the business lose the benefit of limited liability protection.

The CRO is also responsible for the registration of business names for all types of businesses, including sole traders, partnerships, companies and co-operatives.

Name and address of the company

The objectives state the purpose and nature of the business.

The size of the Authorised Share Capital, i.e. the maximum amount of shares the company is allowed to sell.

MEMORANDUM OF ASSOCIATION
FOR ALCHEMY PRODUCTIONS LIMITED

1. **Name:** Alchemy Productions Limited
2. **Address:** 10 Grange Road, Wexford, Republic of Ireland.
3. **Objectives:** To produce television and radio programmes and any other business necessary to achieve the objectives.
4. **Liability:** The liability of the shareholders is limited by shares.
5. **Authorised Share Capital:** €200,000 made up of 200,000 ordinary shares @ €1 each.

We, the undersigned, agree to be the founder shareholders of Alchemy Productions Limited according to the conditions set out in the Memorandum of Association. We also agree to subscribe to the number of shares listed by our name.

Name	Address	Number of shares	Signature
1. Gina Curley	Seaview, Wexford Town	€140,000	Gina Curley
2. Harry Fleming	The Square, Waterford	€50,000	Harry Fleming
3. Marianne Hughes	Clonskeagh, Dublin	€9,900	Marianne Hughes
4. Joan O'Sullivan	Seaview, Wexford Town	€100	Joan O'Sullivan
		€200,000	

The amount of shares held by each of the original shareholders.

The signatures of the original paid-up shareholders.

THE ARTICLES OF ASSOCIATION
FOR ALCHEMY PRODUCTIONS LIMITED

1. Alchemy Productions is a private limited company.
2. The authorised share capital is €200,000 ordinary shares.
3. Additional shares may only be issued by the company with the approval of the majority of existing shareholders.
4. If there are two or more shareholders, then an AGM must be held every 12 months.
5. The company's AGM must be held every year within the Republic of Ireland.
6. There is one vote per share at AGMs and EGMs.
7. Votes at AGMs and EGMs require the support of at least 51% of the votes cast for them to be carried.
8. Any decision to wind up the company requires the support of at least 75% of votes cast.

How are companies run?

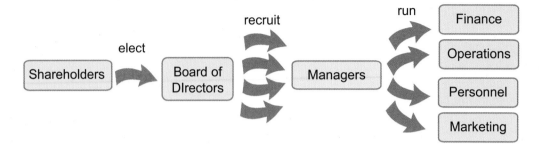

> Companies are owned by shareholders, who elect a board of directors to oversee the running of the business on their behalf.

> The board of directors appoints a managing director or CEO to be the top manager in the business and to achieve the goals set by the board.

★ **Shareholders** are the legal owners of a limited company. By law every company with two or more shareholders is required to hold an Annual General Meeting organised by the board of directors.

★ **Annual General Meetings (AGMs)** *of company shareholders hear reports on the performance of the business from the outgoing directors, elect directors to the board for the coming year and approve a dividend to be paid to shareholders.* AGMs must be held once a year. Sometimes a special **Extraordinary General Meeting (EGM)** of shareholders may be called to deal with a very important matter that cannot wait until the AGM.

★ The **board of directors** are the most senior managers of the company and must:
  - **Set** the overall policy and direction for the firm.
  - **Appoint a chief executive officer (CEO)** *or* **managing director (MD)** *to be responsible for all aspects of the company's activities and achieving the targets set by the board of directors.* The CEO is answerable to the board of directors.
  - **Make** or approve important decisions in consultation with the CEO or managing director.
  - **Report** to the shareholders at the AGM on the performance of the company.
  - **Decide** on the size of the annual dividend to be paid to shareholders.

★ Directors can only be elected or removed from their position by a vote of more than 50% of shareholders at an AGM or EGM.

★ The **company chairperson** *is a director elected by the board of directors to chair the company's board meetings, AGMs and EGMs.* He/she also speaks on behalf of the board of directors.

★ The **company secretary** *ensures that the company meets all the legal requirements as set out under the Companies Acts.* This includes:
  - Maintaining an up-to-date register of names and addresses of shareholders.
  - Organising AGMs and EGMs.
  - Making annual returns to the Companies Registration Office (CRO).
  - Keeping minutes of board meetings, AGMs and EGMs.

★ The **company auditor** *is an external accountant who certifies the company's annual accounts as being correct.*

Case Study

VOLVO SHAREHOLDERS REBEL

The board of directors of Volvo announced that it was planning to merge with Renault to form a new car company. Before the deal could be finalised, it had to get the agreement of a majority of shareholders in both companies. Volvo's board of directors were confident that the company's shareholders would vote in favour of the deal.

However, when the Volvo EGM was held, the board of directors got a shock. Despite a huge amount of planning by Volvo's managers, the company's shareholders were not impressed by the proposal of merging with Renault. The shareholders voted overwhelmingly against the deal, which could not now go ahead.

Advantages of setting up as a private limited company

1. **Formation & dissolution:** Companies are legally independent of their owners and so can continue to exist even if a shareholder dies, for example.

2. **Ownership & control:** The company is owned by its shareholders. It is cheap and easy to transfer the legal ownership of shares from one person to another.

3. **Management & finance:** Companies can raise finance for start-up and expansion through selling shares. Companies can motivate employees by giving them a shareholding in the business. Being 'incorporated' as a private limited company can also improve business image and creditworthiness with suppliers and banks.

4. **Profits & risk:** The owners (shareholders) have the protection of limited liability. If there is just one shareholder, they can keep all the profits and not bother with AGMs.

Disadvantages of setting up as a private limited company

1. **Formation & dissolution: It is** more **complex** to set up as special documents such as a memorandum and articles of association are required, as is registration with the CRO.

2. **Management & finance:** Companies have to deal with ongoing paperwork, including the submission of annual accounts and annual reports to the Companies Registration Office. This information is available to the public, including rivals.

3. **Profits and risks:** Profits must be shared among all the shareholders, depending on the number of shares held.

OL Short Q5, 6, 7, 8
OL Long Q2, 3, 4, 5, 6, 7

HL Short Q2, 5
HL Long Q2, 3, 4, 5, 7

4. What is a co-operative?

Case Study

Greencaps Co-operative

Greencaps is a workers' co-op providing a service to passengers and airlines at Dublin Airport. Its services include baggage portering, a left-luggage service and helping elderly, sick and disabled passengers. Customers are charged a fee for these services. The business was originally started as a limited company by a group of unemployed people. However, the founders later turned their business into a workers' co-operative as they felt that it was a fairer structure.

> Co-operatives are owned by members of one stakeholder group, such as the employees, suppliers or customers. Co-op members have limited liability.

Co-operatives *are businesses that are democratically owned and controlled by their members who may be the firm's workers, suppliers or customers.* However, unlike a limited company, each member can only own one share. This is intended to promote fairness and co-operation among the members. There are several types of co-ops:

* **Worker co-ops** are owned and run by the workers in the business.

* **Credit unions** and mutual building societies are types of financial co-operatives owned by the people who have savings there.

* **Producer co-ops** are owned by producers, such as farmers or fishermen.

* **Consumer co-ops** are retail businesses owned by their consumers.

Summary of the main forms of business legal structure available to entrepreneurs				
	Sole Trader	**Partnership**	**Private Limited Company**	**Co-operative**
Formation & Dissolution	• Easy • Register for tax with Revenue Commissioners. • Business dies with the owner.	• Easy • Register with Revenue Commissioners. • May have to register business name. • Business dies with the partners.	• More complex • Register with Revenue Commissioners. • Register with CRO. • Business continues after death of shareholder(s).	• More complex • Register with Revenue Commissioners. • Register with CRO. • Business continues after death of member(s).

	Sole Trader	Partnership	Private Limited Company	Co-operative
Ownership & Control	• Owned and controlled by sole trader.	• Owned and controlled by partners.	• Owned by shareholders. • Controlled by board of directors elected by shareholders using 'one vote per share' rule. • Annual accounts must be filed with the CRO.	• Owned by members who are the shareholders. • Controlled by management committee elected by members but using a 'one member one vote' rule. • Annual accounts must be filed with the CRO.
Management & Finance	• Decisions made by sole trader. • Without partners, members or shareholders, raising extra finance for expansion can be difficult.	• Decisions made by partners. • Can raise finance by bringing in new partners but this dilutes ownership.	• Decisions made by board of directors with shareholders' approval. • Extra finance can be raised by selling shares. In time, a private company may decide to become a public limited company (PLC) to raise very large sums on the stock market.	• Decisions made by management committee with members' approval. • Extra finance can be raised by bringing in new members but sums are often small.
Profits & Risk	• Sole trader keeps all the profits but pays income tax on earnings. • Sole trader has unlimited liability.	• Partners share all the profits and pay income tax on their earnings. • Partners have unlimited liability.	• Profits are shared among shareholders according to number of shares held. • Company pays corporation tax. Members pay income tax on dividends. • Shareholders benefit from protection of limited liability.	• Profits are shared among members equally. • Co-op pays corporation tax. Members pay income tax on dividends. • Members benefit from protection of limited liability.

OL Short Q9

HL Short Q4, 6

5. What is a state-owned company?

State-owned companies *are owned, financed and controlled by the State on behalf of the taxpayer. They are also referred to as* **'semi-state'** *or* **'state-sponsored' companies**. Well-known examples include Coillte (forestry), RTÉ (media) and CIÉ (transport).

> State-owned companies are owned and controlled by the State. They have limited liability.

❖ **Formation & dissolution:** State companies can be set up using specially written laws and are known as statutory companies. Alternatively, a state-owned company can be registered with the Companies Registration Office as for regular limited companies but with the State as the shareholder.

❖ **Ownership & control:** Each state-owned company is the responsibility of a particular government department.

> Example: Bus Éireann reports to the Department of Transport. The government will also appoint the board of directors to oversee the management of the state company on behalf of the government.

❖ **Management & finance:** The government provides the start-up finance for the business and may also agree to subsidise any losses that may be incurred. The government may **guarantee** the repayment of any loans that the state company may have to take out.

❖ **Profits & risk:** Profits generated may be reinvested in the state enterprise or paid out in dividends to the government. However, any losses suffered by a state company means the taxpayer is losing money.

B. Structures that can be used to expand an existing business

Businesses that were originally set up as sole traders, partnership, co-operatives, private limited companies or state-owned companies may choose additional structures to expand their businesses. These can include:

✪ An existing co-op, private limited company or state-owned company **becoming a public limited company.**

✪ Existing businesses **entering into a strategic alliance** together.

✪ An existing business deciding to **expand by franchising** out the business idea.

✪ Indigenous Irish-owned firms expanding internationally, some **becoming transnational** firms.

6. What is a public limited company?

Glanbia PLC

Glanbia PLC produces well-known Irish brands such as Avonmore milk, cream, fruit juice, cheese, fresh soups and sauces, fresh creamed rice, spreads and butters and the Yoplait range of yogurts and drinks. Glanbia was formerly a producer co-op owned by farmers. However, it changed its legal structure into a PLC to raise the large amounts of

finance needed to develop the economies of scale that are required to expand and compete internationally.

A public limited company (PLC) like Glanbia has at least seven and no maximum number of shareholders. The big difference between it and a private limited company is that shares in a PLC can be freely bought and sold on the stock market. The shares of most Irish PLCs are traded on the Dublin Stock Exchange. However, some Irish companies have also secured stock market listing on the London or New York Stock Exchanges.

> **Public limited companies are owned by shareholders who can buy and sell their shares freely on the stock market.**
> **PLC shareholders have limited liability.**

Advantages of operating as a public limited company

1. **Formation & dissolution:** A PLC must start off as a private limited company before applying to a stock exchange for a listing – also known as a quotation.

2. **Ownership & control:** It is cheap and easy for shareholders to transfer the legal ownership of shares from one person to another.

3. **Management & finance:** PLCs have access to very **large sources of finance** by freely selling more shares on the stock market. **Talented staff** can be rewarded with **options to buy shares** in the business at a discount. Being a PLC can significantly improve a firm's business image and **creditworthiness** with suppliers and banks.

4. **Profits & risk:** The owners (shareholders) have the protection of limited liability. Having a stock market listing provides a PLC with the **prestige and status** that can help the business to expand and grow.

Disadvantages of operating as a public limited company

1. **Formation & dissolution:** The requirements for registering as a PLC are time-consuming and **complex**. Stock market listings are only available to firms with established track records.

2. **Ownership & control:** By having its shares for sale on the stock exchange, a PLC can become an easy target for a takeover.

3. **Management & finance:** PLCs have to comply with very **detailed regulations** in the Companies Acts as well as complex stock exchange regulations. Detailed information must be made public about the PLC's financial and other activities. This **reduces confidentiality** for the business.

4. **Profits and risks:** Many shareholders in PLCs are speculators with a very short-term view of the business and expect very regular and high dividends to be paid. This can put huge pressure on senior managers to perform or be fired.

HL Short Q3, 7, 8
HL Long Q6

7. What are strategic alliances?

> Strategic alliances share the ownership and control of a business project.

Strategic alliances (joint ventures) *are agreements between businesses to co-operate in the establishment of a project or business together.* As a form of business ownership, the firms involved share ownership of the project, as well as pooling their skills and resources.

Example: Hollywood studios Pixar and Disney had a joint venture to produce and market animated movies. Mercedes and Smart Watches formed a strategic alliance to design and build Smart cars.

> **Signpost:** For more information on strategic alliances, see Chapter 17: Business Expansion

Advantages of operating as a strategic alliance

1. **Formation & dissolution:** They are formed by a **contract** negotiated by two separate businesses.
2. **Ownership & control:** Shared ownership and control can mean pooling and sharing of **expertise**.
3. **Management & finance:** Expansion can be faster when two or more firms co-operate in a joint venture. Furthermore, both firms can invest funds and share the costs and financial risks of the venture.
4. **Profits & risk:** Costs are shared; meanwhile, the sharing of staff, technology and other resources can mean less risk than for one individual company.

Disadvantages of operating as a strategic alliance

1. **Formation & dissolution:** Negotiating the contract between two or more separate businesses can be slow and time-consuming. Withdrawal from the contract at a later date by one party will require the consent of the other party to the contract.
2. **Ownership & control** is shared by the partners and any conflicts or differences between the firms can lead to the alliance splitting up before it has had time to become successful.
3. **Management & finance:** The speed of expansion can be delayed due to the need for greater communications and shared decision-making between the firms involved. Disagreements can arise over the sharing of costs.
4. **Profits & risk:** Any profits must also be shared by the partners.

8. What is franchising?

Franchising *means the renting of a complete business formula, including business name, logo and products/services to someone else.* As an ownership structure, a business can become involved as a franchisee or a franchiser. Franchising is becoming more common in service businesses as it is a relatively easy way for entrepreneurs to set up their own business. The **franchisee** owns and runs the business but only according to strict rules set down by the franchiser and in exchange for a share of the sales. If the franchisee breaks the terms of the franchise, the franchiser can withdraw permission to use the business name, idea and products.

> **Franchising means renting a complete business formula out to someone else.**

> **Signpost:** For more information on franchising, see Chapter 17: Business Expansion

Advantages of operating as a franchise

1. **Formation & dissolution:** For the franchisee, renting a business idea with a proven track record and ready-made brand image makes setting up easier. It can be dissolved by cancelling the contract with the franchiser.
2. **Ownership & control:** Ownership of the business idea remains with the franchiser who can withdraw the franchise if they are unhappy with the franchisee.
3. **Management & finance:** The franchisee receives training, advice and other support from the franchiser firm, which can allow rapid business start-up and expansion.
4. **Profits & risk:** For the franchiser, it is a low-cost method of expansion as most of the start-up finance is provided by the franchisee. It is also relatively low-risk to the franchiser because if a franchisee breaks the conditions attached, the contract can be cancelled.

Disadvantages of operating as a franchise

1. **Formation & dissolution:** Franchising is mainly used for service businesses such as retailers.
2. **Ownership & control:** For the franchisee, there is no ultimate ownership or control over the business.
3. **Management & finance:** The franchisee has little real independence in the management of the business. He/she must also put up most of the finance and take most of the financial risk when taking out a franchise. For the franchiser, control is lost over the day-to-day management of franchise outlets.
4. **Profits & risk:** The franchiser receives an annual royalty fee based on a percentage of sales but misses out on the full amount of profit that could be earned if they retained full ownership themselves. An unsuitable franchisee can damage the reputation of the whole business.

OL Short Q12
OL Long Q9

HL Long Q8

9. Why do businesses change their ownership structure over time?

> Some businesses change their legal structures over time to help them raise new finance, bring in new skills or reduce the risks involved in business expansion.

Most new businesses start off as sole traders or partnerships. As they grow, their financial requirements and level of risk can change and they may decide to become co-operatives or limited companies. Subsequent growth may mean that companies and co-ops further alter their legal structure by becoming public limited companies. Businesses often change their legal structures to meet the changing needs of the business and its owners. The main reasons for changing legal structures are as follows:

★ **To raise new finance:** This is the most common reason for changing the legal structure of a business. Sole traders can raise finance by going into partnership. Sole traders and partnerships can become private limited companies in order to sell shares to raise additional finance or reduce their business risks. If a private limited company (or commercial state company) needs to raise very large amounts of finance, it may apply to the stock exchange to become a public limited company (PLC).

★ **To acquire new skills:** Sole traders often change into partnerships to share the workload and also to benefit from the new partners' skills and expertise. If a firm becomes a limited company, it can attract, motivate and reward skilled staff by offering them shares in the business.

★ **To lower the risk for the owners:** As a business grows and the possible risks increase, sole traders and partnerships can become limited liability companies (or co-ops) to get the protection of limited liability for their owners.

★ **To increase sales and profits:** Forming a strategic alliance with another company can give a business the ability to sell more products, leading to increased business for both. Moving from a sole trader or partnership to a private limited company, or from a private limited company to a PLC can enhance the image and reputation of a business, making advertising, public relations and other promotions more effective.

★ **Regain control:** Some owners who turn their firms into limited companies and PLCs to raise finance regret the loss of ownership and control that can occur. They may then buy back the shares they sold and turn the business back into a private limited company. This is what Richard Branson did with his Virgin business (see case study).

Case Study

Virgin changes its legal structure . . . Again

Richard Branson started off in business as a **sole trader**. As the business grew, he considered turning it into a **partnership** but decided instead to set up a **private limited company**, which he called Virgin Ltd.

When Branson decided to start an airline, he needed to raise very large amounts of money. He decided to raise **equity finance** by converting Virgin into a **public limited company** (PLC) and selling

some of his shares on the stock market. This is known as a stock market flotation or 'going public'.

However, Branson became frustrated with the attitude of the new shareholders who were just interested in short-term profits. So, using his own money, he bought back the shares he had previously sold on the stock market and returned Virgin to being a private limited company again. This is known as '**going private**'.

OL Short Q10, 11
OL Long Q10

HL Long Q9

10. What are the main trends in business ownership structures?

Privatisation and nationalisation of companies

Generally, the number of **commercial** state-owned companies has been declining as governments adopted a policy of privatisation (e.g. Aer Lingus, Eircom, Greencore) and very few new commercial state-owned companies have been established. Most new commercial state enterprises that are undertaken as joint ventures with the private sector are known as **public-private partnerships,** e.g. toll bridges on motorways.

However, in recent years, the State has had to fully or partially nationalise some banks to prevent them collapsing and seriously damaging the wider economy.

> Example: Anglo Irish Bank, AIB, Bank of Ireland.

Increase in strategic alliances

Many Irish firms are entering into strategic alliances such as joint ventures with other firms. Such an approach allows firms to achieve greater economies of scale, share risks and compete more effectively in an increasingly globalised economy.

> Example: Tayto Crisps are produced in Libya under a 50:50 joint venture with a local Libyan company.

For more information on privatisation and nationalisation, see Chapter 22: Government & Business

Growth of franchising

Franchising has become a very common method of business expansion for many service firms, such as Supermac's and McDonalds, as it allows firms to expand rapidly in a competitive market at relatively low cost and risk. As a way of setting up or expanding a business, franchising is likely to be very important in the 21st century.

Emergence of Irish Transnational Corporations (TNCs)

Irish firms like Fyffes and Kerry Group have set up operations in many different countries across the globe due to the growth of free trade, membership of the EU and the small size of the Irish market. Such firms are described as **transnational** (or multinational) businesses.

Signpost: For more information on transnational corporations, see Chapter 25: Global Business

OL Long Q8

HL ABQ

HL Long Q1

Coming in the opposite direction, an even larger number of foreign-owned TNCs have located their operations in Ireland to take advantage of our low company tax rates, membership of the EU, well-educated population and availability of State grants.

Key Concepts & Business Terms

After studying this chapter the student should be able to explain the following key concepts and business terms:

1. Sole trader
2. Unlimited liability
3. Partnership
4. Deed of partnership
5. Private limited company
6. Limited liability
7. Memorandum of Association
8. Articles of Association
9. Companies Registration Office (CRO)
10. Shareholders
11. Annual General Meeting (AGM)
12. Board of directors
13. Managing director/chief executive officer (CEO)
14. Company chairperson
15. Company secretary
16. Company auditor
17. Co-operative
18. State-owned companies
19. Public limited companies (PLCs)
20. Strategic alliances
21. Franchising

useful websites

www.cro.ie
www.volvo.com
www.glanbia.com

Leaving Certificate Practice Questions

Ordinary Level

Ordinary Level – Section 1 – Short Questions (10 marks each)

1. As a type of business organisation, describe **three** features of a sole trader. [LCQ]
2. Explain the term 'partnership'. [LCQ]
3. List **one** advantage and **one** disadvantage of a partnership structure.
4. Explain the purpose of a deed of partnership.
5. Define 'limited liability'. [LCQ]
6. Outline the role of the Companies Registration Office (CRO).
7. What does the term 'CEO' mean? [LCQ]
8. Distinguish between Articles of Association and Memorandum of Association. [LCQ]
9. Describe **two** merits of a co-operative as a form of business organisation. [LCQ]
10. List **two** reasons why a business may change its legal structure over time.
11. List **three** reasons why a private limited company would expand to become a public limited company. [LCQ]
12. Explain the term 'franchising' and illustrate your answer with an example. [LCQ]

Ordinary Level – Section 2 – Long Questions

1. Give **two** benefits of a partnership as a type of business organisation. (15 marks)
2. LIst **three** benefits for an entrepreneur in forming a private limited company. (15 marks) [LCQ]
3. People in a company include shareholders, directors, auditors and a company secretary. Explain the role of any **two** of these people. (20 marks) [LCQ]
4. Discuss the benefits of setting up in business as a private limited company. (20 marks)
5. Outline the steps involved in forming a limited company. (20 marks)
6. Define what the term 'shareholders' means. (15 marks) [LCQ]
7. Describe the role of the board of directors in a company. (15 marks) [LCQ]
8. Outline **three** trends affecting business ownership and structure in Ireland. (15 marks)
9. Explain the advantages of franchising for the franchisee and the franchiser. (20 marks)
10. Outline **four** reasons why a business may change its legal structure over time. (20 marks)

Higher Level

Higher Level – Section 1 – Short Questions (10 marks each)

1. List **three** advantages that a partnership has over a sole trader as a legal structure.
2. Explain the purpose of a Memorandum of Association when forming a limited company.
3. Distinguish between a private limited company and a public limited company.
4. Identify **two** advantages of setting up in business as a co-op.
5. What is the role of the managing director in a company?
6. A worker co-operative is . . .
7. Identify the type of company that can sell its shares on the stock market.
8. Distinguish between a state-owned company and a PLC.

Higher Level – Section 2 – Applied Business Question

Molly Malone's Irish Restaurant

Gráinne O'Neill opened a traditional Irish restaurant called Molly Malone's several years ago. An excellent chef, she started off as a sole trader and steadily built up a good reputation for the business. The restaurant became very popular, particularly with tourists, and during the summer season it often had to turn away bookings.

When Gráinne needed to expand her business to cope with the increasing trade, she decided to bring in a business partner, Trevor, to provide the extra finance and people management skills that the business now required. The two work well together and share the workload and decision-making. When one is ill, the other partner is able to continue running the restaurant. Profits are split 60% to Gráinne, 40% to Trevor.

With the help of retained earnings and a bank loan, the business has now expanded to include two more restaurants, and has a combined turnover of over €5 million a year.

Gráinne and Trevor would like to open more restaurants but do not have the finance to do so. They are also aware that as a business grows, so too does the risk. Given the success of the existing restaurants, they are also interested in expanding the business abroad, especially in the US and Germany where they feel there is a demand for traditional Irish restaurants. It has been suggested to them that they consider franchising as a possible route for this expansion.

1. Evaluate the potential risks and benefits of operating the restaurant as a partnership. Refer to the text in your answer. (20 marks)

2. Assess the potential benefits for Trevor and Gráinne of changing their business partnership into a private limited company. Refer to the text in your answer. (30 marks)

3. Explain how Gráinne and Trevor could use franchising to expand the business. (30 marks)

Higher Level – Section 2 – Long Questions

1. Evaluate the legal ownership options open to an entrepreneur seeking to expand his/her enterprise. (20 marks)

2. Compare a private limited company with a partnership as desirable forms of business organisation. (25 marks) [LCQ]

3. Explain why you would recommend a private limited company as a type of business organisation for a new business venture. (20 marks) [LCQ]

4. Explain the steps involved in setting up a private limited company. (20 marks)

5. Draft the agenda for an AGM of a private limited company. (15 marks) [LCQ]

6. Contrast a private limited company with a public limited company as a form of business organisation. (20 marks) [LCQ]

7. Distinguish between the role of directors and shareholders in a company. (20 marks)

8. Contrast a business alliance with a franchise as forms of business organisation. Use examples in your answer. (20 marks) [LCQ]

9. Describe **two** reasons why a business enterprise might change its organisational structure over time. Use illustrations to support your answer. (20 marks) [LCQ]

Chapter 20
Business, the Economy & Community Development

Key Study Questions

Case Study

Tanya Airey started work as a junior travel consultant where she learned all about the travel business from the bottom up. She then became the managing director of Sunway Holidays Limited, a travel agency competing against rivals such as Budget Travel and Falcon Holidays.

The travel **industry**, in the **tertiary sector** of the economy, is a good indicator of the overall health of the **economy**. When the **economic cycle** is on a high, there are lots of jobs and wealth is being created, so more people book

foreign holidays. When the level of economic activity declines and **unemployment** increases, there is less money around so fewer people book foreign holidays. Fluctuations in the economic cycle can be influenced by changes in **interest rates**, changes in **foreign exchange rates** and levels of **taxation**.

Tanya says the secret of business success is being enthusiastic and enjoying what you are doing. 'When you hit the first hurdle, you need enthusiasm from the times that are good to carry you through the times that are bad,' she says. 'People think that being your own boss means that you can doss. But it's not like that – it's a huge responsibility.'

A. Business & the Economy

1. What is the economy?

The **economy** *refers to all the producers, distributors and consumers of goods and services in the country.* Activity in the economy tends to fluctuate in an **economic cycle** (also known as the business cycle), with the level of demand for goods and services in an economy rising and falling over time. For most of the last century, the underlying trend was upwards, as the value of goods and services produced in the economy increased. However, the pattern of economic growth and development can be uneven.

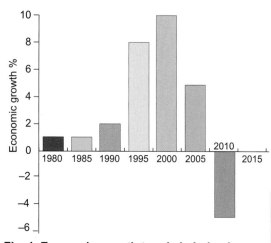

Fig. 1 Economic growth trends in Ireland.

Economic growth *refers to any increases in the financial value of all the goods and services produced from a country's resources.* It is used as an indicator of economic activity.

An **economic boom** *occurs when the level of economic activity is increasing very quickly.* During a boom spending and demand for goods and services such as foreign holidays is high, along with the demand for employees to work in businesses producing the goods and services required.

Example: When Ireland experienced an economic boom, the Irish economy was known as the 'Celtic Tiger'. Businesses and employment grew very quickly and workers from other countries migrated to Ireland looking for jobs.

An **economic recession** *occurs when economic growth ceases or goes into reverse (i.e. the economy starts shrinking).* An economic recession is characterised by falls in sales for businesses and a rise in unemployment. Competition becomes more intense as firms have to try harder to find new opportunities to grow their business. This can result in firms like Sunway Holidays having to cut their labour and other costs to remain competitive.

A **depression** *is a severe and prolonged period of economic decline.* In a depression, demand for the goods and services in the economy falls significantly, unemployment rises sharply and there is a lack of consumer and business confidence in the future.

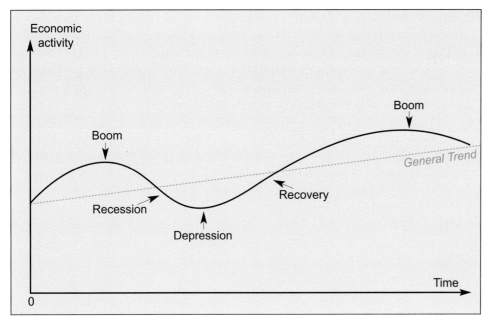

Fig 2: An economic (business) cycle

OL Short Q1

HL Long Q1, 2

2. What economic variables impact on business?

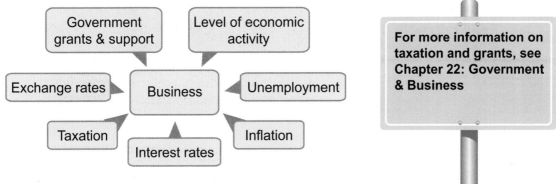

Fig. 3: Key economic variables that impact on business.

For more information on taxation and grants, see **Chapter 22: Government & Business**

Economic variables impact on three key areas of business:

1. Business **sales**
2. Business **costs**
3. Business **confidence** in the future which influences their willingness to invest and expand.

❖ **Sales:** A **rise** in the level of economic activity will generally **increase demand** for most goods and services, including holidays, throughout the economy. However, a **fall** in economic activity can lead to a drop in demand (especially of luxury and non-essentials goods). This can undermine profitability and increase the risk of **redundancies** and possible **business closures**.

❖ **Costs:** A rapid **rise** in economic activity can cause **shortages** of labour and goods as demand exceeds supply. This can cause **prices to rise** sharply, leading in turn to demands for higher wages from staff which **increases costs** and forces firms to raise their prices further. This is referred to as a '**wage-price spiral**' and can destabilise the whole economy.

❖ **Business confidence:** Rising economic activity normally leads to a rise in **government revenue** as more taxes are collected as a result of increased sales (VAT), profits (corporation tax) and employment (PAYE, PRSI). This can allow **increased government spending** on infrastructure, business grants and other areas that will benefit business. This boosts business confidence and the willingness of entrepreneurs to start up or expand.

❖ In contrast, a **decline** in economic activity will **reduce government tax revenue** and force the government to increase tax rates, cut spending or increase borrowing in order to pay for state services. This can undermine business confidence and discourage **investment** in new business projects.

Recall & Review

List the effects that low levels of economic activity could have on Sunway Holidays' business.

---

3. How does the level of unemployment affect business?

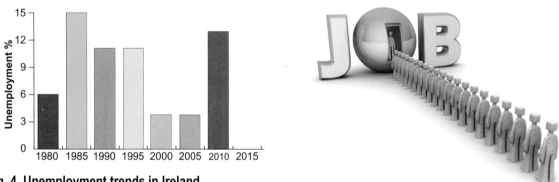

Fig. 4 Unemployment trends in Ireland.

Unemployment *refers to the number of jobless people available for work.* The percentage unemployed is the number of unemployed people expressed as a percentage of the total labour force in the economy.

Impact of unemployment on business

✪ **Sales:** When unemployment is high, sales are lower than they could be as unemployed people have relatively small incomes to spend on goods and services. This reduces overall **demand** in the economy. However, if unemployment is low, more people will have incomes and the level of demand in the economy will be high benefiting firms such as Sunway Holidays.

✪ **Costs:** Demand for wage increases tends to fall during periods of high unemployment. It also becomes easier to recruit staff, which helps to keep wage costs down. However, high unemployment can also lead to higher government taxes to pay for the additional social welfare payments. When unemployment is low, the demand for labour can push up wages as firms are forced to compete to attract and retain skilled staff. Low unemployment can also lead to greater immigration into the country.

❂ **Business confidence:** High unemployment erodes community and national confidence, undermining enterprise in the economy. Additional spending may also be required to deal with the social problems associated with unemployment. All this will put pressure on the government to increase taxes, including taxes on businesses which will reduce their profitability. However, low unemployment reduces pressure on government finances and increases confidence.

OL Long Q6

Recall & Review

List the effects that high levels of unemployment could have on Sunway Holidays' business.

4. How does the level of inflation affect business?

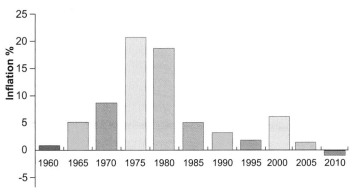

Fig. 5 Inflation trends in Ireland.

Inflation *refers to a rise in the average prices of goods in the economy.* It usually occurs because there is an increasing supply of money or credit circulating in the economy. Inflation reduces the buying power of each euro. It is the reason why a bar of chocolate today costs twice as much as it did 15 years ago.

Impact of inflation on business

★ **Sales:** High inflation makes customers become more price-sensitive and likely to shop around for the best prices. This can result in a fall in sales for firms like Sunway. Low inflation makes consumers less price sensitive and better able to plan their shopping.

★ **Costs:** High inflation increases the cost of raw materials, while employees are more likely to look for **cost-of-living wage increases.** This increases business costs and undermines profitability. When inflation is low, prices and demands for wage increases tend to be low. This helps to keep business costs down.

★ **Business confidence:** High inflation increases uncertainty and erodes business confidence. However, when inflation is low, business confidence is boosted as planning for the future becomes easier for businesses, workers and consumers.

Deflation *refers to a decrease in the average prices of goods in the economy. It typically occurs when there is a shortage of money or credit in the economy.* Deflation means reduced business costs but also reduced sales.

OL Short Q3
OL Long Q2, 3, 4

HL Short Q2, 3, 4

   Ideally, most businesses prefer when there is little or low inflation because prices and costs are relatively stable and predictable. This makes business planning and management easier.

> ### Recall and Review
> List the effects that high inflation could have on Sunway Holidays' sales business.

5. How does the level of interest rates affect business?

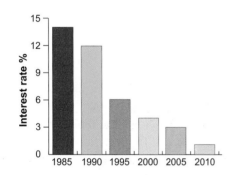

Fig. 6 Interest rate trends in Ireland.

Interest rates *represent the cost of borrowing money.* For countries using the euro currency, the minimum interest rate level is set by the **European Central Bank**. The Irish government has no influence over these interest rates.

Impact of interest rates on business

* **Sales:** High interest rates mean fewer consumers can afford to take out personal loans or buy on hire purchase. As a result, many firms will experience a fall in sales. Low interest rates encourages business and consumer borrowing and spending, which increases overall demand for goods and services.

* **Costs:** High interest rates make borrowing money more expensive for firms and consumers. Since nearly every business borrows money, this will push up business costs and undermine profitability. However, low rates of interest benefit business by making it cheaper for firms to borrow finance for expansion and for consumers to borrow for purchases.

OL Short Q2, 4
OL Long Q5

HL Short Q5, 6
HL Long Q3

* **Business confidence:** Business confidence is eroded when the cost of borrowing becomes, or looks like becoming, more expensive. High interest rates encourage investors to put their money into deposit accounts in financial institutions rather than investing in business projects. Business start-ups and expansions may be postponed or scaled back until interest rates return to a more affordable level. Low interest rates make it more attractive to invest in new business ventures.

6. How does the level of exchange rates affect business?

Exchange rates *are the price of one currency expressed in terms of another currency.* For example, €1 = $1.25 means that one euro can purchase one US dollar and 25 cents. Exchange rates are constantly fluctuating up and down in value on the international currency markets over which the government has no control. This makes doing business outside of the Eurozone more uncertain and risky.

Date	Exchange rate*	Effect
Month 1	€1 : $1	Current € : $US exchange rate
Month 2	€1 : $2	The increased value of the euro makes it cheaper for Sunway to book holiday accommodation in Florida USA.
Month 3	€0.80 : $1 * Fictitious	Depreciation in the value of the euro against the US dollar means more euros are now needed to buy one dollar. This makes it more expensive to book holiday accommodation in Florida.

Impact of exchange rates on business

- ❖ **Sales:** If the euro increases in value against other currencies, Irish exports to countries outside of the Eurozone become more expensive to buy. This is because the Irish seller will want to be paid in euros, which have become more expensive for foreign customers to buy. This will cause sales to these countries to fall. However, if the euro falls in value against other currencies, then Irish goods will become more affordable in these countries and export sales will rise.
- ❖ **Costs:** If the euro increases in value against other currencies, the price of goods imported into Ireland from outside of the Eurozone will become cheaper. This reduces business costs and boosts profitability. If the euro falls in value against other currencies, then imports into Ireland from outside of the Eurozone will become more expensive. This increases business costs and erodes profitability.
- ❖ **Business confidence:** Relatively stable and predictable exchange rates make business planning easier and boost business confidence.

OL Short Q5
OL Long Q1

HL Short Q1, 7
HL Long Q5, 7

Case Study

A DAFT BUSINESS IDEA

When his older sister left home to go to college but had difficulty finding a place to live, Brian Fallon had an idea. The 15-year-old did some **market research** before deciding to design a simple website where people could advertise accommodation for rent. Even though he knew nothing about web design when he started researching his business, he ended up producing a workable site and called it www.daft.ie.

The site quickly became a hit, particularly with students who needed to rent temporary accommodation while in college. 'Landlords were on to us straight away,' says Brian, 'because they liked the idea of paying for an advertisement that would stay on the website for as long as it took to rent out the accommodation.' The price of advertising with daft.ie was also very competitive. Running an Internet business appealed to Brian because selling advertising on the Internet meant that there were no paper, printing or transport costs. It also meant that he could run the business on a part-time basis, as he wanted to go to college and study engineering.

As an **entrepreneur**, Brian Fallon started off as a **sole trader**. As the website became more popular and advertising revenue began to roll in, Brian decided more time and money had to be invested to ensure the long-term success of the site. He decided to turn the business into a **partnership** by bringing his brother in as a business partner.

What started out as a simple website selling advertising to people who had accommodation to rent, is today a sophisticated business with thousands of advertisements for homes, holiday homes, parking spaces and overseas property for sale, as well as houses and apartments for rent. The business has expanded into other Internet-based businesses in Ireland and internationally. A bigger business means bigger risks for the owners, so daft.ie has now adopted a **limited company** as a legal structure.

Recall and Review

1. Explain the terms highlighted in bold.
2. Identify the sector of the economy in which daft.ie is competing.
3. Describe the characteristics that successful entrepreneurs like Brian Fallon possess.
4. Analyse how (a) the level of economic activity, (b) unemployment, (c) inflation and (d) interest rates can impact on the success of daft.ie.

7. How does business impact on the national and local economy?

> **Businesses can have a negative and positive impact on the national and local economy.**

Economic benefits of business

- ✪ **Job creation:** New businesses create jobs and develop employee skills. Indirectly, further jobs are created among suppliers of raw materials and support services, creating further business and employment opportunities. Job creation by businesses means less unemployment.

- ✪ **Boost tax revenue** for local and national government which will also have to spend less on social welfare for the unemployed. This allows more money to be spent on the provision of improved infrastructure and public services, such as schools, hospitals, libraries, etc.

- ✪ **Develop local economic self-reliance and resilience:** Communities with strong local businesses become less exposed to risks, such as the sudden closure of a large local employer or other economic shocks.

- ✪ **Wealth creation:** Businesses create wealth for the entrepreneurs (profits) and employees (wages). This money can be spent or invested in other businesses, thus creating more wealth.

- ✪ **Competition:** Encouraging more competition between businesses in the same industry can lead to lower prices for customers.

Social benefits of business

- ★ **Promote social cohesion:** Economically prosperous communities are less likely to experience the social decay caused by high levels of unemployment (such as crime, ill health and depopulation).

- ★ **Enhances quality of life:** Enterprise and economic activity can result in improved services and higher quality of life for a local community such as postal and banking services, recreational facilities, etc.

- ★ **Sponsorship** of local sporting, arts and cultural activities can be provided by successful local businesses.

Possible negative effects of business

- ✳ **Local economic shocks** can occur when a large business closes down. This can cause a large increase in local unemployment which undermines local quality of life. Business closures also means lower tax revenue and higher welfare spending for the government, which then has less money to spend on other aspects of the economy.

- ✳ **Socially and environmentally irresponsible businesses** may try to cut their costs and increase profits by ignoring environmental regulations and thereby causing environmental damage, e.g. illegally disposing of their waste or not installing proper water treatment facilities.

OL Short Q6
OL Long Q7, 8

HL Short Q9
HL Long Q4, 6

B. Business & Community Development

Case Study

From Dumping to Rockclimbing

Western Kilkenny was a rural area struggling with unemployment and little local enterprise. Some local people with initiative and a vision of a better future decided to do something about it. They called a public meeting from which grew the enthusiasm to revitalise their community.

As a first step, the community decided to set up a **not-for-profit enterprise** to promote local **community development**. Called KBK Community Enterprise Limited, it had a **board of directors** as well as dozens of volunteer members from the local community. Initial efforts included supporting participation in the Tidy Towns competition to attract tourists, renovating an old building for use as a community centre and setting up a small printing business and duck-rearing enterprise.

As their confidence grew, so too did their ambitions and their ability to see new opportunities. Nearby Ballykeeffe Quarry had been a rat-infested dumping place for old car wrecks, washing machines and rotting rubbish. However, a local rock-climbing group was using the quarry walls for climbing practice and the local community realised that it could become an asset instead of an eyesore.

Working closely with Kilkenny County Council and State community development agencies, KBK Community Enterprise Limited drew up ambitious plans to turn the quarry into a multipurpose amenity. With its spectacular cliffs and unique acoustics, the idea for a dramatic amphitheatre in the quarry also caught their imagination.

A detailed plan for the quarry was prepared, and with €50,000 **finance** raised through fundraising from local people and a further €150,000 in **grants**, they swung into action. The car wrecks and all the rubbish were removed and the site landscaped, creating stone seating for 350 people and a terraced grass bank to seat many more. A wood and nature reserve were also added, along with picnic and recreational facilities.

Ballykeeffe is now one of Europe's best rock-climbing centres, attracting rock climbers from all over Europe. It is also a unique and very successful venue hosting musical and dramatic performances that attracts thousands of visitors every year.

The story of Ballykeeffe provides a striking example of what can be achieved when a spirit of enterprise is released – even an old dump can be turned into a hugely valuable asset that creates jobs, enhances local quality of life and benefits the entire community.

8. What is community development?

Community development *refers to local people coming together to identify problems in their area and then developing and implementing a plan to solve the problems themselves.* **Community enterprise development** *means supporting small-scale economic and enterprise development. Typically, this means businesses that employ less than 10 people.*

The signs of a strong and **vibrant local community** are:

- ❖ **Wide variety of local businesses** providing employment to local people. Because the community is not dependent on any one employer, if any business has to lay off staff there should be plenty of other employment opportunities.
- ❖ **Wide range of local services** such as shops, post office, bank, doctor's surgery, etc.
- ❖ **Education and training facilities** for people of all ages, such as schools, evening classes, training courses.
- ❖ **Recreational, social and sporting facilities** for all ages and interests.
- ❖ **Good basic infrastructure** such as electricity, roads, telecommunications and public transport.
- ❖ **A wide variety of voluntary organisations** that allow people to share their interests and also to help others when they are in need. Examples include sports clubs, business association, etc.
- ❖ **A strong sense of community** and willingness to work together to improve everyone's quality of life.

> **Signs of a weak or declining local community:**
> - Few local job opportunities
> - Few social, sporting or cultural activities
> - Derelict sites, graffiti and litter
> - Vandalism, crime, drug abuse
> - Area gets a bad name

HL Short Q8

9. What factors can influence a business's decision to locate in a local community?

Before deciding where to locate, businesses must ensure that the essential financial, production, marketing and human resource needs of the business are fully considered, as well as the needs of the local community and their environment.

A **footloose business** *is a term used to describe a business that is not constrained by particular location factors. Such businesses are free to set up in a wide variety of locations.*

Operational/production considerations
- Close to important suppliers, raw materials and services?
- Availability of good local utilities such as water, energy and waste disposal, postal and telecommunications services, especially in a remote area?
- Suitable local climate, geography and environment?

Financial considerations
- ★ Cost of local land and premises?
- ★ Availability of local grants, tax or financial incentives?

Environmental and social considerations
- Clean and healthy natural environment?
- Little crime or vandalism?
- Supportive local community?

Human resource considerations
- ❖ Local availability of suitable employees?
- ❖ Good transport links and housing if employees need to travel or move to the location?

Fig 7 Factors influencing choice of business location

Marketing considerations
- ✳ Close to customers or markets?
- ✳ Proximity to good transport and infrastructure links?

Case Study

LOCAL COMMUNITY OBJECTS TO PIG BUSINESS

A 6,000-pig farm chose to locate near Lough Erne, in County Cavan due to the availability of affordable land and a suitable transport infrastructure and local supply of labour.

However, before the pig farm could go ahead, the business had to apply for planning permission from Cavan County Council. There were objections from the local community on the grounds that the nearby lake could become a 'slurry tank' for the piggery and result in serious knock-on effects for other more economically important businesses in the area, such as tourism and fishing.

OL Short Q8
OL Long Q11
HL Long Q10

Recall and Review

What factors would be relevant to deciding the location of the following: (a) a major oil refinery, (b) a newsagents shop, (c) a dairy and (d) a computer company?

10. How can a local community develop itself?

Community development requires enterprising people, an organisation, a plan and finance.

Enterprising people

Local people need to get together. The group should be representative of the views of as many local interests as possible (e.g. business, voluntary groups, sports clubs, schools, clubs, etc.) and local government.

> **Example:** In the Ballykeeffe example, a small number of very enterprising people had the initiative and imagination to start talking about their ideas and get others enthusiastic and involved.

An organisation

An organisation with a clear management structure ensures good planning, organisation and control. A management committee could decide to set up a formal business structure, such as a community-owned company or co-op.

> **Example:** In Ballykeeffe the local people set up a limited company, KBK Community Enterprise Ltd., as a means of working together.

A plan

A realistic community development plan should diagnose the problems and needs of the community and identify possible solutions. This can be done by doing a **SWOT analysis** of the local community.

> **Example:** The people of Ballykeeffe worked closely with the local council and state agencies to prepare a detailed plan of what they wanted to do.

Finance

Finance will be needed to implement the plan and can be raised within the community through fundraising events such as raffles and competitions, as well as donations from local individuals and businesses. Local credit unions may also be willing to provide loans at low interest rates for projects that will help their own local community.

Finance from outside the community can come from **grants** from State agencies, such as local authorities, County Enterprise Boards, Area Partnership Companies, Pobal and the EU. Before providing any finance, credit unions and State agencies will want to be convinced that the community development plan is clear and realistic in its aims.

> **Example:** In Ballykeeffe the people raised €50,000 from local fundraising and a further €150,000 in grants from State organisations.

Examples of local development projects:

- Building holiday cottages to rent out.
- Creating an enterprise centre.
- Setting up skills training for local people.
- Restoring an old historic building.
- Cleaning up a local river or lake and restocking it with fish.
- Creating tourist hiking and walking trails.
- Starting a local Tidy Towns group.
- Starting a local festival or summer school.

OL Short Q7

HL Short Q10

HL Long Q8

11. What organisations can assist with community development?

The main organisations assisting community development are:
* County and city enterprise boards
* Pobal
* Area partnership companies
* LEADER programmes.

County and city enterprise boards

County and **city enterprise boards (CEBs)** *are State agencies responsible for assisting entrepreneurs who want to start up a small business (with less than 10 employees) in their own city or county. They all provide the same services and supports to enterprise but in different geographical areas.*

The board of every CEB represents a partnership between various local stakeholders, including local businesses, voluntary groups, trade unions, State agencies and elected public representatives. The main services provided by CEBs are:

* **Conducting local resource audits:** Each CEB is responsible for identifying local assets and resources that can be developed for the benefit of the local economy.
* **Giving grants** for conducting **market research, preparing detailed business plans,** purchasing equipment **or employing or providing training to local people**.
* **Providing training courses** for aspiring and new entrepreneurs in finance, HRM, marketing and other business topics.
* **Providing a mentoring service** to entrepreneurs. **Business mentors** *are experienced business people who are available to provide guidance to entrepreneurs while they are trying to get their business established.*

CEBs provide advice and support for small local enterprises

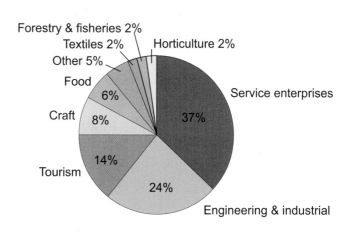

Fig. 8 **Profile of new businesses assisted by county and city enterprise boards.**

Pobal

Pobal is the State agency responsible for distributing specific national and EU finance for supporting projects that assist community development. Pobal's focus is on funding social initiatives that will improve **local quality of life** rather than commercial projects. Pobal provides the funding to run local area partnership development companies.

Area partnership companies

Area partnership companies (APCs) *encourage and support local enterprise and quality of life in local communities.* Examples include the Dundalk Employment Partnership, the Ballymun Partnership and the West Cork Development Partnership.

> Examples of the types of community social projects supported by Pobal and area partnership companies include graffiti removal, computer training, community childcare facilities and installing community CCTV systems.

LEADER Programmes

LEADER *is an EU-funded programme designed to encourage and assist* **rural** *communities to develop enterprises suitable to their own local area.* Specifically its aim is to:

* **Improve competitiveness of agriculture** and forestry businesses.

> Example: Assisting a farmer to produce and sell his own ice cream.

* **Improve the environment** and quality of life in the countryside.

Farmer Tom Baldwin got LEADER funding to produce his own brand of farmhouse ice cream.

> Example: Funding woodland walks and restoring heritage houses and castles.

* **Encourage diversification** of business activities in rural areas.

> Example: Supporting the development of Ballykeeffe Amphitheatre, artisan food businesses like Baldwin's Farmhouse Ice Cream and local craft businesses.

Funding is available for activities such as market research, prototype development and feasibility studies.

| OL Short Q9, 10 |
| OL Long Q9, 10 |
| HL ABQ |
| HL Long Q9 |

Key Concepts & Business Terms

After studying this chapter the student should be able to explain the following key concepts and business terms:

1. The economy
2. Economic (or business) cycle
3. Economic growth
4. Economic boom
5. Economic recession
6. Economic depression
7. Unemployment
8. Inflation
9. Deflation
10. Interest rates
11. Exchange rates
12. Business impact on the economy
13. Community development
14. Community enterprise development
15. Footloose business
16. Factors influencing the location of businesses
17. Community development plan
18. County and city enterprise boards
19. Business mentors
20. Pobal
21. Area partnership companies
22. LEADER programme

 useful websites

www.sunway.ie
www.ecb.int
www.ballykeeffe.com
www.pobal.ie
ec.europa.eu

Leaving Certificate Practice Questions

Ordinary Level

Ordinary Level – Section 1 – Short Questions (10 marks each)

1. Explain what is meant by an economic recession.
2. Outline **two** ways in which high interest rates can affect business. [LCQ]
3. Outline the meaning of the term 'inflation'.
4. Explain what is meant by interest rates.
5. What is meant by the term 'exchange rate'.
6. List **two** benefits that business can bring to a community [LCQ]
7. Identify **three** elements needed by a community that wants to develop local enterprise.
8. List **three** factors a business may consider before choosing to locate in an area.
9. Identify **three** possible sources of finance for community development.
10. List **three** organisations that assist local community development

Ordinary Level – Section 2 – Long Questions

1. Identify **four** economic variables that impact on business. (20 marks)
2. Define the term 'inflation' and cite the approximate percentage rate of inflation in Ireland at present. (10 marks) [LCQ]
3. Outline **two** benefits of low inflation to Ireland. (20 marks) [LCQ]
4. Outline **two** effects that a high rate of inflation would have on business. (20 marks) [LCQ]
5. Explain the importance of interest rates to business. (15 marks)
6. Explain **three** benefits to the economy of low unemployment. (15 marks) [LCQ]
7. Local community enterprise has increased in recent years. Explain why local community enterprise is important. (15 marks) [LCQ]
8. Describe the opportunities to local business that would result from more tourists visiting an area. (30 marks) [LCQ]
9. Name **two** agencies that can help local community development and outline the role of **one** of them. (20 marks) [LCQ]
10. Describe the role of LEADER and city/county enterprise boards in encouraging community development. (20 marks)
11. Chemphar is an American transnational company which manufactures chemical and pharmaceutical products for the world market. The company is considering setting up a new factory in the industrial estate in Rosstown, Co. Waterford.

    (a) Outline **three** factors a business should consider before choosing a location. (15 marks)

    (b) List **three** reasons why Chemphar might like to locate a new factory in Rosstown. (15 marks) [LCQ]

    (c) Outline **three** benefits to the local community of Rosstown if Chemphar were to locate their factory there. (15 marks) [LCQ]

    (d) Describe **two** environmental responsibilities that Chemphar may have if they locate their factory in Rosstown. (20 marks) [LCQ]

Higher Level

Higher Level – Section 1 – Short Questions (10 marks each)

1. Outline **two** economic variables that affect the Irish economy. [LCQ]

2. Illustrate your understanding of the term 'inflation'. [LCQ]

3. Identify **three** effects that a high rate of inflation can have on business.

4. Distinguish between inflation and economic growth.

5. List **three** effects that low interest rates would have on business.

6. Identify **two** effects on business if the European Central Bank announces a sharp rise in interest rates.

7. Explain the term 'exchange rate'. [LCQ]

8. Define 'community development'. [LCQ]

9. Identify **three** benefits of community enterprise.

10. Illustrate the difference between a community enterprise and a State enterprise. [LCQ]

Higher Level – Section 2 – Applied Business Question

Carrigbawn

Carrigbawn is a small coastal town located at the foot of a scenic mountain range. With little local employment, most local people have to leave the town for work, or else commute long distances every day into the nearest city located over 50 kilometres away. Aside from a few shops, the last remaining employer is a small local dairy. However, it has been announced that due to rationalisation in the agribusiness industry, it is to close at the end of the year.

Over the years, many of the buildings have become derelict and litter and graffiti is an increasing problem in the town which seems to be facing a bleak future. Residents decided to organise a local meeting to discuss the town's future. A large crowd turned up and a wide-ranging discussion was held as people shared ideas about what to do. Many of the participants mentioned the different skills and talents that existed among residents which could help to generate local enterprises.

For example, one person suggested opening a local seafood restaurant while another suggested organising an annual town festival. An unemployed mechanic suggested opening a Vintage car museum in a derelict building while a local musician suggested that it could be used as a performance venue. A local farmer suggested organising a weekly farmers' market selling organic foods and arts and craft in the town square.

From the meeting, the residents of Carrigbawn realised that the town had lots of ideas and that the future did not have to be bleak. They also realised that, whatever community enterprises were set up, the town needed a facelift. A Tidy Towns committee would be a good place to start, as it would help to get the town looking good and to inspire more confidence and self-respect in the community.

1. Conduct a SWOT analysis of Carrigbawn using the above information. Refer to the text in your answer. (20 marks)

2. Outline the steps that the residents of Carrigbawn could take to promote the development and prosperity of their town. (20 marks)

3. Explain the possible implications for Carrigbawn of (a) a drop in interest rates, (b) a sharp rise in unemployment. (20 marks)

4. Identify **two** State agencies that could assist Carrigbawn's development and outline **two** specific ways that they could assist the local community. (20 marks)

Higher Level – Section 2 – Long Questions

1. Illustrate with a diagram your understanding of the term 'business cycle'. (15 marks)

2. Discuss the importance of economic growth on the level of business activity. (15 marks)

3. Describe the impact of interest rates on business in Ireland. (20 marks) [LCQ]

4. Explain, using an example where appropriate, the impact that business activity has in the development of the Irish economy. (30 marks) [LCQ]

5. Analyse how the economic variables (factors) in the Irish economy have an impact on business. (25 marks) [LCQ]

6. Analyse how local communities and local businesses can benefit from each other's presence in an area. Use an example in each case to illustrate your answer. (20 marks) [LCQ]

7. Analyse how the economic variables (factors) in the Irish economy have an impact on a local economy. (20 marks) [LCQ]

8. Describe the steps a local community can take to generate local enterprise and employment. (20 marks)

9. Discuss how the services provided by **one** community development organisation in your locality helps business enterprises. (20 marks) [LCQ]

10. A manufacturer of fire extinguishers is expanding and wants to build a new, state-of-the-art factory. Discuss the factors that will influence the choice of local community in which this factory may be located. (30 marks)

UNIT 6

Chapter 21

Ethical, Social & Environmental Responsibilities in Business

'Only when the last tree has died and the last river been poisoned and the last fish been caught will we realise we cannot eat money.'

Cree Indian Proverb

Key Study Questions

SHELL SHOCKED!

Case Study

Public outrage erupted across Europe when the **transnational company** Shell Oil announced plans to dump a massive, obsolete oil rig 500 kilometres off the Donegal coast. Many people regarded the company as using the Atlantic as a cheap dump for giant rubbish and this led to an international customer boycott of Shell petrol stations, estimated to have cost the company €12 million a day in lost sales. Many political leaders in Ireland and other European countries condemned Shell's plan, while newspapers compared the plan to 'dumping rusty old cars in the local duck pond'. So much **bad publicity** was generated for Shell that the company decided to abandon its plans.

The incident proved very damaging to Shell's international reputation and led to a major rethink by the company about how it does business. To prevent such events occurring again, the company decided to build a much closer relationship with its **stakeholders** in society, including environmentalists and local communities. For example, in order to find a solution to the problem of disposing of the oilrig, Shell organised a series of meetings with various stakeholders, including environmentalists and scientific experts. As a result of this process the company decided to finally dispose of the rig by recycling it as part of a quay extension in Norway.

Shell also learned a number of important business lessons from these events. Firstly, although something may be technically legal, it may not be morally acceptable to customers or the public. Secondly, the ability to identify and resolve conflicts between business and society is becoming critical to the long-term success of every business.

A. Business Ethics

1. What is meant by business ethics?

Shell Oil learned that although something may be legal, it might still not be ethically acceptable to customers or the wider public. **Business ethics** *refers to the moral rules that guide business decision-making. It helps people in business to decide whether a decision is right or wrong, honest and fair, regardless of whether it is profitable or not.* An ethical business decision might reject the most profitable solution in favour of one that provides a greater benefit to society.

Examples of ethically motivated decisions include:

∗ A business deciding not to sell a tasty and legal, but also unhealthy, food product.

∗ A business deciding to install solar panels to produce its own electricity without generating any carbon emissions that contribute to climate change.

● Reasons for unethical decision-making

Unethical decision-making usually arises from human weaknesses. Firms and individuals are more likely to behave in an unethical and irresponsible manner for the following reasons:

❖ **Greed:** Firms that put maximising profits and growth above everything else are far more likely to make unethical decisions.

❖ **Fear:** Employees who are working in a fearful atmosphere under threat of punishment such as demotion, pay cuts or job losses may be forced to make unethical business decisions to avoid suffering these actions.

❖ **Apathy:** The lack of proper leadership and management control of how staff do their jobs can lead to an 'anything goes' attitude where ethical considerations get ignored.

Example: Over the years, the narrow focus on profits of US transnational company General Electric has resulted in convictions for deliberately overcharging the US government for supplies, bribing politicians in Puerto Rico, as well as many fines for pollution.

✪ **Bad examples set by senior managers** are likely lead to similar behaviour by others throughout the business.

OL Short Q1, 2
OL Long Q4

✪ **Lack of regulations** or **weak penalties** and **enforcement** can tempt wrongdoers to justify their actions because, strictly speaking, they may not have been acting illegally.

The Personal Ethics Test

When making a business decision, if the answer to any of these questions is 'No', then a person should think carefully about their decision and its effects on others.

1. Will it be **legal**? Will this decision or action uphold the law?
2. Will it be **fair**? Will this decision or action be fair in the long term to all the stakeholders in the business?
3. Will it make me feel **proud**? How would I feel about this if it was reported in the media and all my family and friends found out?

2. How can ethical business behaviour be encouraged?

High ethical standards can be encouraged in business through the following:

★ **Using a code of ethics:** *A code of ethics is a document setting out guidelines for employees to follow when making decisions.* It contains guidelines for employees when dealing with different stakeholders, e.g. 'staff will never knowingly mislead customers or members of the public'. In some businesses, this code is signed by staff when they are recruited and any breaches of the code can provide legally acceptable grounds for dismissal.

★ **Encouraging employees to report unethical behaviour** without fear that their careers will be jeopardised. If staff concerns are ignored, they may be forced to become whistleblowers. **Whistleblowers** *are staff whose ethical concerns are ignored within the business and who have the courage to report the wrongdoing to the authorities or the media.*

> **Example:** A pilot with Eastern Airlines in the USA discovered a potentially fatal flaw in the design of the automatic pilot device in the airline's aircraft. The airline's managers ignored his fears and subsequently one of the planes crashed, killing 103 people. The company, wanting to save money, still ignored his concerns. The pilot then decided to whistleblow by going public about the faulty aircraft design. This led him to being demoted and grounded by his managers. He successfully sued the airline and won millions of dollars in compensation.

✳ **Senior managers must lead by example** by being seen to act with honesty, fairness and respect for others and encourage all staff to do likewise.

✳ **Clear disciplinary procedures** and penalties need to be in place for staff who are found to have acted unethically. Unethical behaviour should be discouraged by the use of deterrents, such as fines, demotion or dismissal. Ethical behaviour should be recognised and rewarded, possibly through giving bonus payments or promotion.

Case Study

FRESH MILK?

A British dairy was discovered to be secretly re-pasteurising out-of-date, unsold milk and reselling it as fresh milk to supermarkets. The dairy operated in a very competitive market and was under pressure from large supermarket chains to reduce its prices. As a result, the dairy was barely profitable and managers were being forced to cut costs to ensure that the dairy – and their jobs – survived.

Unsold milk cartons were seen being returned from supermarkets, opened and tipped into a pasteurising vat where the contents were mixed with fresh milk. Staff were also told to mix fresh milk with milk contaminated by contact with machinery and dirty wet floors. It was then packaged as 'farm fresh' milk before being transported to supermarkets. The managers of the dairy said they have since stopped reselling the old milk because 'we realised that it puts the customer in a bad position'.

OL Short Q3, 4
OL Long Q3

HL Short Q1, 2
HL Long Q1, 2, 3

Recall and Review

1. List the effects that reusing old milk could have on the business above and its different stakeholder groups.

2. Identify the reasons that you think may have tempted the dairy's managers to take this action.

3. Recommend the steps that could be taken to prevent a repeat of this incident in the dairy.

B. Business Social Responsibility

3. What is business social responsibility?

Business social responsibility *refers to the obligation of every business to respect the interests of all the stakeholder groups.* Also known as corporate social responsibility, it means looking at the wider effects of business decisions on others. Whereas business ethics is more concerned with how a specific business decision is made, social responsibility refers to the overall behaviour of the **whole business** towards stakeholders.

> **Business ethics looks at the behaviour and decisions of individuals.**
>
> **Business social responsibility looks at the overall behaviour of the business towards stakeholders.**

Social responsibility towards **employees**

❖ No toleration of discrimination, bullying or harassment in the workplace.
❖ Fair pay and safe working conditions.
❖ Secure and continuous employment wherever possible.
❖ Jobs designed to be interesting and challenging.

> **Example:** The Irish Civil Service allows employees with school-going children to take unpaid leave every year so that they can look after their children during school summer holidays. Those caring for someone with a disability can also avail of the leave scheme.

2 Social responsibility towards **investors**

∗ Provide open and honest financial information.

∗ Pay a fair dividend to shareholders.

∗ Keep honest and accurate financial accounts.

∗ No excessive salaries or perks paid to managers.

> **Example:** US telecommunications firm WorldCom was discovered to have deliberately falsified its accounts so that investors would invest money in the business.

3 Social responsibility towards **suppliers**

❖ Fair negotiations, free of pressure or duress.

❖ Bills paid in full and on time.

❖ Suppliers treated fairly and all contracts and agreements honoured.

❖ Avoiding suppliers that use child labour or other unethical practices.

> **Example:** Tesco was accused by Irish farmer suppliers of putting huge pressure on them to supply produce at uneconomical prices.

4 Social responsibility towards **customers**

✪ Production of safe and reliable goods and services.

✪ Fair prices.

✪ Truthful and accurate advertising.

✪ No advertising targeted at impressionable and vulnerable consumers, e.g. children.

✪ Good after-sales service in which complaints are dealt with speedily and helpfully.

✪ All consumer protection legislation obeyed.

> **Example:** NIB Bank was discovered to be deliberately overcharging customers for banking services without their customers' knowledge.

5 Social responsibility towards **government**

★ Ensure that the correct taxes are paid on the firm's profits (e.g. Corporation Tax, Capital Gains Tax).

★ Collect all the taxes required by the government and pass them onto the Revenue Commissioners on time (e.g. PAYE and PRSI from employees, DIRT and VAT from customers).

★ Local, national and EU laws obeyed, both in letter and spirit.

★ No use of bribery or corruption of politicians or public officials.

> **Example:** Anglo Irish Bank was found to have provided misleading information to the government in order to qualify for State aid.

Social responsibility towards **local communities**

6

* No pollution of the local environment.
* Protect the quality of life of local communities (e.g. be sensitive to noise, traffic and aesthetic concerns).
* Support the employment of local people.
* Support local suppliers wherever possible.
* Consult openly and honestly with the local community regarding business decisions that may affect them, such as a new building extension.
* Support local community activities such as sponsoring sports, arts and cultural activities.

Example: Saehan Media, a Korean transnational, was fined in the Irish courts for allowing its factory in Sligo to pollute the local Garavogue river.

Social responsibility towards **society** and **the planet**

7

* Produce safe, durable goods in an environmentally responsible way with minimal pollution or waste.
* Run the business in an environmentally sustainable manner.
* Do not trade with or operate in countries with corrupt governments.
* Do not produce socially undesirable products (e.g. landmines, cigarettes, etc.).
* Compete ethically and fairly against other firms in the market.
* Be open and transparent with the public about the activities of the business.
* Support good causes in society such as sponsoring sports, art and cultural events.

Example: Transnational oil company Exxon/Esso has been fined billions of dollars for the ecological and economic damage caused by oil spillages and pollution from the firm's activities. Shell Oil became embroiled in controversy over its plans to dump an old oil rig at sea.

OL Short Q5
OL Long Q1, 2, 5, 7

HL Short Q3
HL Long Q4

Case Study

A Tale of Two Civilisations . . .

Easter Island in the Pacific Ocean, famous for its hundreds of giant carved stone heads, was once home to a flourishing and sophisticated civilisation with a detailed knowledge of astronomy and construction. As the economy expanded, more and more of the island's trees were cut down to make space for building and agriculture and to provide fuel and construction material for houses, household goods and boats. The society and economy of Easter Island flourished, with the population peaking at about 10,000.

However, because the trees were cut down faster than new ones could grow, the island became almost completely deforested. People had to live in caves or flimsy reed huts and could only build fragile and unstable reed boats for fishing. Without the trees to bind it, the soil began to erode, reducing food supplies and nutrients.

Eventually, the entire economy and society collapsed and the

population rapidly declined to just 2,000 people, who were reduced to living in squalor and resorting to warfare and cannibalism to survive.

Similarly, the sand dunes in areas bordering the Sahara desert in North Africa were once fertile plains, home to extensive grain fields and olive orchards supplying the ancient Roman Empire. However by about 250AD the use of environmentally unsustainable agricultural practices led to massive and permanent soil erosion. Where once there were great cities with coliseums seating 65,000 spectators, there now remains only sandy desert and the ruins of cities.

By taking more from the natural environment than they put back, the societies on Easter Island and in North Africa were living beyond their means and pushing the environment beyond its ability to renew itself. Through this unsustainable use of natural resources, these people destroyed their own civilisations. No one individual was responsible, but together they created an environmentally unsustainable economy that led to their eventual destruction.

4. What is environmentally sustainable business?

> **Sustainable development means not damaging the environment for future generations.**

The events of Easter Island and the Roman Empire in the Sahara region are lessons from history to modern business of what happens when the products and activities in an economy are not environmentally (or ecologically) sustainable. Yet today, businesses and consumers are destroying the natural environment faster than the Earth can cope. This is happening through the use of raw materials that cannot be replaced (such as oil, gas, tropical timber) or by producing products that damage the environment (such as plastics, pesticides, cars, aircraft, batteries, toxic chemicals or carbon dioxide emissions).

Sustainable development *is economic development that can continue indefinitely without causing permanent harm to the environment or reducing the quality of life for future generations.* In other words, sustainable development means being able to grow enough food and source our energy and raw material needs without doing irreversible damage to the environment for present and future generations.

5. What are the important environmental issues facing businesses?

● Climate change

The biggest environmental challenge facing the planet is a changing climate, caused by increasing levels of 'greenhouse gases', such as carbon dioxide from economic activities like the burning of fossil fuels (e.g. oil and gas) to power our cars, aircraft and power stations. Rising temperatures are predicted to lead to more severe weather events (e.g. storms, floods), melting polar ice caps and a resulting rise in sea levels which will affect coastal cities around the world. In order to reduce emissions of greenhouse gases, businesses and households need to switch over to more energy-efficient goods and renewable sources of energy, such as wind, wave, solar and bio-fuels.

Energy

As supplies of non-renewable fossil fuels such as oil and gas will be exhausted within decades, there is a real possibility of energy shortages unless businesses and households become much more energy efficient and start using renewable sources of energy.

Waste

Waste dumped in landfills or at sea will eventually end up contaminating soil and underground water supplies and this dumping cannot continue indefinitely. Alternatives such as the burning of waste produces highly toxic waste ash and can also release harmful chemicals into the air. Plastics, in particular, can have a very long-lasting and toxic effect on the environment. Businesses and consumers must therefore find ways to **reduce, reuse** and **recycle** as much of their waste as possible. This includes eliminating throwaway goods marketed for convenience and all unnecessary and excessive packaging.

Pollution

Waste emissions of chemicals from factories and vehicles can be polluting to the environment and damage human and animal health. The leaking or dumping of waste materials such as chemicals, farm slurry and other materials from industry, intensive agriculture and households into rivers, lakes and seas can seriously pollute the environment.

> **Examples:** Local drinking water was contaminated and thousands of fish killed when the Shournagh River in Co. Cork was seriously polluted by over 160,000 tonnes of slurry from a farm business. In the USA, an Eastman Kodak factory was found to be dumping so many chemicals into the river beside it that it was actually possible to develop photographs in the water.

Destruction of natural resources

The pollution and destruction of natural habitats, including forests, bogs, rivers and coastlines, damages the habitats of thousands of plant and animal species, driving many to extinction. Recreational and tourist resources can also be lost in this way.

> **Example:** Orangutans are being forced into extinction as their forest homes are cleared to make way for plantations to grow palm oil, a common ingredient in food products and cosmetics. Meanwhile, one unscrupulous Japanese company was even discovered to be cutting down irreplaceable, thousand-year-old tropical rainforests to make toilet paper.

OL Short Q6, 7

OL Long Q6

HL Short Q4, 5

HL Long Q5, 6, 10

AN OPPORTUNITY BLOWING IN THE WIND

Case Study

Eddie O'Connor was working for Bord na Móna, a **commercial state company** when he became very concerned about the likely effects of **climate change** for Ireland and the planet.

He saw wind energy as a way to tackle the problem because it allows the generation of unlimited amounts of electricity without any negative climate-change-causing pollution. He tried to persuade the **board of directors** of Bord na Móna to invest in wind energy as an environmentally friendly way to make money, but at the time they were not interested. So he quit the company and decided to do it himself.

Eddie raise **equity finance** of €500,000 from family, friends and associates and began looking for suitable sites to locate wind turbines. He then needed another €13 million to buy his first set of wind turbines. He did this by negotiating a **bank loan** for €7 million and raising another €10 million by selling a 51% stake in his company to investors. Airtricity **Limited** was now up and running.

Over the next few years, Eddie established a network of wind farms across Ireland. These include Airtricity's most advanced wind farm located 12 kilometres off the coast of Arklow, County Wicklow, which uses the largest wind turbines in the world. This offshore wind farm is spread out over three kilometres, rises 120 metres out of the ocean, with rotors that slice the air at 300 kph. To make this happen, Eddie persuaded the turbine manufacturers, GE, to provide the turbines for free. In exchange, GE benefit from an excellent **public relations** (PR) showcase for the world's most advanced turbines. According to a senior GE manager, 'Airtricity came up with one of the best offshore sites I've seen . . . and we see them as a growing customer.'

Airtricity is now expanding throughout Europe and North America and generating sales of hundreds of millions of euro. According to Eddie: 'The preservation of a sustainable global environment capable of supporting 8 billion people is high on the agenda of all countries. It follows that it should also be high on the agenda of each business and its employees.'

As the issues of climate change and dwindling oil reserves become more acute, they are also opening more doors than ever for entrepreneurs. Eddie O'Connor is just one of many **entrepreneurs** demonstrating how serious money can be made by being very environmentally responsible.

HL ## 6. What are the characteristics of an environmentally responsible business?

Business has a particularly important responsibility in ensuring environmental sustainability because a business, such as Airtricity, can have a much greater impact and influence on the world than a single individual. Steps that a business can take to become more environmentally responsible are as follows:

Produce durable goods

✳ Products should be designed to be **durable** and capable of lasting for the maximum possible lifespan. 'Built-in-obsolescence', or deliberately designing goods to wear out after a short period of time, is irresponsible and unsustainable.

Produce in an ecologically sustainable manner

❖ **Locate** production away from ecologically sensitive areas – for instance, it would be highly undesirable to build an oil refinery beside a nature reserve.

❖ Become **energy efficient** and aim to use renewable resources such as wind and solar power instead of non-renewable sources such as fossil fuels.

❖ Aim to eliminate **pollution** and **waste** from all parts of the production process. Any waste produced (e.g. paper, glass, metals, food) should be reused, recycled or composted where possible.

❖ Seek the advice of the **Environmental Protection Agency (EPA)** to ensure compliance with environmental laws or to seek advice on new developments. The law requires many new business developments to produce an Environmental Impact Assessment (EIA). An **Environmental Impact Assessment** *is a report that looks at the effect that the business can be expected to have on the pollution of land, air and water, wildlife and their habitats, trees and other plant life, noise levels and the health of local people.*

❖ Goods should be sold without unnecessary and wasteful packaging.

Example: The Cully & Sully food company package some of their meals in reusable ceramic bowls instead of non renewable, disposable packaging.

Plan for disposal after use

⚙ Goods produced should be easy to **reuse, repair or recycle** after use. Parts should be interchangeable with those in similar products.

Example: BMW design their cars so that they can be easily disassembled for recycling. The company is aiming for 100% parts reusability.

⚙ If a firm's products cannot be recycled then they should be designed for **safe disposal** back into the natural environment. This means that, wherever possible, only natural raw materials or ingredients should be used.

Conduct regular environmental audits

✳ Environmentally responsible firms conduct regular environmental audits to guide management decision-making. An **environmental audit** *is a study of the impact of the business on the environment.* It focuses on four basic areas: what is produced, how it is produced, how it is marketed and how it will be disposed of.

Example: IKEA conducts regular environmental audits of its business.

HL Short Q6

HL Long Q7

Case Study

IKEA's sustainable supply chain

IKEA is a Swedish transnational company that **manufactures** and **retails** furniture and other products for the home all over the world. It has sales of billions of euro and conducts regular **environmental audits** to ensure that the business is operating in an environmentally responsible manner.

The company works closely with **suppliers** around the world and insists that all its suppliers comply with local laws, follow proper health and safety and environmental procedures and do not employ child labour. The company sources **environmentally sustainable** raw materials wherever possible. About half of IKEA's products are made of wood that is both a **renewable** and **recyclable** resource. The firm also produces tables made from recycled plastic and rugs made from scrap cloth. The company encourages staff to cycle to work, only uses electric or hybrid vehicles as company cars and aims to recycle over 90% of all its waste.

HL

7. What are the costs and benefits to a business of meeting its social and environmental responsibilities?

Case Study

Wasting Less Saves Money for SPAR

When Louis Byrne took over a SPAR **franchise** shop in Tralee, County Kerry, the first thing he did was to put a proper waste management system in place. Instead of sending all his waste to landfill, he began sorting it into paper, cardboard and plastics and sending them for recycling. He then contacted **suppliers** and requested that all future deliveries be made in crates that could be reused or recycled. His next step was to begin composting all the food waste from the shop's deli counter. His efforts have paid off as he has cut his shop's operating **costs** by thousands of euro a year and increased his **profits** at the same time.

Costs to business

- ❖ Paying fair **wages** to staff and providing good working conditions costs extra.
- ❖ Providing **investors** with full and honest financial information may reduce the amount of finance that they can be persuaded to provide.
- ❖ Providing customers with honest information without any **exaggerated advertising claims** may mean sales will not be as high as they could be in the short term.
- ❖ **Investing in equipment** and production processes that minimise waste and pollution costs money.
- ❖ Not engaging in unfair **anti-competitive practices** such as price-fixing reduces the amount of profit that can be made.
- ❖ **Obeying the law** and paying the correct amount of taxes can reduce business profitability.

Benefits to business

- ★ Proper waste management can **save money in the long term** by reducing the amount of raw materials that are wasted.

Example: Louis Byrne's SPAR store saves thousands of euro by recycling its packaging.

- ★ Businesses **avoid being fined** for breaking laws relating to pollution, evading tax or engaging in anti-competitive practices. This also helps to protect the reputation of the business.
- ★ Businesses with positive social and environmental reputations **attract more loyal customers** who are not just influenced by price or fashion.

Example: Airtricity has attracted loyal customers because it offers clean, renewable electricity.

- ★ Businesses with strong ethical and responsible reputations and brand images usually find it much easier **to recruit and motivate skilled staff**.
- ★ **Access to business finance** can be easier as investors become more concerned about what their money is used for and want to avoid funding harmful or unethical business activities. There are now many investment funds that specialise in only providing finance for ethical and socially responsible businesses.
- ★ A genuine commitment to ethics and social responsibility can boost a firm's reputation and assist **marketing promotion**.

HL Short Q7
HL ABQ
HL Long Q8, 9

Key Concepts & Business Terms

After studying this chapter the student should be able to explain the following key concepts and business terms:

1. Business ethics
2. Reasons for unethical behaviour
3. Encouraging ethical behaviour
4. Code of ethics
5. Whistleblowers
6. Business social responsibility
7. Sustainable development
8. Climate change
9. Characteristics of an environmentally responsible business **HL**
10. Environmental Impact Assessment **HL**
11. Environmental audit **HL**
12. Benefits of socially responsible business **HL**
13. Costs of socially responsible business **HL**

 useful websites

www.shell.com
www.airtricity.com
www.epa.ie
www.ikea.com

Leaving Certificate Practice Questions

Ordinary Level

Ordinary Level – Section 1 – Short Questions (10 marks each)

1. Explain the term 'business ethics'. [LCQ]
2. Illustrate **two** examples of unethical behaviour in business.
3. List **two** causes of unethical behaviour in business.
4. Outline what is meant by a code of ethics.
5. Identify **three** examples of socially irresponsible behaviour by a business.
6. Identify **two** environmental issues facing business.
7. Tee Limited has just bought a site to build a hotel and golf course in Ballytown. Identify **two** environmental issues that the local community may consider important if the hotel and golf course are built. [LCQ]

Ordinary Level – Section 2 – Long Questions

1. Define 'business social responsibility'. (15 marks)
2. Using examples, describe how a business can behave ethically towards (a) employees and (b) its customers. (20 marks) [LCQ]

3. Describe an ethical problem that a manager could encounter. (15 marks)
4. Describe a simple ethical test that can be applied to business decision-making. (20 marks)
5. Outline **two** environmental responsibilities of business. [LCQ]
6. Identify and explain **five** environmental issues facing business today. (25 marks)
7. Explain the ways in which a socially responsible firm could deal with:
    (a) employees, (b) investors, (c) suppliers and (d) customers. (20 marks)

Higher Level

Higher Level – Section 1 – Short Questions (10 marks each)

1. Illustrate your understanding of unethical behaviour by a business person.
2. Define the term 'code of ethics' for a business. [LCQ]
3. List **three** characteristics of a socially responsible business.
4. List **four** environmental issues facing business.
5. Define 'sustainable development'.
6. List **three** issues that a business needs to address if it is to be environmentally responsible.
7. Outline **two** benefits and **two** costs of behaving in a socially and environmentally responsible manner.

Higher Level – Section 2 – Applied Business Question 1

Spiroz Chemicals

The Spiroz Chemical Corporation has purchased a site in Drumcooley, a scenic rural area, where it intends to build a chemical plant. The company, which has a poor environmental record internationally, does not anticipate any difficulties in obtaining planning permission for the plant as it expects to be a substantial local employer and some local people have welcomed the news.

However, the proposal has met with opposition from others. The Spiroz chemical factory will produce emissions into the atmosphere and local farmers are concerned about how these emissions will affect the purity and reputation of their meat, dairy and vegetable produce. They are concerned about the negative reputation that similar chemical plants have acquired in other parts of the country. Local residents and environmentalists are concerned about the health effects on local people of the emissions from the factory. Some local businesses are also concerned about the impact of the proposed location on tourism and related businesses.

However, not all the locals are against the new industry as some businesses see it as bringing valuable employment and income to the local community. Tensions are increasing as the level of local opposition has already seriously delayed the commencement of construction work on the site.

1. Discuss the social responsibilities of Spiroz to its stakeholders. (30 marks)
2. Describe the steps that Spiroz Chemicals should take to become an environmentally responsible company. (30 marks)
3. Evaluate the possible effects on Spiroz's costs and profitability of meeting its environmental responsibilities. (20 marks)

Higher Level – Section 2 – Long Questions

1. Explain, using examples, what is meant by the term 'business ethics'. (20 marks)
2. Discuss the main causes of unethical behaviour in business. (25 marks)
3. Explain how a business could encourage ethical behaviour among staff. (20 marks)
4. Discuss the social responsibilities that a business has towards its various stakeholders. (20 marks) [LCQ]
5. Illustrate how environmental issues can have an impact on businesses. (15 marks) [LCQ]
6. Explain what is meant by the term 'sustainable development'. Use an example to support your answer. (20 marks)
7. Illustrate the characteristics of an environmentally responsible business. (20 marks) {LCQ}
8. Evaluate the effect on a firm's revenue and costs of meeting its social responsibilities. (25 marks) [LCQ]
9. Evaluate the potential benefits for a firm in attempting to meet its social and environmental responsibilities. (20 marks)
10. 'Demand for greater social and environmental responsibility from business will be a major challenge to business in the 21st century.' Discuss the reasons for this growing pressure on business. (30 marks)

Chapter 22
Government & Business

Key Study Questions

SEAHORSE
AQUARIUMS
AQUATIC SPECIALISTS

Case Study

Seahorse Aquariums

Seahorses are an unusual species of small fish where the males become pregnant, not females, giving birth to as many as 800 offspring a month. There is a very high demand for seahorses for use in traditional Chinese medicine and for display in aquariums, and the **global market** for these creatures is estimated to be worth hundreds of millions of euro. Unfortunately, demand is so high that stocks of wild seahorses are seriously depleted and catching them in the wild has been banned.

However, a young Irish marine biologist, Kealan Doyle saw an opportunity to use his expertise to set up a business breeding seahorses in captivity. He conducted **market research** and discovered that the main competitor in the market was based in Hawaii and sold seahorses over the Internet. With a friend as a business partner, Kealan decided to set up his own seahorse farming business.

As entrepreneurs, they had only a small **budget** to start the business so they based their business in a remote part of Connemara where rents were very low. While the local **infrastructure** was poor, they qualified for an enterprise development **grant** from **a state agency,** as the business was setting up in an Irish-speaking area.

The business initially concentrated mainly on selling to the lucrative aquarium market in Europe. A business website was developed to take orders and they secured a deal with Federal Express whereby seahorses bought online before noon could be delivered to the customer by nine o'clock the next morning. Their very first sale netted them a whopping €18,000 and gave the business a much needed boost. However, after paying **taxes**, all initial profits earned had to be **ploughed back** into the business in further **research and development.**

The life of an **entrepreneur** was tough, and Kealan's business partner decided that working '15 hour days, seven days a week' trying to make the business work was too much for him and he left to take up a regular job. Kealan was left running the business on his own but financial and technical problems meant that the business was losing more and more money.

Kealan came up with a new **strategic plan** for the business. He decided to move from Connemara and open premises in Dublin selling seahorses, exotic fish and aquariums mainly to domestic consumers. The dramatic change of direction worked, the business finally began making a **profit** and extra staff had to be hired to cope with consumer demand.

1. Why do governments intervene in business and economic affairs?

> The public expects the State to intervene to ensure that the economy is run fairly and in the best interests of citizens.

Governments intervene in business and economic affairs for various reasons:

* **To encourage enterprises** like Seahorse Aquariums to grow, create jobs and generate tax revenue.

* **To regulate the conduct of business and economic** affairs to ensure **fairness** and protection from exploitation or irresponsible behaviour.

* **To provide essential services** that may not be provided by businesses, such as health care, education, policing and support for enterprise development.

* **To provide essential physical infrastructure** such as public lighting, roads, sewerage systems and water supplies. **Infrastructure** *refers to the basic network of supports needed for economic activity to develop, such as road, rail, sea and air links, waste disposal, water systems and educational facilities.*

> **Example:** A good transport and telecommunications infrastructure is essential to Seahorses Aquariums to allow customers to visit their premises or their online store.

- ❖ **To achieve fairer distribution of wealth** by collecting money in taxes and spending money on social welfare and other services.
- ❖ **To achieve more balanced regional development** so that people in all parts of the country benefit from jobs and economic activity.
- ❖ **To protect strategic resources** such as electricity, water and public transport that are critically important to the economy.
- ❖ **To develop a natural resource** that may be too risky or long term for the private sector.

coillte

> **Example:** The government set up Coillte to develop Ireland's long-term potential to become a major producer of timber and forestry products.

OL Short Q1, 2

OL Long Q1

HL Short Q1, 2

2. How does government taxation affect business?

Like all businesses, Seahorse Aquariums has to pay taxes on any profits earned. **Taxes** *are compulsory payments of money to the State.* Taxes are raised by the government to pay for the provision of State services such as schools, hospitals, Gardaí, roads, etc. Taxes are also needed to fund repayments on government borrowings. Different taxes can affect a business in different ways.

> **Main sources of tax revenue:**
> - **Income tax**
> - **VAT**
> - **Excise duties**
> - **Corporation tax**

Impact of taxes on business

- ⭕ **Sales:** High **PAYE income taxes** reduce the amount of disposable income available to consumers, thus reducing demand. By increasing the price of goods, **VAT** can also discourage consumers from purchasing goods.

- ⭕ **Costs:** High PAYE taxes can encourage workers to look for higher wages, thereby increasing business **labour costs.** High **employers' PRSI** increases the costs of employing staff and is effectively a tax on employment. For firms with a large number of employees, this extra business cost can significantly reduce profitability and discourage firms from recruiting extra staff. High **corporation taxes** reduces the amount of profit for entrepreneurs and also reduces the amount of money that can be reinvested in the business. High corporation taxes in Ireland could force businesses to locate in lower tax countries. Costs are also incurred as businesses have to carry the financial and **administrative burden** of collecting VAT, PAYE and other taxes for the Revenue Commissioners.

> **For more information on taxation and grants, see Chapter 11: Managing Business & Household Insurance and Tax.**

- ⭕ **Business confidence:** High taxes can erode business confidence and discourage foreign companies from setting up in Ireland. High personal taxes, especially for low wage earners, can act as a deterrent to work, as employees may be financially better off living on social welfare. High levels of employers' PRSI can discourage firms like Seahorse Aquariums from employing more staff. High **corporation tax** reduces the amount of profits that the owners of a business can earn, thereby discouraging business activity, enterprise and risk taking.

OL Short Q4

OL Long Q3

HL Long Q4

3. How does government expenditure affect business?

Every year the government spends billions of euro on providing goods and services such as schools, hospitals and other public services. Providing these services means that the government is also a huge consumer of goods and services. For instance, the Gardaí need uniforms and equipment, schools need buildings and furniture, and civil servants need offices, computers and stationery. The government also spends hundreds of millions of euro every year providing grants to new and existing businesses. Government spending is divided into current expenditure and capital expenditure.

★ **Current expenditure** is *spending on day-to-day running costs*, such as paying wages of public sector employees, social welfare payments, uniforms, stationery, lighting and heating.

★ **Capital expenditure** *is spending on infrastructure*. Approximately every five years the government prepares a **national development plan** setting out how much will be invested in developing the country's infrastructure over the following five years.

Glossary of government budget terms

- **Fiscal policy** refers to the approach followed by the government when raising and spending money.

- **'The budget'** refers to the government's financial plans for the next year. It sets out how much it plans to spend, what it will spend it on and where the money is going to come from.

- A **balanced budget** occurs when government expenditure equals income. It is also known as a **neutral budget.**

- A **budget surplus** means the government's income is greater than its expenditure, i.e. it is collecting more in taxes than it is spending.

- A **budget deficit** means government expenditure exceeds revenue, i.e. it is spending more than it is receiving. In the short term, budget deficits must be funded from government reserves or by borrowing money. Large budget deficits can only be reduced by increasing taxes and/or reducing the levels of government expenditure.

- The **bond market** *refers to the place where governments (and very large companies) borrow money by issuing bonds*. **Bonds** *are a type of IOU issued by governments promising to repay the loan at an agreed date and also to pay a fixed rate of interest*. The main buyers of bonds are banks, insurance companies, pension and investment funds.

Impact of government spending on business

Main areas of government spending:

- **Servicing national debt**
- **Social welfare**
- **Health**
- **Education**
- **Agriculture**
- **Environment**
- **Security**
- **EU contributions**

❋ **Sales:** Generally, the more money the government spends, then the more money there will be circulating in the economy. This means more money is available to consumers, which will boost the overall level of economic activity and business sales.

❋ **Costs:** Government expenditure on infrastructure and services for businesses can reduce business costs and assist their international competitiveness. However, government spending that is considered wasteful or not necessary, must ultimately be financed by taxation, including taxes on businesses.

* **Business confidence:** If government spending is perceived to be well managed and without the need for increased taxes, business confidence in the future is enhanced. However, if government spending is seen as excessive or wasteful, then this will undermine business confidence. If the government is **borrowing** large sums to finance its spending, then this government debt will ultimately have to be repaid. Reducing large government debts can usually only be done by reducing government spending and/or increasing taxes. This can undermine business confidence.

OL Short Q3
OL Long Q2
HL Short Q3, 4
HL Long Q5

4. How do government services affect business?

Besides planning, raising taxes and spending money, the government also provides many State services that directly or indirectly assist businesses.

SERVICES	STATE ORGANISATION
Policy and planning	• Government departments
Financial management	• **Revenue Commissioners** (collects taxes for the government) • National Treasury Management Agency (NTMA) (borrows money on behalf of the government; manages the national debt) • National Asset Management Agency (NAMA)
Regulating	• **Equality Authority** • Environmental Protection Agency • Health & Safety Authority
Business development	• **Enterprise Ireland** • **IDA Ireland** • **County enterprise boards** • Údarás na Gaeltachta (in Gaeltacht areas)
Transport	• Bus Éireann • Iarnród Éireann
Marketing	• Fáilte Ireland • Bord Bia
Research	• Central Statistics Office • Economic & Social Research Institute (ESRI)
Human resources	• FÁS • **Labour Relations Commission** • **Labour Court** • **Equality Authority**
Energy	• ESB • Bord Gáis
Industry sector development	• Coillte (forestry) • Bord Iascaigh Mhara (fishing) • Teagasc (horticulture)
Infrastructure development	• Local city and county councils (e.g. roads, water supplies, waste disposal, sewerage) • National Roads Authority (NRA)
Community development	• **Area partnership companies** • **Pobal** • **LEADER**

Government support for business

Government policy is designed to encourage enterprise, wealth and job creation, whether by Irish entrepreneurs or through foreign investment in Ireland. A number of State agencies exist to promote business development including Enterprise Ireland, IDA Ireland and county enterprise boards. One of their most important roles is to distribute **grants** and **venture capital investmen**t to promote enterprise and business development. The amount of finance available depends on the size of the business, purpose of the grant, where the business will locate and whether the business is large or small, indigenous or a foreign transnational. It will also depend on the general state of the economy and what the government can afford.

Enterprise Ireland assists existing businesses to grow

Impact of government services on business

❖ **Sales:** Advice and grants are available to businesses to conduct market research and to market their products internationally. This can help to boost sales.

❖ **Costs:** Advice and grants help to reduce the start-up costs for entrepreneurs. Although they will only cover part of the costs, grants help to ensure survival during the start-up phase, when failure rates are highest. Grants to existing firms to expand or to encourage transnationals to locate in Ireland help to cover business costs and increase business profitability.

❖ **Business confidence:** As advice and grants reduce the risks involved, entrepreneurs and businesses will be more confident about taking commercial risks.

OL Short Q8, 9
OL Long Q4, 5

HL Short Q9

LOCALLY	NATIONALLY	INTERNATIONALLY
County & City Enterprise Boards	**Enterprise Ireland**	**IDA Ireland**
Assist small local businesses with **less than 10 employees**. Provide advice and small grants. Example: County enterprise boards gave financial support to The Bliss Bakery to set up.	Assist Irish-owned enterprises that employ, or are capable of employing, **more than 10 people** and are capable of **exporting** their goods/services. Enterprise Ireland provides assistance with:	Attracts foreign **transnational companies** to locate in Ireland as a base for **exporting**. Promotes Ireland as a low-tax, English-speaking and business-friendly location for foreign firms looking for an EU base.
Údarás na Gaeltachta	– Market research and new product development	
Supports enterprise in Gaeltacht areas. Example: It gave a start-up grant to Seahorse Aquariums.	– International marketing – Finance through grants and venture capital investment. Example: Enterprise Ireland supported Cully & Sully and Vitz Drinks when they were setting up and expanding.	Example: IDA Ireland have given grants to transnational companies such as Microsoft, Intel and Google to persuade them to locate their European headquarters in Ireland.

Fig. 1 The main State agencies that encourage enterprise and economic development.

5. How do government laws and regulations affect business?

Seahorse Aquariums has to comply with many different laws and regulations covering such areas such as:

THE EQUALITY AUTHORITY
AN tÚDARÁS COMHIONANNAIS

❖ **Employment and industrial relations**

> **Example:** The Employment Equality Act 1998 prevents employers from discriminating against employees on the basis of age, gender, marital status, etc. The Unfair Dismissals Acts 1977 to 2007 state that businesses cannot dismiss employees without a just reason.

❖ **Consumer protection**

> **Example:** The Consumer Protection Act 2007 protects consumers from unfair or misleading commercial practices, such as false advertising.

❖ **Data protection**

> **Example:** The Data Protection Acts 1988 & 2003 require businesses to abide by certain conditions relating to any data or records they keep about private individuals (e.g. give information when requested, keep data safe, etc.)

❖ **Company law**

> **Example:** The Companies Act 1990 ensures that companies are correctly set up and also monitored regularly by the Companies Registration Office.

The government also regulates the rules for doing business in many different markets:

Commission for
Communications Regulation

- ◆ **Commission for Energy Regulation** regulates competition in the energy supply market.
- ◆ **Commission for Communications Regulation (ComReg)** regulates competition in the telecommunications market (such as fixed line, mobile and broadband services).
- ◆ **Central Bank and Financial Services Authority** is responsible for regulating the banks and the financial services industries.

OL Long Q6
HL Short Q5
HL Long Q2

6. What is the public sector?

Goods and services can be provided by public sector or private sector organisations.

★ The **public sector** *is made up of all organisations and activities that are owned or financed by the State.* The public sector employs thousands of people in State-funded hospitals, schools, universities, semi-state companies (e.g. Enterprise Ireland, FÁS and CIÉ), **the civil service** (government departments), local authorities, Gardaí and the Defence Forces. The public sector is the controlled part of the economy and its role is to protect the public interest and provide public services for everyone, usually without profit.

★ The **private sector** *describes all economic activities not owned or financed by the State.* Private enterprise provides most goods including food, clothing, cars, music and computer goods and services.

> Example: Seahorse Aquariums is an enterprise operating in the private sector.

★ **Public-private partnerships (PPPs)** *are agreements where a private sector business may build and operate a service, such as a road or toll bridge, on behalf of the government for a profit.* Typically, such agreements last a fixed number of years after which the full ownership of the service, building, etc. will pass back to the State (the public sector).

Public sector is a major employer

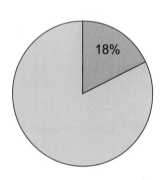

Fig. 2 In Ireland, approximately 18% of the workforce is employed in the public sector.

The public sector provides direct employment to hundreds of thousands of people. The government also indirectly supports thousands more jobs in firms that sell goods and services to the public sector (e.g. computers, stationery, uniforms, buildings). Being such a large employer, the government has the following effects on business:

＊ **Job creation:** By creating jobs in the public sector, the government reduces unemployment in the economy.

＊ **Taxation:** The more people it employs, the larger the government's wage bill, which must be paid out of taxation that is paid mainly by the much larger private sector and/or from reduced spending in other areas.

＊ **Wages:** The State pays the wages of a large percentage of the population. This money gets spent on things like housing, food and consumer goods, which boosts sales for businesses and activities throughout the economy.

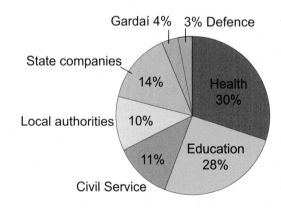

Fig. 3 Public sector employment.

OL Short Q5
OL Long Q7

HL Short Q6, 7
HL Long Q1, 3

7. What is privatisation and nationalisation?

> **Nationalisation transfers ownership of a firm from the private sector to the public sector.**
>
> **Privatisation transfers the ownership of State firms from the public to the private sector.**

Semi-State companies (also known State companies or State-sponsored bodies) *are organisations established by the government for various purposes.* There are two types:

1. **Commercial State companies** provide their services for a price. This may enable them to make a profit or at least contribute towards their costs.

> Examples: RTÉ, ESB, Coillte.

2. **Non-commercial semi-state companies** provide services that cannot be sold for a price and that are regarded as essential or desirable for the well-being of the country.

> Examples: Enterprise Ireland, IDA Ireland, the Labour Relations Commission.

Privatisation *is the selling of State companies to buyers in the private sector.* This is done either to raise money or to allow the State to concentrate on being regulators rather than providers of services. In Ireland dozens of commercial State companies have been privatised, including telecommunications, shipping and food companies. Eircom was originally set up as a State telecommunications company but was sold off by the government to raise finance. In other countries, previously free services such as water supplies have been sold to private companies which now charge for the water.

Nationalisation *refers to the transfer of ownership of firms from the private sector to the public sector.*

> Example: The government fully and partially nationalised a number of banks to prevent them collapsing and damaging other banks and the wider economy.

Arguments in favour of privatisation

- Privatised firms are free from **possible political interference.**

> Example: When Eircom was State-owned, central government demanded that the company pay large annual dividends to the State even though the company argued that it needed these funds to reinvest in the business.

- Privatisation can **reduce the waste and inefficiency** that can be common in some State-owned firms as managers are motivated to concentrate on maximising profits for shareholders.
- **Privatised firms find it easier to raise money for expansion.**

> Example: Greencore was once a State-owned company. Since privatisation, Greencore has sold millions of shares on the Dublin Stock Exchange to raise additional finance for expansion.

- **Privatisation raises money** for government.
- **Ideological: leave business to business.** Some argue that the government should concentrate on making laws and regulating businesses, rather than running them.

Arguments against privatisation

- ★ **Nationalisation protects important services** that privatised companies may be unwilling to provide as they are unprofitable (e.g. some rural bus services, post offices or loans to small businesses).

> Example: The need to ensure that banks would continue providing loans to businesses forced the Irish government to partially nationalise AIB and Bank of Ireland.

- ★ **Nationalisation of strategically important industries** like telecommunications, electricity production or water supplies can prevent them being purchased by foreign investors with no loyalty to the country.
- ★ **Nationalisation can protect employment** as privatised firms may cut jobs and costs purely to boost profitability.

OL Short Q6, 7, 10
OL Long Q8, 9, 10

HL Short Q8, 10
HL ABQ
HL Long Q6, 7

Key Concepts & Business Terms

After studying this chapter the student should be able to explain the following key concepts and business terms:

1. Reasons for government intervention in the economy
2. Infrastructure
3. Taxes
4. Current expenditure
5. Capital expenditure
6. Fiscal policy
7. The budget
8. Balanced budget
9. Budget surplus
10. Budget deficit
11. Bond market
12. Bonds
13. Government expenditure
14. Government services to business
15. Government regulations
16. The public sector
17. The private sector
18. Public-private partnerships
19. State-sponsored bodies
20. Commercial State bodies
21. Non-commercial semi-state bodies
22. Nationalisation
23. Privatisation

useful websites

www.seahorseaquariums.com
www.comreg.ie (Commission for Communications Regulation)
www.cer.ie (Commission for Energy Regulation)

Leaving Certificate Practice Questions

Ordinary Level

Ordinary Level – Section 1 – Short Questions (10 marks each)

1. List **three** examples of infrastructure in a country.
2. List **two** ways in which government affects business. [LCQ]
3. List **two** areas where government spends taxpayers' money.
4. Identify **one** tax and briefly outline how a rise in that tax could affect business.
5. Explain what is meant by the public sector of the economy.
6. What are State-sponsored (semi-state) bodies?
7. Explain the benefits of State-owned enterprises. [LCQ]
8. Identify **three** semi-state organisations that help Irish businesses. [LCQ]
9. Explain the role of IDA Ireland.
10. Define the term 'privatisation'. [LCQ]

Ordinary Level – Section 2 – Long Questions

1. Explain **three** reasons why the government intervenes in the economy. (15 marks)
2. Describe **two** ways in which government expenditure (fiscal) policies can impact on business. (20 marks)
3. Describe **three** effects of taxation on business. (15 marks)
4. List and explain the role of **two** State organisations providing business support at (a) national level and (b) international level. (20 marks)
5. Explain the role of the following State agencies (a) IDA Ireland, (b) Enterprise Ireland. (20 marks)
6. Outline **four** areas where government regulations impact on business. (20 marks)
7. Outline the importance of the government as an employer. (20 marks)
8. Outline **two** benefits of State ownership of business enterprise. Give an example. (15 marks) [LCQ]
9. Outline **two** disadvantages of State-owned enterprises. (15 marks) [LCQ]
10. Outline **three** benefits of privatisation of a State enterprise. Give an example of one company that has been privatised. (20 marks) [LCQ]

Higher Level

Higher Level – Section 1 – Short Questions (10 marks each)

1. List **four** ways in which government affects the climate for business.
2. Explain what is meant by the term 'infrastructure'.
3. Identify **three** ways in which the level of government spending can affect business.
4. Distinguish between a budget surplus and a budget deficit.
5. List **three** pieces of legislation that affect business.
6. Distinguish between a public sector and a private sector employee.
7. Explain what is meant by a public-private partnership.
8. Identify **three** commercial semi-state bodies.
9. Identify **four** State agencies that can assist a business in expanding. In the case of **one**, briefly outline the type of support available.
10. Illustrate the impact of privatisation on the development of the Irish economy.

Higher Level – Section 2 – Applied Business Question

ALPHA SYSTEMS

Alpha Systems produces electronic gates and security equipment. Founded by entrepreneur Brian Loughrey with help from his local county enterprise board, the firm has grown steadily and now controls nearly 50% of the market in Ireland for such products. It is a very profitable firm and pays millions in taxes every year. It recently secured a contract to supply security equipment to a large semi-state company.

Alpha is currently considering taking over another Irish firm with a 20% share of the domestic market. If it goes ahead, this expansion will give Alpha control of over 70% of the Irish market.

As the Irish market is quite small, in recent years the firm has focused most of its attention on exporting as a means of expanding the business. With the assistance of Enterprise Ireland, this strategy has been very successful and export sales to European countries are now a significant and growing part of the business. If this trend continues, the firm sees its future in exporting most of its output.

The company expects that the future expansion of the business will be financed using a combination of retained earnings and venture capital from Enterprise Ireland. This funding will allow Alpha to proceed with building a new state-of-the-art factory that will be among the most modern and efficient in Europe.

A site for the new factory has been purchased close to major roads with easy access to a port to accommodate the steady stream of trucks coming to and from the factory. However, before construction can proceed, an environmental impact statement will have to be completed before planning permission can be secured.

1. Analyse the impact that changes in government tax **and** expenditure can have on the success of Alpha Systems. Use examples to support your answer. (30 marks)

2. Discuss the steps the government takes to make it more attractive for Irish entrepreneurs like Brian Loughrey to set up new businesses in Ireland. (30 marks)

3. Contrast the role of Enterprise Ireland and IDA Ireland in encouraging business development. (20 marks)

Higher Level – Section 2 – Long Questions

1. Analyse the way in which the government creates a suitable climate for business enterprises in the country. Use examples in your analysis. (25 marks) [LCQ]

2. Discuss, using examples, the importance of the government's role as regulator of business activity. (20 marks)

3. The government is the largest single employer in the State. Analyse the impact this has for business. (15 marks)

4. Discuss how the Irish government could use the tax system to create a positive climate for business in Ireland. Use examples to illustrate your answer. (20 marks) [LCQ]

5. Outline the effect that the government's spending policies can have on business. (20 marks)

6. Identify **four** government agencies, laws or actions that support and encourage business enterprise. (20 marks)

7. Evaluate, using examples, the arguments in favour or against the privatisation of commercial State enterprises. (20 marks) [LCQ]

Chapter 23
Ireland & the Global Economy

Key Study Questions

Case Study

When his farming businesses went into decline, Raymond Coyle was forced to sell up. He used the money from the sale of his farm to clear his debts and had just enough money to set up a modest new enterprise, Largo Foods, making potato crisps. At the time the market was dominated by big players like Tayto, and Largo captured just a small share.

Raymond's big break came when he won the contract to make **own-brand** crisps for SuperQuinn and expanded to employ nine people. He then bought the Perri brand name from a company that had closed down. He used this name to launch a range of 'Supercrisp' in a bigger foil pack, which set its packaging distinctly apart from that of Tayto, its main rival.

Raymond Coyle went on to create new brands, such as Hunky Dory's, Sam Spudz, Kezzil and McCoy's. His ability to put together a very effective **marketing mix** for each brand means that all these products have proved to be very successful.

Largo Foods continued to expand using a range of **organic** and **inorganic expansion** strategies. It eventually took over its main Irish

3 OUT OF 4 PEOPLE PREFER TAYTO

THANKS TO THE GOODNESS OF FRESH IRISH POTATOES COOKED IN PURE SUNFLOWER OIL

rival, Tayto, which made it the largest snack food company in Ireland with dozens of different product lines including crisps, popcorn, peanuts and other snacks.

The company employs nearly 1,000 people with plants in Meath, Donegal and the Czech Republic. Sales run into many millions of euro and the firm now **exports** most of its output.

Raymond Coyle is well known for visiting **international trade fairs** to promote the company and win export orders. He now supplies supermarkets in Britain with own-brand crisps and also exports to many countries, including Lebanon, Singapore, Iceland, Dubai, Malta, Russia and Canada.

As the Irish market is small, access to international markets has been critical to the **growth** of Largo Foods and exports are essential to its future success. From his farming experience, Coyle has learned not to be dependent on any one single market.

1. What is international trade?

By exporting crisps, Largo is engaging in international trade. **International trade** *refers to the buying (importing) and selling (exporting) of different products between countries.* International trade has existed for thousands of years but the last 50 years has seen a huge increase due to improvements in transport and telecommunications technology.

Over the past 75 years, Ireland has gone from being a country with very little foreign trade to being one of the most open economies in the world. **An open economy** *is an economy that engages in international trade.* For most European countries today, international trade accounts for about a quarter of all business activity in their economies. However, in Ireland, nearly 60% of all the goods and services produced in the economy are now exported.

Imports *are goods/services bought from other countries and they can be visible or invisible.* Imports must be paid for using foreign currency.

* **Visible imports** *are physical goods, such as cars, books and computers.*

* **Invisible imports** *are services, such as banking, insurance and tourism, that are provided to Irish customers by foreign firms.*

> **Ireland buying products from abroad = visible imports**
> **Ireland buying services from abroad = invisible imports**

Why import? Ireland imports goods because it is a small country and we do not have the resources, skills or economies of scale to produce all of the goods that consumers or businesses need. Importing provides oil, machinery and components needed by industry. It also provides consumers with a wider variety of goods to choose from when shopping. However, importing costs money. To earn the money needed to pay for imports, Ireland must **export** products that customers in other countries want to buy.

Exports *are goods or services sold by Irish firms to customers in other countries.* Exporting goods and services brings foreign currency into the country and benefits the national economy. Exports are also important as they allow us to earn the foreign currency we need to pay for the imports we want.

- ❖ **Visible exports** are physical goods, such as food, pharmaceuticals and engine components.
- ❖ **Invisible exports** are services that can be sold to foreign customers, such as financial services or selling holidays in Ireland to foreign tourists.

> Ireland selling products abroad = visible exports
> Ireland selling services abroad = invisible exports

Why export? Ireland needs to export to earn the money to pay for imports. Exporting also generates economies of scale and increased employment in the firms producing goods and services for export.

Ireland's main exports are:
- **Medical equipment**
- **Chemicals and pharmaceuticals**
- **Electronics**
- **Software**
- **Food and drink**
- **Financial services**

Import or Export?
Ask yourself which way is the money going?
- ✪ If the money is coming into Ireland, it's an export.
- ✪ If the money is going out of Ireland, it's an import.

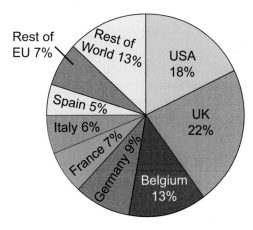

Fig. 1 Destination of Ireland's exports (goods and services)

OL Short Q1, 3
OL Long Q1, 2, 3
HL Short Q2

2. How is international trade measured?

How a country is performing in international trade is measured using the **balance of payments.** The balance of payments *sets out all the flows of money into and out of a country in a year.*

A **balance of payments surplus** is favourable as it *means Ireland is earning more than it is spending internationally.*

A **balance of payments deficit** is unfavourable as it *means the country is paying out more than it is earning.*

Sample Balance of Payments (in € billions)		
Visible Trade	Exports of goods	€100
	Less imports of goods	€(80)
	Balance of trade	**€20 surplus**
Invisible Trade	Exports of services	€25
	Less imports of services	€(30)
	Balance of invisible trade	€(5) deficit
Balance of Payments		**€15 surplus**

The balance of payments is made up of the **balance of trade** and the **balance of invisible trade**:

> ✳ The **balance of trade** *refers to the difference between all visible imports into and visible exports out of a country.* Invisibles are excluded. In the example above, the country has a balance of trade surplus of €20 billion.

OL Short Q2, 4, 5

OL Long Q4, 5

HL Short Q1, 3

> ✳ The **balance of invisible trade** *refers to all the money flowing into the Irish economy* (from tourist revenues, EU grants, foreign loans, etc.) *and flowing out of the economy* (from Irish people taking foreign holidays, repayments of foreign loans, etc.).

3. What are the benefits to Ireland of free international trade?

Free trade occurs when trade between countries is not restricted in any way by barriers such as tariffs (import taxes) or quotas. It is based on the theory that countries will be better off if each specialises in the goods it is most efficient at producing. Free trade exists between members of the EU. This means firms like Largo Foods can freely export their goods to other EU markets without having to deal with obstacles like tariffs or quotas.

● Benefits for businesses

> ❖ **Access to raw materials:** Firms can **import** raw materials (e.g. oil) and essential finished goods (e.g. machinery) that are not available in Ireland.
>
> ❖ **Increase sales:** Firms like Largo Foods can expand their sales and profits beyond the domestic market through **exporting.**
>
> ❖ **Economies of scale: Exports** help firms to gain economies of scale and become more efficient, such as lowering per-unit costs and prices. This improves their ability to compete and survive against multinational rivals.
>
> ❖ **Spreads business risk: Exporting** spreads a firm's business risk by reducing its reliance on sales in a single country.

● Benefits for consumers

> ✪ **Choice: Imports** of goods can lead to more competition and a wider choice of goods for consumers.
>
> ✪ **Quality:** A wider choice of goods for consumers puts pressure on domestic firms to ensure their products can match or exceed the quality of imports at competitive prices.

● Benefits for the economy

★ **Jobs:** Successful **exporting** generates jobs and incomes in Ireland.

★ **Foreign exchange earnings:** Ireland must **export** goods to earn the foreign currency needed to pay for imports.

★ **International understanding:** International trade encourages communication, understanding and co-operation between countries and was one of the major reasons for the establishment of the EU. Countries that trade a lot with each other are far less likely to go to war.

OL Short Q6
OL Long Q6, 8
HL Short Q4
HL Long Q1

4. What is protectionism?

Case Study

China Copies Japan

After the Second World War, Japan adopted **protectionist** policies to discourage imports into the country. This allowed Japanese firms to grow and develop free from foreign competition in their home market. When the Japanese economy was rebuilt and its firms were large enough to compete internationally, the government relaxed some of the protectionist policies. However, from time to time the Japanese government still uses protectionist policies to safeguard Japanese firms and jobs, especially in new or still-growing sectors of the economy.

Today, China has copied Japan's example and is using many protectionist policies to protect its industries from foreign competition. This allows it to build up strong companies with the economies of scale needed to compete internationally. It is using protectionism as part of its strategy to become an economic superpower.

Protectionism *refers to barriers imposed by governments to prevent free trade.* Governments are often tempted to introduce protectionist policies, especially against imports, for the following reasons:

✳ **Business growth:** Protectionism can help shelter young and growing firms from cheap foreign competition.

> Example: the US government imposed tariffs on imports of Japanese motorbike brands such as Yamaha in order to protect the US Harley-Davidson brand of motorbike.

✳ **Business survival:** Protectionism can protect essential industries such as agriculture, media, steel and transport from being undermined or destroyed by cheaper foreign competition.

> Example: The removal of protectionist policies when Ireland joined the EU meant that thousands of jobs in traditional industries like footwear and clothing were lost due to cheaper European imports.

* **Protect employment:** Protectionism can be used to protect employment in industries under threat from cheap imports. This can be important if competition is coming from countries with cost advantages such as low wages (e.g. China) or large government subsidies (e.g. South Korea).

* **Improve balance of payments:** Protectionism can improve a country's balance of payments by reducing the amount of money flowing out of the country. Protectionist measures such as tariffs can also **raise tax revenue** for a government.

Methods of protectionism

❖ **Tariffs** *are taxes put on imported goods.* This makes imports more expensive and less competitive against the products and services of domestic firms.

Example: If Largo Foods tried to export goods to China, it would find a tariff tax of between 25–35% being placed on its crisps before they could be sold.

❖ **Quotas** *establish a limit on the quantity of certain goods that can be imported.* The aim of a quota is to discourage imports and promote sales of domestically produced goods.

Example: The EU has imposed a limit on the quantity of bananas that can be imported from non-EU member countries.

❖ **Embargoes** *are bans preventing the importation or export of specified goods.*

Example: Ireland and other EU countries were forced to place an embargo on the import of cattle and meat from the UK because of the very high levels of BSE ('mad cow' disease) in that country.

❖ **Rules and regulations:** Governments can restrict international trade by imposing rules and regulations on the import or export of goods. There may be good health, safety or environmental reasons for these rules but governments sometimes use them as a concealed method of deliberately frustrating the importation of foreign goods.

Example: If Largo Foods tried to export their products to China, it could be forced to wait up to three years before the Chinese government would issue a licence allowing the goods to be imported. By setting up its own factory in China, Largo Foods could bypass this protectionist barrier.

❖ **Subsidies** *are money paid by governments to help firms cover their operating costs and keep their prices competitive.* They can take the form of grants or special low-interest loans.

Example: The EU has given subsidies to help aircraft manufacturer Airbus to compete internationally on price against rival US firms such as Boeing.

❖ **Retaliation:** The introduction of protectionist policies by one country can provoke retaliation from another country that introduces similar policies in response. Both countries then miss out on the benefits of free trade.

OL Short Q8, 9
OL Long Q9

HL Short Q5, 6, 7

5. What are the main trends in international trade?

The huge increase in international trade over the last 50 years is due to a number of interrelated factors.

- ✪ **Improvements in transport and ICT:** Modern shipping and air transport have made exporting and importing cheaper and faster. Improvements in information and communications technology (ICT) allow businesses to communicate globally with staff, customers and suppliers. Goods can also be bought and sold over the Internet, with payments made electronically.

- ✪ **Development of global advertising** using television and the Internet. This allows firms to develop **global brands** that can be promoted globally for a global audience.

- ✪ **The emergence of trading blocs: A trading bloc** *is a group of countries that agree to remove protectionist barriers to free trade between themselves. However, they impose tariffs and other protectionist barriers on all imports coming in from countries that are not members of the bloc.* The **European Union (EU)** started as a trading bloc, and the USA, Canada and Mexico have come together to form the **North American Free Trade Agreement (NAFTA).**

- ✪ **Emergence of new markets:** Eastern Europe is a growing market. Further east, the Pacific Rim region is a fast growing economic region and includes China, Japan, South Korea, Taiwan, Singapore, Thailand, Malaysia and Indonesia.

- ✪ **Increasing power and influence of transnational corporations (TNCs):** Transnational corporations are companies that produce and sell goods or services in many different countries. Since the Second World War, the number and size of TNCs has increased and many are now huge **global companies** that treat the world as one single market for their products. These companies can lobby governments for greater free trade policies and fewer restrictions on their activities.

- ✪ **Deregulation** *refers to the removal of government rules and regulations from the workings of business, including the ability to trade freely internationally without any protectionist barriers.*

Example: In Ireland the deregulation of air travel allowed new operators like Ryanair to enter the market and sell tickets up to 80% cheaper than Aer Lingus. Deregulation normally means increased competition in markets and lower prices. However, jobs in the previously protected firms and industries may be threatened. Countries that do not comply with demands for deregulation can be subject to fines or other sanctions, for example from the EU or World Trade Organisation (see page 406).

- ✪ **The level of international competition is becoming intense.** As a result, firms must be constantly vigilant about business developments and strive to adapt and compete to the highest possible international standards.

- ✪ **More businesses are relocating production and other activities to lower-cost countries.** They can avail of the lowest taxes, labour and other costs to save money but this can undermine existing jobs in the higher-cost countries.

Example: Toymaker Hornby, maker of model trains and Scalextric, relocated all its manufacturing to China to save on labour and other costs.

- ✪ **Businesses can relocate production to countries with more lax regulation** to avoid strict labour, environmental or other laws that apply in their home countries.

Example: Many American companies have relocated factories across the border to Mexico to take advantage of very cheap labour as well as very low environmental and safety standards.

○ **Increasing power of the World Trade Organisation (WTO).** National governments have less national control as organisations such as the WTO now make the trade rules. **The World Trade Organisation (WTO)** *is responsible for setting the rules of international trade among its 150 member countries. It does this by organising* **negotiations** *between member countries to reduce protectionism and allow free trade.* Once rules are agreed, every member is expected to comply.

Example: The EU banned the importation of genetically modified food from the USA because of health concerns. However the USA complained to the WTO which decided that it was a form of protectionism and imposed a fine of $150 million a year on the EU. Under WTO rules, free-trade rules take precedence over national health concerns.

○ **Globalisation.** The result of the massive growth of international trade and communications is globalisation. **Globalisation** *refers to the emergence of the world as one single interconnected marketplace.* Decisions or events in one part of the world can now quickly affect people in other parts of the globe.

OL Short Q7
OL Long Q7, 12

HL Short Q8, 9, 10
HL Long Q5

> **Globalisation refers to the emergence of the world as one single interconnected marketplace.**

6. Where are the major global markets in the 21st century?

European Union – As a very successful trading bloc, the EU has reduced the barriers, expense and risks involved in international trade for member countries. This gives Irish firms relatively easy access to markets in all EU countries.

Russia and former Soviet Union – The collapse of communism at the end of the 20th century means that markets in these countries are now open for business to Irish firms. However, doing business in these countries can be difficult, as government inefficiency and corruption remain a problem.

North America – The United States is the biggest exporter and importer of goods in the world. Together with Canada and Mexico, the North American region has massive consumer buying power. The main drawbacks for Ireland are the distances and trans-Atlantic transport costs involved.

Middle East – Oil wealth has increased demand and opportunities for Irish exports to the Middle East, especially food, healthcare products and professional services.

Developing countries – Other Asian countries, along with those of Africa and most of South America have yet to develop significant export opportunities, partly because they are handicapped by corruption, bad economic management and huge inequalities of wealth.

China & the Pacific Rim – The Pacific Rim countries are growing very fast and the region is becoming the most economically important in the world in the 21st century. Obstacles to trade in the Pacific Rim for Irish firms include long-distance transport costs, language and cultural barriers. Furthermore, many Asian governments such as China operate 'hidden barriers' to discourage foreign goods.

7. What are the main opportunities for Irish businesses in international trade?

Ireland is a small island in the Atlantic Ocean on the edge of Europe. However, despite this peripheral geographical position, we have a number of distinct advantages that can be used by businesses like Largo Foods to survive and prosper in the global economy of the 21st century. These advantages are:

* **EU membership:** Ireland is a member of the EU trading bloc, which allows us free access to a market of 480 million high-income consumers. This provides us with the opportunity to develop the **economies of scale** that would not be possible selling to a domestic market of just four million. EU membership has also attracted hundreds of non-EU companies to set up operations here.

* **Euro currency** makes trade within the eurozone easy. As the euro is a very stable currency, the risk of exchange rate fluctuations with countries outside the eurozone is reduced.

* **Educated citizens:** Ireland's relatively well-educated population provides us with a huge resource in terms of intelligent and adaptable entrepreneurs and workers. This is one of the main reasons why so many foreign hi-tech firms have located their factories in Ireland.

* **Language/culture:** As a predominantly English-speaking country, Ireland speaks the international business language. Furthermore, our ancient Gaelic and Celtic heritage – in terms of art, music and literature – provides us with a unique and attractive selling point to distinguish Irish products in a global market.

* **Green image:** To date, Ireland has had a unique image as a relatively green, unspoilt and pollution-free country. This has benefited us in terms of rapidly growing tourism, food products and the environmental services industries but needs to be protected for the future.

* **Low corporation taxes** on company profits attract many foreign firms to locate in Ireland even though they export most of their output to other countries.

* **Government assistance** to business such as grants, training and advice helps to reduce the cost and risk to TNCs of locating here. IDA Ireland has many years of experience in attracting TNCs to locate operations in this country and has a global network of contacts. **Trade missions** *occur when a group of business people visit a foreign country to meet with potential customers and distributors and to negotiate deals and sales.* Trade missions from Ireland are often organised by Enterprise Ireland.

OL Short Q10
OL Long Q10

HL Long Q6

| Case Study | **A HIGH-FLYING GLOBAL NICHE** |

Joining the EU brought many opportunities for Ireland. However, the arrival of **free trade** and the removal of **protectionist** barriers also led to the rapid decline of once-large Irish indigenous firms in areas such as furniture, textiles, clothing and footwear manufacturing because they could not compete with lower-cost European **imports**.

One textile firm that has survived and prospered in the new **global**

market is the Botany Weaving Mill in Dublin's Liberties. This firm traditionally produced fabric to cover chairs and other furniture. To survive in the global marketplace, Botany could no longer compete on price so the firm changed its **marketing strategy**. With help from **Enterprise Ireland**, it saw an opportunity to become the global experts in producing specialist fabric for aircraft seats. This is a very technical area because, for safety reasons, aircraft seat covers have to be flame resistant, tough and extremely lightweight. They also need to be comfortable to sit on, pleasing to the eye, have extremely low static and also be stain-resistant. The firm used international trade fairs and trade missions to contact new customers.

Botany's strategy worked and the firm's customers now include over eighty airlines such as Aer Lingus, Virgin Atlantic, British Airways, Gulf Air and Quantas. Before entering the specialist aviation niche of the textile market, the business was struggling against competitors from dozens of lower-cost countries. Now it has just one competitor, a Swiss firm, and business is booming.

Recall & Review

1. Explain the terms in bold.
2. List the challenges that face a firm like Botany Weaving when trying to sell to international markets.

8. What are the main challenges for Irish business in international trade?

To survive and fully avail of the opportunities presented by the global marketplace, Irish firms like Botany Weaving and Largo Foods must successfully overcome certain barriers to trading successfully in this marketplace. These include the following:

★ **High costs:** As an island on the edge of Europe, Ireland has higher transport costs than most other EU firms doing business in Europe. We also have very high labour costs and so Irish firms must operate as efficiently as possible to remain competitive.

★ **Competition:** Irish firms tend to be small by international standards but still need to be able to operate competitively to the highest international standards. This may mean concentrating on filling niches in the global marketplace (such as fabric for airline seats) and competing on the basis of superior design, quality, branding or after-sales service, rather than price.

★ **Lack of economies of scale:** Because the Irish market is small, Irish firms tend to be small by international standards. This makes it very difficult to develop the economies of scale needed to compete against larger firms producing mass-market products. Most Irish firms need to concentrate on niche markets where price is not the most important consideration for customers.

Example: By concentrating on a specialist niche with few international competitors, Botany Weaving has survived and thrived in the global marketplace.

★ **Foreign languages:** To sell successfully to foreign customers, Irish businesses need to be able to speak their language.

Example: Language problems caused difficulties when the US company General Motors launched the Opel Nova car in Spanish-speaking South American countries. In Spanish, Nova means 'Won't go' and the car was a flop. Similarly, Largo Foods must be careful about the brand name it uses for its products in foreign markets.

★ **Cultural differences** between countries can present challenges and even result in lost sales or offended customers.

Example: Using images of cows in advertising and packaging in India could cause offence to some Hindus who regard the cow as a sacred animal.

★ **Product designs and standards** may need to be adapted to suit the safety laws and different requirements of foreign markets, especially those outside the EU.

Example: A British car manufacturer tried to export cars to Saudi Arabia but failed miserably as the cars were not equipped with air conditioning, essential for a hot country.

★ **Payment difficulties:** Collecting debts from customers in other countries is more difficult than at home, especially if they are far away or have a very different culture or legal system.

Example: If a Taiwanese customer does not pay Largo Foods the money owed, it can be very difficult and expensive to go to Taiwan and try to collect the money.

★ **Exchange Rates:** Further difficulties can be caused by fluctuations in exchange rates for different currencies.

Example: When an American customer is buying goods from Largo Foods, they must buy euro currency to pay for them. If the value of the euro rises against the dollar on foreign exchange markets, it will cost the American customer more to pay for the Irish exports. For firms such as Largo Foods, this can result in lost sales and possible job cuts.

OL Long Q11

HL ABQ

HL Long Q2, 3, 4

Key Concepts & Business Terms

After studying this chapter the student should be able to explain the following key concepts and business terms:

1. International trade
2. An open economy
3. Imports (visible and invisible)
4. Exports (visible and invisible)
5. Balance of payments
6. Balance of payments surplus
7. Balance of payments deficit
8. Balance of trade
9. Benefits of international trade
10. Free trade
11. Protectionism
12. Tariffs
13. Quotas
14. Embargoes
15. Subsidies
16. A trading bloc
17. Deregulation
18. World Trade Organisation
19. Globalisation
20. Trade missions

useful websites

www.largofoods.ie
www.wto.org
www.botanyweaving.com

Leaving Certificate Practice Questions

Ordinary Level

Ordinary Level – Section 1 – Short Questions (10 marks each)

1. Explain what is meant by the term 'open economy'.
2. Distinguish between balance of trade and balance of payments. [LCQ]
3. Distinguish between firms exporting and importing goods. Illustrate with an example of each. [LCQ]
4. If visible exports are worth €16,000m and visible imports €13,000m, does the country have a deficit or a surplus on its balance of trade?
5. Visible exports are €1,138 million, visible imports are €1,235. (a) Calculate the balance of trade. (b) State whether it is a surplus or a deficit.
6. Identify **two** benefits of free international trade.
7. Explain what is meant by a trading bloc and illustrate your answer with an example.
8. List **two** examples of protectionist policies that can be used by the European Union.
9. What is a tariff?
10. Identify **two** advantages Ireland has in the international marketplace.

Ordinary Level – Section 2 – Long Questions

1. What is international trade? (15 marks) [LCQ]

2. Explain what is meant by invisible exports and give **two** examples of invisible exports. (25 marks) [LCQ]

3. Outline two reasons why goods are imported into Ireland and give two examples of imported goods. (15 marks) [LCQ]

4. Describe what is meant by Ireland's balance of payments. (20 marks) [LCQ]

5. Visible exports are worth €16,000m, invisible exports €4,000m, visible imports €13,000m and invisible imports are €6,000m (a) Calculate the balance of trade. (b) Calculate the balance of payments. (c) Is the balance of payments in surplus or deficit? (15 marks)

6. Explain what is meant by free trade. (20 marks)

7. Identify and explain **two** reasons for the growth of international trade. (20 marks)

8. Outline the benefits of free trade for (a) consumers and (b) businesses in Ireland. (20 marks)

9. Outline the actions a country can take to protect its own industries from foreign competition. (15 marks)

10. Outline **three** opportunities faced by Irish firms engaged in international trade. (20 marks) [LCQ]

11. Discuss **three** challenges faced by Irish business engaged in international trade. (20 marks) [LCQ]

12. Describe **three** ways in which information and communications technology (ICT) has helped international trade. Use an example in each of your answers. (15 marks) [LCQ]

Higher Level

Higher Level – Section 1 – Short Questions (10 marks each)

1. Explain what is meant by a country's balance of trade.

2. Illustrate **three** types of invisible export.

3. Using the following information, calculate (a) the balance of trade and (b) the balance of payments:

   Total imports €16 billion Invisible exports €11 billion

   Total exports €19 billion Invisible imports €9 billion

4. Identify **three** benefits of international trade to business.

5. Explain what is meant by the term 'protectionism'?

6. Distinguish between (a) a quota and an embargo and (b) a tariff and a subsidy.

7. List **four** examples of protectionist practices that can be used by governments.

8. What is a trading bloc? State **one** example.

9. Define deregulation. [LCQ]

10. Explain the term 'globalisation'.

Higher Level – Section 2 – Applied Business Question

SLIEVEMORE CHEESE COMPANY

The Slievemore Cheese Company is an agribusiness firm producing high-quality cheese products. Currently, all of the firm's sales are in Ireland. However, Lynn Keogh, the firm's managing director, feels that sales in Ireland have reached maturity and that continued business growth will have to come from export markets.

Lynn instructed Slievemore's marketing manager to prepare a market research report on possible foreign market opportunities. The report has now been completed and has identified a number of large supermarket chains in the UK, France and Russia who may be interested in stocking the firm's products. However, the report pointed out that marketing staff in the firm have very poor foreign language skills. The firm is also highly geared and cannot afford to invest large sums trying to build up sales in a foreign market.

International trade has its risks and Lynn is keen to tackle just one foreign market initially. However, she is unsure about what country to select first. The UK is English-speaking, France is in the eurozone while Russia has the largest potential population.

Lynn has heard lots of stories of big companies who have made expensive mistakes when trying to sell goods to foreign countries. She is therefore keen to get advice from Enterprise Ireland about how to successfully manage the move into export markets.

1. Evaluate the main opportunities open to Slievemore for engaging in international trade. (20 marks)
2. Analyse the possible barriers to trade that Slievemore could encounter when trying to enter new export markets. Refer to the text in your answer. (40 marks)
3. Describe the possible role of Enterprise Ireland in assisting Slievemore as it prepares to trade internationally. (20 marks)

Higher Level – Section 2 – Long Questions

1. Outline the significance of international trade for Ireland. (15 marks) [LCQ]
2. Analyse the problems that Irish firms face when trying to compete globally. (30 marks)
3. Analyse the significance or otherwise of international trade for Ireland. Refer to the development of trading blocs and transnational companies in your answer. (35 marks) [LCQ]
4. Discuss the changing nature of the international economy. Include in your response the effects it has on Irish business. (30 marks) [LCQ]
5. Describe the role of the World Trade Organisation in promoting international trade. (20 marks)
6. Identify and explain the advantages that Ireland has when competing in the global marketplace. (20 marks)

Chapter 24

Ireland & the European Union

'Those who do not learn from the mistakes of history are doomed to repeat them.'

George Santayana

Key Study Questions

Case Study

Kingspan PLC

Kingspan PLC specialises in manufacturing insulation and energy-saving products used in the construction of environmentally friendly buildings. Headquartered in County Cavan, it started off as a small engineering business. However, Ireland's membership of the European Union provided the business with opportunities to grow and develop.

Kingspan's management took a strategic decision to reduce the risk of relying just on the small and vulnerable Irish market. They put together a **strategic plan** to sell their products to every country in the EU. By spreading the company's sales among many different countries, management wanted to reduce the risk of relying on just one market.

Kingspan®

Kingspan's strategic plan has proved very successful and today it sells its products to customers in every country in the EU. This success has encouraged the firm to think globally and it has continued to expand further and now also sells its products in Russia, Canada, the USA and in the Far East.

Kingspan is run by a **board of directors** that meets approximately once a month to provide strategic direction to the business and to make important decisions such as the appointment of senior managers, to approve large investment decisions or to sell valuable assets. The board employ a **chief executive officer** (CEO) to oversee the day-to-day management of the business. Currently Kingspan uses a product **organisational structure.**

Kingspan PLC now operates in dozens of countries around the world, but the EU is the most important market for its products.

Recall & Review

Explain the terms highlighted in bold.

1. What is the European Union?

Ireland's membership of the European Union has been very important to Kingpsan's success. The **European Union** *is an international trading bloc and political alliance of European nations designed to promote closer political, economic and social co-operation among its member countries.* Each member country contributes tax revenue towards the cost of running the EU and, in return, shares economic and political policies intended to benefit all the members.

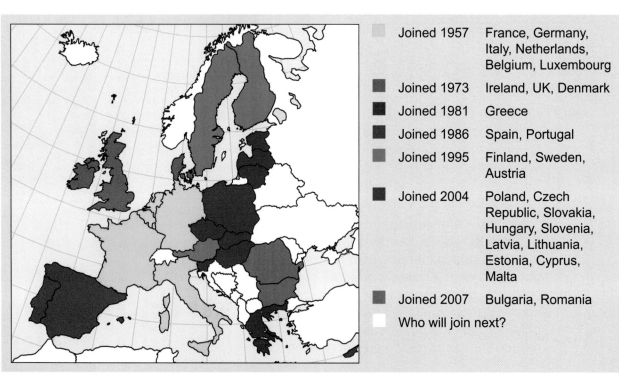

	Joined 1957	France, Germany, Italy, Netherlands, Belgium, Luxembourg
	Joined 1973	Ireland, UK, Denmark
	Joined 1981	Greece
	Joined 1986	Spain, Portugal
	Joined 1995	Finland, Sweden, Austria
	Joined 2004	Poland, Czech Republic, Slovakia, Hungary, Slovenia, Latvia, Lithuania, Estonia, Cyprus, Malta
	Joined 2007	Bulgaria, Romania
	Who will join next?	

2. How are EU policies and laws made?

EU policies and laws are made as a result of decisions taken by the EU's 'institutional triangle', composed of:

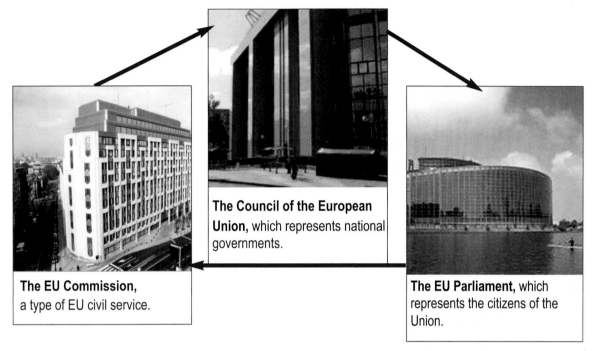

The Council of the European Union, which represents national governments.

The EU Commission, a type of EU civil service.

The EU Parliament, which represents the citizens of the Union.

The Council of the European Union (Council of Ministers)

The **Council of the European Union** *(formerly the Council of Ministers) is the EU's most important decision-making body and is made up of representatives from each member state government.* Its meetings are attended by the relevant minister from each member state for the topic being discussed, e.g. if foreign policy is to be discussed, the foreign affairs minister from each country will attend. The government of each EU country takes turns presiding over the Council for a six-month period. The main functions of the Council are:

> **Council of the EU**
> - **Most important decision making body in the EU.**
> - **Represents national governments.**
> - **Qualified majority voting.**
> - **Important decisions must be unanimous.**

* **Sets goals** and plans for the EU.
* **Approves the budget** for the EU together with the European Parliament.
* **Approves laws** drafted by the Commission and in conjunction with the European Parliament (known as 'co-decision').

The European Commission

The **European Commission** *is the institution responsible for the day-to-day management of the European Union.* The **EU commissioners** *are the senior managers who are appointed by national governments to run the European Union.* Each commissioner is allocated a different Directorate-General (DG), which is an area of responsibility such as transport, competition, agriculture, social affairs, etc.

The main functions of the European Commission are:

❖ **Proposing new laws:** The Commission is the only EU institution that can initiate new laws but must consult with interest groups and experts on any proposed new legislation to ensure that the interests of the European Union as a whole are served.

❖ **Implementing EU laws and policies:** The Commission supervises member states to ensure all EU legislation is fully implemented. If member states do not comply, the Commission can take a case against them to the European Court of Justice.

❖ **Managing the EU budget:** The Commission decides on the amount of money required to run the EU and manages spending.

The European Parliament

The **European Parliament** *is directly elected by EU citizens to act as a supervisory 'watchdog' over all aspects of the EU's activities.* It is made up of over 700 MEPs. **MEPs** *are Members of the European Parliament who are elected in EU-wide elections every five years.* The Republic of Ireland elects 13 MEPs. Unlike other parliaments, the European Parliament does not have the power to draft its own legislation. This is known as the EU's **'democratic deficit'.** The European Parliament:

✪ **Represents:** MEPs are directly elected to represent the views of the people of the EU.

✪ **Legislates:** The Parliament debates and votes on all new policies and laws proposed by the Commission. Without the Parliament's approval, proposals cannot become law.

✪ **Supervises:** The Parliament supervises the running of the EU such as:

◎ **Funding and spending activities** of the EU. This includes approving the EU budget in conjunction with the Council of the European Union.

◎ **Interviewing** all candidates for the jobs as EU Commissioners and has the power to dismiss the entire Commission if unhappy with its functioning.

The European Parliament

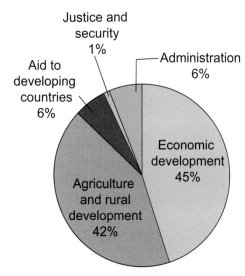

Fig. 1 Where the EU spends its budget

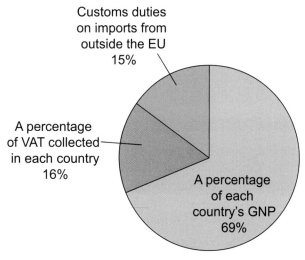

Fig. 2 How the EU is financed

The Court of Auditors

The **Court of Auditors** *is responsible for ensuring that the EU* **budget is spent efficiently** and **for the purpose intended.** It checks that all the European Union's revenue has been received from member countries and that all the expenditure incurred is lawful and has been well managed. It can **audit the accounts** of any organisation that is handling EU funds, and looks for areas where there may be possible waste, mismanagement or fraud with EU funds.

> Example: The Court of Auditors discovered that the EU Commission gave money to the Irish government to conserve a scientifically and ecologically important bog in Co. Kilkenny. At the same time, however, another part of the Commission was giving money for the same bog to be harvested for turf fuel.

The European Court of Justice

The European Court of Justice *is responsible for ensuring that EU laws are applied the same way in all EU countries.* It is made up of one judge from each of the member states. It tries to iron out any differences between European and national laws. When there is a dispute over EU law, governments, companies and individuals can bring cases to the Court for resolution.

> Example: The EU Commission took the Irish government to the European Court of Justice for improperly spending EU agriculture funds. Ireland has also been prosecuted for ignoring EU laws requiring that the quality of fishing waters be protected.

The European Court of Justice

The European Central Bank

The **European Central Bank (ECB),** *based in Frankfurt, is the central bank for all countries that have adopted the euro as their common currency.* Its main roles are to keep inflation low and to safeguard the value of the euro. It does this by setting the interest rates that apply in the eurozone.

> The ECB sets interest rates for the eurozone.

OL Short Q1, 2

HL Short Q1

HL Long Q2

3. How are new EU laws introduced?

There are five stages involved in introducing new laws in the EU:

1. Proposal by the Commission

Proposals for new laws are prepared by the European Commission.

2. Consultation with the EU Parliament and relevant stakeholder groups

The proposal is sent for discussion to the European Parliament, national governments and any other relevant bodies. At this stage considerable lobbying and campaigning may be undertaken by people, such as national governments, MEPs, and special interest groups. **Lobbying** *refers to a deliberate effort to influence decision-making by promoting a particular point of view.*

3. Redrafting by the Commission

Comments and feedback are received by the Commission which may make changes to the original proposal in light of arguments made.

4. Approval by the Council

A final version of the proposed law is sent to the European Council for approval or rejection.

5. Implementation by the Commission and national governments

The Council of the EU (Council of Ministers) will also decide how the law should be implemented. This can be done by issuing a **regulation**, a **directive** or a **decision**.

> * **EU Regulations** *are legally binding decisions that become effective in law immediately and take precedence over national laws.*
> * **EU Directives** *set out a goal to be achieved by member states and a deadline for its achievement. However, each country is **free to decide** how best to achieve the goal. This allows each country to introduce or amend its own laws to achieve the goal. Directives aim to* **harmonise** *laws among EU members.*
> * **EU Decisions** *are only binding on specifically named countries, companies or organisations.*

> **EU Regulations are immediately binding in law.**
> **EU Directives set out a goal to be achieved by all member countries but methods of achievement are left to the discretion of national governments.**
> **EU decisions only apply to specific countries or organisations.**

> **Example:** In the past, the Commission has issued Decisions declaring that Irish companies such as CRH and Aer Lingus must pay fines for unfair competitive behaviour.

OL Long Q1, 2

HL Long Q1, 3

4. What is the role of special interest groups in EU decision-making?

Case Study

The **European Commission** proposed a ban on Harley-Davidson and similar motorbikes on the grounds that they were 'unsafe'. When motorbike enthusiasts heard of this proposal, they formed an interest group and began **lobbying** MEPs and the Commission to persuade them to drop the plans. The campaign succeeded as the Commission dropped the proposal just before it was due to go to the European Council for final approval.

> **Many different interest groups try to influence the EU's decision-making process.**

EU laws can have major effects on governments, businesses, industries, organisations and individuals. As a result, many interest groups try to influence these decisions to suit their own members. These include:

* **National governments,** who will always try to get support for their own views and to protect national interests.

* **Industry bodies** representing particular industries such as chemicals, automobiles or agriculture.
* **Employer organisations** such as IBEC.
* **Trade unions** representing workers.
* **Large transnational companies.**
* **Consumer** protection organisations.
* **Environmental** organisations.
* **Regional groups** representing specific regions of the EU.
* **Individuals** or small groups with specific concerns, such as equality or health issues.

Methods of persuasion used by interest groups

Interest groups can influence EU decision-making in the following ways:

* **Lobbying the key decision-makers** – these are the ministers, commissioners and MEPs.
* **Setting up an office in Brussels and Strasbourg makes lobbying easier.** The larger interest groups have permanent staff working close to the Commission and Parliament to monitor all EU developments and to stay close to the decision-making process.
* **Using public relations** and other information campaigns can help to publicise an interest group's views in order to win over public opinion and, hopefully, influence the decision-makers.
* **Protests and public demonstrations** are sometimes used by interest groups to attract media attention and get publicity for their views.

5. What are the main EU policies?

THE EU HAS A NUMBER OF IMPORTANT POLICIES TO HELP IT ACHIEVE ITS OBJECTIVES	
Policy	**Objective**
Single European Market Policy	Promotion of **free trade** between member states
European Monetary Union Policy	Promotion and protection of the **euro currency**
Social Policy	Protecting **worker, consumer and citizen rights**
Environmental Policy	Ensuring **environmental protection**
Common Agricultural Policy	Developing **agriculture** and rural life
Common Fisheries Policy	Developing and protecting **fishing**
Structural Policy	Promoting **regional economic development**
Competition Policy	Promoting **competition** in the marketplace

Single European Market Policy

Case Study — Before the EU's Single European Market policy was introduced, firms like Kingpsan had to complete lots of paperwork when exporting Irish goods to other EU countries. Different customs forms in different languages had to be completed for each country and the whole process was a very slow and complicated affair. But the introduction of the single market has eliminated most of the paperwork involved and has made exporting much simpler. There are no more document checks or customs delays at frontiers, aside from occasional searches for illegal goods. This allows imports and exports to reach customers faster and reduces business transport costs.

The Single European Market is extremely important to business.

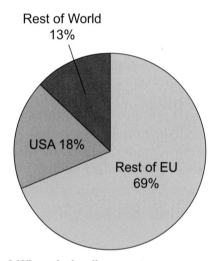

Rest of World 13%

USA 18%

Rest of EU 69%

Fig. 3 Where Ireland's exports go

The purpose of the **Single European Market (SEM) policy** *is to remove barriers to the free movement of goods, services, people and capital between member states.* It is intended to boost free trade within the Union by allowing businesses to treat the entire EU as their home market.

● Benefits of the SEM for business

✪ **Creation of a huge market:** Nearly 480 million consumers across the EU can be easily accessed by Irish firms, allowing them to export and benefit from economies of scale and reduced dependence on the small Irish market.

✪ **Free movement of goods:** Trade barriers such as frontier controls, tariffs, physical checks on goods at border crossings and regulations regarding product testing have been removed. Standards are being harmonised on thousands of products, ranging from chocolate and lawnmowers to cars and bananas. These measures are intended to make it easier for a firm in one EU country to do business in any other member state. However, governments are still allowed to restrict the movement of some goods on health or security grounds.

- ✪ **Free movement of capital:** Firms and citizens can invest their money wherever it can earn the greatest return within the EU. As a result, Irish interest rates move in line with those in other EU countries, especially Germany. For example, it is possible for Kingpsan to buy foreign businesses, open a French bank account or negotiate a loan from a Dutch bank.

- ✪ **Free movement of labour:** EU citizens are free to travel, live and work in most member countries without immigration or passport controls.

- ✪ **Tax harmonisation:** EU governments have harmonised some of their tax rates, especially on goods and services. For example, VAT in all EU countries will eventually be at the same rate of 15%.

- ✪ **Protectionism for EU firms:** For goods imported from outside the EU, a common external tariff is applied. It helps to protect firms like Kingpsan from cheap competition from outside the European Union.

- ✪ **Foreign direct investment:** Membership of the EU and access to the Single European Market has made Ireland an attractive, low-tax European base for many transnational firms. This has created thousands of jobs in Ireland.

Drawbacks of the SEM for business

- ★ **Public procurement:** Governments are not allowed to show favouritism towards their own firms when buying goods. If the Irish government wants to buy uniforms for the army it must buy from the most competitive source and cannot try to protect Irish jobs by favouring an Irish firm if an Italian firm is cheaper.

> **Example:** A 'Buy Irish' advertising campaign run by the Irish government was found by the European Court of Justice to be contrary to the Single European Market and was declared illegal.

- ★ **Greater competition:** The SEM means increased competition for Irish businesses from European firms.

European Monetary Union (EMU) Policy

Case Study

Before the European Monetary Union (EMU) policy was introduced, firms like Kingpsan that engaged in international trade had to use different currencies when buying goods in different countries. They also had to deal with changing currency exchange rates, making financial planning more complicated and risky. The EMU resulted in the introduction of the euro as a common currency shared by most EU members. For businesses like Kingpsan, using the euro makes buying and selling goods among countries very easy.

> **EMU introduced the euro as a shared currency among many EU countries.**

The Single European Market allows for the free movement of goods, money and people within the EU. However, to work effectively, the single market requires a common currency within the EU. **European Monetary Union (EMU)** *refers to the introduction of the euro as a common currency for EU* *members.* Most EU countries have become part of the EMU. **The eurozone** *is the name given to those EU countries that have replaced their national currencies with the euro currency.*

To become a member of the eurozone, member countries must meet economic conditions set by the European Central Bank. These include strict rules about having low inflation and tight control over government spending and borrowing.

● Benefits of EMU policy for business

* ✳ **International payments** within the eurozone are simpler, cheaper and free from exchange-rate risk.

* ✳ **Increased trade within the eurozone has been stimulated** creating additional jobs for European workers.

* ✳ **International travel** within the eurozone is easier as people no longer need to change currencies when moving between countries. Price comparisons between different countries have also become easier.

● Drawbacks of EMU policy for business

* ❖ **Ireland's biggest export customers, the UK and the USA, are not in the eurozone.** If the euro increases in value against the pound sterling and the US dollar, this makes Irish exports to the UK and USA more expensive and uncompetitive.

* ❖ As a member of the eurozone, the Irish government has to comply with strict EU rules concerning government spending and taxation.

EU Social Policy (social charter)

Besides promoting international trade and business, the EU has also brought in measures to protect the rights of workers and consumers, and to create a better quality of life for all its citizens. **EU Social Policy** *is intended to improve and harmonise working conditions and consumer rights throughout the EU.*

● Benefits of EU Social Policy for business

* ✪ **Improved work conditions** through the implementation of minimum standards of working hours, holiday entitlements, protection and safety of employees, especially for children and adolescents at work.

* ✪ The **European Social Fund** *provides funding to train and retrain workers and increase their adaptability to change.* Many third-level courses in Ireland have been funded by the ESF.

* ✪ EU Social Policy has also brought about greater **equality of treatment for men and women**, especially in the area of employee rights. The European Social Fund finances the training and retraining of workers and young people.

* ✪ **Consumer rights** have been improved significantly as EU social policy directives are implemented in Ireland through laws such as the Consumer Protection Act and the Sale of Goods & Supply of Services Act.

- ## Drawbacks of EU Social Policy

  ★ **Increased costs:** To comply with rules and regulations resulting from the social policy, businesses such as Kingpsan are subject to greater costs and expenses. This particularly affects smaller businesses.

EU Common Agricultural Policy (CAP)

> The CAP is very important to the primary sector of the economy.

The **Common Agricultural Policy (CAP)** *is designed to make the EU self-sufficient in food and maintain the incomes of farmers and rural communities.* It achieves this by modernising farming practices and stabilising the prices of agricultural produce. The **Common Fisheries Policy** *aims to improve the management of the community's fishery resources.* It is mainly concerned with ensuring freedom of access to EU waters for member states, modernisation of the industry and conservation of dwindling fish stocks due to over-fishing.

- ## Benefits of the CAP for business

  ✳ **A single market** has been created for agricultural products with guaranteed prices for farmer producers.

  ✳ EU **farmers have been protected against low-cost food imports from outside the EU** through various protectionist measures such as quotas and tariffs.

  ✳ The CAP has also **encouraged the development** of Irish agribusiness into a major exporting industry. This has encouraged the growth of firms like Kingpsan.

  ✳ **Food production for the EU is more secure,** while food quality has been raised to very high standards. The **Common Fisheries Policy** is attempting to conserve fish stocks from over-fishing.

  ✳ **Farmers' incomes have increased,** benefiting the national economy due to the relatively large size of our agricultural industry.

  ✳ Large CAP payments to farmers by the EU have **improved Ireland's balance of payments.**

- ## Drawbacks of the CAP for business

  ❖ Grants for the modernisation of agriculture and economies of scale has led to the **loss of many small farm businesses** in favour of large-scale intensive agriculture.

❖ Mechanisation and rationalisation of the industry has led to a **reduction of direct employment in agriculture.**

❖ The CAP is the EU's **most** expensive **policy,** costing EU taxpayers billions of euro every year.

EU Environment Policy

Case Study

Before joining the European Union, building standards in Ireland were very low and the market for insulation and energy-efficiency products was very small. However, over the years the EU has introduced regulations and directives requiring member countries to improve their environmental standards. This has led to increased demand for environmentally friendly products across the EU and, as a producer of insulation and energy-saving products, has created business opportunities for Kingspan.

Increased foreign trade and economic growth have a number of serious environmental side-effects, including increasing amounts of waste and carbon emissions. **EU Environment Policy** *aims to ensure that economic development within the Union is ecologically sustainable and is not at the expense of the quality of Europe's environment.* It does this by:

⚙ Making governments and businesses responsible for their impact on the environment through the **'polluter pays' principle.**

⚙ Ensuring that EU decisions and EU-funded projects take into account the **environmental consequences** of the actions involved.

⚙ Making sure that all large industrial or infrastructure projects **are evaluated** in terms of their environmental impact before planning approval is given.

⚙ Promoting the move towards the **use of renewable sources of energy** such as wind and solar power instead of fossil fuels.

EU Structural Policies

EU structural policies *are designed to improve the competitiveness and wealth of the EU's poorer regions and vulnerable industries.* In the past, Ireland was a major beneficiary of these funds but today most of this aid is directed towards the poorer regions of eastern and southern Europe. Structural funds are provided to countries mainly through the **European Regional Development Fund,** the **European Social Fund** and the **European Cohesion Fund.**

★ The **European Regional Development Fund** *aims to reduce differences between rich and poor regions of the EU, especially areas lagging behind in development or those in industrial decline.* Finance is targeted at improving economic infrastructures (e.g. roads, ports, sewerage systems and telecommunications), improving production methods, developing new industries, reversing economic decline and tackling unemployment.

★ The **European Cohesion Fund** *provides grants to economically poorer countries for infrastructure and environmental improvement projects.*

EU Competition Policy

The larger the number of firms competing in a market, the more likely consumers are to benefit from a wider choice of high-quality goods and competitive prices. **EU Competition Policy** *sets out rules designed to ensure free and fair competition between firms in the Single European Market.* The European Commission only investigates complaints of anti-competitive behaviour by large companies and where trade between EU member states is affected. Firms found guilty by the EU of unfair practices can face large fines. EU Competition Policy rules cover issues such as:

* **Large mergers or takeovers:** These must be approved by the EU Commissioner for Competition to ensure they do not violate the EU's competition policy.

> **Example:** The EU investigated Tesco's takeover of an Irish supermarket chain to ensure it conformed to the principles of free and fair competition.

* **Monopolies and cartels:** Firms are not allowed to form anti-competitive cartels to fix prices, share markets, or block new firms from entering the market. **Dominant firms** in a market are not allowed to use their power to increase consumer prices, restrict the growth of smaller firms or prevent new firms entering the market.

> **Example:** Irish food company Greencore's offices were raided by EU officials as part of an investigation into unfair competition arising from its dominant position in the Irish sugar market. It was subsequently fined €8m by the EU Commission for abusing its monopoly position in the market.

* **Governments** are prohibited from giving special aid, such as subsidies, to firms if this is likely to give such firms an unfair advantage over their European competitors.

> **Example:** The EU restricted the amount of cheap financial aid the Irish government could provide to the Irish Steel Company when it was in financial trouble.

* **Deregulation of monopolies:** Governments are required to allow competition into monopolies, whether state-owned or private.

> **Example:** In Ireland, this is why state-owned firms like ESB, RTÉ, VHI and Bus Éireann have competition.

| OL Short Q3, 4 |
| OL Long Q3, 4, 5, 7 |
| HL Short Q2, 3, 4, 5, 6, 7 |
| HL Long Q4, 5, 6, 8, 10 |

6. What are the benefits of EU membership to Ireland?

● Businesses

❖ Irish firms have easy **access to a large and wealthy market.**
❖ **EU grants to industry** have helped many Irish businesses to grow.
❖ Irish **agriculture** continues to receive large amounts of financial support through the Common Agricultural Policy.

● Employees

✪ Membership of the EU has encouraged many **TNCs to invest in Ireland** by setting up their EU operations here. This has **created thousands of jobs** and pumped billions of euro into the Irish economy.

✪ EU social policy has enhanced **employees' legal rights.**

● Consumers

★ Consumers benefit from being able to use the same currency when travelling in many other EU countries.

★ Competition policy has provided **increased choice** and keeps prices low.

★ EU directives have resulted in strong **consumer protection legislation** being introduced.

● Economy and environment

✳ Membership rules of the eurozone mean that Irish governments have to follow **more responsible taxation and spending policies.** Large budget deficits are not allowed among eurozone members.

✳ The Irish economy has benefited from billions of euro in CAP and structural fund payments over the past few decades.

OL Short Q5
OL Long Q6, 8

✳ EU policies have forced Irish businesses and the government to become much more environmentally responsible.

Case Study

MICROSOFT'S EU base is Ireland

The giant American **transnational company** Microsoft employs over 1,000 staff in its EU base in Dublin. Even though most of the software products it produces in Ireland are exported to other EU countries, it chose to locate its EU base in Dublin because:

★ Ireland's access to the EU's **Single European Market** makes exporting to other EU countries easy.

★ Ireland's use of the **euro** as its currency makes paying and getting paid in the EU easy.

★ Ireland has low **corporation tax** on company profits compared to many other countries.

★ Ireland has a skilled, computer literate workforce.

If Ireland was not a member of the EU, transnational companies like Microsoft would not set up their European exporting bases in this country. This would mean that there would be far fewer jobs, far less tax revenue for the government to pay for State services, and Ireland would be a far less prosperous country.

Microsoft®

Recall and Review

1. Explain the terms highlighted in bold.
2. Evaluate the benefits of the Single European Market to Ireland.
3. Evaluate the benefits of the European Monetary Union (EMU) to Ireland.

7. What challenges face Ireland and the EU in the future?

Specific issues facing Ireland as a member of the EU

❖ **Ireland needs to take greater advantage of the eurozone.** Despite having access to the EU's huge Single European Market, Ireland still does more than half of its trade with non-eurozone countries, especially the UK and the USA.

❖ **Ireland needs to conform with EU rules regarding proper management of the economy.** Poor government regulation and excessive spending by Irish governments in the past caused a major banking and property crisis. The resulting collapse in tax revenues meant that the Irish government was forced to request emergency loans from the European Central Bank. The ECB provides the loans but with strict conditions attached about how Irish governments manage the economy in future.

❖ **Net contributor to EU budget:** Every member of the EU is required to contribute a percentage of its annual income towards the EU budget. In the past, for every €1 Ireland contributed to running the EU, we received €4 in return in grants and other payments, mainly from the CAP and regional policies. However, as Ireland has become wealthier, it has become a net contributor of funds to the EU budget, that is, Ireland will pay in more than we receive back.

❖ **Increased competition for investment:** More recent EU member countries from eastern Europe have much lower labour costs and low levels of corporate taxation. This will make IDA Ireland's job of attracting TNCs to Ireland potentially much harder than before.

Issues facing the entire EU

⊙ **Protecting the stability of the euro currency** by ensuring that all members of the eurozone follow responsible economic policies.

⊙ **Tax harmonisation** *means having the same rates of taxation in all EU countries.* Powerful, high-tax countries such as France and Germany do not like countries such as Ireland having low corporation taxes which tempt TNCs away from their own countries.

⊙ **Institutional reform:** With the expansion of the EU to over two dozen countries there is a need to reform EU structures and institutions to ensure greater democracy, accountability and transparency, as well as greater **decentralisation** of power.

⊙ **Budget reform:** Further reform of the very expensive Common Agricultural Policy will be necessary to reduce its cost to the EU taxpayer and to free up funds for other areas, such as R&D, environmental protection, enterprise development and the fight against international crime and terrorism.

⊙ **Tackling climate change** and promoting sustainable development and environmental protection across industry, agriculture and other areas of the economy is a major priority for the EU.

OL Short Q6

HL Short Q8

HL ABQ

HL Long Q7, 9, 11

Key Concepts & Business Terms

After studying this chapter the student should be able to explain the following key concepts and business terms:

1. European Union (EU)
2. Council of the European Union
3. European Commission
4. EU Commissioners
5. European Parliament
6. MEPs
7. Court of Auditors
8. European Court of Justice
9. European Central Bank (ECB)
10. Lobbying
11. EU Regulations
12. EU Directives
13. EU Decisions
14. Single European Market (SEM)
15. European Monetary Union (EMU)
16. Eurozone
17. EU Social policy
18. EU Common Agricultural Policy (CAP)
19. EU Common Fisheries Policy
20. EU Environment Policy
21. EU Structural Policies
22. European Regional Development Fund
23. European Social Fund
24. European Cohesion Fund
25. EU Competition Policy
26. Benefits of EU membership
27. Challenges facing Ireland and the EU

useful websites

www.kingspan.com
www.europa.eu
www.harley-davidson.com
www.idaireland.com

Leaving Certificate Practice Questions

Ordinary Level

Ordinary Level – Section 1 – Short Questions (10 marks each)

1. Explain the role of the EU Commission.
2. Outline the role of the EU Court of Auditors.
3. Name **two** important EU policies.
4. Identify **two** effects of the Single European Market on Irish business. [LCQ]
5. List **two** benefits of EU membership for Irish business. [LCQ]
6. List **two** challenges facing the future of the EU.

Ordinary Level – Section 2 – Long Questions

1. Describe the roles of the main EU institutions in the decision-making process. Illustrate your answer using an example. (20 marks)

2. Explain the role of the Council of the European Union in EU decision-making. (15 marks)
3. List **three** EU policies and explain the role of one of them. [LCQ] (20 marks)
4. Outline **three** effects of the Single European Market on Irish firms. [LCQ] (15 marks)
5. Illustrate how having a single European currency assists firms exporting to other EU countries. (20 marks)
6. Explain what is meant by 'international trade' and why the EU is important for Irish trade. [LCQ] (20 marks)
7. Outline the purpose of the EU's Competition Policy. (20 marks)
8. State **three** advantages to Ireland of membership of the European Union. [LCQ] (15 marks)

Higher Level

Higher Level – Section 1 – Short Questions (10 marks each)

1. Identify the EU institution that can issue fines for breaches of EU law.
2. List **three** aims of the Single European Market.
3. Identify **two** disadvantages for Ireland of the Single European Market.
4. List **one** advantage and **one** disadvantage of the CAP to Ireland.
5. Explain what is meant by the free movement of labour in the EU.
6. The Single European Market helps business because it . . . [LCQ]
7. Outline the purpose of the European Union's Competition Policy. [LCQ]
8. List **two** challenges facing Ireland as a member of the EU.

Higher Level – Section 1 – Applied Business Question

NatureVite Healthcare Ltd. was started by Eugene Redmond when he identified a niche in the market for an Irish producer of natural vitamin and mineral supplements. 'The Irish market was dominated by brands from other EU countries,' according to Eugene, who studied biochemistry in university. 'After conducting some market research I knew there was room in the vitamins market for a quality Irish product.' So, with help from Enterprise Ireland, he set up his own business.

NatureVite Healthcare began by selling to small grocery stores and pharmacies before persuading the big supermarkets to stock their products. The company now supplies all the leading Irish supermarkets. The company does all its own R&D, manufacturing, quality control, marketing, distribution and package design.

Eugene emphasises the importance of good product packaging. 'In this market I think using bright colours and a distinctive design is important to give our company's products a definite sense of identity and vibrancy. 'NatureVite now has a sales turnover of nearly €15 million, a staff of 100 and over 50 different products ranging from vitamin and mineral food supplements to skin-care and baby-care products.

> NatureVite is a member of a healthcare trade association that represents the interests of all the Irish firms in this industry. Changes to EU laws regarding permitted ingredients and labelling are having a big impact on the vitamin and supplement market and Eugene is concerned about the possible negative implications for his business of some of the changes proposed by the European Commission.
>
> Sales in the Irish market are now beginning to level out and Eugene is aware that the firm will need to look abroad for new markets and business opportunities. He is particularly keen for NatureVite to take advantage of the opportunities offered by the EU's Single European Market. He is considering targeting France and the UK initially.

1. Compare the challenges NatureVite Heathcare will face in exporting to Britain compared to France. (30 marks)
2. Explain how NatureVite's trade association could influence EU decision-making. Refer to the main EU decision-making bodies in your answer. (30 marks)
3. Evaluate the potential implications for NatureVite Healthcare of **two** EU policies. (20 marks)

Higher Level – Section 2 – Long Questions

1. Explain the decision-making process of the European Union. Include the relevant institutions in your answer. [LCQ] (25 marks]
2. Explain the functions of **two** of the following: (a) The European Parliament, (b) The Council of Ministers/EU Council, (c) the European Commission. (20 marks) [LCQ]
3. Distinguish between an EU (a) regulation, (b) directive and (c) decision. (15 marks)
4. (a) Discuss the main elements of the EU's Single European Market.
   (b) Evaluate the significance of the Single European Market for Irish business. [LCQ] (40 marks)
5. Illustrate with a relevant example the impact of a European Union policy on economic activity in Ireland. [LCQ] (20 marks]
6. Discuss the importance for Ireland of any **two** of the following EU policies: (a) Common Agricultural Policy, (b) Competition Policy and (c) Social Policy. (30 marks)
7. Evaluate the opportunities and challenges for Irish business in the EU market. (20 marks) [LCQ]
8. Discuss the main reasons why a country would want to join the EU. (30 marks)
9. Explain the opportunities **and** challenges for Irish business as a result of new member states joining the European Union. [LCQ] (25 marks]
10. With reference to the various EU policies, evaluate the pros and cons of EU membership for Ireland. (40 marks)
11. Outline the possible implications for Ireland of the harmonisation of EU corporation tax rates. (20 marks)

Chapter 25
Global Business

'The empires of the future will be the empires of the mind.'

Winston Churchill

Case Study

Unilever

Unilever is one of the world's largest **transnational corporations** (TNCs). It owns and controls over 500 **subsidiary companies** worldwide, employs tens of thousands of staff and sells thousands of different product lines, such as detergents, dairy products, drinks, ice cream and hair care products. Among its well-known **global brands** are:

- Lynx deodorants
- Bird's Eye frozen foods
- Domestos cleaners
- Comfort fabric conditioner
- Knorr soups
- Hellman's
- Vaseline
- Timotei shampoo
- Signal toothpaste
- John West tinned foods
- Sunsilk
- Dove soap

Unilever controls most of the **global market** for washing powders and detergent products. Many brands which look like they are competing against each other, such as Persil and Surf washing powders and Blue

Band, Flora and Stork margarines – are actually all owned by Unilever.

Every year the company spends millions of euro on **advertising** these different brands of practically identical products. This advertising is designed to capture different types of buyers such as parents, male shoppers or the health conscious. With annual global sales of billions of euro, this single company sells more goods than every single Irish business combined.

Unilever's annual budget is also larger than that of many national governments, including Ireland's. In its pursuit of growth, the company purchased Ben & Jerry's ice cream company in a deal worth €326m, adding the ice cream to its massive product range.

1. What are transnational corporations?

> Transnational corporations produce and market goods in more than one country.

> The role of TNCs in the Irish economy is covered in detail in Chapter 18: Industries and Sectors in the Economy

Major global companies
- Unilever
- Shell
- Toyota
- Johnson & Johnson
- Coca-Cola
- Microsoft
- Ford
- Dell

> A global business is the most internationally focused type of transnational corporation.

OL Short Q1, 2   **HL Short Q1**

Transnational corporations (TNCs) *are firms that produce and market goods in more than one country, such as Unilever, Microsoft, McDonald's, Ford and Toyota.* Also known as **multinationals,** these businesses have a **global perspective**, which means they see the world as one giant market. TNCs do not have strong ties to any particular country. Instead, they carry out research, raise finance, source raw materials and manufacture wherever they can maximise their profits. Most transnationals have their headquarters in the USA, Europe or Japan from where they are firmly controlled. However TNCs are also emerging in countries like South Korea and Taiwan. Some Irish companies, such as the Kerry Group and Greencore are also expanding to become transnational businesses but are still small by international standards.

With the globalisation of the international economy, many TNCs are now behaving like global companies. A **global company** *treats the world as one single, giant production location and marketplace.* Specific characterisics of global companies include:

* **Global market**: A global company sees the world as a single marketplace, regardless of geographic and cultural differences.

* **Standardised products:** Global businesses sell the same standardised product in broadly the same way throughout the world with only minor variations to accommodate unavoidable local differences such as language or left/right hand drive.

* **Economies of scale:** By mass producing huge quantities of goods wherever it is cheapest, huge economies of scale can be achieved. This reduces production costs per unit to a very low level.

* **Global branding:** Global businesses invest heavily in developing distinctive, globally recognisable brands. To build up and reinforce global branding, all the elements of the marketing mix are similar throughout the world.

2. What are the reasons for the development of global companies?

Since the end of the Second World War, the size and number of global companies has grown rapidly. Reasons for the growth of global companies include:

> **Global companies now dominate international trade and most global economic activity.**

❖ **Own market saturation:** Firms are forced to expand internationally when their home markets become saturated and are unable to provide any further increases in sales or profits.

❖ **Spread risk:** Selling globally reduces the risk associated with being too dependent on any one country. This was the main motivation for Unilever to expand internationally.

❖ **Economies of scale:** Firms are attracted to the economies of scale that can be achieved by selling to very large markets.

❖ **Deregulation and opening up of global markets** as a result of free trade agreements (e.g. European Union, World Trade Organisation).

❖ **Faster transport and telecommunications links** have made it far easier for businesses to communicate with subsidiaries, customers, and suppliers around the world using information and communication technology (ICT) such as as email, Internet, electronic data interchange (EDI) and video conferencing.

OL Short Q3
OL Long Q1

HL Short Q2
HL Long Q1

❖ **E-business:** Firms can use the Internet to sell goods to a global market.

3. What is a global marketing mix?

Case Study

FORD'S GLOBAL MARKETING MIX

Ford was one of the first **global companies**. The company's best-selling Fiesta, Focus and Mondeo car models were designed by teams of engineers and designers spread across the USA, Europe and Australia, all working together and communicating using **information and communication technologies (ICT)**. Ford deliberately tries to develop **standardised products** that will be basically the same in all parts of the world with only small variations. A **global marketing mix** is put together that will help to maximise global sales. For example, its **global marketing promotions** have included paying to have their cars featured in James Bond movies because such films are popular with a global audience. By adopting a global approach to marketing, Ford is able to keep production and marketing costs down and achieve huge **economies of scale**. This helps to make the firm more competitive against other car producers.

Global marketing means having
- **Global product**
- **Global pricing**
- **Global distribution/place**
- **Global promotion**

Global marketing *means marketing a product globally with broadly the same marketing mix, as though the world were a single marketplace.* Global companies, such as Ford, Pepsi and Microsoft, brand their products with a common global image and global marketing mix. Having a global marketing mix provides two strong advantages to a company:

✪ **Cost savings:** Product design and advertising can be used globally with only minor adjustments for different countries.

✪ **Recognition:** Global marketing builds global brand names. This level of recognition builds strong consumer loyalty to a brand.

Some transnationals use a standardised global marketing mix, while others use an adapted global marketing mix.

✪ A **standardised global marketing mix** *means using the same basic mix in different countries.* This approach is used by Unilever, Coca-Cola and Microsoft. However, to ensure commercial success, global companies sometimes have to take account of local market conditions and make some adjustments to their marketing strategy for each country.

> **Example:** When first entering the Japanese market, Apple took a very standardised approach and did not even bother to translate its computer manuals into Japanese. As a result, its computers sold poorly compared to other global competitors who used an adapted marketing mix.

✪ An **adapted global marketing mix** *means adjusting the mix to take account of cultural, geographic, economic and other differences in various countries.*

> **Example:** Ford has to adapt its products by offering left/right hand drive vehicles in different countries.

Global product

Typically a global marketing mix will offer a standardised global product to all customers regardless of the country they are in. A **global product** *is a product that is the same all over the world.* This makes it easier for consumers to recognise and trust the brand when they travel abroad. **Production sharing** *means that part of a product is made in one country, then shipped to another for further assembly, with the finished product sold in yet another country.*

★ **Product design may need to be slightly adapted** for some countries due to differences in culture or climate.

Product marketing is covered in detail in Chapter 15: Marketing

> **Example:** Ford cars sold in the Middle East all have air conditioning as standard. Wherever you go in the world, a Big Mac will taste exactly the same but McDonald's adjusts its global marketing mix for different cultures by, for example, serving beer in Germany, wine in France and McSpaghetti in the Philippines.

★ **Brand names** may also need to be adapted to avoid confusion.

> **Example:** Kellogg's Bran Buds cereal means 'burnt farmer' in Swedish and Esso means 'breakdown' in Japanese, so these names had to be changed for those countries.

Global price

Despite having a standardised product design, the prices charged may vary from country to country due to factors such as:

* Different **standards of living** in different countries.
* Different distances and **transport costs** involved in getting to the local market.
* Different rates of **import** and **sales taxes** in different countries.
* Different **levels of competition** and prices charged by local competitors.
* Different **adjustments** needed to ensure products comply with local laws or culture.

Pricing is covered in detail in Chapter 15: Marketing

Global distribution/place

A global channel of distribution tends to be longer and more complex given the many different countries involved. The channels of distribution available to global businesses include:

* **Export directly to customers** from the factory. Example: Dell computers are manufactured in Poland but sold online to customers all over the world.
* **Use distribution agents: An agent** *is an independent person or firm who will sell the goods in the target market in return for a commission on every sale.*

> **Example:** Ford uses local car dealers in different countries as agents to distribute their cars globally. Many global businesses will use local wholesalers or retailers.

* **Licensing: A foreign licensing arrangement** *is a deal that gives permission to a local firm to manufacture or distribute a global firm's goods or services, or to use their global brand name. In return the global business receives a commission on sales.*

> **Example:** Global cola brand Pepsi gave a licence to Britvic to produce and sell Pepsi in Ireland. While this is a low-cost method, it involves some loss of control over the product.

Channels of distribution are covered in detail in Chapter 15: Marketing

* **Joint venture** with a local business that better understands the local market. In a **joint venture,** *resources and capital are invested by both companies and profits are shared.* Many countries, such as China, will only allow foreign firms to invest if it is done as part of a joint venture with one of their own indigenous firms. This approach suits many businesses as risks are shared.

> **Example:** Irish food company Glanbia established a joint venture with a Hungarian partner to set up a cheese-making factory in Hungary.

glanbia
NUTRITIONALS

❖ **Set up a foreign subsidiary** in the target country to manage the distribution of the goods. If the market is big enough, some global companies set up a manufacturing plant in the country concerned.

Example: Unilever set up subsidiaries all over the world to produce and distribute their products.

❖ **Use an export trading house** to handle the distribution in specific countries. **An export trading house** *is a company that buys goods in one country and then, like an international merchant, resells the goods at a profit in another country.*

Global promotion

Instead of designing different campaigns for each country, one standardised global promotion campaign can be implemented. This can then be recycled from one country to another at very little extra cost.

✪ **Global advertising.** Posters and websites can simply be translated into local languages, and radio and television advertisements can be dubbed.

Example: Coca-Cola uses very similar advertisements in many different countries.

✪ **Global public relations** can use a firm's good reputation in one part of the world to improve its image in others.

Example: Global companies particularly like to sponsor global events such as the Olympics or the World Cup. Although these events can cost hundreds of millions of euro to sponsor, they are still regarded as value for money because a global audience of billions will be watching.

✪ **Internet:** The Internet is a low-cost and highly effective media for firms to advertise and sell their goods to a global market.

Example: A company website can have different language pages for different countries. Potential customers anywhere in the world can browse through online catalogues and e-mail **orders** to the exporter's computer from anywhere around the globe at very low cost.

✪ A **trade fair** *is a business exhibition where suppliers in a particular industry (e.g. food industry) display their products to potential customers, such as supermarkets, wholesalers, etc.* Trade fairs are very useful promotional tools as many customers are gathered together in one location.

Example: Enterprise Ireland often provides grants towards the cost of Irish firms attending trade fairs and selling internationally.

Marketing promotions are covered in detail in Chapter 15: Marketing

Duh! Global promotional blunders

Effective global marketing requires being sensitive to local language and cultural differences. Sometimes firms that try to go global ignore this advice and end up making embarrassing and costly mistakes:

'Come alive with Pepsi!' was translated in China into advertising that proclaimed **'Pepsi brings your ancestors back from the dead!'**

In China, fast-food chain KFC mistranslated their slogan 'Finger licking good' into posters that said **'Eat your fingers off'**.

A beer company with the slogan 'Turn it loose!' mistranslated their advertising into Spanish as **'Get diarrhoea!'**

Nissan launched a car called 'Moco' but did not realise that this means **'snot'** in Spanish.

Case Study

Kerry Goes Global

From very modest beginnings in the south west of Ireland, the Kerry Group Plc has become a **transnational business** with annual sales of billions of euro. Over time, the firm changed its legal structure from being a **private limited company**, to a **co-operative** and then, to raise finance for global expansion, into a **public limited company**. Today the firm is a global business with factories and offices on five continents, generating over 80% of its sales from outside of Ireland.

The Kerry Group's first international project was a dairy plant in the USA. The firm then steadily expanded through a combination of **organic growth** and **acquisitions**. It is now a major global supplier of food ingredients, selling directly to large fast-food restaurant chains and food and drinks companies such as Pepsi. It is following a highly successful expansion strategy that has allowed it to become the world's largest producer of cheese and dairy ingredients for convenience foods. Another important element in the company's success is its continuous investment in **R&D** of new products and careful **market research**.

Like any business expanding into international markets, the Kerry Group has come up against

KERRY

OL Short Q4, 5
OL Long Q3, 4, 5, 6

HL Short Q3, 4
HL Long Q2, 3, 4, 5, 6

many different barriers to trade, such as foreign languages and geographical distance. The company has also had to deal with many artificial **'protectionist' barriers** imposed by foreign governments. However, this has not deterred the company, which has seen its determination pay off in terms of a growing global market share.

Recall and Review

1. Explain the terms highlighted in bold.
2. Describe how a global marketing mix could assist Kerry Group when launching a new brand of yoghurt.

4. What are the benefits and risks for a business operating globally?

For firms like Unilever and Kerry Group, there are both benefits and risks of becoming a global company:

● Benefits

❋ **Access to a global market** means bigger sales and potentially larger profits.

❋ Global companies can generate huge **economies of scale** by **producing** and selling the same standardised product in broadly the same way throughout the world. Cost savings can also be achieved by locating factories in low-cost countries, or by subcontracting to low-cost firms in those countries. Purchasing raw materials in massive quantities can generate **very large discounts** from suppliers.

❋ **Global brand recognition** means cheaper global marketing. Global firms can use the same advertising, public relations, sponsorship and other promotional campaigns and materials (with minor changes) in different countries.

❋ **Expansion** and **business survival** are more likely for firms that can compete on a global basis.

● Risks

❖ **Customer needs may not be properly met** by standardised products and marketing mixes. Customers in different countries may prefer or need more customised products and services even if it means higher marketing costs. Some TNCs prefer to use well-established and successful local brands and products in different countries rather than risk switching to a standardised, global alternative. Example: Unilever's Lynx range of deodorants is sold under the Axe brand name in France.

❖ **Diseconomies of scale** may also be incurred if a business becomes too big. For instance, larger firms will have more complex organisational structures. This can slow down communications and impede management decision-making compared to smaller firms.

❖ **Increased risk:** If a global marketing campaign does not work, then the costs can be huge.

> **Example:** Pharmaceutical companies deliberately avoid using global branding for medicines to avoid the impact that negative publicity for a brand in one country might have for sales of the same brand in other countries.

Helping Irish Business to go Global

Enterprise Ireland is the State agency responsible for assisting Irish-owned firms to grow and expand by exporting internationally. Using its network of overseas offices, it assists Irish firms to compete in the global market by:

★ Providing **market research** information.
★ Assisting with **international advertising** and promotions.
★ Setting up international **distribution channels**.
★ Providing **translation services**.
★ Providing **advice** on dealing with export regulations and documentation, methods of international payment and how to minimise foreign-exchange risks.
★ Providing **grants** and **venture capital investment** to firms that want to export.

| OL Long Q2 |
| HL ABQ |
| HL Long Q7, 8 |

Key Concepts & Business Terms

After studying this chapter the student should be able to explain the following key concepts and business terms:

1. Transnational corporations (TNCs)
2. Global companies
3. Reasons for the development of global companies
4. Global marketing
5. Standardised global marketing mix
6. Adapted global marketing mix
7. Global product
8. Production sharing
9. Agent
10. Foreign licensing arrangement
11. Joint venture
12. Export trading house
13. Trade fair
14. Enterprise Ireland
15. Benefits and risks of operating globally

www.unilever.co.uk
www.ford.com
www.kerrygroup.com

Leaving Certificate Practice Questions

Ordinary Level

Ordinary Level – Section 1 – Short Questions (10 marks each)

1. Distinguish between a transnational company and a trading bloc. [LCQ]
2. Explain what is meant by a global company.
3. List **two** reasons for the development of transnational companies.
4. List the **four** Ps of global marketing.
5. List **three** examples of well-known global brands.

Ordinary Level – Section 2 – Long Questions

1. TNCs now dominate global business. Explain why they have achieved this level of dominance. (20 marks)
2. Explain the benefits to a firm of expanding to become a transnational or global company. (20 marks)
3. Outline the factors that need to be considered when putting together a global marketing mix. (20 marks)
4. Why might a global company adjust its marketing mix in different countries? (15 marks)
5. Distinguish between a standardised and an adapted global marketing mix. (20 marks)
6. Language skills are essential if Irish firms are to succeed internationally. Explain this statement. (20 marks)

Higher Level

Higher Level – Section 1 – Short Questions (10 marks each)

1. List **three** characteristics of a transnational company.
2. Identify **one** reason for the growth of transnational companies.
3. What is global marketing? Name **two** global businesses. [LCQ]
4. Identify **one** advantage of adopting a global approach to marketing.

Higher Level – Section 2 – Applied Business Question

Soft-Tech, MediWorld and Cottonland

Soft Tech is a transnational firm employing hundreds of highly skilled employees in an industrial estate located outside a small town on the banks of the Shannon. Since setting up in Ireland it has signed contracts with many local firms to supply goods such as computers, stationery, packaging, food and services such as cleaning, security and insurance services. Every year it also pumps millions in wages into the local economy, which further benefits many local enterprises. As a result, the town is a thriving and prosperous place.

However, a downturn in the global economy and increasing low-cost competition from Asia means that Soft Tech's head office in the USA is considering relocating the factory to India where labour costs are a fraction of the costs in Ireland.

At the same time in a nearby town, Medi-World, a local indigenous firm producing medical equipment is looking at a more exciting future. With help from Enterprise Ireland and linkages with the local Institute of Technology, it has successfully developed a new life-saving product that it expects will be in huge demand by hospitals and doctors worldwide. The company is very excited about this development and is preparing a global marketing plan to ensure it becomes a success.

However, the news is not so good at Cottonland, an indigenous clothing company in the same town. Despite having award-winning fashion designs, this long established local firm has been struggling to survive in recent years due to low-cost competition from foreign firms. The latest sales figures are very poor and the board of directors are meeting to discuss the future of the business

1. Discuss the factors that the management of Soft Tech will consider when deciding the future of their Irish operations within a global context. (30 marks)
2. Analyse how a global marketing mix can assist Medi-World in successfully launching their new product. (20 marks)
3. Evaluate the challenges facing Irish industry within a globalised business environment. Refer to the case study in your answer. (30 marks)

Higher Level – Section 2 – Long Questions

1. Explain the reasons for the global spread of transnational corporations. (25 marks)
2. Explain, using examples, the importance of global marketing for a global business. [LCQ] (20 marks)
3. 'Marketing a product for the Irish market and marketing globally are basically the same.' Evaluate this statement using examples to illustrate your answer. (30 marks)
4. Explain the term 'global marketing' and its role in international business. (25 marks) [LCQ]
5. Describe how information technology can assist in the global marketing of products. (25 marks)
6. Explain why firms may adjust their marketing mix in different countries. (25 marks)
7. A business involved in global markets faces additional marketing challenges. Discuss these challenges, using examples to support your answer. (30 marks) [LCQ]
8. Evaluate the potential benefits and risks for a business of operating globally. (30 marks)

> 'Once the game is over, the king and the pawn go back into the same box.'
> *Italian Proverb*

Index

Notes

Director of Consumer Affairs (Functions).
- To view advertisements in general Comply with the Law.
- To request advertisers to Create advertising.
- To request advertisement be altered.
- To receive and investigate Complaints.

Notes

Notes